Zend Framework in Action

Zend Framework
in Action

ROB ALLEN
NICK LO
STEVEN BROWN

MANNING

Greenwich
(74° w. long.)

For online information and ordering of this and other Manning books, please visit
www.manning.com. The publisher offers discounts on this book when ordered in quantity.
For more information, please contact:

>Special Sales Department
>Manning Publications Co.
>Sound View Court 3B   Fax: (609) 877-8256
>Greenwick, CT 06830   Email: orders@manning.com

Many of the designations used by manufacturers and sellers to distinguish their products are
claimed as trademarks. Where those designations appear in the book, and Manning
Publications was aware of a trademark claim, the designations have been printed in initial caps
or all caps.

♾ Recognizing the importance of preserving what has been written, it is Manning's policy to have
the books we publish printed on acid-free paper, and we exert our best efforts to that end.
Recognizing also our responsibility to conserve the resources of our planet, Manning books are
printed on paper that is at least 15% recycled and processed elemental chlorine-free

>Manning Publications Co.   Copyeditor: Andy Carroll
>Sound View Court 3B   Typesetter: Tony Roberts
>Greenwich, CT 06830   Cover designer: Leslie Haimes

ISBN: 1933988320
Printed in the United States of America
1 2 3 4 5 6 7 8 9 10 – MAL – 13 12 11 10 09 08

To Georgina, Jon, and Ben,
for the love and support that you give me
—R.A.

To the Cookie Fairy and her two little helpers, Cory and Cass,
for the nourishment you give me
—N.L.

To Grandma, for believing in me
—S.B.

brief contents

contents

preface

Small things lead to big things. In August 2006, I decided to write a short getting-started tutorial on Zend Framework (for version 0.1.4!). Many people read it and fixed my errors for me, which was nice. In October 2006, Ben Ramsey contacted me via IRC and asked if I were interested in writing a book about Zend Framework. Apparently Chris Shiflett had recommended me, as he'd read my tutorial and other musings on Zend Framework-related topics and thought I could write. Simple mistake, really!

Ben put me in touch with Mike Stephens of Manning, and I agreed to outline a book about Zend Framework. He introduced me to Marjan Bace who worked with me through the process of getting the outline together. Marjan's kind words and encouragement helped tremendously. By the time we knew what the book would be about, I believed I could write it, and I started in January 2007.

By May, we all realized that I'm not the fastest writer in the world, and if we wanted a book out this decade, we needed some help! Nick Lo and, later, Steven Brown kindly answered the call for help, and their enthusiasm has ensured that the book was completed. Nick also proved much more capable at graphics than I, and the diagrams are a pleasure to look at as a result!

While writing the book, Zend Framework matured with 1.0, 1.5, and 1.6 releases. (Version 1.6 was released late into the development cycle of the book, and while we cover it, we do not cover the new Dojo integration features.) We have watched Zend Framework grow from a collection of essentially untested code into the mature, stable code base that it is now. Thousands of developers, myself included, use Zend Framework as the base upon which they build their websites and applications. I hope that this book will enable you to join us.

ROB ALLEN

acknowledgments

It was not until we actually tried to write a book that we discovered why the acknowledgments section of every book explains that the book is more than the work of the author (or authors) whose name(s) appears on the front cover! True to form, this book was also a group effort by more than just Rob, Nick, and Steven. We would like to thank everyone who helped us turn the original idea into the book you are now holding.

We are indebted to our development editors, Joyce King, Douglas Pundick, and Nermina Miller, who offered advice and encouragement throughout the writing phase. We would never have completed it without you guys. Late-night/early-morning chats on Skype enlightened us on the book-writing process and the organization required to complete the manuscript.

A host of other people at Manning also worked very hard behind the scenes to ensure that the book made it through to publication. We would like to thank them all, including our publisher Marjan Bace, our associate publisher Mike Stephens, our review editor Karen Tegtmeyer, and Megan Yockey who kept on top of the paperwork. When the manuscript entered the production stage, Mary Piergies, our project editor, provided invaluable guidance. The rest of the production team (Tony Roberts, Dottie Marsico, Tiffany Taylor, Leslie Haimes, Elizabeth Martin, Gabriel Dobrescu, and Steven Hong) all had a hand in bringing this book to you.

We are also thankful to all the reviewers of the manuscript at its various stages of completeness: Deepak Vohra, Jonathon Bloomer, Horaci Macias, Jeff Watkins, Greg Donald, Peter Pavlovich, Pete Helgren, Marcus Baker, Edmon Begoli, Doug Warren,

Thomas Weidner, Michal Minicki, Ralf Eggert, David Hanson, Andries Seutens, and Dagfinn Reiersøl.

We would also like to thank the many people who preordered the book and joined the MEAP program. Your feedback has made the book much better than it would have been.

The quality and readability of the text in your hands is so much better than our initial efforts thanks to the sterling efforts of Andy Carroll, our copy editor. The writing is now much tighter and easier to read due to his work.

Finally, we would like to thank Matthew Weier O'Phinney for checking the technical content for us. He has given generously of his time and advice, though, of course, all errors and omissions are ours alone.

Rob Allen

I would like to thank my wife, Georgina, and sons for putting up with me through this project. Georgina's support and encouragement have enabled me to get through to the end. I promise not to write another book until the decorating is done! I would also like to thank my parents for listening to my inane ramblings about something they don't understand and for instilling in me a desire to see things through to the end. My boss, Carl, and the rest of the team at Big Room Internet also deserve my thanks for listening to my progress reports and coping when I wasn't as alert as I should have been, due to late-night and early-morning writing sessions.

I would also like to thank the many contributors to Zend Framework who have provided the code, documentation, and help on mailing lists, forums, and the #zftalk IRC channel. The community has made Zend Framework what it is, and it's great to be part of it.

Nick Lo

My first thanks must go to Rob for giving me the opportunity to be part of this project, and for his patience as I bumbled through it. I have to also reiterate the thanks to our editors—it's impressive just how much a good editor can squeeze out of your writing even after you've been over and over it.

Personal thanks go to all my family for the initial excitement they had and will have again when I hand them a copy of the book. I won't mind if your eyes glaze over when you realize the book has as much interest to you, as my brother put it, as a refrigerator manual!

Finally, thanks to all our fellow developers who offer their knowledge to the development community. It's heartening to see how much help is shared amongst often total strangers for no apparent gain. That spirit contributed to the book, with suggestions like early-access reader Antonio Ruiz Zwollo's .htaccess setting, which we used in chapter 11.

Steven Brown

I must thank Michael Stephens for recommending that I join Rob and Nick in writing this book. Thanks to Rob and Nick for allowing me to come on board, and for understanding when personal disruptions prevented me from contributing as much as I had hoped. Thanks to Nermina Miller for making my writing look good, and thanks to Nick for making my diagrams look good.

Most importantly, I thank my wife, Tamara, who is still waiting for the landscaping to be finished and who smiles and nods politely when I ramble on about coding problems. Tamara has always been there to support me through the hard times, and to make the good times even more enjoyable.

about this book

In 2005, Andi Gutmans of Zend Technologies announced Zend's PHP Collaboration Project, and with it launched Zend Framework. By March 2006, there was some initial code, and version 1.0 was released in July 2007 with regular releases since then. Zend Framework has provided PHP with a high-quality framework that is different from most others due to its use-at-will philosophy, allowing the developer to pick and choose which parts to use for any given project.

This book shows how to use Zend Framework to your best advantage, and the techniques are demonstrated on an example website that is developed over the course of the book. We look at the major components of Zend Framework and show how to use each one in the context of a real-world application. As a result, this book supplements the online manual's functional view of the framework by showing you how it all fits together, allowing you to produce high-quality websites and applications.

Who should read this book?

This book is for PHP developers who want to or are using Zend Framework. As Zend Framework has a use-at-will philosophy, not all chapters will be useful to every reader immediately. However, we believe that all readers will gain something from every chapter, even if you have to read it again to pick up the details when you start using that component!

This is not a beginner's book; we assume that you are familiar with PHP and have an understanding of object-oriented programming. Appendix A, "A Whistle-Stop

Tour of PHP Syntax," and appendix B, "Object-Oriented PHP," provide a useful overview of the fundamentals, but they are not substitutes for a full book on the subject.

Further information about Zend Framework

In addition to this book, the Zend Framework website at http://framework.zend.com/ is an excellent resource. The online manual at http://framework.zend.com/manual/en/ is the definitive reference documentation for all the components in the framework. For help and discussion on Zend Framework, we recommend subscribing to the mailing lists. The details can be found at http://framework.zend.com/wiki/display/ZFDEV/Contributing+to+Zend+Framework, and the archives are at http://framework.zend.com/archives. Finally, interactive, real-time chat about Zend Framework can be found on the Freenode IRC network in the #zf-talk channel.

Road map

This book is organized into three parts. Part 1 introduces Zend Framework and shows how to implement a simple "hello world" application using Zend Framework components. Part 2 looks at the components in the framework that are useful to most web applications, and part 3 introduces the less frequently used components that will be cherry-picked for particular projects.

THE ESSENTIALS

Chapter 1 looks at what components Zend Framework provides to help us build websites quickly and efficiently. It also looks at why we use the framework in the first place and what advantages it brings.

Chapter 2 puts some code on the table. Starting slowly, we build the simplest, complete website that we can using the Model View Controller (MVC) design pattern. This chapter sets the stage and introduces core concepts about the code and design of Zend Framework that serve as a foundation for parts 2 and 3.

A CORE APPLICATION

Chapter 3 develops the initial design and code for the *Places to take the kids!*, a real-world community website using Zend Framework. We start by looking at bootstrapping and code organization and build up to the home page controller code.

Chapter 4 builds on the work in chapter 3 to develop the frontend look and feel of the website. We use the `Zend_View` and `Zend_Layout` components to develop a Composite View system that separates the display elements that are specific to a given page from those that are common across all pages.

Chapter 5 introduces Ajax from first principles, then looks at integrating an Ajax request into a Zend Framework MVC application.

Chapter 6 considers interaction with a database, using the Zend Framework database components, from database abstraction to the higher-level table abstraction.

Chapter 7 is all about the users and how to authenticate access and then control their access to specific sections of a website.

Chapter 8 explains how to take control of forms on your website by using the Zend_Form component.

Chapter 9 tackles the thorny subject of site-wide searching to help your users find what they are looking for on your website.

Chapter 10 discusses the Zend_Mail component that allows for sending and reading of email.

Chapter 11 completes this part of the book by looking at management issues including version control, deployment, and testing.

MORE POWER TO YOUR APPLICATION

Chapter 12 looks at integrating web applications together with XML_RPC and REST protocols. It also looks at integrating RSS and Atom feeds into an application.

Chapter 13 explains how to add value to your website by integrating the plethora of data from public web services available on the Internet.

Chapter 14 goes behind the scenes and shows how caching can be used to speed up a website and allow an application to scale.

Chapter 15 considers how to provide a multilingual website that is also aware of the local idioms that your users' expect on a polished website.

Chapter 16 shows how to create PDF documents with text and graphics in them.

THE APPENDICES

Appendix A provides a short tour of the PHP syntax, mostly aimed at people coming from another language.

Appendix B describes the PHP5 object model and so provides a leg up for those who have mainly programmed procedurally before using Zend Framework.

Appendix C offers tips and tricks that allow you to develop your Zend Framework applications more easily.

Code conventions and downloads

All source code in the book is in a fixed-width font like this, which sets it off from the surrounding text. For most listings, the code is annotated to point out the key concepts, and numbered bullets are sometimes used in the text to provide additional information about the code. We have tried to format the code so that it fits within the available page space in the book by adding line breaks and using indentation carefully. Sometimes, very long lines will include line-continuation markers.

Source code for all the working examples is available for download from http://www.manning.com/ZendFrameworkinAction. A readme.txt file is provided in the root folder and also in each chapter folder; they provide details on how to install and run the code. In cases where we have not been able to show every detail in the book, the accompanying source code has the full details. You will need a working PHP installation on the Apache web server and a MySQL database for the examples to run.

Author Online

Purchase of *Zend Framework in Action* includes free access to a private web forum run by Manning Publications where you can make comments about the book, ask technical questions, and receive help from the lead author and from other users. To access the forum and subscribe to it, point your web browser to www.manning.com/ZendFrameworkinAction or www.manning.com/allen. This page provides information on how to get on the forum once you're registered, what kind of help is available, and the rules of conduct on the forum.

Manning's commitment to our readers is to provide a venue where a meaningful dialog between individual readers and between readers and the authors can take place. It's not a commitment to any specific amount of participation on the part of the authors, whose contribution to the AO remains voluntary (and unpaid). We suggest you try asking the authors some challenging questions lest their interest stray!

The Author Online forum and the archives of previous discussions will be accessible from the publisher's website as long as the book is in print.

About the title

By combining introductions, overviews, and how-to examples, the *In Action* books are designed to help learning and remembering. According to research in cognitive science, the things people remember are things they discover during self-motivated exploration.

Although no one at Manning is a cognitive scientist, we are convinced that for learning to become permanent it must pass through stages of exploration, play, and, interestingly, retelling of what is being learned. People understand and remember new things, which is to say they master them, only after actively exploring them. Humans learn in action. An essential part of an *In Action* guide is that it is example-driven. It encourages the reader to try things out, to play with new code, and explore new ideas.

There is another, more mundane, reason for the title of this book: our readers are busy. They use books to do a job or to solve a problem. They need books that allow them to jump in and jump out easily and learn just what they want just when they want it. They need books that aid them *in action*. The books in this series are designed for such readers.

about the cover illustration

The illustration on the cover of *Zend Framework in Action* is taken from the 1805 edition of Sylvain Maréchal's four-volume compendium of regional dress customs. This book was first published in Paris in 1788, one year before the French Revolution. Each illustration is colored by hand.

The colorful variety of Maréchal's collection reminds us vividly of how culturally apart the world's towns and regions were just 200 years ago. Isolated from each other, people spoke different dialects and languages. In the streets or the countryside, they were easy to place—sometimes with an error of no more than a dozen miles—just by their dress. Dress codes have changed everywhere with time and the diversity by region, so rich at the time, has faded away. It is now hard to tell apart the inhabitants of different continents, let alone different towns or regions. Perhaps we have traded cultural diversity for a more varied personal life—certainly a more varied and faster-paced technological life.

At a time when it is hard to tell one computer book from another, Manning celebrates the inventiveness and initiative of the computer business with book covers based on the rich diversity of regional life of two centuries ago, brought back to life by Maréchal's pictures.

Part 1

The essentials

The first two chapters of this book introduce Zend Framework. Chapter 1 considers what Zend Framework is and why you would want to use it in your PHP web development process. Chapter 2 builds a simple Zend Framework application that shows how the parts fit together. The introduction of the Model View Controller (MVC) design pattern will bring order to your application and set the foundations for the rest of the book.

Introducing Zend Framework

PHP has been used to develop dynamic websites for over 10 years. Initially, all PHP websites were written as PHP code interspersed within HTML on the same page. This worked very well, as there is immediate feedback, and for simple scripts this was what was needed. PHP grew in popularity through versions 3 and 4, so it was inevitable that larger and larger applications would be written in PHP. It quickly became obvious that intermixing PHP code and HTML was not a long-term solution for large websites.

The problems are obvious in hindsight: maintainability and extensibility. While PHP intermixed with HTML allows for extremely rapid results, it is hard to continue to update the website in the longer term. One of the really cool features of publishing on the web is that it is dynamic, with content and site layouts changing. Large websites change all the time, and the look and feel of most sites is updated regularly, as the needs of the users (and advertisers!) change. Something had to be done.

Zend Framework was created to help ensure that the production of PHP-based websites is easier and more maintainable in the long term. It contains a rich set of reusable components including everything from a set of Model-View-Controller (MVC) application components to PDF generation classes. Over the course of this book, we will look at how to use all the Zend Framework components within the context of a real website.

In this chapter, we will discuss what Zend Framework is and why you should use it, and we'll look at some of the design philosophies behind it. This introduction to the framework will act as a guide for the rest of the book and it will help make the design decisions behind each component clearer. Let's start by looking at how Zend Framework can provide structure for a website's code base.

1.1 *Introducing structure to PHP websites*

The solution to this tangled mess of PHP code and HTML on a website is structure. The most basic approach to structuring applications within PHP sites is applying the concept of "separation of concerns." This means that the code that does the display should not be in the same file as the code that connects to the database and collects the data. The usual novice approach mixes the two types of code, as shown in figure 1.1.

Figure 1.1 The organization of a typical PHP file created by a novice interleaves HTML and PHP code in a linear fashion as the file is created.

Most developers begin to introduce structure to a website's code by default, and the concept of reusability dawns. Generally, this means that the code that connects to the database is separated into a file called something like db.inc.php. Having separated out the database code, it then seems logical to separate out the code that displays the common header and footer elements on every page. Functions are then introduced to help solve the problem of global variables affecting one another by ensuring that variables live only within the scope of their own function.

As the website grows, common functionality shared between multiple pages is grouped into libraries. Before you know it, the application is much easier to maintain, and adding new features without breaking existing code becomes simpler. The website continues to expand until it gets to the point where the supporting code is so large that you can't hold a picture in your head of how it all works.

PHP coders are used to standing on the shoulders of giants because our language provides easy access to libraries such as the GD image library, the many database client access libraries, and even system-specific libraries such as COM on Microsoft Windows. It was inevitable that object-oriented programming, known as OOP, would enter the

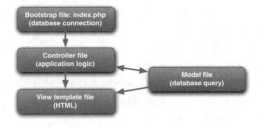

Figure 1.2 A typical MVC application separates the code of an application into separate concerns.

PHP landscape. While classes in PHP4 provided limited OOP features, PHP5 provides excellent support for all the things you'd expect in an object-oriented language. There are visibility specifiers for class members (public, private, and protected) along with interfaces, abstract classes, and support for exceptions.

PHP's improved object-oriented support allowed for more complicated libraries (known as frameworks) to evolve, such as Zend Framework, which supports the Model-View-Controller design pattern—a way of organizing web application files. This design pattern is shown in figure 1.2.

An application designed using MVC principles results in more files, but each file is specialized in what it does, which makes maintenance much easier. For example, all the code that performs database queries is stored in classes known as *models*. The actual HTML code is known as the *view* (which may also contain simple PHP logic), and the *controller* files handle the connection of the correct models to the correct views to display the desired page.

Zend Framework isn't the only option for organizing a website based on MVC principles; there are many others in the PHP world. Let's look at what Zend Framework contains and why it should be considered.

1.2 Why use Zend Framework?

Before we dive into using it, we will first look at why we use Zend Framework over all the other PHP frameworks out there. In a nutshell, Zend Framework introduces a standardized set of components that allow for easy development of web applications that can be easily developed, maintained, and enhanced.

Zend Framework has a number of key features that make it worth investigating:

- Everything is in the box.
- It has a modern design.
- It is easy to learn.
- It has full documentation.
- Development is simple.
- Development is rapid.

That list is rather stark, so let's look at each item in turn and see what it means to us as website developers.

1.2.1   Everything is in the box

Zend Framework is a comprehensive loosely coupled framework that contains everything you need to develop your application. This includes a robust MVC component to ensure that your website is structured according to best practices and other components for authentication, searching, localization, PDF creation, email, and connecting to web services, along with a few more esoteric items. These components can be grouped into the six categories shown in figure 1.3.

Figure 1.3   There are many components in Zend Framework, but we can group them into these six categories for ease of reference.

That's not to say that Zend Framework doesn't play nice with other libraries; it does that too. A core feature of the design of the framework is that it is easy to use just those bits you want to use with your application or with other libraries such as PEAR, the Doctrine ORM database library, or the Smarty template library. You can even use Zend Framework components with other PHP MVC frameworks, such as Symfony, CakePHP, or CodeIgniter.

1.2.2   Modern design

Zend Framework is written in object-oriented PHP5 using modern design techniques known as design patterns. Software design patterns are recognized high-level solutions to design problems and, as such, are not specific implementations of the solutions. The actual implementation depends on the nature of the rest of the design. Zend Framework makes use of many design patterns, and its implementation has been carefully designed to allow the maximum flexibility for application developers without making them do too much work!

The framework recognizes the PHP way and doesn't force you into using all the components, so you are free to pick and choose. This is especially important as it allows you to introduce specific components into an existing site. The key is that each component within the framework has few dependencies on other components. This allows you to introduce specific Zend Framework components, such as `Zend_Search`, `Zend_Pdf`, or `Zend_Cache` into your current project without having to replace all the rest of your project code.

1.2.3   Easy to learn

If you are anything like us, learning how a vast body of code works is difficult! Fortunately, Zend Framework is modular, encouraging developers with a "use at will" design philosophy that helps make it easy to learn, one step at a time. Individual components don't depend on lots of other components, so they are easy to study. The design of each component is such that you do not need to understand how it works in its entirety before you can use it and benefit from it. Once you have some experience in using the component, learning to use the more advanced features is straightforward, as it can be done in steps. This reduces the barrier to entry.

For example, the `Zend_Config` configuration component is used to provide an object-oriented interface to a configuration file. It supports two advanced features: section overloading and nested keys, but neither of these features needs to be understood in order to use the component. Once the user has a working implementation of `Zend_Config` in her code, confidence increases, and using the advanced features is a small step.

1.2.4   *Full documentation*

No matter how good the code is, lack of documentation can kill a project through lack of adoption. As Zend Framework is aimed at developers who do not want to have to dig through all the source code to get their job done, Zend Framework puts documentation on an equal footing with the code. This means that the core team will not allow new code into the framework unless it has accompanying documentation.

Two types of documentation are supplied with the framework: API and end-user. The API documentation is created using phpDocumenter and is automatically generated using special DocBlock comments in the source code. These comments are typically found just above every class, function, and member variable declaration. One key advantage of using DocBlocks is that IDEs such as the Eclipse PDT project or Zend's Studio are able to supply autocompletion tool tips while coding, which can improve developer productivity.

Included documentation

Zend Framework supplies a full manual that can be downloaded, and it's also available online at http://framework.zend.com/manual. The manual provides details on all components of the framework and shows what functionality is available. Examples are provided to help you get started in using the component in an application. More importantly, in the case of the more complicated components (such as `Zend_Controller`), the theory of operation is also covered, so that you can understand why the component works the way it does.

The documentation provided with the framework does not explain how to fit all the components together to make a complete application. As a result, a number of tutorials have sprung up on the web, created by community members to help developers get started on the framework. These have been collated on a web page on Zend Framework's wiki at http://framework.zend.com/wiki/x/q. The tutorials, while a useful starting point, do not tend to go in depth with each component or show how it works within a nontrivial application, which is why this book exists.

1.2.5   Simple development

As we have noted, one of PHP's strengths is that developing simple, dynamic web pages is very easy. This ease of use has enabled millions of people to have fantastic websites who may not have had them otherwise. As a result, PHP programmers range in ability from beginner hobbyists through to enterprise developers. Zend Framework is designed to make development simpler and easier for developers of all levels.

So how does it make development simpler? The key feature that the framework brings to the table is tested, reliable code that does the grunt work of an application. This means that the code you write is the code you need for your application. The code that does the boring bits is taken care of for you and does not clutter up your code.

1.2.6   Rapid development

Zend Framework makes it easy to get going on your web application or to add new functionality to a current website. The framework provides many of the underlying components of an application, so you are free to concentrate on the core parts of your application. You can get started quickly on a given piece of functionality and immediately see the results.

Another way the framework speeds up development is that the default use of most components is the most common case. In other words, you don't have to set lots of configuration settings for each component just to get started using it. For example, the most simplistic use of the whole MVC is bootstrapped with just the following code:

```
require_once('Zend/Loader.php');
Zend_Loader::registerAutoload();
Zend_Controller_Front::run('/path/to/controllers');
```

Once it's up and running, adding a new page to your application can be as easy as adding a new function to a class, along with a new view script file in the correct directory. Similarly, `Zend_Session` provides a multitude of options that can be set so that you can manage your session exactly as you want to; however, none need to be set in order to use the component for most use-cases.

1.2.7   Structured code is easy to maintain

As we have seen, separating out different responsibilities makes for a structured application. It also means that when you are fixing bugs, it's easier to find what you are looking for. Similarly, when you need to add a new feature to the display code, the only files you need to look at are related to the display logic. This helps to avoid bugs that might be created by breaking something else while adding the new feature. The framework also encourages you to write object-oriented code, which makes maintaining your application simpler.

We have now looked at why Zend Framework has been developed and at the key advantages it brings to developing PHP websites and applications. We'll now turn our attention to the components Zend Framework contains and how they will help us to build websites more easily.

1.3   *What is Zend Framework?*

Zend Framework is a PHP glue library for building PHP web applications. The components fit together to provide a full-stack framework with all the components required to build modern, easily built, maintainable applications. That rather simple description doesn't tell the whole story though, so we'll look at where this framework came from and what it actually contains.

1.3.1   *Where did it come from?*

Frameworks have been around for years. The very first web framework Rob used in a real project was Fusebox, which was originally written for ColdFusion. Many other frameworks have come along since then, with the next major highlight being Struts, written in Java. A number of PHP clones of Struts were written, but didn't translate well to PHP. The biggest problem was that Java web applications run in a virtual machine that runs continuously, so the startup time of the web application is not a factor for every web request. PHP initializes each request from a clean slate, so the large initiation required for Struts clones made them relatively slow as a result.

A couple of years ago, a new framework called Rails entered the world, based on a relatively unknown language called Ruby. Rails (or Ruby on Rails as it is also known) promoted the concept of convention over configuration and has taken the web development world by storm. Shortly after Rails came along, a number of direct PHP clones appeared, along with a number of frameworks inspired by Rails, rather than direct copies.

In late 2005, Zend Technologies, a company that specializes in PHP, started Zend Framework as part of its PHP Collaboration project to advance the use of PHP. Zend Framework is an open source project that provides a web framework for PHP and is intended to become one of the standard frameworks that PHP applications of the future will be based on.

1.3.2   *What's in it?*

Zend Framework is composed of many distinct components that can be grouped into six top-level categories. Because it is a complete framework, you have everything you need to build enterprise-ready web applications. However, the system is very flexible and has been designed so that you can pick and choose to use those bits of the framework that are applicable to your situation. Following on from the high-level overview shown earlier in figure 1.3, figure 1.4 lists the main components within each category of the framework.

Each component of the framework contains a number of classes, including the main class for which the component is named. For example, the `Zend_Config` component contains the `Zend_Config` class along with the `Zend_Config_Ini` and `Zend_Config_Xml` classes. Each component also contains a number of other classes that are not listed in figure 1.4. We will discuss the classes as we go through the book and learn about each component.

Figure 1.4   Zend Framework contains lots of components that include everything required to build an enterprise application.

THE MVC COMPONENTS

The MVC components provide a full-featured MVC system for building applications that separates out the view templates from the business logic and controller files. Zend Framework's MVC system is made up of Zend_Controller (the controller) and Zend_View (the view) with Zend_Db and the Zend_Service classes forming the model. Figure 1.5 shows the basics of Zend Framework's MVC system, using Zend_Db as a model.

The Zend_Controller family of classes provides a Front Controller design pattern, which dispatches requests to controller actions (also known as commands) so that all processing is centralized. As you'd expect from a fully featured system, the controller supports plug-ins at all levels of the process and has built-in flex points to enable you to change specific parts of the behavior without having to do too much work.

The view script system is called Zend_View, which provides a PHP-based template system. This means that, unlike Smarty or PHPTAL, all the view scripts are written in PHP. Zend_View provides a helper plug-in system to allow for the creation of reusable display code. It is designed to allow for overriding for specific requirements, or even for using another template system entirely, such as Smarty. Working in conjunction with Zend_View is Zend_Layout, which provides for aggregating multiple view scripts to build the entire web page.

Zend_Db_Table implements a Table Data Gateway pattern which, along with the web services components, can be used to form the basis of the model within the MVC system. The model provides the business logic for the application, which is usually but

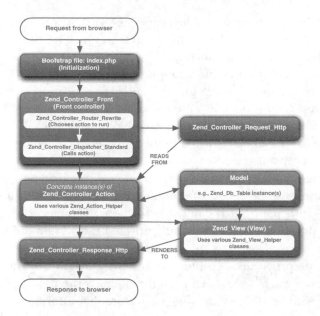

Figure 1.5   The MVC flow in a Zend Framework application uses a front controller to process the request and delegate to a specific action controller that uses models and views to craft the response.

not always database-based in a web application. `Zend_Db_Table` uses `Zend_Db`, which provides object-oriented database-independent access to a variety of different databases, such as MySQL, PostgreSQL, SQL Server, Oracle, and SQLite.

The most simplistic setup of the MVC components can be done with this code:

```
require_once 'Zend/Controller/Front.php';
Zend_Controller_Front::run('/path/to/your/controllers');
```

It is more likely, however, that a more complicated bootstrap file will be required for a nontrivial application. We will explore this in chapter 2 when we build a complete application with Zend Framework.

The MVC classes work in combination with some of the core classes that create the nucleus of a complete application. The framework itself does not require configuration, but some configuration of your application is invariably required (such as database login details). `Zend_Config` allows an application to read configuration data from PHP arrays or INI or XML files and includes a useful inheritance system for supporting different configuration settings on different servers, such as production, staging, and test servers.

Security is very much on the minds of every PHP developer worth his salt. Input data validation and filtering is the key to a secure application. `Zend_Filter` and `Zend_Validate` are provided to help the developer ensure that input data is safe for use in the application.

The `Zend_Filter` class provides a set of filters that typically remove or transform unwanted data from the input as it passes through the filter. For example, a numeric filter will remove any characters that are not numbers from the input, and an HTML entities filter will convert the "<" character to the sequence "<". Appropriate filters can be set up to ensure that the data is valid for the context in which it will be used.

`Zend_Validate` provides a very similar function to `Zend_Filter`, except that it provides a yes/no answer to the question, "Is this data what I expect?" Validation is generally used to ensure that the data is correctly formed, such as ensuring that the data entered in an email address field is actually an email address. In the case of failure, `Zend_Validate` also provides a message indicating why the input failed validation so that appropriate error messages can be returned to the end user.

AUTHENTICATION AND ACCESS COMPONENTS

Not every application needs to identify its users, but it is a surprisingly common requirement. Authentication is the process of identifying a user, usually via a token, such as a username/password pair, but it could equally be via a fingerprint. Access control is the process of deciding whether the authenticated user is allowed to have access to, and operate on, a given resource, such as a database record.

As there are two separate processes, Zend Framework provides two separate components: `Zend_Acl` and `Zend_Auth`. `Zend_Auth` is used to identify the user and is typically used in conjunction with `Zend_Session`, which can store that information across multiple page requests (known as token persistence). `Zend_Acl` then uses the authentication token to provide access to private information using a role-based access control (RBACL) system.

Flexibility is a key design goal within the `Zend_Auth` component. There are so many ways to authenticate a user that the `Zend_Auth` system is built with the intention that the user will provide his own method if none of the provided solutions are suitable. Authentication adapters are provided for HTTP digest, database tables, OpenID, Info-Card, and LDAP. For any other method, you must create a class that extends `Zend_Auth_Adapter`. Fortunately, this is not difficult, as we will see in chapter 7.

As `Zend_Acl` is an implementation of an RBACL system, the manual describes this component in abstract terms. RBACL is a generic system that can provide access to anything by anyone, so specific terms are discouraged. Hence, we talk about *roles* requesting access to *resources*. A *role* is anything that may want to access something that is under the protection of the `Zend_Acl` system. Generally, for a web application, this means that a role is a user group that has been identified using `Zend_Auth`. A *resource* is anything that is to be protected. This is generally a record in a database, but could equally be an image file stored on disk. As there is such a variety of resources, the `Zend_Acl` system enables us to create our own very simply by implementing `Zend_Acl_Role_Interface` within our class.

INTERNATIONALIZATION COMPONENTS

We live in a multicultural world with multiple languages, so Zend Framework provides a rich set of functionality for localizing your applications to match your target users. This covers minor issues, like ensuring that the correct currency symbol is used throughout, to full support for changing all the text on the page to the correct language. Date and time routines are also provided with a simple, object-oriented interface, as are settings for the many ways that a calendar can be displayed.

Zend Framework provides the `Zend_Locale` class, which is responsible, along with `Zend_Currency` and `Zend_Measure`, for ensuring that the correct language and idioms are used. The `Zend_Translate` component is concerned with the actual translation of a website's text into the desired language.

INTERAPPLICATION COMMUNICATION COMPONENTS

Zend Framework provides a component to read data from other websites. `Zend_Http_Client` makes it easy to collect data from other websites and services and then present it on your site. This component works much like the curl PHP extension, but it is implemented in PHP and so can be used in situations where curl is not enabled.

When you need to communicate with another application over HTTP, the most common transfer format is one of two flavors of XML: XML-RPC and SOAP. PHP5 contains excellent built-in SOAP support, and Zend Framework provides `Zend_XmlRpc_Client` to allow for easy processing of XML-RPC. More recently, the lightweight JSON (JavaScript Object Notation) protocol has been gaining favor, mainly due to how easy it is to process within the JavaScript of an Ajax application. `Zend_Json` provides a nice solution to both creating and reading JSON data.

WEB SERVICES COMPONENTS

Zend Framework provides a rich set of functionality to allow access to services provided by other suppliers. These components cover generic RSS feeds along with specific components for working with the public APIs from Google, Yahoo!, and Amazon. RSS has come a long way from its niche among the more technologically minded bloggers and is now used by the majority of news sites. `Zend_Feed` provides a consistent interface to reading feeds in the various RSS and Atom versions that are available without having to worry about the details.

Google, Yahoo!, Amazon, and other websites have provided public APIs to their online services in order to encourage developers to create extended applications around the core service. For Amazon, the API provides access to the data on amazon.com in the hope that the new application will encourage more sales. Similarly, Yahoo! provides API access to its Flickr photo data in order to allow additional services for Flickr users, such as the print service provided by moo.com. The traditional Yahoo! properties such as search, news, and images are also available. Zend Framework groups these and many more components into a set of classes prefixed with `Zend_Service`. There is `Zend_Service_Amazon`, `Zend_Service_Delicious`, `Zend_Service_Simpy`, `Zend_Service_SlideShare`, and `Zend_Service_Yahoo` to name but a few within this family.

Google has a number of online applications allowing for API access that are supported by the `Zend_Gdata` component. `Zend_Gdata` provides access to Google's Blogger, Calendar, Base, YouTube, and Code Search applications. In order to provide consistency, the `Zend_Gdata` component provides the data using `Zend_Feed`, so if you can process an RSS feed, you can process Google Calendar data too.

CORE COMPONENTS

There is a set of other components provided with Zend Framework that do not fit easily into any category, so we have grouped them together into the core category. This potpourri of components includes classes for caching, searching, and PDF creation. The rather esoteric measurement class is also in this category.

Everyone wants a faster website, and caching is one tool that can be used to help speed up your site. While it's not a sexy component, the Zend_Cache component provides a generic and consistent interface for caching any data in a variety of backend systems, such as disks, databases, or even APC's shared memory. This flexibility ensures that you can start small with Zend_Cache, and as the load on your site increases, the caching solution can grow to help ensure you get the most out of your server hardware.

Every modern website provides a search facility, but most are so terrible that the site's users would rather search Google than use the site's own system. Zend_Search_Lucene is based on the Apache Lucene search engine for Java and provides an industrial-strength text-search system that will allow your users to find what they are looking for. As required by a good search system, Zend_Search_Lucene supports ranked searching (so that the best results are at the top) along with a powerful query system.

Another core component is Zend_Pdf, which can create PDF files programmatically. PDF is a very portable format for documents intended for printing. You can control the position of everything on the page with pixel-perfect precision, without having to worry about differences in the way web browsers render the page. Zend_Pdf is written entirely in PHP and can create new PDF documents or load existing ones for editing.

Zend Framework provides a strong email component, Zend_Mail, to allow for sending emails in plain text or HTML. As with all Zend Framework components, the emphasis is on flexibility and sensible defaults. Within the world of email, this means that the component allows for sending email using SMTP or via the standard PHP mail() command. Additional transports can easily be slotted into the system by writing a new class that implements Zend_Mail_Transport_Interface. When sending email, an object-oriented interface is used:

```
$mail = new Zend_Mail();
$mail->setBodyText('My first email!')
 ->setBodyHtml('My <b>first</b> email!')
 ->setFrom('rob@akrabat.com', 'Rob Allen')
 ->addTo('somebody@example.com', 'Some Recipient')
 ->setSubject('Hello from Zend Framework in Action!')
 ->send();
```

This snippet also shows the use of fluent interfaces—each member function returns an object instance so that the functions can be chained together to make the code more readable. Fluent interfaces are commonly used in Zend Framework classes in order to make the classes easier to use.

As you can appreciate, Zend Framework contains a comprehensive set of components that provide most of the foundations for a website. As the framework continues to grow, even more components will be added, and all components will follow Zend Framework's design philosophy, which ensures the quality and consistency of the framework.

1.4 Zend Framework design philosophy

Zend Framework has a number of published goals that make up the design philosophy of the framework. If these goals do not mesh with your views on developing PHP applications, Zend Framework is unlikely to be a good fit for your way of doing things. All components in the framework meet these goals, which ensures the usefulness of the framework code going into the future.

1.4.1 High-quality components

All code within the Zend Framework library will be of high quality. This means that it will be written using PHP5's features and will not generate any messages from the PHP parser (that is, it is E_STRICT compliant). This means that any PHP parser messages in your logs come from your code, not the framework, which helps considerably when debugging! Zend Framework also defines high quality to include documentation, so the manual for a given component is as important as the code.

It is intended that entire applications can be developed with no external library dependencies (unless you want them). This means that Zend Framework is a "full stack" framework (like Ruby on Rails or the Django Python framework) rather than a set of disjointed components, though much less tightly coupled. This will ensure that there will be consistency in the components: how they are named, how they work, and how the files are laid out in subdirectories. Having said that, it is important to emphasize that Zend Framework is modular with few dependencies between modules. This ensures that it plays well with other frameworks and libraries and that you can use as much or as little as you want. For example, if you only want PDF generation, you don't have to use the MVC system.

1.4.2 Pragmatism and Flexibility

Another design goal for the framework is the mantra "Don't change PHP." The PHP way is simple, with pragmatic solutions, and Zend Framework is intended to reflect that and to provide a simple solution for mainstream developers. Zend Framework is also powerful enough to allow for specialized usage via extensions. The core developers have done a great job in covering the common scenarios and providing "flex points" to easily allow changes to be made to the default behavior by those who want something more powerful or specialized.

1.4.3   Clean IP

All contributors to Zend Framework have signed a Contributor License Agreement (CLA). This is an agreement with Zend that ensures the intellectual property status of the contribution. That is, the contributors warrant that (to the best of their knowledge), they are entitled to make the contribution and that no one else's intellectual property rights are being infringed upon. This is intended to help protect all users of the framework from potential legal issues related to intellectual property and copyright. The risk is minimal, but the legal action brought by SCO against AutoZone showed that a litigator going after the user of the allegedly copyright-infringing code is a possibility. As with everything, it is better to be prepared.

Zend Framework's source code is licensed under the new BSD license. This provides users with a lot of freedom to use the code in many different applications from open source projects to commercial products. When combined with the clean IP requirements, Zend Framework is well-positioned for use by anyone for any purpose.

1.4.4   Support from Zend Technologies

An obvious but important consideration is that Zend Framework is supported by Zend Technologies. This means that the framework is unlikely to die due to inactivity of the core developers or by not being updated to the latest and greatest version of PHP. Zend Technologies also has the resources to provide full-time developers on the project to help move it forward at a consistent pace.

We have now covered Zend Framework in some detail, looking at why it exists, what it contains, and its overall goals. A lot of PHP frameworks meet the needs of different programmers, so let's look at where Zend Framework sits compared to some other frameworks.

1.5   Alternative PHP frameworks

Considering that the usage of PHP is so broad, no one framework is going to suit everyone. There are many other frameworks vying for your attention in the PHP world, and all have their strengths and weaknesses. Table 1.1 lists some of the strengths and weaknesses of these frameworks. We have rather arbitrarily picked four frameworks that all have some traction in the community, but these are by no means the only choices.

While this book is about Zend Framework, the other frameworks are worth investigating to see if they better match your requirements. If you still need to support PHP4, you will need to use either CakePHP or CodeIgniter because the rest do not support PHP4. In this day and age, however, it's time to leave PHP4 behind us as it has been officially discontinued.

Table 1.1   Key features of Zend Framework, CakePHP, CodeIgniter, Solar, and Symfony

Feature	Zend Framework	CakePHP	CodeIgniter	Solar	Symfony
Uses PHP5 to full advantage	Yes	No	No	Yes	Yes
Prescribed directory structure	No (Optional recommended structure)	Yes	Yes	No	Yes
Official international-ization support	Yes	In progress for version 1.2	No	Yes	Yes
Command line scripts required to setup framework	No	No	No	No	Yes
Requires configuration	Yes (minor amount)	No	No	Yes	Yes
Comprehensive ORM provided	No	Yes	No	No	Yes (Propel)
Good documentation and tutorials	Yes	Yes	Yes	Yes	Yes
Unit tests for source available	Yes	No	No	Yes	Yes
Community support	Yes	Yes	Yes	Yes (some)	Yes
License	New BSD	MIT	BSD-style	New BSD	MIT

1.6   Summary

In this chapter, we have looked at what Zend Framework is and why it is useful for writing web applications. It enables rapid development of enterprise applications by providing a comprehensive set of components using best practices in object-oriented design. The framework contains many components, from an MVC controller through to a PDF generator to a powerful search tool. Zend Framework has a set of design principles that ensure the code is of high quality and is well documented. A CLA is in place for all contributions, so the risk of IP issues with the framework is minimized, and with Zend Technologies committed to maintaining the framework, we can be sure of the long-term future for applications built on this technology.

This book is about providing real-world examples, so we'll have Ajax technology built in wherever it is appropriate. Now, let's move on to the core topic of this book and look at a how to build a simple, but complete, Zend Framework application in chapter 2.

Hello Zend Framework!

2

This chapter covers

- An introduction to the Model-View-Controller design pattern
- Zend Framework's controller components
- The `Zend_View` component
- Databases as models

Before we can investigate in detail all the components of Zend Framework, we must get our bearings, and this is best done by building a simple website that uses the MVC) components. For a standard PHP application, the code to display the text "Hello World" constitutes just one line in one file:

```
<?php echo 'Hello World';
```

In this chapter, we will build a Hello World application using Zend Framework. We will also consider how to organize the website's files on disk to make sure we can find what we are looking for, and we will look at Zend Framework files required to create an application that uses the MVC design pattern.

NOTE   Zend Framework requires many files to create the foundation from which a full website can be created. This means the code for our Hello

18

World application may appear unnecessarily verbose as we set the stage for the full-blown website that will follow in later chapters.

This chapter will walk through all the files required to build Hello World. We will also discuss Zend Framework's MVC design and the core components it provides for building the controller, view, and model in our application. Let's dive right in and look at what the Model-View-Controller design pattern is all about.

2.1 *The Model-View-Controller design pattern*

In order to enable you to make sense of a Zend Framework application, we need to cover a little bit of theory. Zend Framework provides an implementation of the Model-View-Controller software design pattern coupled to another design pattern known as Front Controller. A software design pattern is a standard general solution to a common problem. This means that while implementations will vary, the concepts used to solve problems using a given pattern will be the same.

The Front Controller pattern is a mechanism that centralizes the entrance point to your application. The front controller handler (usually index.php) accepts all server requests and runs the correct action function within the action command. This process is known as routing and dispatching. Zend Framework implements the front controller pattern over a number of subcomponents. The important ones are the `router` and the `dispatcher`. The `router` determines which action needs to be run, then the `dispatcher` runs the requested action and any other action that may be required.

The MVC pattern describes a way to separate out the key parts of an application into three main sections: the model, view, and controller. These are the sections that you write in order to create an application. Figure 2.1 shows how the Front Controller's router and dispatcher are attached to the model, controller, and view to produce a response to a web browser's request.

Within the Zend Framework MVC implementation, we have five main areas of concern. The router and dispatcher work together to determine which controller is to be run based on the contents of the URL. The controller works with the model and the view to create the final web page, which is sent back to the browser. Let's look at the model, view, and controller in more detail.

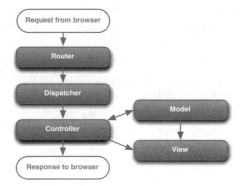

Figure 2.1 Zend Framework's Front Controller and MVC components work together to serve a web page. The router and dispatcher find the correct controller, which builds the page in conjunction with the model and view.

2.1.1   *The model*

The model part of the MVC pattern is all the business-logic code that works behind the scenes in the application. This is the code that decides how to apply the shipping costs to an e-commerce order, or knows that a user has a first name and a surname. Retrieving data from and storing it in a database falls within the model layer.

In terms of the code, Zend Framework provides the `Zend_Db_Table` and `Zend_Service` components. `Zend_Db_Table` provides table-level access to databases and allows for easily manipulating the data used by the application. `Zend_Service` provides a suite of components for easily accessing both public and private web services and integrating them into your application.

2.1.2   *The view*

The view is the display logic of the application. For a web application, this is usually the HTML code that makes up the web pages, but it can include, say, XML that is used for an RSS feed. Also, if the website allows for exporting in CSV (comma-separated values) format, the generation of the CSV data would be part of the view.

The view files are known as templates or scripts, because they usually have some code that allows for the display of data created by the model. It is also usual to move the more complex template-related code into functions known as *view helpers*, which improve the reusability of the view code. By default, Zend Framework's view class (`Zend_View`) uses PHP within the script files, but another template engine, such as Smarty or PHPTAL, may be substituted.

2.1.3   *The controller*

The controller is the rest of the code that makes up the application. For web applications, the controller code determines what should be done in response to a web request.

As we have discussed, Zend Framework's controller system is based on the Front Controller design pattern. which uses a handler (`Zend_Controller_Front`) to dispatch action commands (`Zend_Controller_Action`) that work in tandem. The dispatcher component allows for multiple action commands to be processed within a single request, which provides for flexible application architectures. The action class is responsible for a group of related action functions, which perform the real work required by the request. Within Zend Framework's front controller, it is possible to have a single request result in the dispatch of multiple actions.

Now that we understand a little about Zend Framework's MVC implementation, we can start looking at the nitty gritty of how the files fit together. As we mentioned earlier, there are a lot of files in a Zend Framework application, so we need to organize them into directories.

2.2   The anatomy of a Zend Framework application

A typical Zend Framework application has many directories. This helps to ensure that the different parts of the application are separated. The top-level directory structure is shown in figure 2.2.

There are four top-level directories within an application's folder:

- application
- library
- public
- tests

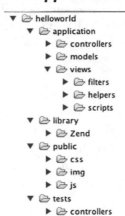

Figure 2.2   A typical Zend Framework application's directory layout groups the files by their role in the application, so it is easy to find the file you are looking for.

The application, library, and public directories are used when processing a request from the user. The tests directory is used to store unit test files that enable you to ensure that your code operates correctly.

2.2.1   The application directory

The application directory contains all the code required to run the application, and it is not directly accessed by the web server. In order to emphasize the separation between business, display, and control logic, there are three separate directories within the application directory to contain the model, view, and controller files. Other directories may be created as required, such as for configuration files.

2.2.2   The library directory

All applications use library code because *everyone* reuses previously written code! In a Zend Framework application, the framework itself is obviously stored in the library directory. However, other libraries, such as a custom superset of the framework, a database ORM library such as Propel, or a template engine such as Smarty, may also be used.

Libraries can be stored anywhere that the application can find them—either in a global directory or a local one. A global include directory is one that is accessible to all PHP applications on the server, such as /usr/php_include (or c:\code\php_include for Windows) and is set using the include_path setting within the php.ini configuration file. Alternatively, each application can store its libraries locally within the application's directory. In a Zend Framework application, we use a directory called library, though it is common to see this directory called lib, include, or inc.

2.2.3   The tests directory

The tests directory is used to store all unit tests. Unit tests are used to help ensure that the code continues to work as it grows and changes throughout the lifetime of the application. As the application is developed, existing code often needs to be changed (known as *refactoring*) to allow for the addition of new functionality or as a result of other code being added to the application. While test code is rarely considered important within the PHP world, you will thank yourself over and over again if you have unit tests for your code.

2.2.4 *The public directory*

To improve the security of a web application, the web server should only have direct access to the files that it needs to serve. As Zend Framework uses the Front Controller pattern, all web requests are channeled though a single file, usually called index.php. This file is the only PHP file that needs to be accessible by the web server, so it is stored in the public directory. Other common files that are accessed directly are image, Cascading Style Sheets (CSS), and JavaScript files, so each has its own subdirectory within the public directory.

Now that we looked at the directory system used by a Zend Framework web application, we can proceed to add the files required to create a very simple application that displays some text on the page.

2.3 *Hello World: file by file*

To create a simple Hello World application, we need to create four files within our directory structure: a bootstrap file, an Apache control file (.htaccess), a controller file, and a view template. A copy of Zend Framework, itself, also needs to be added to the library directory. The final program will display the page shown in figure 2.3.

The result is a web page with very little text, and the code required to do this seemingly simple task appears to be long and daunting. As an application's complexity grows, the additional code required to provide the new functionality is relatively small, showing benefits of the MVC system that are not apparent in a small example like this.

Let's start with the bootstrap file, which is used to start the application.

2.3.1 *Bootstrapping*

Bootstrapping is the term used to describe the code that initializes the application and configures it. With the Front Controller pattern, the bootstrap file is the only file

Figure 2.3   The Hello World application produces the words "Hello World!" in our browser. A minimal Zend Framework application requires .htaccess, bootstrap, controller, and view files working together to produce this.

needed in the public directory, and so is usually called index.php. Because this file is used for all page requests, it is also used for setting up the application's environment, setting up Zend Framework's controller system, then running the application itself, as shown in listing 2.1.

Listing 2.1 The bootstrap file, index.php, initializes and runs the application

```php
<?php
error_reporting(E_ALL|E_STRICT);
ini_set('display_errors', true);
date_default_timezone_set('Europe/London');

$rootDir = dirname(dirname(__FILE__));
set_include_path($rootDir . '/library'
        . PATH_SEPARATOR . get_include_path());

require_once 'Zend/Loader.php';
Zend_Loader::loadClass('Zend_Debug');
Zend_Loader::loadClass('Zend_Controller_Front');

// set up controller
$frontController = Zend_Controller_Front::getInstance();
$frontController->setControllerDirectory('../application/controllers');

// run!
$frontController->dispatch();
```

1 Sets up environment

2 Sets the path

3 Retrieves **Zend_Controller_Front** instance

Let's look at this file in more detail. Most of the work done in the bootstrap file is initialization of one form or another. Initially, the environment is set up correctly **1** to ensure that all errors or notices are displayed. (Don't do this on your production server!) PHP 5.1 introduced new time and date functionality that needs to know where in the world we are. There are several ways to set this, but the easiest method is to call date_default_timezone_set().

Zend Framework assumes that the library directory is available on the php_include path. The fastest way of setting this for a global library is to alter the include_path setting directly in php.ini. A more portable method, especially if you use multiple versions of the framework on one server, is to set the include path within the bootstrap file as we do here **2**.

Zend Framework applications do not depend on any particular file, but it is useful to have a couple of helper classes loaded early. Zend_Loader::loadClass() is used to "include" the correct file for the supplied class name. The function converts the underscores in the class's name to directory separators and then, after error checking, includes the file. As a result the code lines

```php
Zend_Loader::loadClass('Zend_Controller_Front');
```

and

```php
include_once 'Zend/Controller/Front.php';
```

have the same end result. Zend_Debug::dump() is used to output debugging information about a variable by providing a formatted var_dump() output.

The final section of the bootstrap file sets up the front controller and runs it. The front controller class, Zend_Controller_Front, implements the Singleton design pattern, so we use the getInstance() static function to retrieve it ❸. A Singleton design is appropriate for a front controller, as it ensures that there can only be one instance of the object processing the request.

The front controller, by default, captures all exceptions thrown and stores them in the response object that it creates. This response object holds all information about the response to the requested URL, and for HTML applications this includes the HTTP headers, the page content, and any exceptions that were thrown. The front controller automatically sends the headers and displays the page content when it finishes processing the request. In the case of exceptions, Zend Framework's ErrorHandler plugin will redirect the request to an action method called error in a controller called ErrorController. This ensures that we can control the error displayed to the user and possibly even offer additional help. We will implement this feature later.

To run the application, we call the front controller's dispatch() method. This function will automatically create a request and response object to encapsulate the input and output of the application. It will then create a router to work out which controller and action the user has asked for. A dispatcher object is then created to load the correct controller class and call the action member function that does the "real" work.

Finally, as we noted earlier, the front controller outputs the data within the response object and a web page is displayed to the user.

2.3.2 *Apache .htaccess*

To ensure that all web requests that are not for images, scripts, or stylesheets are directed to the bootstrap file, Apache's mod_rewrite module is used. This can be configured directly in Apache's httpd.conf file or in a local Apache configuration file named .htaccess that is placed in the public directory. Listing 2.2 shows the .htaccess file required for Zend Framework.

Listing 2.2   The bootstrap file: public/.htaccess

```
# Rewrite rules for Zend Framework
RewriteEngine on
RewriteCond %{REQUEST_FILENAME} !-f
RewriteRule .* index.php
```

Continues only if requested URL is not a file on disk

Redirects request to index.php on disk

Fortunately, this is not the most complicated set of Apache mod_rewrite rules, so they can be easily explained. The RewriteCond statement and the RewriteRule command between them instruct Apache to route all requests to index.php unless the request maps exactly to a file that exists within the public directory tree. This will allow us to serve any static resources placed in the public directory, such as JavaScript, CSS, and image files, while directing any other requests to our bootstrap file, where the front controller can work out what to display to the user.

2.3.3 Index controller

The Front Controller pattern maps the URL requested by the user to a particular member function (the action) within a specific controller class. This process is known as *routing and dispatching*.

The controller classes have a strict naming convention requirement in order for the dispatcher to find the correct function. The router expects to call a function named {actionName}Action() within the {ControllerName}Controller class. This class must be within a file called {ControllerName}Controller.php. If either the controller or the action name is not provided as part of the request, then the default, "index" is used. A call to http://zfia.example.com/ will result in the "index" action of the index controller running. Similarly, a call to http://zfia.example.com/test will result in the index action of the test controller running. As you will see later, this mapping is very flexible, but the default covers most scenarios.

Within Zend Framework's front controller implementation, the dispatcher expects to find a file called IndexController.php within the application/controllers directory. This file must contain a class called IndexController and, as a minimum, this class must contain a function called indexAction(). Listing 2.3 shows the IndexController.php required for our Hello World application.

Listing 2.3 The index controller: application/controllers/IndexController.php

```php
<?php

class IndexController extends Zend_Controller_Action
{
    public function indexAction()
    {
        $ this->view->assign('title', 'Hello World!');
    }

}
```

As you can see, IndexController is a child class of Zend_Controller_Action, which contains the request and response objects for access to the date received by the application and to set the data that will be sent back to the user, along with a few useful helper functions to control the program flow. For Hello World, our indexAction() function needs to assign a variable to the view property, which is provided for us by an action helper called Zend_Controller_Action_ViewRenderer (known as ViewRenderer).

NOTE An *action helper* is a class that plugs into the controller to provide services specific to actions. They expand a controller's functionality without using inheritance and so can be reused across multiple controllers and projects.

The ViewRenderer action helper performs two useful functions for us. First, before our action is called, it creates a Zend_View object and sets it to the action's $view property, allowing us to assign data to the view within the action. Second, after our action finishes, it automatically renders the correct view template into the response object after the controller action has completed. This ensures that our controller's action functions can concentrate on the real work and not on the framework's plumbing.

What is the "correct view template" though? The ViewRenderer looks in the view/ scripts directory for a template file named after the action, with a .phtml extension, within a folder named after the controller. This means that for the index action within the index controller, it will look for the view template file view/scripts/index/ index.phtml.

As we noted previously, the response's body is automatically printed by the front controller, so anything we assign to the body will be displayed in the browser. We do not need to echo ourselves.

Zend_View is the view component of the MVC troika and is a fairly simple PHP-based template system. As we have seen, the assign() function is used to pass variables from the main code body to the template, which can then be used within the view template file.

2.3.4   *View template*

The view script for our application, index.phtml, is stored within the views/scripts/ index subdirectory. A useful convention that ViewRenderer follows is to name all view files with an extension of .phtml as a visual indication that they are for display only. Of course, this is easily changed by setting the $_viewSuffix property of ViewRenderer.

Even though this is a simple application, we have a separate directory for each controller's view templates, because this will make it much easier to manage as the application grows. Listing 2.4 shows the view template.

Listing 2.4   The view template: views/scripts/index/index.phtml

```
<!DOCTYPE html PUBLIC "-//W3C//DTD XHTML 1.0 Strict//EN"
    "http://www.w3.org/TR/xhtml1/DTD/xhtml1-strict.dtd">
<html xmlns="http://www.w3.org/1999/xhtml" lang="en" xml:lang="en">
<head>
    <meta http-equiv="Content-Type" content="text/html;charset=utf-8" />
    <title>
        <?php echo $this->escape($this->title);?>      ◁——— Converts special
    </title>                                                   characters to HTML
</head>                                                         entity representations
<body>
    <h1><?php echo $this->escape($this->title);?></h1>
</body>
</html>
```

As Zend_View is a PHP-based template engine, we use PHP within the file to display data from the model and controller. The template file, index.phtml in this case, is executed within a member function of Zend_View, so $this is available within the template file, and it is the gateway to Zend_View's functionality. All variables assigned to the view from within the controller are available directly as properties of $this, as can be seen by the use of $this->title within index.phtml. Also, a number of helper functions are provided via templates, which makes them easier to write.

The most commonly used helper function is escape(). This function ensures that the output is HTML-safe and helps to secure your site from cross-site scripting (XSS) attacks. All variables that are not expected to contain displayable HTML should be displayed via the escape() function. Zend_View is designed to encourage the creation of new helper functions. For maximum flexibility, the convention is that view helper functions return their data, and then the template file echoes it to the browser.

With these four files in place, we have created a minimal Zend Framework application with all the pieces in place for a full-scale website. You should now have a fundamental understanding of how the pieces fit together. Next, we will look at what is happening within Zend Framework's code, which provides the MVC foundation our code is built upon.

2.4 *How MVC applies to Zend Framework*

While there appear to be many different ways of routing web requests to code within web applications, they can all be grouped into two camps: page controllers and front controllers.

A page controller uses separate files for every page (or group of pages) that make up the website, and this is traditionally how most PHP websites have been built. This means that the control of the application is decentralized across lots of different files, which can result in repeated code, or, worse, repeated and slightly altered code leading to issues such as lost sessions when one of the files doesn't do a session_start().

A front controller, on the other hand, centralizes all web requests into a single file, typically called index.php, which lives in the root directory of the website. There are numerous advantages to this system; the most obvious are that there is less duplicated code and it is easier to separate the URLs that a website has from the actual code that is used to generate the pages. Usually, the pages are displayed using two additional GET parameters passed to the index.php file to create URLs such as this to display a list page:

```
index.php?controller=news&action=list
```

As we explained in chapter 1, Zend Framework uses a Front Controller pattern coupled to the Model-View-Controller pattern to respond to a request from the browser. Each pattern is made up of multiple classes, as shown in figure 2.4.

One important goal of most modern web applications is that the URLs should look "good," so that they are more memorable for users and it is easier for search engines like Yahoo! or Google to index the pages of the website. An example of a friendly URL would be http://www.example.com/news/list, because this URL does not include any ? or & characters, and the user can infer what will be displayed (a list of news items). Zend Framework's front controller uses a subcomponent known as a router that supports friendly URLs by default.

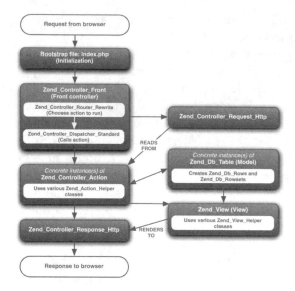

Figure 2.4   The interaction of the various Zend Framework classes in an MVC application

2.4.1   *Zend Framework's controller*

Zend Framework's front controller code is spread over a number of classes that work together to provide a very flexible solution to the problem of routing a web request to the correct place. Zend_Controller_Front is the foundation, and it processes all requests received by the application and delegates that actual work to action controllers.

THE REQUEST

The request is encapsulated within an instance of Zend_Controller_Request_Http, which provides access to the entire HTTP request environment. What is a request environment? It is all the variables received by the application, along with relevant controller parameters, such as the controller and action router variables.

The HTTP request environment contains all the superglobals ($_GET, $_POST, $_COOKIE, $_SERVER, and $_ENV) along with the base path to the application. The router also places the module, controller, and action names into the request object once it has worked them out. Zend_Controller_Request_Http provides the get-Param() function to allow the application to collect the request variables, and so the rest of the application is protected from a change in environment. For example, a command-line request environment wouldn't contain the HTTP-specific items, but would include the command-line arguments passed to the script. Thus, this code will work unchanged when run as a web request or as a command-line script:

```
$items = $request->getParam('items');
```

In general, the request object should be treated as read-only to the application, because the values set by the user shouldn't be changed. Having said that, Zend_Controller_Request_Http also contains parameters that can be set in the startup phase of the application and then retrieved by the action functions as required. This can be used to pass additional information from the front controller to the action methods, if required.

After the front controller has set up the request object from the superglobals, it then starts the router.

ROUTING

The router determines which code to run, based on the parameters within the request. This is done by a class that implements `Zend_Controller_Router_-Interface`. The framework also supplies `Zend_Controller_Router_Rewrite`, which handles most routing requirements.

Routing works by taking the part of the URI after the base URL (known as the *URI endpoint*) and decomposing it into separate parameters. For a standard URL, such as http://example.com/index.php?controller=news&action=list the decomposition is done by simply reading the `$_GET` array and looking for the controller and action elements. It is expected that most applications built using Zend Framework (like other modern applications) will use pretty URLs of the form http://example.com/news/list. In this case, the router will use the relevant variables in the `$_SERVER` super-global array to determine which controller and action have been requested.

After the controller and action have been determined, the correct controller action method is run, along with any other controller action methods that may be specified by the application. This is known as *dispatching* and is performed by the front controller after the router has completed.

DISPATCHING

Dispatching is the process of calling the correct method in the correct class. Like all components in Zend Framework, the standard dispatcher provides enough functionality for nearly every situation, but if you need something special, it is easy to write your own dispatcher and fit it into the front controller. The key things that the dispatcher controls are formatting the controller class name, formatting the action method name, and calling the action method itself.

`Zend_Controller_Dispatcher_Standard` is where the rules concerning case are enforced, such that the name format of the controller is always TitleCase and only contains alphanumeric characters (and the underscore character). The dispatcher's `dispatch()` method is responsible for loading the controller class file, instantiating the class and then calling the action method within that class. If you decided that you wanted to reorganize the structure so that each action lived in its own class within a directory named after the controller, you would need to supply your own dispatcher.

At this point, the dispatcher passes control to the controller class's action function. Action controllers are separate classes that are stored within the controllers subdirectory of the application directory.

THE ACTION

`Zend_Controller_Action` is an abstract class that all action controllers are derived from. The dispatcher enforces that your action controllers derive from this class to ensure that it can expect certain methods to be available. The action contains an instance of the request, for reading parameters from, and an instance of the response, for writing to. The rest of the class concentrates on ensuring that writing actions and managing changes from one action to another are easy to do. There are accessor functions to get and set parameters, and redirection functions to redirect to another action or another URL entirely.

Assuming that the standard dispatcher is used, the action functions are all named after the action's name with the word "Action" appended. You can therefore expect a controller action class to contain functions such as `indexAction()`, `viewAction()`, `editAction()`, `deleteAction()`, and so on. Each of these is a discrete method run in response to a specific URL.

There are also a number of tasks that you will want to do regardless of which action is run. `Zend_Controller_Action` provides two levels of functionality to accommodate this requirement: `init()` and the `preDispatch()` and `postDispatch()` pair.

The `init()` method is called whenever the controller class is constructed. This makes it very similar to the standard constructor, except that it does not take any parameters and does not require the parent method to be called.

`preDispatch()` and `postDispatch()` are a complementary pair of methods that are run before and after each action method is called. For an application where only one action is run in response to a request, there is no difference between `init()` and `preDispatch()`, as each is only called once. If the first action method uses the `_forward()` function to pass control to another action method, `preDispatch()` will be run again, but `init()` will not be. To illustrate this point, we could use `init()` to ensure that only administrators are allowed access to any action method in the controller, and we could use `preDispatch()` to set the correct view script file that would be used by the action.

After the action method has finished, control is returned to the dispatcher, which will then run other actions as required. When all actions are complete, the created output is returned to the user via the response object.

THE RESPONSE

The final link in the front controller chain is the response. For a web application, `Zend_Controller_Response_Http` is provided, but if you are writing a command-line application, `Zend_Controller_Response_Cli` would be more appropriate. The response object is very simple and is essentially a bucket to hold all the output until the controller processing is finished. This can be very useful when using front controller plug-ins, as they could alter the output of the action before it is sent back to the client.

`Zend_Controller_Response_Http` contains three types of information: header, body, and exception. In the context of the response, the headers are HTTP headers, not HTML headers. Each header is an array containing a name, along with its value, and it is possible to have two headers with the same name but different values within the response's container. The response also holds the HTTP response code (as defined in RFC 2616), which is sent to the client at the end of processing. By default, this is set to 200, which means OK. Other common response codes are 404 (Not

Found) and 302 (Found), which is used when redirecting to a new URL. As we will see later, the use of status code 304 (Not Modified) can be very useful when responding to requests for RSS feeds, as it can save considerable bandwidth.

The body container within the response is used to contain everything else that needs to be sent back to the client. For a web application, this means everything you see when you view the source on a web page. If you are sending a file to a client, the body would contain the contents of the file. For example, to send a PDF file to the client, the following code would be used:

```
$filename = 'example.pdf';
$response = new Zend_Controller_Response_Http();

// set the HTTP headers
$response->setHeader('Content-Type', 'application/pdf');
$response->setHeader('Content-Disposition',
   'attachment; filename="'.$filename.'"');
$response->setHeader('Accept-Ranges', 'bytes');
$response->setHeader('Content-Length', filesize($filename));

// load the file to send into the body
$response->setBody(file_get_contents($filename));

echo $response;
```

The final container within the response object houses the exceptions. This is an array that can be added to by calling `$response->setException()`, and it is used by `Zend_Controller_Front` to ensure that errors within the code are not sent to the client, possibly exposing private information that could be used to compromise your application. Of course, during development you will want to see the errors, so the response has a setting, `renderExceptions`, that you can set to `true` so that the exception text is displayed.

In order to extend the front controller, a plug-in system has been developed.

FRONT CONTROLLER PLUG-INS

The front controller's architecture contains a plug-in system to allow user code to be executed automatically at certain points in the routing and dispatching process. Plug-ins allow you to change the functionality of the front controller's routing and dispatching system in a modular fashion, and they are designed to be easily transferred from one project to another.

All plug-ins are derived from `Zend_Controller_Plugin_Abstract`, and there are six event methods that can be overridden:

- `routeStartup()` is called just before the router is executed.
- `routeShutdown()` is called after the router has finished.
- `dispatchLoopStartup()` is called just before the dispatcher starts executing.
- `preDispatch()` is called before each action is executed.
- `postDispatch()` is called after each action is executed.
- `dispatchLoopShutdown()` is called after all actions have been dispatched.

As you can see, there are three pairs of hooks into the process at three different points, which allow for increasingly finer control of the process.

One problem with the current router is that if you specify a controller that does not exist, an exception is thrown. A front controller plug-in is a good way to inject a solution into the routing process and redirect the application to a more useful page. Zend Framework supplies the `ErrorHandler` plug-in for this purpose, and its use is very well explained in the manual.

Now that we have looked in detail at the controller part of MVC, it's time to look at the view part, as provided for by the `Zend_View` component.

2.4.2   *Understanding Zend_View*

The `Zend_View` class keeps the view portion of an MVC application separate from the rest of the application. It is a PHP template library, which means that the code in the view scripts is in PHP rather than another pseudo-language, like Smarty for instance. However, it is easy to extend `Zend_View` to support any other template system.

Let's start our exploration of `Zend_View` by looking at how to assign data to the view. `Zend_View`'s `assign()` method is used to display data from the model. Simple variables can be assigned to a view variable like this:

```
$view->assign('title', 'Hello World!');
```

This assigns the string "Hello World!" to the `title` variable. Alternatively, you can assign multiple variables simultaneously using an associative array:

```
$music = array('title'=>'Abbey Road', 'artist'=>'The Beatles');
$music = array('title'=>'The Wall', 'artist'=>'Pink Floyd');
$view->assign($music);
```

As we are using PHP5, we can also take advantage of the __set() magic method to write

```
$view->title = 'Hello World!';
```

which will also assign the string to the `title` variable. Whichever of the preceding two methods you use for assigning data, the data from the model or controller is now available for use in the view script, which is the file that contains output HTML and code.

THE VIEW SCRIPT

A view script is just like any other regular PHP file, except that its scope is contained within an instance of a `Zend_View` object. This means that it has access to all the methods and data of `Zend_View` as if it were a function within the class. The data assigned to the view is public property of the view class and so is directly accessible. In addition, the view provides helper functions to make writing view scripts easier.

A typical view script might look like this:

```
<h1>Glossary</h1>
<?php if ($this->glossary) :?>
<dl>
<?php foreach ($this->glossary as $item) : ?>
```

```
<dt><?php echo $this->escape($item['term']);?></dt>
<dd><?php echo $this->escape($item['description']);?></dd>
<?php endforeach; ?>
</dl>
<?php endif; ?>
```

As you can see, this is a PHP script with an HTML bias, as the PHP commands are always contained within their own <?php and ?> tags. Also, we have used the alternative convention for control loops so that we don't have braces within separate PHP tags—matching braces can be quite tricky when using lots of separate PHP tags.

Note that we do not trust the glossary data that has been assigned to the script. It could have come from anywhere! In the code accompanying this book, the data is created using an array, but it could equally have come from the users of a website. To avoid any XSS vulnerabilities in our website, we use the escape() helper function to ensure the term and description do not have any embedded HTML.

To avoid repeating lots of similar PHP code in multiple view scripts, view helper functions are used to provide common functionality.

VIEW HELPER FUNCTIONS

Zend_View contains a number of helpful methods to make writing your view scripts easier. These methods are known as view helpers and exist in their own classes within the application/views/helpers subdirectory. As we have already seen, the most common view helper is the escape() method, which is built into the Zend_View class itself. Every other helper exists in its own class and is automatically loaded by Zend_View.

Let's create a simple formatting helper for displaying a cash amount. Consider that we need to display a monetary value that may be negative. In the UK, for a value of 10, the display would be £10.00, and for a value of –10, the display would be –£10.00.

We would use the helper in our view scripts like this:

```
<p>He gave me <?php echo $this->formatCurrency(10);?>.</p>
```

Which outputs the correctly formatted amount as shown in figure 2.5.

All default view helpers use the class prefix Zend_View_Helper and are stored in the applications/views/helpers subdirectory. You can store view helpers elsewhere, in which case you would use your own class prefix. Our formatting helper class is called Zend_View_Helper_FormatCurrency and is stored in the file application/views/helpers/Format-Currency.php, as shown in listing 2.5. In a break

Figure 2.5 The FormatCurrency view helper is used to display the correct currency symbol in the correct place.

from the usual convention within the framework, this is one of the few cases where the class name is not the same as the file path.

Listing 2.5   The FormatCurrency view helper

```
class Zend_View_Helper_FormatCurrency {

    public function formatCurrency($value, $symbol='&pound;')
    {
        $output = '';
        $value = trim($value);
        if (is_numeric($value)) {
            if ($value >= 0) {
                $output = $symbol . number_format($value, 2);
            } else {
                $output = '-' . $symbol . number_format(abs($value), 2);
            }
        }
        return $output;
    }
}
```

❶ Ignores $value if it is not a number

As you can see, if we don't know that $value is a number, we do not return it as part of the output ❶. This helps to ensure that we do not inadvertently introduce an XSS vulnerability.

The name of the method within the helper class is the same as the method that is called within the view script: formatCurrency() in our case. Internally, Zend_View has an implementation of the __call() magic function to find our helper class and execute the formatCurrency() method.

TIP   When you create your view helpers, the names are case-sensitive. The class name is in CamelCase with underscores, but the method name is in camelCase. The class name must start with an uppercase letter, and the method name starts with a lowercase one.

View helpers are the key to extracting common code from your view scripts and ensuring that they are easy to maintain, so view helpers should be used whenever possible to simplify the view script files. As view script files contain the output of the application, it is important to always keep security issues in mind when sending data to the web browser.

SECURITY CONSIDERATIONS

When writing view code, the most important security issue you need to be aware of is XSS. Its vulnerabilities occur when unexpected HTML, CSS, or JavaScript is displayed by your website. Generally, this happens when a website displays data created by a user without checking that it is safe for display. This could happen when the text from a comment form contains HTML and is displayed on a guestbook page "as is."

One of the more famous XSS exploits is the Samy MySpace worm. This exploit used specially crafted JavaScript in the profile that was displayed on a page which lists all the user's friends. The JavaScript would run automatically whenever anyone else viewed the victim's friends page, and if that user was logged into MySpace, it made Samy their "friend" too. Thus, whenever anyone looked at your page, they were also made "friends" of Samy's. This resulted in an exponential increase in friends for

Samy—over one million MySpace profiles were infected within 20 hours. Fortunately, the code wasn't too malicious and didn't steal each user's password along the way.

The easiest way to prevent XSS vulnerabilities is to encode the characters that have special meaning in HTML. That is, you should change all instances of < to <, & to & and > to > so that the browser treats them as literals rather than HTML. Within Zend Framework, you can use the escape() helper function to do this. Every time that you display a PHP variable within a template file, you should use escape() unless you need it to contain HTML. If it does need to contain HTML, you should write a sanitizing function to allow only HTML code that you trust.

We have completed our look at the view, so now let's look at the model. This is where the guts of the application are, including interaction with databases and files.

2.4.3   The model in MVC

We have spent a lot of time in this chapter looking at the controller and the view, as these are the minimum required for a Hello World application. In a real application, though, the model element of the MVC pattern takes on more importance as this is where the business logic of the application resides. In most cases, the model is linked in some way to a database that holds data to be manipulated and displayed by the application.

DATABASE ABSTRACTION WITH ZEND_DB

Zend_Db is Zend Framework's database abstraction library, which provides a suite of functions that insulate your code from the underlying database engine. This is most useful when you need to switch your application from using something like SQLite to MySQL or Oracle.

Zend_Db uses the Factory design pattern to provide the correct database-specific class, based on the parameters passed into the factory() static method. For example, to create a Zend_Db object for MySQL, you would use code like this:

```
$params = array ('host'     => '127.0.0.1',
                 'username' => 'rob',
                 'password' => '******',
                 'dbname'   => 'zfia');
$db = Zend_Db::factory('PDO_MYSQL', $params);
```

The Zend_Db abstraction is mostly built upon PHP's PDO extension, which supports a wide range of databases. There is also support for DB2 and Oracle outside of PDO; they all extend from Zend_Db_Adapter_Abstract, so the interface is essentially the same, regardless of the underlying database.

What you do get in Zend_Db that you don't get in PDO itself? Well, you get lots of helper functions to manipulate the database, and also a profiler to work out why your code is so slow. There are all the standard functions for inserting, updating, and deleting rows, along with fetching rows. The manual is particularly good at describing all these functions, so let's move on and consider database security.

SECURITY ISSUES WITH DATABASES

The most common database security problems are known as SQL injection security breaches. These occur when your user is able to trick your code into running a database query that you didn't intend to allow. Consider this code:

```
$result = $db->query("SELECT * FROM users
WHERE name='" . $_POST['name'] . "'");
```

This typical code might be used to authorize a user after they have submitted a login form. The coder has ensured that the correct superglobal, $_POST, is used, but hasn't checked what it contains. Suppose that $_POST['name'] contains this string:

```
' OR 1 OR name = '
```

This would result in the following perfectly legal SQL statement:

```
SELECT * from users where name='' OR 1 OR name= ''
```

As you can see, the OR 1 in the SQL statement will result in all the users being returned from the database table. With SQL injection vulnerabilities like this, it is possible for an attacker to retrieve username and password information or to maliciously delete database rows causing your application to stop working.

As should be obvious, the way to avoid SQL injection attacks is to ensure that the data you are putting into the SQL statement has been escaped using the correct functionality for your database. For MySQL, you would use the mysql_real_escape_string() function, and for PostgreSQL, you would use pg_escape_string(). As we are using Zend_Db, we can use the quote() member function to take care of this issue. The quote() method will call the correct underlying database-specific function, and if there isn't one, it will escape the string using the correct rules for the database involved. Using it is very easy:

```
$value = $db->quote("It's a kind of magic");
```

An alternative solution is to use parameterized queries, where variables are denoted by placeholders and the values are substituted by the database engine. Zend_Db provides the quoteInto() function for this:

```
$sql = $db->quoteInto('SELECT * FROM table WHERE id = ?', 1);
$result = $db->query($sql);
```

Parameterized queries are generally considered best practice, as they result in faster database accesses, especially if you use prepared statements.

Within the Zend_Db component, Zend Framework provides a higher-level access to the database using the Zend_Db_Table component, which provides an object-oriented interface to a database table and its associated rows, thereby avoiding the necessity of writing common SQL statements in every model.

HIGHER-LEVEL INTERACTION WITH ZEND_DB_TABLE

When coding the model of an MVC application, we don't tend to want to work at the level of database queries if we can help it because we are thinking about the business logic of the application, rather than the nitty gritty of how to interact with a database. The framework provides Zend_Db_Table, an implementation of the Table Data Gateway pattern that provides a higher-level abstraction for thinking about data from the database. Zend_Db_Table uses Zend_Db behind the scenes and provides a static class function, setDefaultAdapter(), for setting the database adapter to be used for all instances of Zend_Db_Table. This is usually set up in the bootstrap file like this:

```
$db = Zend_Db::factory('PDO_MYSQL', $params);
Zend_Db_Table::setDefaultAdapter($db);
```

We don't use Zend_Db_Table directly. Instead, we create a child class that represents the database table we wish to work with. For the purposes of this discussion, we will assume that we have a database table called news with the columns id, date_created, created_by, title, and body to work with. We now create a class called News:

```
Class News extends Zend_Db_Table
{
    protected $_name = 'news';
}
```

The $_name property is used to specify the name of the table. If it is not provided, Zend_Db_Table will use the name of the class, and it is case sensitive. Zend_Db_Table also expects a primary key called id (which is preferably automatically incremented on an insert). Both these default expectations can be changed by initializing the protected member variables $_name and $_primary respectively. Here's an example:

```
class LatestNews extends Zend_Db_Table
{
    protected $_name = 'news';
    protected $_primary = 'article_id';
}
```

The LatestNews class uses a database table called news that has a primary key called article_id. As Zend_Db_Table implements the Table Data Gateway design pattern, it provides a number of functions for collecting data, including find(), fetchRow(), and fetchAll(). The find() function finds rows by primary key, and the fetch methods find rows using other criteria. The only difference between fetchRow() and fetchAll() is that fetchRow() returns a single row object, whereas fetchAll() returns an object, known as a *rowset*, that contains a set of rows. Zend_Db_Table also has helper functions for inserting, updating, and deleting rows with the functions insert(), update(), and delete().

While Zend_Db_Table is interesting in its own right, its usefulness becomes apparent when we add business logic to it. This is the point when we enter the realm of the model within MVC. There are lots of things you can do, and we'll start with overriding insert() and update() for our News model.

First of all, let's assume that our news database table has the following definition (in MySQL):

```
CREATE TABLE `news` (
`id` INT NOT NULL AUTO_INCREMENT PRIMARY KEY ,
`date_created` DATETIME NOT NULL ,
`date_updated` DATETIME NULL ,
`title` VARCHAR(100) NULL ,
`body` MEDIUMTEXT NOT NULL
)
```

The first business logic that we will implement in our News class, which is our model, will automatically manage the date_created and date_updated fields when inserting and updating records, as shown in listing 2.6. These are "behind the scenes" details that the rest of the system doesn't need to worry about, so they are ideal for placing in the model.

Listing 2.6   Automatically maintaining date fields in a model

```
class News extends Zend_Db_Table
{
    protected $_name = 'news';

    public function insert($data)
    {
        if (empty($data['date_created'])) {
            $data['date_created'] = date('Y-m-d H:i:s');
        }
        return parent::insert($data);                    Calls Zend_DB_Table's
    }                                              ❶  insert() function

    public function update($data)
    {
        if (empty($data['date_updated'])) {
            $data['date_updated'] = date('Y-m-d H:i:s');        Sets date field if
        }                                                       not already set
        return parent::update($data);
    }

}
```

This code is self-explanatory. When inserting, if date_created hasn't been supplied by the caller, we fill in today's date and call Zend_Db_Table's insert() function ❶. For updating, the story is similar, except we change the date_updated field instead.

We can also write our own functions for retrieving data according to the business logic required by the application. Let's assume that for our website, we want to display the five most recently created news items (within the last three months) displayed on the home page. This could be done using $news->fetchAll() in the home page controller, but it is better to move the logic down into the News model to maintain the correct layering of the application, so that it can be reused by other controllers if required:

```
public function fetchLatest($count = 5)
{
    $cutOff = date('Y-m-', strtotime('-3 months'))
    $where = array('date_created > ?' => $cutOff);
    $order = "date_created DESC";
```

```
    return $this->fetchAll($where, $order, $count);
}
```

Again, this is very simple functionality that becomes much more powerful when placed in the right layer of the MVC triumvirate. Note that we use a parameterized array for the $where variable, which ensures that Zend_Db will protect us against SQL injection attacks.

2.5 Summary

We have now written a simple Hello World application using Zend Framework, and we have explored the way the Model-View-Controller design pattern is applied to our applications. You should now have a good idea of how Zend Framework can make our applications maintainable and easy to write.

One ideal that the framework developers try to adhere to is known as the 80/20 rule. Each component is intended to solve 80 percent of the problem space it addresses, and provides flex points to enable developers who need to work with the other 20 percent. For example, the front controller system provides a router that covers nearly all requirements. If you need a more specialized router, it is very easy to insert your own into the rest of the front controller setup. Similarly, Zend_View_Abstract allows for adding other template engines, such as Smarty or PHPTAL, if the supplied Zend_View is not suitable for your application.

We will now move on to build a fully functioning community website that will utilize most of the components supplied with the framework.

Part 2

A core application

Now that we know what Zend Framework is and understand the basics of creating a Zend Framework application, in chapters 3-11 we'll build a real-world application to use throughout the rest of the book. While looking at the core Zend Framework components that are used for building a typical website, we'll see how they are integrated into a coherent whole.

Along with authentication, access control, forms, searching, and email, we'll cover implementing Ajax within an MVC application. Finally, we'll look at management and deployment issues, including version control and testing.

Building a website
with Zend Framework

3

This chapter covers

- Developing a large Zend Framework application
- Building a maintainable Bootstrap class
- Writing and testing database model classes

To show off the features of the framework in this chapter, we are going to build a community website where parents can find out about pro-child tourist attractions. We will call it *Places to take the kids!*.

Building such a community website requires a lot of time and effort, and it will be tempting to take the easy road toward intermingled PHP and HTML. We expect our website to be a key resource for many years, and following good software engineering principles now will pay off many times over the lifetime of the project. Zend Framework's MVC system will help us to do things the right way. There is even a side benefit of being quicker, as we can take advantage of the simplicity and convention-over-configuration principles to ensure that our code is easy to write and refactor.

Before we build the basic website, we will focus on what we intend to build and the features it will need. We will then be able to set up an initial database and code the first pages.

3.1   *Initial planning of a website*

We can't build a website without some sort of specification, but a whole specification would take too long. Instead, we will describe our site's goals with a simple story. After looking at what the site will achieve, we will then look at any issues within the UI of the website that will lead us into the code.

3.1.1   *The site's goals*

For any website, there is only one question that needs to be answered from the user's point of view: *What does this site do for me?* If we can identify who will give positive answers to this question, then we have a potential audience. There are secondary questions to ask too, including how to fund the site, but these are relatively minor compared to ensuring that the site can get visitors.

One way to describe features of a website is to use paragraphs that explain how a certain feature works from a very high-level perspective. The main benefit these "stories" have over a proper specification is that they are written in easy-to-understand language. Without jargon. We can use the same mechanism to describe the entire website too:

> *Places to take the kids!* is a website that enables parents to fully enjoy a day out, confident that the places they visit will be suitable for their children. The site will welcome a community of users who can review and recommend places to visit. The site provides simple mechanisms for finding places to visit by browsing through categories or by searching. The user will be able to save different places as part of a planned trip, and then can print out the details of their trip later.

Our site story conveys all we need to know to create a good website, and we are now able to start planning. Clearly, we could write even more about what the site could do, but that can be left for future phases of development. We will start looking at the main functionality of the website and at how we will use testing to improve our code.

MAIN FUNCTIONALITY

Let's brainstorm a list of the things that the website will need using a mind map. Our initial thoughts are shown in figure 3.1.

Another nice thing about mind maps is that they can be easily added to. In this case, the Locations (or places) section is key to the site and so has had the most thought put into it. We will not worry too much about competitions, because they are a "nice to have" feature rather than a core requirement to meet the site's goals.

We have now developed our initial plans for the website, so we will turn our thoughts to the build process. We intend to build our website by implementing one feature at time. As the site grows, the initial code will be changed to accommodate

Figure 3.1 Mind maps are a good way to brainstorm features for a new website. For this site, we have found that seven main areas of the website will be required to meet our main goals. The Locations section has been fleshed out the most.

new features, and we will need to ensure that we do not break any existing functionality. Unit testing can help ensure that.

THE UNIT TESTING PROCESS

We will write tests for anything we are unsure about as we go along. This will give us confidence in our code and allow us to refactor it as we improve the design. Improving the design shouldn't be hard, as we have barely done any! Even if we did lots of up-front design, it is certain that what we learn while building will be of immeasurable value; we want to incorporate what we learn as we go along. While we won't be discussing each of the tests within these pages, the accompanying source code contains all the tests required for us to have confidence in the code.

Testing provides confidence that our code will continue work as we add new features. The testing for *Places* will be done mainly using unit tests, which can be automated, because testing that requires someone to follow a written procedure would not be done often enough to catch errors that result from code changes. Zend Framework's MVC system provides a response object, so we can use unit testing to check that the HTML output has the correct data in it and test elements of the page rendering too.

3.1.2 Designing the user interface

We need to consider how our new website is going to work in terms of the user interface (UI). I'm a software engineer, not a creative designer, so it's probably best if I don't provide many thoughts on design! A good user interface is much more than appearance; you also have to consider how it operates for the user. We need to ensure that our users can navigate easily to the information they are looking for.

The key UI features we will be considering on our *Places* website are navigation via a menu and a search system. The navigation will use a drill-down approach, with the main menu always being visible and the current level menu also being shown. This allows for a lot of flexibility while not creating a cluttered menu. We could also display a breadcrumb trail so that the user understands where they are in the site and which route they took from the home page to get to the page they are currently viewing.

When designing a UI for the site, we need to think about the features of the site, such as:

- menus and navigation
- page layout
- accessibility
- images

We will now look at the key issues to consider for these elements which form part of the design brief for creation of the actual look and feel of the website.

MENUS AND NAVIGATION

The key feature we will be considering on our *Places* website is navigation, both via a menu and a search system.

The navigation will use a drill-down approach with the main menu across the top of the site always being visible, and the current level vertical submenu also being shown. This allows for a lot of flexibility while not creating a cluttered menu. We could also display a breadcrumb trail so that the user has an appreciation of where they are in the site and which route they took from the home page to get to the page they are currently viewing.

This will give us a site that is easy to navigate and that also has plenty of expansion room for building new features.

PAGE LAYOUT

As this is a community site, we want to make sure that there is plenty of room for content and also room for discretely placed advertisements that will help pay the bandwidth bills. The site's basic look and feel will be long-lived, because we want to build a brand and because communities don't tend to like change. This means we will need a design that can grow as we improve the site with new features.

ACCESSIBILITY

A modern site needs to be accessible to all. This means that our site needs to be standards-compliant so that it works in all modern browsers and also that we must consider users with less than perfect eyesight and mouse coordination. We need to keep the Web Accessibility Initiative (WAI) standard in mind at all times when building the front end of the website.

IMAGES

They say that an image is worth a thousand words, but it costs a lot of time and bandwidth compared to those words! We will use images to improve how the site looks and to add value for our users. Obviously, we will provide images of the locations for each review. Images also work well for feature lists and to mark different sections of the pages.

Putting all this together into a design, we have a site that looks like figure 3.2.

There are four sections to this design: the header (including menu) across the top, the main content on the left, a banner ad on the right, and a footer. We are now ready to look at the code required to build the site, starting with the initial setup of the

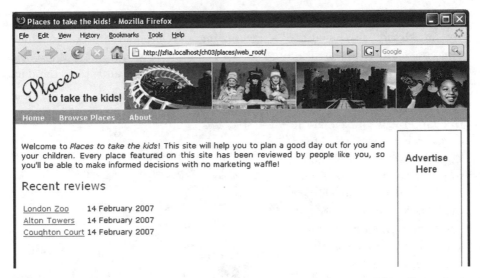

Figure 3.2 *PLACES TO TAKE THE KIDS!* **home page maximizes the amount of space for content while ensuring ease of use.**

directory structure, bootstrap, and loading of configuration information. We will also look at how we build the view scripts to ensure that we do not repeat the header and footer code within every action view script.

3.1.3 Planning the code

We have looked at the goals of the site and at how the user interface will work, so we can now look at how we will organize the PHP code. As with the UI, we need to ensure that our code will not be "hemmed in" when the site's functionality and feature lists grow. We also want the system to do as much of the plumbing automatically for us, so, for instance, we don't have to worry about finding the correct class in the file structure, choosing the name of a view script, or struggling to relate to database tables. We will also be using Ajax and so will need to change the output format of the view from HTML at times.

Zend Framework is a good choice to meet these requirements. As we discussed in chapter 1, Zend Framework is a flexible, robust, and supported platform that will be around for as long as our site is.

Zend Framework's MVC system ensures that we will organize our site into separate controllers, each with a set of view scripts. We will also access our database tables via models that will allow us to write code in the language of the problem rather than in the language of the database. Another feature of the MVC system is modules that allow us to group a set of related controllers, views, and models together. We will use this functionality to separate out different logical concerns of the *Places* website.

With this initial planning in place, we can now start creating code and tests, just as soon as we know where to put it!

3.2   *Initial coding*

We can kick off the initial coding by creating a skeleton structure onto which we can build the features that are required. This means that we will set up the directories we will need, write the bootstrap file, consider configuration issues, and create the database.

3.2.1   *The directory structure*

In chapter 2, we looked at the core directories we need for a Zend Framework application, so we'll start from there. Our *Places* website is a bit bigger than Hello World, so we will need additional directories to keep the files manageable, as shown in figure 3.3.

As with Hello World, we organize our directory structure with the goal of ensuring we can find the files again. This means that we separate out all the functionality both logically, using modules, and by concern, into separate

Figure 3.3   Directory structure of the *Places* website, showing key files for the home page

models, views, and controllers directories. For security, the public directory is the only directory that the web server can directly serve files from, so it only contains one file: the index.php file that will load the Bootstrap class, which is the next thing we will look at.

3.2.2   *The Bootstrap class*

The Hello World application's bootstrap file was very simplistic, so it was stored in index.php. As an application grows, more flexibility is required. We will therefore create a Bootstrap class in application/bootstrap.php, which is then referenced from public/index.php. We will start with the bootstrap code from Hello World and augment it to load configuration data, initialize the database, and automatically load classes as we use them. Our initial Bootstrap class is shown in listing 3.1—we will discuss the details in the following sections.

Listing 3.1   The initial Bootstrap class: `application/bootstrap.php`

```php
<?php
class Bootstrap
{
    public function __construct($configSection)
    {
        $rootDir = dirname(dirname(__FILE__));          Sets up
        define('ROOT_DIR', $rootDir);                   include path
        set_include_path(get_include_path()
            . PATH_SEPARATOR . ROOT_DIR . '/library/'
            . PATH_SEPARATOR . ROOT_DIR .
                '/application/models/'
        );

        include 'Zend/Loader.php';              ❶  Enables automatic
        Zend_Loader::registerAutoload();            class loading

        // Load configuration
        Zend_Registry::set('configSection',     ❷  Loads configuration
            $configSection);                        file, stores to registry
        $config = new Zend_Config_Ini(
            ROOT_DIR.'/application/config.ini',
            $configSection);
        Zend_Registry::set('config', $config);

        date_default_timezone_set(               Sets default time zone
            $config->date_default_timezone);     from configuration file

        // configure database and store to the registry
        $db = Zend_Db::factory($config->db);        ❸  Configures
        Zend_Db_Table_Abstract::setDefaultAdapter($db);  database, stores
        Zend_Registry::set('db', $db);
    }

    public function configureFrontController()      ◁─────        Sets up
    {                                                             front
        $frontController = Zend_Controller_Front::getInstance();  controller
        $frontController->setControllerDirectory(ROOT_DIR .
            '/application/controllers');
    }

    public function runApp()
    {
        $this->configureFrontController();

        // run!
        $frontController = Zend_Controller_Front::getInstance();
        $frontController->dispatch();       ◁───    Runs the
    }                                               application
```

The Bootstrap class has three methods: the constructor, which initializes the environment; configureFrontController(), which sets up the front controller; and runApp(), which runs the MVC application itself. This allows us to reuse this code when testing our application.

The constructor prepares the environment for our application, so let's look in detail at the functionality in the constructor.

AUTOMATICALLY LOADING CLASSES

One less than ideal aspect of the bootstrap file in the original Hello World is that there are a lot of `Zend_Loader::loadClass()` calls to load up the classes we need before we use them. In larger applications, there are even more classes in use, resulting in clutter throughout the application just to ensure that the right classes are included at the right time.

For our *Places* website, we use PHP's `__autoload()` functionality so that PHP will automatically load our classes for us. PHP5 introduced the `__autoload()` magic function that is called whenever you try to instantiate a class that hasn't yet been defined. The `Zend_Loader` class has a special `registerAutoload()` method specifically for use with `__autoload()`, as shown in listing 3.1 ❶. This method will automatically use PHP5's Standard PHP Library (SPL) `spl_autoload_register()` function so that multiple autoloaders can be used. After `Zend_Loader::registerAutoload()` has been called, whenever a class is instantiated that has not yet been defined, the file containing the class is included. This solves the problem of `Zend_Loader::loadClass()` clutter and ensures that only the needed files are loaded for any given request.

CONFIGURATION WITH ZEND_CONFIG

There is an implicit requirement that our *Places* website will store its data to a database, such as MySQL. We need to store the database connection settings, and we'll use `Zend_Config` for this purpose. `Zend_Config` provides for three configuration file formats: XML, INI, and PHP arrays. We will use the INI format because it is easy to maintain.

`Zend_Config` provides an object-oriented interface to the configuration data regardless of which file format has been loaded. Consider an INI file called config.ini containing the following information:

```
[db]
adapter = PDO_MYSQL
database.host = localhost
database.username = user1234
database.password = 1234
database.name = db_one
```

When this file is loaded, the data can be accessed like this:

```
$config = new Zend_Config_Ini('config.ini', 'db');
$adapter = $config->adapter;
$databaseHost = $config->database->host;
```

Note how the period (.) within the key name of a setting is automatically turned into a hierarchical separator by `Zend_Config`. This allows us to group our configuration data easily within the confines of the INI file format.

Another extension to the INI format that `Zend_Config` supports is section inheritance, using the colon character (:) as a separator within the section name. This allows us to define a base set of configuration settings and then provide specific changes for different parent sections, as shown in listing 3.2.

Listing 3.2   An example `Zend_Config` INI file

```
[general]            ◁────────────┐   Specifies main
db.adapter = PDO_MYSQL            │   settings within
db.params.host = localhost            [general]
db.params.username = user1234
db.params.password = 1234
db.params.dbname = db_one

[live : general]     ◁───────────┐    [live] inherits
db.params.host = livedb.example.com   from [general]

[dev : general]
db.params.host = devdb.example.com
```

We can now load this INI file in two ways. On the live site, the INI file is loaded with this command, which loads the live configuration:

```
$config = new Zend_Config_Ini('config.ini', 'live');
```

To load the dev configuration for use on a developer's local workstation, this load statement would be used:

```
$config = new Zend_Config_Ini('config.ini', 'dev');
```

In both cases, `Zend_Config` will load the general section first, then apply the settings in the live or dev section. This will have the effect of selecting a different database depending on whether the application is running on the live or development server.

THE PLACES CONFIGURATION FILE

Because we will have only one configuration file for our *Places* website, we will call it config.ini, as shown in listing 3.3, and place it in the application directory.

Listing 3.3   The initial config.ini file for *Places*: application/config.ini

```
[general]
db.adapter = PDO_MYSQL
db.params.host = localhost
db.params.username = zfia
db.params.password = 123456
db.params.dbname = places         ◁──────────┐   Sets
date_default_timezone = "Europe/London"           standard
                                                  database
[live : general]

[dev : general]                              Sets different
                                             database for unit
[test : general]                             tests
db.params.dbname = places_test    ◁──────┘
```

The only thing we need to set up at this point is the connection to the database. The test section is for automatic testing of our application. While we are testing, we don't want to touch our main database, so we will use a separate database that we can overwrite at will while testing different scenarios. The configuration section from the config.ini file is loaded in the `Bootstrap` class (listing 3.1 ❷), and then the resulting `Zend_Config` object is stored in the `Zend_Registry` class so that the configuration data can be retrieved wherever we need it.

ZEND_REGISTRY

Using global variables is generally considered unwise for large applications, as it introduces coupling between modules and it is very difficult to track down where and when a given global variable is modified during the processing of a script. The solution is to pass variables as parameters through functions to where the data is required. This causes a problem in that you can end up with lots of pass-through parameters that clutter function signatures for functions that do not use the data, except to pass it on to the next function.

One solution is to consolidate the storage of such data into a single object that is easy to find; this is known as the registry. As its name implies, `Zend_Registry` implements the Registry design pattern and so is a handy place to store objects that are required in different parts of the application.

`Zend_Registry::set()` is used to store objects in the registry. Internally, the registry is implemented as an associative array, so when you register an object with it, you have to supply the key name that you want to identify it with. To retrieve the object at a different place in the code, `Zend_Registry::get()` is used—you supply the key name, and a reference to the object is returned. There is also a helper method, `Zend_Registry::isRegistered()`, which enables you to check whether or not a given object key is registered.

A bit of warning is in order: using the registry is very similar to using a global variable, and unwanted coupling between the registered objects and the rest of the code can occur if you are not careful. `Zend_Registry` should be used with caution. We will use it with confidence for two objects: `$config` and `$db`. These two objects are ideal for storing to a registry because they are generally only read from and not written to; we can be confident that they are unlikely to change during the course of a request. Even though the data is in the registry, we will still pass the relevant configuration data around our application if it minimizes coupling or makes a given section easier to test.

Now that the configuration file is loaded, we can look at the final section of the `Bootstrap` constructor in listing 3.1. The initialization of the database will ensure that we can access the database from any of our models throughout the rest of the application.

DATABASE INITIALIZATION

As we discussed in chapter 2, we can use the `Zend_Db` factory class to create a `Zend_Db_Adapter` specific to our database. In this case, we'll receive an object of type `Zend_Db_Adapter_Pdo_Mysql`.

To create the object, we need to pass the adapter name and an array of configuration parameters or a `Zend_Config` object that has been set up correctly. `Zend_Config`'s nested parameter system is used to provide the expected data for the `Zend_Db::factory()` method. We use a top-level key of `db` in listing 3.3, and the subkeys are adapter, to tell the factory which instance of Zend_Db_Adapter to load, and params, which is passed to the adapter to connect to the database. The keys required within params are specific to the adapter that is loaded, with host, dbname, username, and password being common requirements for all databases.

The database initialization in Bootstrap passes the configuration object $config->db to Zend_Db::factory(), and the returned adapter is set as the default adapter for the Zend_Db_Table objects that we will use (listing 3.1 ❸). It also registers the adapter with the Zend_Registry so that we can retrieve it for ad hoc SQL queries.

3.2.3 Running the application

We have now created a Bootstrap object that initializes the environment and can run our application. The code that uses this object is in public/index.php and is shown in listing 3.4.

> **Listing 3.4 public/index.php is used to run the application**

```php
<?php
include '../application/bootstrap.php';

$configSection = getenv('PLACES_CONFIG') ?
    ➥ getenv('PLACES_CONFIG') : 'general';      ← ❶ Chooses the config section to load
$bootstrap = new Bootstrap($configSection);
$bootstrap->runApp();        ← ❷ Runs the application
```

To ensure that we load the correct section, we use the PLACES_CONFIG environment variable. This is set on a per server basis using the Apache configuration command SetEnv PLACE_CONFIG {section_name}. For a development server, we configure the Apache configuration with SetEnv PLACE_CONFIG dev and on the live site, we use SetEnv PLACE_CONFIG live. If the environment variable does not exist, we fall back to the general section ❶. Running the application is as simple as instantiating Bootstrap and calling runApp() ❷.

The configureFrontController() method (listing 3.1 ❸) sets up the front controller in the same manner as in the bootstrap file for Hello World (listing 2.1 in chapter 2). Again, we use the applications/controllers directory to store the controller files, and finally, the runApp() method calls the front controller's dispatch() method to run the application.

We have now set up the code necessary to run the website. We can concentrate on the controllers next.

3.3 The home page

The home page is the shop front to our application, so we want to ensure that we provide an attractive page with easy-to-use navigation. There are four main sections to the page: At the top, there is a header with logo and main navigation menu. The main content area is in the middle, and a column on the right side provides space for advertising. There is also a footer, which is not shown in figure 3.2, to provide contact and copyright information on all pages.

To build the home page, we will first create the initial models and the unit tests required to validate them. We will write unit tests as we go along, so that we can be confident that as we refactor to add new functionality, we do not break what we know to be working.

The centerpiece of the *Places* website is reviews of places to take children, so we will start there.

3.3.1 *The initial models*

We need a list of reviews on the home page, so let's start with a database table called Reviews, with each row representing a review of a place. Each place will have more than one review, so we will need a list of locations in a table called Places. The initial database schema is shown in figure 3.4.

We can now go ahead and create our initial model classes, `Reviews` and `Places`. To keep things organized and easy to find, the `Reviews` model is stored in application/ models/Reviews.php and the `Places` model is stored in application/models/ Places.php. The classes are initially very simple:

```
class Reviews extends Zend_Db_Table
{
    protected $_name = 'reviews';
}
class Places extends Zend_Db_Table
{
    protected $_name = 'places';
}
```

As we explained in chapter 2, `Zend_Db_Table` gives us all the functionality of a Table Data Gateway pattern without our having to write any code. This allows us to read, write, and delete from the database table by calling methods in the parent class. We have no intention of writing code that isn't going to be used, so we will not expand our model classes until we need to. For now, we'll populate the database directly with a few rows so we have something to display on the home page, as shown in listing 3.5.

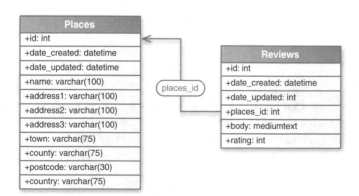

Figure 3.4 In order to build the initial pages, the database consists of two tables with a foreign key from Reviews to Places.

```
CREATE TABLE places (
  id int(11) NOT NULL auto_increment,        ◄—————  Increments
  date_created datetime NOT NULL,                     primary key
  date_updated datetime NOT NULL,                     automatically
  name varchar(100) NOT NULL,
  address1 varchar(100) default NULL,
  address2 varchar(100) default NULL,
  address3 varchar(100) default NULL,
  town varchar(75) default NULL,
  county varchar(75) default NULL,
  postcode varchar(30) default NULL,
  country varchar(75) default NULL,
  PRIMARY KEY  (`id`)
);

INSERT INTO places (name, address1, town, county, postcode, date_created)
VALUES
('London Zoo', 'Regent\'s Park', 'London', '', 'NW1 4RY',
   '2007-02-14 00:00:00')
,('Alton Towers', 'Regent\'s Park', 'Alton', 'Staffordshire',
   'ST10 4DB', '2007-02-14 00:00:00')
,('Coughton Court', '', 'Alcester', 'Warwickshire', 'B49 5JA',
   '2007-02-14 00:00:00');

CREATE TABLE reviews (
  id int(11) NOT NULL auto_increment,
  date_created datetime NOT NULL,
  date_updated datetime NOT NULL,
  place_id int(11) NOT NULL,          ◄—————  Creates foreign
  user_name varchar(50) NOT NULL,              key to Places
  body mediumtext NOT NULL,                    table
  rating int(11) default NULL,
  helpful_yes int(11) NOT NULL default '0',
  helpful_total int(11) NOT NULL default '0',
  PRIMARY KEY  (`id`)
);

INSERT INTO reviews (place_id, body, rating, date_created)
VALUES
(1, 'The facilities here are really good. All the family enjoyed it', 4,
   '2007-02-14 00:00:00')
,(1, 'Good day out, but not so many big animals now.', 2,
   '2007-02-14 00:00:00')
,(1, 'Excellent food in the cafeteria. Even my 2 year old ate her lunch!',
   4, '2007-02-14 00:00:00');
```

The SQL in listing 3.5 needs to be seeded into the database using a MySQL client, such as the command-line mysql application or another one like phpMyAdmin. Obviously, if you are using another database server, the SQL will have to be tweaked appropriately.

Now that we have data in the database, we can write tests using the PHPUnit framework, which will enable us to ensure that the models work as intended.

3.3.2   *Testing our models*

In section 3.1, we looked at the importance of testing our code. We use unit tests to ensure that the code works the way we intend it to. Unit testing is the process of testing individual functionality separately from the rest of the code.

The tests have to run quickly, as we want to run them whenever we make changes to the code to make sure the code functions correctly. This gives us a safety net when making changes to improve our program. If the tests still work, the changes were good. If the tests no longer work, the changes can be backed out.

The process of changing already-working code to make it better and easier to understand is known as *refactoring*. This is an important skill, and it's required for maintaining an application over a long period of time. Refactoring without tests to check that the changes haven't broken anything can be an extremely risky business, and because of this, refactoring sometimes doesn't get done and the application's source becomes harder to understand. With tests, refactoring is easy and possibly even fun; everything changes because of your confidence in the code.

Because we are going to write tests for the majority of our code, we need a system to run the tests. PHPUnit (http://www.phpunit.de) is a testing framework for PHP that runs each test in isolation and provides functionality to allow us to organize the test code.

NOTE   In order to run the unit tests, you need to install PHPUnit. The instructions can be found on the PHPUnit website (http://www.phpunit.de).

Listing 3.6 shows the initial testing of our models, although at this stage we do not have much to test!

Listing 3.6   A Places model unit test: tests/Models/PlacesTest.php

```php
<?php
require_once dirname(__FILE__) . '/../TestConfiguration.php';
require_once '../application/models/Places.php';

class models_PlacesTest extends PHPUnit_Framework_TestCase
{
    public function setUp()                              ❶ Calls setUp()
    {                                                      before every test
        // reset database to known state
        TestConfiguration::setupDatabase();
    }

    public function testFetchAll()
    {
        $placesFinder = new Places();
        $places = $placesFinder->fetchAll();            ❷ Checks row
                                                           count is correct
        $this->assertSame(3, $places->count());
    }
}
```

A PHPUnit test case consists of a number of separate methods that contain each test. These methods all start with the word `test`, so that PHPUnit can identify them. The setUp() method **❶** is run before each test and so can be used to initialize the system for the test. This helps to ensure that tests are not dependant upon other tests and also that one text does not cause problems for subsequent tests. The tearDown() method is run after each test and so can perform any cleanup required.

We name the test class using the same convention as for Zend Framework classes, and we include the subdirectory name separated using underscores. In this case, the test is called models_PlacesTest because it is stored in the models/PlacesTest.php file within the tests directory. We run the test using the command-line phpunit script from the tests directory:

```
phpunit models_PlacesTest
```

For testing our models, we want to ensure that the database is in a known state for every test. We have written a separate class, TestConfiguration, which contains the setupDatabase() method to do this. It is not part of this class because it will be used for testing other models too.

Figure 3.5 **The unit tests are run from the command line using the `phpunit` script, which displays the number of tests and details of any failures.**

Our initial test, testFetchAll(), does a simple sanity check to ensure that everything is working **❷**. It collects all the places in our test database and counts them. In this case, we are expecting three places, and that's what we get, as shown in figure 3.5. Of course, Zend Framework's own unit tests ensure that the fetchAll() method works, so in your own applications, you would only test functionality that you create.

PHPUnit maps the name of the test to the correct file, runs it, and tells us about any errors. This means that we can run any test class in isolation. In general, we will run all the tests as often as we can to ensure we do not create regressions in the application. To do this, we need to organize our tests into a hierarchy of test suites.

Figure 3.6 **The unit tests are divided into controllers and models. The controllers/ AllTests.php and models/ AllTests.php scripts allow each group of tests to be run independently if required.**

TEST ORGANIZATION

For our test case to work and to support multiple test-case classes, we will organize our tests into two suites: one for models and one for controllers. We will group these suites into an encompassing suite, so that we can run all the tests with the simple command phpunit AllTests.php. A certain amount of initialization is required, so we will put this into a separate file called TestConfiguration.php, as shown in figure 3.6.

The TestConfiguration.php file contains the `TestConfiguration` class, which contains two methods, `setup()` and `setupDatabase()`, as shown in listing 3.7.

Listing 3.7 The `TestConfiguration` class

```php
<?php                                                        ❶ Runs setup function
                                                               when file is required
TestConfiguration::setup();  ◀──────────────

class TestConfiguration
{
    static function setup()
    {                                                        ❷ Puts Zend Framework
        $lib = realpath(dirname(__FILE__)                      library on the path
               . '/../../../lib/');  ◀──────────
        set_include_path(get_include_path()
               . PATH_SEPARATOR . $lib);

        require_once dirname(__FILE__)                       ❸ Loads Bootstrap using
               . '/../application/bootstrap.php';              test configuration
        self::$bootstrap = new Bootstrap('test');  ◀────────
    }

    static function setupDatabase()  ◀──────────
    {                                                          Sets database
        $db = Zend_Registry::get('db');                        to a known
        $db->query(<<<EOT                              ❹       state
DROP TABLE IF EXISTS places;
EOT
        );

        $db->query(<<<EOT
CREATE TABLE places (
id INT NOT NULL AUTO_INCREMENT PRIMARY KEY ,
date_created DATETIME NOT NULL ,
date_updated DATETIME NOT NULL ,
name VARCHAR( 100 ) NOT NULL ,
address1 VARCHAR( 100 ) NULL ,
address2 VARCHAR( 100 ) NULL ,
address3 VARCHAR( 100 ) NULL ,
town VARCHAR( 75 ) NULL ,
county VARCHAR( 75 ) NULL ,
postcode VARCHAR( 30 ) NULL ,
country VARCHAR( 75 ) NULL
)
EOT
        );

$db->query(<<<EOT
INSERT INTO places (name, address1, town, county, postcode,
   date_created, date_updated)
VALUES
('London Zoo', 'Regent''s Park', 'London', '', 'NW1 4RY',
   '2007-02-14 00:00:00', '2007-02-14 00:00:00')
,('Alton Towers', 'Regent''s Park', 'Alton', 'Staffordshire',
   'ST10 4DB', '2007-02-20 00:00:00', '2007-02-20 00:00:00')
,('Coughton Court', '', 'Alcester', 'Warwickshire', 'B49 5JA',
```

```
    '2007-02-16 00:00:00', '2007-02-16 00:00:00')
  ;
  EOT
      );

      // continues
  }
}
```

The setUp() method is run when the TestConfiguration.php file is included ❶. It sets up the include path ❷ so that Zend Framework is on the path. Then it reuses the Boot-strap class from listing 3.1 to set up the application using the loads in the config.ini file's test section ❸. The test section is used so that we can specify a different database (places_test), to ensure that we don't accidentally affect our main database.

We use the TestConfiguration::setupDatabase() method ❹ to ensure that we start each test from a clean database. This function is simply a set of SQL queries that drops the table, creates it again, and populates it with the same data. This means that for any given test, you can be sure that the database is in the correct state. The source code supplied with the book contains the test suite files and the full SQL code that resets the database.

With the models defined and tested, we'll now turn our attention to the controller part of the MVC system and create our home-page controller and update the Places model to provide the required data.

3.3.3 *The home-page controller*

The home-page controller's action is the default action of the default controller, so the /index/index URL will also display the home page in addition to just /. Either URL maps to the indexAction() method within the IndexController class. In this method, we need to collect a list of the most recently updated places from the Places model and assign it to the view. The view will then take care of displaying the content to the user.

UPDATING THE PLACES MODEL

Zend_Db_Table provides the fetchAll() function to retrieve multiple rows from the database, so we could directly call it from the controller. However, we're going to encapsulate the requirements for the home page's list within the Places class. This is so we keep the database code where it belongs: in the model. It also provides us with a class where we can add further functionality that is specific to the concept of places.

We'll add a new function, fetchLatest(), to the Places class, which will automati-cally order the results by reverse date of update, as shown in listing 3.8.

Listing 3.8 fetchLatest() ensures the business logic is kept in the model layer

```
class Places extends Zend_Db_Table            Specifies database
{                                             table name
   protected $_name = 'places';  ←─────────────

   function fetchLatest($count = 10)
```

```
    {
        return $this->fetchAll(null,          Orders by reverse date,
            'date_created DESC', $count);      limits to $count
    }
}
```

This simple function ensures that the data is ordered correctly and allows the caller to specify how many records they want to retrieve.

It is a good rule of thumb to write at least one test for every piece of functionality that you add to the model. This means that you write tests for each discrete behavior of the model class. A behavior may be implemented using multiple methods, or simply describe one use of a single method that takes multiple arguments. In this case, we add one test for `fetchLatest()` to the tests/models/PlacesTest.php file, as shown in listing 3.9.

Listing 3.9   The test case for the `fetchLatest()` method

```
class Models_PlacesTest extends PHPUnit_Framework_TestCase
{
    // ...

    public function testFetchLatestShouldFetchLatestEntriesInReverseOrder()
    {
        $placesFinder = new Places();                         Calls function
        $places = $placesFinder->fetchLatest(1);    ⟵         being tested

        $this->assertSame(1, $places->count());    ⟵    ❶  Tests
                                                            limit
        $thisPlace = $places->current();
        $this->assertSame(2, (int)$thisPlace->id);  ⟵         Tests
    }                                                       ❷  ordering
}
```

This test method exercises the two features of the `fetchLatest()` method. First, we check that the number of records returned is correct ❶, then we check the ordering by ensuring that the correct record is returned ❷. The second test shows why we need to control our dataset and ensure that tests do not interact with each other. I have set up the test data so that the second database row, with an ID of 2, has the most recent `date_created`. If this changed, the test would fail.

We have created our model for the data that will be displayed on the home page, so we'll now move on to the controller function itself.

THE CONTROLLER ACTION

The controller's `indexAction()` method needs to ensure that the view contains everything it will display to the user. Note that this is the data specific to the main content on this page, and does not include the data that is created elsewhere, such as the ads to be displayed or any of the header or footer data.

Naming your test methods

Test names should describe the behavior tested. As you can see, we have named our test `testFetchLatestShouldFetchLatestEntriesInReverseOrder()`. While really long and somewhat hard to read, PHPUnit contains a feature called testdox that will translate the camelCasedWords to separate words. This gives you a really nice specification to read in the end. A well-named test method also makes it clear what specific behavior is tested in the method, which makes refactoring and bug fixing easier later.

PHPUnit also supports the use of DocBlock annotations. One useful annotation is `@group`, which can be used to group sets of related tests. It is often used for metadata, such as recording bug numbers to allow the name of the test to describe the behavior under test.

The `fetchLatest()` function returns a `Zend_Db_Table_Rowset`, which can be iterated over using the `foreach()` construct in our view script. In listing 3.10, we assign it to the view within `indexAction()`.

Listing 3.10 `indexAction()` displays a list of recently added places

```
class IndexController extends Zend_Controller_Action
{
    public function indexAction()
    {
        $this->view->title = 'Welcome';          ◁——— Sets title for web
        $placesFinder = new Places();                     browser's title bar
        $this->view->places = $places->fetchLatest();   ◁——— Assigns recent
    }                                                          places to the view
}
```

The `IndexController`'s `indexAction` method is quite simple. All it does is assign a couple of member variables to the view. The model has encapsulated all the details of dealing with the database, leaving the controller to work at the business-logic level. This is MVC separation at work, and the controller only needs to worry about linking the model data to the view and letting the view render itself.

As with the model, we now need to write unit tests for the controller so that we can ensure that it continues to work as the site grows.

TESTING THE CONTROLLER

To round off our initial work on the home-page controller, we'll write a test to ensure that it works. We do this in the tests/controllers/IndexControllerTest.php file. The controller's subdirectory of the tests directory allows us to separate our tests in much the same manner as we separate our application code.

We'll create a new test case class called `controllers_IndexControllerTest`, as shown in listing 3.11.

Listing 3.11   Testing the index controller

```php
<?php
require_once dirname(__FILE__) . '/../TestConfiguration.php';

class controllers_IndexControllerTest extends
        Zend_Test_PHPUnit_ControllerTestCase
{
    public function setUp()
    {
        $bootstrap = TestConfiguration::$bootstrap;      ❶ Sets front controller
        $this->bootstrap = array($bootstrap,               initialization method
            'configureFrontController');
        parent::setUp();
    }

    public function testHomePageIsASuccessfulRequest()
    {
        $this->dispatch('/');      ❷ Runs application

        $this->assertFalse($this->response      ❸ Tests that no exceptions
            ->isException());                      are generated

        $this->assertNotRedirect();      ◁──────────  Tests for
    }                                                 redirection to
    public function testHomePageDisplaysCorrectContent()  the error
    {                                              ❹ handler
        // set up request
        $this->dispatch('/');

        // test the output
        $this->assertQueryContentContains('h1',
            'Welcome');
        $this->assertQueryContentContains('h2',      ❺ Tests data assigned
            'Recent reviews');                          to view is rendered
        $this->assertQueryCount('td a', 3);
        $this->assertQueryContentContains('td a',
            'Alton Towers');
    }
}
```

Fortunately, testing controllers is made simple by Zend Framework's Zend_Test_PHP-
Unit_ControllerTestCase class. This class does the heavy lifting of setting up the
front controller to enable testing of specific controller functionality. In our case, we
want to test that the home page doesn't cause an error, by using testHomePageIsA-
SuccessfulRequest(), and that it displays the expected content, by using testHome-
PageDisplaysCorrectContent().

We need to ensure that the front controller is set up the same way for every test in
the test case. This is done by the parent's setUp() method, but before we call it, we
need to provide a method for configuring the front controller after it has been set up.
Our Bootstrap class in listing 3.1 has a function called setupFrontController(),
which is exactly what we need here. We use it by setting the local member variable

bootstrap to an array containing the instance of the `Bootstrap` class that we created in `TestConfiguration`'s `setup()` method and the name of the `Bootstrap`'s method that we want to be called ❶.

The first test, `testHomePageIsASuccessfulRequest()`, ensures that the request was successful. First, we use the `dispatch()` method to run the application against the `/` URL ❷. This method mimics the user navigating to the home page. We then test that no exceptions occurred by asserting that the response object does not have any exceptions stored ❸. We also check that the error handler plug-in hasn't redirected the page to an error action by using the built-in `assertNotRedirect()` test ❹.

The second test for the home page, `testHomePageDisplaysCorrectContent()`, ensures that the page displays the expected data. We take advantage of the assertQuery family of methods that are built into `Zend_Test_PHPUnit_Controller-TestCase`. These methods allow us to specify where to find some given text using CSS-like specifications ❺. In the first assertion, we check that the `h1` tag contains the word "Welcome". The other assertions ensure that the other parts of the view script rendered as expected.

This completes the testing of the home-page controller. With that test in place, we are able to confidently move forward.

3.4 Summary

This chapter has introduced a real application, *Places to take the kids!*, which will be expanded upon throughout the rest of the book as we discuss all the components of Zend Framework. In keeping with some modern design practices, we haven't tried to design *Places* up front; instead we have a story that describes what the site is about, and from that we have an initial list of functional ideas. We then concentrated on the model and controller for the home page and have put unit tests in place. Testing is vitally important—we need the freedom to be able to change our code to suit each new piece of added functionality and to be sure that existing code still works!

We have set up the directory structure for *Places* and have also created the first model required. For simplicity, our model directly extends `Zend_Db_Table` to provide database access and it is where we have implemented the business logic required to retrieve a list of the most recently updated locations.

We are now ready to look in detail at the view components of Zend Framework, which will introduce the Composite View design pattern to allow us to create and maintain a common look and feel across the website.

Managing the view 4

This chapter covers

- Understanding the Composite View design pattern
- Using the `Zend_Layout` component
- Building a front controller plug-in to initialize the view
- Creating cleaner scripts by using view helpers

In chapter 3, we created a project, the *Places to take the kids!* website, that will showcase features of Zend Framework over the course of this book, and will demonstrate how to integrate components into a proper web application. We have looked at the directory structure, creating a model and a controller for the home page, and also at how to test these. To complete the first stage of the website, we now need to create view scripts.

The view is the section of your application that the user interacts with, so it is important that you get it right. All but the smallest of websites have common display elements on all pages. Usually this includes the header, footer, and navigation elements, but it could also include advertising banners and other elements required by the site's design. Zend Framework provides a suite of components that help make the visual part of your website both powerful and flexible and also easy to maintain in the long term.

We have already looked at the basics of `Zend_View` in chapters 2 and 3. In this chapter, we will look in more detail at the more advanced view helpers supplied with the framework. We'll also look at the `Zend_Layout` component, which provides for a Two Step View integrated with a Composite View system allowing for very flexible page displays. First, though, let's look at what the Composite View design pattern is and why we would want to use it.

4.1 Introducing the Two Step View and Composite View patterns

We need to ensure that the common display elements of our website are consistent across all pages, so we need a way to avoid copying and pasting the same HTML code across all view scripts. One way to do this is to add two includes to every view script, like this:

```
<?php include('header.phtml');?>
<h1>page title</h1>
<p>body copy here</p>
<?php include('footer.phtml');?>
```

The main problem with this approach is that we are repeating those two lines of code in every single view script. This clutters up the view script with code that is not relevant to the job in hand, and because it happens all the time, it is ripe for automation. A better solution is to separate out the common sections automatically. There are two design patterns that cover this area, Two Step View and Composite View.

The Two Step View pattern is documented by Martin Fowler like this:

Two Step View deals with this problem by splitting the transformation into two stages. The first transforms the model data into a logical presentation without any specific formatting; the second converts that logical presentation with the actual formatting needed. This way you can make a global change by altering the second stage, or you can support multiple output looks and feels with one second stage each.

> —(From http://martinfowler.com/eaaCatalog/twoStepView.html)

Composite View is documented by Sun like this:

[Composite View] provides for the creation of a composite view based on the inclusion and substitution of modular dynamic and static template fragments. It promotes the reuse of atomic portions of the view by encouraging modular design. It is appropriate to use a composite view to generate pages containing display components that may be combined in a variety of ways.

> —(From http://java.sun.com/blueprints/corej2eepatterns/Patterns/
> CompositeView.html)

In terms of building a website with Zend Framework, this means that the view script attached to the action should only contain the HTML related to that action. The rest of the page is built up independently, and the content of the controller action is placed into it. This is shown in figure 4.1, where we have a master template (layout.phtml) providing the overall layout and an action template containing the action-specific content.

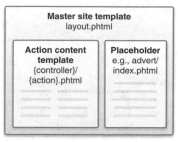

Figure 4.1 Multiple templates are used to build up the complete page.

The layout script contains those parts of the page that are not directly related to the current action, such as the header, footer, and menu sections. The action view script contains the display code specific to the action being dispatched. The Zend_Layout component of Zend Framework is used to manage this process. Along with the ViewRenderer action helper and the action()_view helper, it provides a complete and very flexible composite display system.

The ViewRenderer expects that all action view scripts are stored in the views/scripts subdirectory (though this is configurable). They are further subdivided into separate subdirectories per controller. As we saw in chapter 2, by default the template file is named after the action with an extension of .phtml. That is, if we have a controller called reviews, the index action's view script is called index.phtml and resides in the reviews subdirectory. Zend_Layout adds to this by storing the layout templates in a central layouts directory. By default, this is the views/scripts/ directory, though it is usual to specify a separate directory, such as views/layouts.

4.2 *View handling with Zend_Layout*

The Zend_Layout component manages rendering of a master layout script, which contains content placeholders for embedding content generated by actions or other view scripts. As with all Zend Framework components, Zend_Layout works with the minimum of configuration for most uses, but if your requirements are more specialized, it is very flexible.

When using Zend_Layout with the MVC components, the startMvc() method is used to initialize it. This is done in the bootstrap file like this:

```
Zend_Layout::startMvc(array('layoutPath' => '/path/to/layouts'));
```

As you can see, this is a static method, so you don't need to create an instance of the Zend_Layout class first. Behind the scenes, startMvc() creates a Singleton instance of Zend_Layout and registers a front controller plug-in and an action helper that can then be interfaced with from the rest of the application. The front controller plug-in, Zend_Layout_Controller_Plugin_Layout, has a postDispatch() hook function that renders the layout template at the end of the last dispatched action. The action helper, Zend_Layout_Controller_Action_Helper_Layout, is used to provide easy access to the Zend_Layout object from within a controller.

The startMvc() function takes an array of options, but only layoutPath is required. This specifies the directory where the layout files are stored. By default, the layout.phtml file is rendered by Zend_Layout. However, you can easily change this in any controller method, such as init(), with this statement:

```
$this->_helper->layout->setLayout('layout2');
```

This will cause layout2.phtml to be rendered instead.

4.3   Integrating Zend_Layout into Places

The functionality provided by Zend_Layout is very desirable, so let's put it into our *Places* application.

4.3.1   Setup

To integrate Zend_Layout into the *Places* website, we need to start with the bootstrap class. Listing 4.1 shows the change we need to make to the runApp() function.

> **Listing 4.1   Starting Zend_Layout in application/bootstrap.php**

```
public function runApp()
{
   // setup front controller
   // ...

   // setup the layout
   Zend_Layout::startMvc(array(              ❶ Sets layoutPath to
      'layoutPath' => ROOT_DIR                  layouts directory
               . '/application/views/layouts',
   ));

   // ...
```

As explained in section 4.2, we use the startMvc() method to set up the Zend_Layout object and also register the associated front controller plug-in and action helper. The default settings for Zend_Layout are acceptable for the *Places* site, except that we need to specify the directory for the layout scripts ❶. We have chosen views/layouts in the application directory, as this separates the layout files from our script files.

We also need to configure our view object with information about the current request and set up our initial CSS and output-encoding requirements. This could easily be done within the bootstrap class, but to keep that class simpler and to promote reusability, we will create a front controller plug-in to handle view setup. This class, Places_Controller_Plugin_ViewSetup, follows Zend Framework naming conventions and so is stored in lib/Places/Controller/Plugin/ViewSetup.php.

Initially, the work we need to do only needs to be done once, so we can use the dispatchLoopStartup() hook as shown in listing 4.2.

Listing 4.2 The `Places_Controller_Plugin_ViewSetup` front controller

```
class Places_Controller_Plugin_ViewSetup extends
   Zend_Controller_Plugin_Abstract
{
   /**
    * @var Zend_View
    */
   protected $_view;

   public function dispatchLoopStartup(
          Zend_Controller_Request_Abstract $request)
   {
      $viewRenderer = Zend_Controller_Action_HelperBroker::
                 getStaticHelper('viewRenderer');
      $viewRenderer->init();                                      Initializes
                                                                  ViewRenderer
           $view = $viewRenderer->view;
      $this->_view = $view;

      $view->originalModule =                                 ❶ Sets variables
             $request->getModuleName();                          that may be
      $view->originalController =                                required in view
             $request->getControllerName();
      $view->originalAction =
             $request->getActionName();                       ❷ Sets doctype for
      $view->doctype('XHTML1_STRICT');                           view helpers

      $prefix = 'Places_View_Helper';          ❸
      $dir = dirname(__FILE__)                      Adds new helper
             . '/../../View/Helper';                path to Places
      $view->addHelperPath($dir, $prefix);          view helpers

      $view->headMeta()->setName('Content-Type',
             'text/html;charset=utf-8');          ❹ Sets content type

      $view->headLink()->appendStylesheet(
             $view->baseUrl().'/css/site.css');
   }                                             ❺ Includes
                                                    standard CSS file

}
```

In this method, we do four distinct things. First, we assign the module, controller, and action from the request object into the view ❶. Because the dispatch loop hasn't started yet, these variables are the ones originally requested by the user via the URL and will get overwritten if any other actions are dispatched during the request cycle.

We then add support for an additional view helper directory, /lib/Places/View/Helper, to provide a place where we can store view helpers that are used across both the front and admin sections of the website ❷. The class names of the view helpers stored within the lib/Places/View/Helper directory will be named `Places_View_Helper_{helper name}`, so we also set the $prefix to this ❸. Otherwise, the view would try to load a helper using the standard `Zend_View_Helper` prefix, which does not make sense for classes in the `Places` directory subtree.

We then register the new plug-in with the front controller. This is done in the `runApp()` function of the `Bootstrap` class in application/bootstrap.php, immediately after setting the controller directory like this:

```
$frontController->registerPlugin(new Places_Controller_Plugin_ViewSetup());
```

Finally, Zend Framework provides a number of view helpers that help manage the `<head>` section of the web page. These view helpers are unusual, as they have two modes of operation, setting and rendering, where most view helpers only render. We use the `headMeta()` view helper to set the content type of the page ❹, but it can also be used for setting any of the meta fields in a web page, such as description and keywords. We use another "head" view script, `headLink()`, to store the default CSS file for the page; site.css in this case ❺. The `headLink()` helper allows us to add both a stylesheet and alternative stylesheets, should we wish to.

Now that we have initialized the view system, we can look at the scripts that we require to build the website.

4.3.2 Layout scripts

The master layout script is called layout.phtml and is stored in view/layouts/layout.phtml. This file serves as the holder for all the content to be displayed, so it only contains the fundamental structure of the page design and then delegates the rest of the content to other files. The master layout is shown in listing 4.3.

Listing 4.3   The master layout script: view/layouts/layout.phtml

```
<?php echo $this->doctype(); ?>          ◀──❶ Sets output doctype
<html xmlns="http://www.w3.org/1999/xhtml" lang="en" xml:lang="en">
<head>
    <?php echo $this->headMeta(); ?>       ❷ Specifies head view
    <?php echo $this->headTitle(); ?>         helpers to registry
    <?php echo $this->headLink(); ?>
</head>
<body>                                             ❸ Renders header
    <?php echo $this->partial("_header.phtml"); ?>  ◀   in separate file
    <?php echo $this->layout()->menu; ?>     ◀──
    <div id="container">                       ❹ Renders content
        <div id="content" class="column"><div id="pad">  placeholder for menu
            <?php echo $this->layout()->content; ?>  ◀──
        </div></div>                            ❺ Renders main content
        <div id="right" class="column">            for this page
            <?php echo $this->layout()->advert; ?>  ◀──
        </div>                                  ❻ Renders content
    </div>                                         placeholder for
    <?php echo $this->partial("_footer.phtml"); ?>  ◀  advertisement
</body>
</html>                                         ❼ Renders footer in
                                                   separate file
```

We set up which doctype to use earlier, so when rendering we just call the `doctype()` view helper ❶, and it will produce the correct doctype. This saves having to look it up in Google, as no one ever remembers them! The `doctype()` view helper supports all three HTML 4 and all three XHTML 1.0 document types, which covers pretty much all web pages at the moment. When HTML 5 is released and supported in browsers, we can expect that it will also be supported.

In the <head> section, we use the so-called head* view helpers. There are a number of these view helpers, and we make use of three of them ❷. These were set initially in the `Places_Controller_Plugin_ViewSetup` front controller plug-in (listing 4.2), but they can be added to during the dispatch of the request in the action controller or another plug-in.

The visible page is contained within the <body> tag, and we have further separated out the data to improve maintenance. The header and footer sections are stored in their own view script files and are included in the layout using the `partial()` view helper for _header.phtml ❸ and _footer.phtml ❼. The `partial()` view helper renders another view script within a "sandbox," where only passed-in variables are available. This limits the scope of the variables to the one view script, so they are accessed directly using $this->variableName, and we are confident that they will not conflict with variables in another script.

A note about `partial()`

The view script used within the `partial()` or `partialLoop()` view helpers does not have access to any of the variables that have been assigned to the view within the controller or other helpers and plug-ins. You need to pass all variables that you need for the view script as an array to the `partial()` call, like this:

```php
<?php
echo $this->partial('myscript.phtml', array('var'=>$this->var));
?>
```

All the view helper functions are available, though, with no extra work.

The ViewRenderer action helper stores the content from the action's view script into a named segment in the response. The `layout()` view helper is then used to retrieve and render the content from the named segments within the response. This provides the mechanism that enables display of the action view scripts within the master view script. The default response segment name is content, so we can render the main action's view script like this ❺:

```php
<?php echo $this->layout()->content; ?>
```

The placeholder name can be anything we like. For the *Places* website, we make use of two other placeholders: menu ❹ and advert ❻, which provide the menu display and the advertisement respectively. We'll look at how these placeholders are populated in section 4.3.3.

We will continue our discussion of the master layout template from listing 4.3 by looking at separating out view scripts using "partials."

PARTIAL VIEW SCRIPTS

As we saw in listing 4.3, we use two view scripts within `partial()` view helpers to help maintenance. The two scripts, _header.phtml and _footer.phtml, simply keep the relevant HTML logically separate from our layout template and are shown in listings 4.4 and 4.6.

Listing 4.4   The header view script: view/layouts/_header.phtml

```
<a name="top" id="top"></a>
<div id="scrn-read" title="links to aid navigation for screen readers">
  [<a href="#content" accesskey="s">Skip to main content</a>]
</div>
<div id="header">
  <img id="first"
     src="<?php echo $this->baseUrl(); ?>/img/rollercoaster.jpg"
     title="" alt="header image of a roller coaster"/>
  <img src="<?php echo $this->baseUrl(); ?>/img/family2.jpg"
     title="" alt="header image of a family"/>
  <img src="<?php echo $this->baseUrl(); ?>/img/castle.jpg"
     title="" alt="header image of a castle"/>
  <img src="<?php echo $this->baseUrl(); ?>/img/family3.jpg"
     title="" alt="header image of a family"/>
</div>
```

The header essentially contains a couple of links for accessibility (hidden via CSS for most users) and then the main images used at the top of the page. It is nicely contained within its own file so that if we did decide to change it for different sections of the site, we would just need to change the call to `partial()` (listing 4.3 ❸).

In order to create the correct path to the image files, we need to refer to the website's root URL. We could do this work directly in the view script, but this is a common requirement that lends itself to factoring into a view helper. We will call our view helper `baseUrl()`, so its class name is `Places_View_Helper_BaseUrl` and it is stored in library/Places/View/Helper/BaseUrl.php as shown in listing 4.5. This means that it is available from the earliest part of the dispatch process, when we add the Places/View/helper directory to the view object within the `ViewSetup` front controller plug-in in listing 4.2.

Listing 4.5   The `Places_View_Helper_BaseUrl` view helper

```
class Places_View_Helper_BaseUrl
{
   function baseUrl()
   {                                                        ❶ Retrieves front
     $fc = Zend_Controller_Front::getInstance();                controller
     return $fc->getBaseUrl();          Returns base
   }                                     URL value
}
```

The actual work of creating the correct path to the web server's root URL is already done by the request object so the path is available from the front controller directly.

This means that the `BaseUrl` view helper has to retrieve it and return it to the view script. The front controller is easily accessible because it is a Singleton, so we use the static `getInstance()` method ❶ and then simply return the result of the `get-BaseUrl()` member function.

By contrast, the footer view script, _footer.phtml, is very basic, as shown in listing 4.6.

Listing 4.6   The footer view script: views/layouts/_footer.phtml

```
<div id="footer-wrapper">
  <div id="footer">Copyright &copy;2008 Rob Allen, Nick Lo &amp; Steven
  Brown.</div>
</div>
```

The footer script contains just the copyright notice now, but it may be extended later to include other items to round out the site's functionality.

This completes our exploration of the view scripts required by our layout. We have looked at the HTML that's used to build up the main outer template script. Now, we can move on and look at the actions that will be used to create the content for the `menu` and `advert` placeholders.

4.3.3   *Common actions using placeholders*

It's quite common to need to run code on every page—code that is relatively complex and doesn't lend itself to being placed into a helper class. For *Places*, we need to create the menu and also the advertisement on the right side of the page. One of the more obvious ways to do this is to use actions, because these provide a mechanism for accessing models directly and have an associated view script to hold the HTML required.

We need to run these actions, and our initial solution is to use the `_forward()` method of the controller. This allows us to run another action at the end of our current action, so we could forward from the main action to the menu creation action, and from there to the advertisement creation action. The biggest problem is that we have to remember to write the `_forward()` call at the end of every other action in our application.

The developers of Zend Framework foresaw this problem, and the ActionStack front controller plug-in is provided to solve this problem. Its full name is `Zend_Controller_Plugin_ActionStack`, and it runs a list of actions that it holds internally. Actions can be easily added to it, and, as its name implies, it operates a stack-based system where the last action added is the first action run. This is known as Last In, First Out (LIFO), and it enables us to control the order in which the actions run, if we need to. The ActionStack plug-in has a `postDispatch()` hook that is used to add another action to the dispatch loop if no actions are currently being run.

In order to initially populate the ActionStack with the two actions that we need, we will create our own front controller plug-in called ActionSetup. This enables us to keep the setting up of the ActionStack separate from the bootstrap code, and as we only need to add two actions to the stack, we only need to hook into `dispatchLoop-`

`Startup()`. As ActionSetup is stored in the file lib/Places/Controller/Plugin/Action-Setup.php, the full class name is `Places_Controller_Plugin_ActionSetup`. The code is shown in listing 4.7.

Listing 4.7   The `Places_Controller_Plugin_ActionSetup` front controller plug-in

```
class Places_Controller_Plugin_ActionSetup extends
      Zend_Controller_Plugin_Abstract
{
   public function dispatchLoopStartup(
          Zend_Controller_Request_Abstract $request)
   {
      $front = Zend_Controller_Front::getInstance();
      if (!$front->hasPlugin(
          'Zend_Controller_Plugin_ActionStack')) {
         $actionStack = new
           Zend_Controller_Plugin_ActionStack();            ❶ Creates
         $front->registerPlugin($actionStack, 97);             ActionStack
      } else {                                                  if required
         $actionStack = $front->getPlugin(
           'Zend_Controller_Plugin_ActionStack');
      }
      $menuAction = clone($request);
      $menuAction->setActionName('menu')               ❷ Adds menu
          ->setControllerName('index');                   action
      $actionStack->pushStack($menuAction);

      $advertAction = clone($request);                 ❸ Adds advert
      $advertAction->setActionName('advert')              action
          ->setControllerName('index');
      $actionStack->pushStack($advertAction);
   }
}
```

The ActionSetup front controller plug-in is very simple and starts by initializing the ActionStack plug-in if required ❶. We use the `hasPlugin()` function to check that it hasn't already been created, and if not, we instantiate it and add it to the end of the plug-in stack so that it runs after pretty much all the other plug-ins (`Zend_Layout` and the `ErrorHandler` plug-ins come after it). This section of code is defensive, as we don't expect that the ActionStack will have been created, but if we introduce another third-party plug-in to our application, we do not want to have to edit this file again.

As with the ViewSetup plug-in, we need to register the ActionSetup plug-in with the front controller. This is done in the `runApp()` function of the `Bootstrap` class, immediately after registering the ActionSetup plug-in like this:

```
$frontController->registerPlugin(
   new Places_Controller_Plugin_ActionSetup(), 98);
```

Note that we want the ActionSetup's `postDispatch()` hook to run after all other plug-ins except `Zend_Layout`, so we explicitly set the position of the plug-in to 98. We choose 98 because 99 is already used by Zend_Layout and we want ViewSetup to run just before Zend_Layout renders the action's view.

To add an action to the ActionStack, we clone the current request object to get a new copy of it, then alter it appropriately. For the menu action ❷ we set the action name to menu and the controller name to index. Finally, we use the pushStack() method to add the action to the ActionStack. We then repeat the process for the advert action ❸, except that we set a different action name within the request object. The net result is that the main action, as requested by the user, will run, and then any subsequent forwards in that action will run. After that, due to the LIFO stack, the advert action will run, then the menu action.

We have now successfully automated the running of the actions required to build the whole page. As *Places* is a simple application, the menu action is part of the Index-Controller, and the menu itself is hard coded. In a bigger application, it is likely that the menu would be built from a database. As it is part of IndexController, the menu-Action() function is stored in application/controllers/IndexController.php and is shown in listing 4.8.

Listing 4.8   The IndexController's menuAction() function

```
class IndexController extends Zend_Controller_Action
{
   // ...

   public function menuAction()
   {                                        ┌─ Hard-codes
      $mainMenu = array(     ◁──────────────┤  menu items
         array('title'=>'Home',
            'url'=>$this->view->url(array(), null, true)),
         array('title'=>'Browse Places',
            'url'=>$this->view->url(
               array('controller'=>'place',
               'action'=>'browse'),
               null, true)),
         array('title'=>'Articles',
            'url'=>$this->view->url(
               array('controller'=>'articles'),
               null, true)),
         array('title'=>'About',
            'url'=>$this->view->url(
               array('controller'=>'about'),
               null, true)),
      );
                                          ❶ Assigns
                                            to view
      $this->view->menu = $mainMenu;   ◁─────┘
      $this->_helper->viewRenderer->
         ⮕    setResponseSegment('menu');      ❷ Changes the response
   }                                              placeholder
}
```

As you can see, the bulk of the action code is creating the $mainMenu array and assigning it to view ❶ to be rendered. The layout script is expecting the menu to be in a placeholder called `menu`. To set this up, we access the ViewRenderer view helper using the `_helper` property of the `Zend_Controller_Action` class and call the `setRespons⁃ eSegment()` method ❷. This means that the view script for this action (application/ views/scripts/index/menu.phtml) will be rendered to the `menu` segment of the response object so that it can be collected by the layout script later.

The HTML that renders the menu is shown in listings 4.9 and 4.10.

Listing 4.9   The menu's view script: application/views/scripts/index/menu.phtml

```
<?php $this->headLink()->appendStylesheet(           ❶ Sets CSS file
       $this->baseUrl() . '/css/menu.css') ?>    ←        for menu

<div id="menu">
<ul id="main-menu">
<?php echo $this->partialLoop('index/_menuItem.phtml',
       $this->menu) ?>                              ❷ Iterates using
</ul>                                                  partialLoop()
</div>
```

In the menu's view script, we use the `headLink()` view helper to set an additional stylesheet in the header of the layout file ❶. This is possible because the layout is rendered after all the actions have rendered, so we can affect the head section in each action as it runs. In this case, we need to style the menu we are generating, and this is best achieved using a separate CSS file, again using the `baseUrl()` view helper to retrieve the path to the website's root.

The menu itself is quite simple, and as we are iterating over a record set, we can take advantage of the `partialLoop()` view helper, ❷ which will render the _menuItem.phtml view script for each item in the menu. This view script is stored in view/scripts/index/_menuItem.phtml and is shown in listing 4.10.

Listing 4.10   A partial menu item script

```
<li>
  <a href="<?php echo $this->url ?>">           ❶ Links menu
      <?php echo $this->escape($this->title); ?></a>   ←   title to URL
</li>
```

The template that is rendered for each menu item simply wraps the menu's title in a link ❶ and places it within the `<li>` tag to create the list element. As usual, we use the `escape()` view helper to ensure that any unusual characters within the menu's title are encoded.

The other action that is run for every displayed page is the advert action. This works exactly the same way as the menu action, except that it renders to the place‑ holder called `advert`. There is no need for any other controller logic, as shown in listing 4.11.

Listing 4.11   The IndexController's advertAction() function

```
class IndexController extends Zend_Controller_Action
{
    // ...

    public function advertAction()
    {
        $this->_helper->viewRenderer->
            ➥ setResponseSegment('advert');        ⟵───┤ Sets response
    }                                                   placeholder
```

We just have a graphic in the advertisement section, so the HTML is done entirely within the view script, views/scripts/index/advert.phtml, as shown in listing 4.12.

Listing 4.12   The advertAction() method's view script: advert.phtml

```
<a id="right-ad"
    href="<?php echo $this->url(array('controller'=>'contact'),
    ➥ null, true); ?>">
    <img src="<?php echo $this->baseUrl(); ?>
        ➥ /img/advert.gif"                         Displays
        title="" alt="advertise here" />           single image
</a>
```

As you can see, the advertisement we use is just an image with a link to the contact controller. The third parameter to the url() view helper is used to reset the assembly so that only those parameters in the array are used in the construction of the URL. If we did not do this, the current action would be used in the construction of the URL, which we do not want. Alternatively, we could set the action within the url() view helper itself.

This completes the creation of the master layout template, so we can now turn our attention to the view content of the controller action itself. As we discovered in chapter 2, the view script for the current action is stored in the views/scripts/{controller name}/{action name}.phtml file. In chapter 3 we implemented the home page action (the index action of the index controller), so we shall now implement the associated view script.

4.3.4   *The homepage view script*

The view script for the home page is stored in the views/scripts/index/index.phtml file and is shown in listing 4.13.

Listing 4.13   The home page's view script: index.phtml

```
<h1><?php echo $this->escape($this->title);?></h1>
<p>Welcome to <em>Places to take the kids</em>! This
site will help you to plan a good day out for you and
your children. Every place featured on this site has
been reviewed by people like you, so you'll be able to
make informed decisions with no marketing waffle!</p>
```
 Displays welcome content

```php
<?php if(count($this->places)) : ?>
<h2>Recent places</h2>
<table>
<?php echo $this->partialLoop('index/_placeRow.phtml',
           $this->places) ?>
</table>
<?php endif; ?>
```

❷ Displays reviews only if we have some

Iterates over items within $this->places

In the home page view script, we first add general content text at the top ❶, which sets the stage for the website, and then we present a list of places that have been recently updated ❷. This list uses the $places member variable that was set in the controller's indexAction() in chapter 3 (listing 3.8). To iterate over the items in the places rowset, we again make use of the partialLoop view helper, which eliminates the need for a foreach() loop. Each item in the rowset is extracted into local variables within the _placeRow.phtml view script. Note that we use the naming convention of a preceding underscore to indicate that _placeRow.phtml is a partial script used in conjunction with another script. The _placeRow.phtml script is shown in listing 4.14.

Listing 4.14   A partial view script for the home page listing: _placeRow.phtml

```php
<?php $url = $this->url(array('controller'=>'place',
           'action'=>'index',
           'id'=>$this->id)); ?>
<tr>
   <td><a href="<?php echo $url ;?>">
      <?php echo $this->escape($this->name);?></a></td>
   <td><?php echo $this->displayDate(
           $this->date_updated); ?></td>
</tr>
```

❶ Creates URL for use in link

❷ Formats date using view helper

The _placeRow.phtml view script creates a single table row containing two columns: the name of the place, and the date that the information about it was updated. As with all links, we again use the url() view helper to generate the link ❶. This will ease maintenance if we decide to use custom routes, because the url() view helper will continue to generate the correct URLs.

We also factor the date-formatting code into a view helper ❷ so we can reuse it on other pages. This view helper is stored in application/views/helpers/Display-Date.php, and the code is shown in listing 4.15.

Listing 4.15   The DisplayDate view helper

```php
class Zend_View_Helper_DisplayDate
{
   function displayDate($timestamp, $format=Zend_Date::DATE_LONG)
   {
      $date = new Zend_Date($timestamp, 'en_GB');
      return $date->get($format);
   }
}
```

❶ Creates Zend_Date object

❷ Retrieves date in correct format

One thing about creating view helpers is that you must get the case of the names correct. The filename must start with an uppercase letter to match the class name but the method name must start with a lowercase letter. This is a very common issue that can trip you up if you develop on a case-insensitive filesystem, such as Windows' NTFS or Mac OS X's HFS+ and then deploy to a case-sensitive filesystem on Linux or Solaris.

For `displayDate()`, we instantiate a `Zend_Date` object with the required timestamp and locale ❶, and then use the `get()` member function to retrieve the data in the correct format ❷. `Zend_Date` is a very useful component for handling dates and times, as it is locale-aware so that when we come to localize our application into other languages, the date format will automatically change to a format that is correct for that locale.

We have now built the entire view for the home page using a composite approach. `Zend_Layout` is controlling the outer template that contains all the common elements for the site, so that the view script for each specific action is only concerned with the specific output related to the action.

`Zend_View` also provides a useful set of view helpers that we can use to make development faster. We have looked at some of these while integrating `Zend_Layout` into *Places*, but we will now look at each one in turn to see what it is used for and how to use it.

4.4   Advanced view helpers

A variety of view helpers are provided as part of the `Zend_View` component to improve the development of view scripts. These view helpers allow for easier integration with controllers, management of view scripts, and creation of common HTML headers. We'll start with the `action()` and `url()` view helpers, which help integrate view scripts with controllers.

4.4.1   Controller integration

There are two supplied view helpers that interact with the controller. The `action()` view helper is used to run actions directly, and the `url()` view helper is able to generate URLs to controller actions.

THE ACTION() VIEW HELPER

The `action()` view helper is used to run a controller action from within a view script. The result is returned and can be echoed. This is generally used in the same way as placeholders to render subsections of pages in a reusable manner.

For example, we could use `action()` to display the advertisement in layout.phtml. In listing 4.3, the following code was used to display the advertisement:

```
<div id="right" class="column">
   <?php echo $this->layout()->advert; ?>
</div>
```

As discussed in section 4.3.3, this code assumes that the `IndexController::advert-Action()` action has already been dispatched by the ActionStack, as shown in listing 4.7. As an alternative, we could use the `action()` view helper to dispatch the `avertAction()` directly within the layout.phtml file, like this:

```
<div id="right" class="column">
    <?php echo $this->action('advert', 'index'); ?>
</div>
```

The result that is displayed to the user in the browser is exactly the same in both cases, and the choice of whether to use the `action()` view helper or layout placeholders is entirely up to the developer. In general, it depends on how active you consider the view object should be in your application. Some developers see the view as very active and so use `action()`, and others treat it as more passive and ensure that the controller does the work using the ActionStack plug-in.

As it is fundamental to creating usable links within a template, let's look at the `url()` view helper in a bit more detail.

THE URL() VIEW HELPER

The `url()` view helper creates URL strings based on a named route. This is the method signature:

```
public function url($urlOptions = array(), $name = null, $reset = false,
                $encode = true)
```

The parameters are shown in table 4.1.

Table 4.1   Parameters for the `url()` view helper

Parameter	Description
`$urlOptions`	Array of options that are used to create the URL string.
`$name`	Name of the route to use to create the URL string. If `null`, the route name that originally matched the current page's URL is used.
`$reset`	Set to `true` to reset all the parameters when creating the URL string.
`$encode`	Set to `true` to `urlencode()` all the parameter values in `$urlOptions`.

When using the default route, you can pass in the action, module, controller, and other parameters required, and the correct URL will be generated. If you do not pass in some of these fields, it will use the current known ones. If we want to generate a URL to the browse action in the place controller, then we would use this line:

```
<?php echo $this->url(array('controller'=>'place', 'action'=>'browse')); ?>
```

However, if the current page is within the place controller, we can omit that part and use only this:

```
<?php echo $this->url(array('action'=>'browse')); ?>
```

To pass other parameters to the controller action, such as the page number of the list of places we wish to browse, we include them as additional keys in the array:

```php
<?php echo $this->url(array('controller'=>'place', 'action'=>'browse',
    'page'=>'2')); ?>
```

This generates the URL /base-url/place/browse/page/2. One side effect is that if you then generate links using `url()`, all the URL strings created will have /page/2 included unless you override. Overriding can be done in two ways. First, you can set the parameter to `null`:

```php
<?php echo $this->url(array('controller'=>'place', 'action'=>'browse',
    'page'=>null)); ?>
```

Alternatively, you can use the third parameter of the `url()` view helper, which is `$reset`. This parameter ensures that none of the known parameters are used when creating the URL. It is used like this:

```php
<?php echo $this->url(array('controller'=>'place', 'action'=>'browse'),
    null, true); ?>
```

As you can see, `url()` is very powerful and allows for flexible and maintainable URL creation within view scripts.

The next set of provided view helpers make it easier to separate view scripts into separate files. The `partial()` and `partialLoop()` view helpers help us manage our view scripts and avoid having too much code in any one file.

4.4.2   *View script management*

It is not unusual to have multiple view scripts making up a single response. We have seen this already in listing 4.3, where the header and footer view scripts are linked into layout.phtml. There are two related view script management view helpers: `partial()` and `partialLoop()`.

THE PARTIAL() VIEW HELPER

The `partial()` view helper renders a separate view script within its own scope. This means that none of the variables that have been assigned to the view are available in the targeted view script, and only the variables specifically passed in are there. If you need to render a separate view script within the same context as the current view script, the `render()` method of `Zend_View` would be used.

Standard usage of `partial()` is like this:

```php
<?php echo $this->partial("menu.phtml",
    array('title'=>'home', 'url'=>'/')); ?>
```

This will render the `menu.phtml` view script, and the only two variables available within it are `$this->title` and `$this->url`. The parameters that you pass to a partial are known as the model and may be either arrays or objects. If an object is used, either the `toArray()` method or all the public variables are assigned to the view partial.

The `partialLoop()` view helper extends `partial()`, allowing the same view script to be called multiple times.

THE PARTIALLOOP() VIEW HELPER

One common use-case of partial view scripts is iterating over a list of data like this:

```php
<?php
foreach $this->menu as $menuItem) {
    echo $this->partial("menu.phtml", $menuItem);
}
?>
```

This is so common that the `partialLoop()` view helper is provided to simplify this code to this:

```php
<?php echo $this->partialLoop('menu.phtml', $this->menu) ?>
```

Behind the scenes, `partialLoop()` calls `partial()`, so it works in exactly the same way.

> ### Placing a row object into a partial
>
> By default, if you use a rowset with a `partialLoop()`, you will notice that the row object is turned into a set of member variables when used in the view script. If you want the object itself, then you can do this:
>
> ```php
> <?php echo $this->partialLoop()->setObjectKey('menu')
>     ->partialLoop('menu.phtml', $this->menu) ?>
> ```
>
> The variables are now available within the view script by using `$this->menu->{variable name}`.

Using `partial()` and `partialLoop()` can significantly improve the reusability of HTML view scripts in the same way that classes and functions allow reusability of PHP code.

We will now turn our attention to managing the header section of an HTML page with the many `head*()` view helpers.

4.4.3 *HTML header helpers*

Zend Framework provides a set of helpers to manage the <head> section of an HTML page. These helpers enable you to set up the information in advance and output it within the layout view script. There are a variety of helpers that mostly begin with the word *head*, and two, `json()` and `doctype()`, which are also used at the head of a document.

JSON() HELPER

The `json()` view helper is used when sending JSON data to the web browser, usually in response to an Ajax request. It does three things:

- Encodes the data into JSON format.
- Disables layout rendering.
- Sets the HTTP header `content-type` to `application/json`.

The usage is very simple. Given an array or object called data, it is encoded and sent to the browser using this code:

```php
<?php echo $this->json($this->data)); ?>
```

This view helper uses the Zend_Json component to encode the data. This component will use the json PHP extension if it is available; otherwise it will fall back to a native PHP implementation.

All the other HTML head view helpers output text into the HTML page. Let's start by looking at the doctype() view helper, as this one is used at the very top of the page.

DOCTYPE() HELPER

The doctype() view helper is a convenience helper for creating the doc type in the HTML file. It mainly solves the problem of having to look up the correct document type from the W3C website. As with all view helpers, you simply echo it out:

```php
<?php echo $this->doctype('XHTML1_TRANSITIONAL'); ?>
```

The doctype() view helper understands all XHTML 1 and HTML 4 doctype declarations, and this also affects the rendering of the relevant head*() view helpers so that they are compliant with the doctype specified. You can also test for XHTML or not in other view scripts using the isXhtml() member function.

TIP   Some view helpers, especially the form-related ones, will output either HTML- or XHTML-compliant code, depending on the value passed into the doctype() view helper. For that reason, it's best to set the doc type early in the dispatch process, such as in dispatchLoopStartup() of your ViewSetup front controller plug-in. You still need to echo it at the top of your (X)HTML output, but you don't need to pass in the value again.

HEADLINK() HELPER

HeadLink() manages <link> elements in the <head> section of the document. This includes CSS stylesheets, favicons, RSS feeds, and trackbacks. It aggregates the elements together while rendering each view script and is later used to render the elements into the layout.

We used this functionality in listing 4.9, the menu.phtml view script that specified a CSS file for the menu:

```php
<?php $this->headLink()->appendStylesheet($this->baseUrl()
     . '/css/menu.css') ?>
```

There is also a prependStylesheet() member function for controlling the order of output, and for alternative stylesheets appendAlternate() and prependAlternate() can be used. We can also set the media for the stylesheet by setting the second parameter, so for a print stylesheet, the following code is used:

```php
<?php $this->headLink()->appendStylesheet($this->baseUrl().
     '/css/menu.print.css', 'print') ?>
```

Favicons are attached in a similar way, only we use the generic `headLink()` member function, rather than the CSS-specific functions:

```php
<?php $this->headLink()->headLink(array('rel' => 'favicon',
    'href' => $this->baseUrl().'/favicon.ico'))?>
```

All the links that have been specified are then rendered using this line:

```php
<?php echo $this->headLink(); ?>
```

HEADSCRIPT() HELPER

Similar to the `headLink()` view helper, `headScript()` is used to manage JavaScript files. This allows us to add the relevant files to the helper as the views are rendered, and then to render the final output later. This is important for maintenance, as it means that the references to the JavaScript are within the correct action's view script rather than being separate in the layout.

Adding JavaScript files is very similar to adding CSS files and is done like this:

```php
$this->headScript()->appendScript($this->baseUrl().'/js/autocomplete.js');
```

When all the scripts have been added, they are rendered by echoing the helper:

```php
<?php echo $this->headScript(); ?>
```

One useful thing that `headScript()` does for us is ensure that we only include one reference to an external JavaScript file, even though we may have added it more than once. With an emphasis on ensuring minimum page-load times, this is a good optimization and means that we don't have to manage it ourselves.

HEADMETA() HELPER

As you would expect, `headMeta()` is used to set all the `<meta>` tags in the `<head>` section of the page. There are two types of meta tags: *name* and *http-equiv*, so there are two sets of functions, as shown in table 4.2.

The `$keyValue` field sets either the name or the http-equiv key for the tag. The `$content` parameter is used for the value attribute of a name tag or the content

Table 4.2   The `headMeta()` view helper functions

Name version	http-equiv version
appendName($keyValue, $content, $conditionalName)	appendHttpEquiv($keyValue, $content, $conditionalHttpEquiv)
prependName($keyValue, $content, $conditionalName)	prependHttpEquiv($keyValue, $content, $conditionalHttpEquiv)
setName($keyValue, $content, $modifiers)	setHttpEquiv ($keyValue, $content, $modifiers)
offsetSetName ($index, $keyValue, $content, $conditionalName)	offsetSetHttpEquiv($index, $keyValue, $content, $conditionalHttpEquiv)

attribute of an http-equiv tag, and the `$modifiers` parameter is an associative array that can contain the `lang` and `scheme` attributes if required.

Let's look the `keywords` meta tag. Usually, this would be set in the action view script based on the content being rendered by the action. In *Places*, we set the keywords for each place during the index action of the place controller, as this is the controller that displays a page containing a single place. The keywords are stored in the database and so are assigned to the view along with all the other data about the place. The action view script then renders the information for the visitor, such as title and description, and also sets up the `keywords` meta tag using this code:

```
$this->headMeta()->appendName('keywords', $this->place->keywords);
```

We also want the browser to cache the page, but not for too long, because there will be new reviews added to it, so we also add the `expires` http-equiv meta tag using the code in listing 14.16.

Listing 4.16   Setting up the `expires` meta tag using `Zend_Date`

```
$date = new Zend_Date();
$date->add('3', Zend_Date::HOUR);        ←——  ❶  Adds 3 hours to
$this->headMeta()->appendHttpEquiv('expires',       current date/time
        $date->get(Zend_Date::RFC_1123));    ❷  Requires RFC 1123
                                                 format date
```

We have chosen to use an expiry time 3 hours into the future, and this is easily done using `Zend_Date`'s `add()` function ❶, as it is very easy to add and subtract any amount of time from a `Zend_Date` object. The expires meta tag requires a date format of the type defined in RFC 1123, which is directly supported by `Zend_Date`'s `get()` function ❷.

As we saw in listing 4.3, the layout.phtml file prints out the meta tags using this line:

```
<?php echo $this->headMeta(); ?>
```

This picks up all the meta tags that have been added over the course of rendering the page and formats them correctly for us.

HEADTITLE() HELPER

The `headTitle()` helper sets the `<title>` tag within the `<head>` section. This helper allows you to build up a multi-section title while the front controller's dispatch loop runs and displays it. Typical usage is to display the title of the page and the name of the website; for example: "London Zoo - Places to take the kids."

In *Places*, we achieve this by adding to the `Places_Controller_Plugin_ViewSetup` front controller plug-in introduced in listing 4.2. To add the page title, we call the `headTitle()` view script directly in the action controller, so for the home page, we need to add the following code in `indexAction()` of the `IndexController`:

```
$this->view->headTitle('Welcome');
```

We now need to add the website's name to the end. This is done in the `postDispatch()` function of `Places Controller_Plugin_ViewSetup`, which runs after every dispatch. This function is shown in listing 4.17.

Listing 4.17 Adding a website name with the postDispatch() method

```
public function postDispatch(Zend_Controller_Request_Abstract $request)
{
    if (!$request->isDispatched()) {          ❶ Checks for
        return;                                   more actions
    }

    $view = $this->_view;

    if (count($view->headTitle()->getValue()) == 0) {    ❷ Assigns view's
        $view->headTitle($view->title);                     $title if nothing
    }                                                       has been set

    $view->headTitle()->setSeparator(' - ');        ◄────────┐
                                                       ❸ Sets separator
    $view->headTitle('Places to take the kids!');   ◄──┐
}                                                   ❸ Sets site name
```

We want only the website's name to be added to the title if this is the last action to be dispatched. This allows for other actions to add additional information to the title if needed. We check this by looking at the request's `isDispatched()` method and returning if it is `false` ❶. We have already set in place the convention that the main `<h1>` tag for the page is filled with the value of the `$view->title`, so as a convenience, we check if the head title has been set, and if not, we use the page's title ❷. By default, there is no separator between each segment of the title, so we need to set one ❸. For *Places*, we have chosen a hyphen, though you could also use a colon or a slash character. Finally, we add the website's name ❸. Again, we display the title in listing 4.3 using this code:

```
<?php echo $this->headTitle(); ?>
```

We have now looked at all the commonly used `head*()` view helpers that are designed to bring management and maintainability to the `<head>bt` section of your web page. The most significant advantage of using the `headLink()` and `headScript()` view helpers is that you can keep the per-action CSS and JavaScript within the action's view script while still rendering them in the correct place in the document.

There are numerous other view helpers provided by the framework that we have not covered here because they are appropriate for `Zend_Form` and `Zend_Translate`. They are covered in those chapters.

4.5　*Summary*

We have now looked at a complete application that uses Zend Frameworks MVC components to separate the code and ensure that it is maintainable. Concentrating on the view, we have seen that the Composite View design pattern is a powerful tool for ensuring that we have a consistent look and feel to the site. The Zend_Layout component helps to make implementing a layout script with content placeholders easy. The advanced view helpers ensure that the layout is as flexible as required, with the ability to call other controller actions directly. This separation ensures that each controller action has only one responsibility and thus is easier to maintain and develop.

Through chapters 3 and 4, we have built the foundations of *Places to take the kids!* to make it into a fully working website. The accompanying source code for this book shows the full code that has been created. We are now ready to look at how Zend Framework can interact with Ajax.

5

Ajax

This chapter covers

- Using Ajax in web applications
- Creating a simple Ajax example
- Intergrating YUI into Ajax
- Integrating Ajax elements into a Zend Framework application

Ajax is a way of using JavaScript to create interactive web pages that send data to and from the server behind the scenes. This means that the user doesn't see the full page refresh and that a website is more responsive and feels faster to the user. As a result, a web application, such as a web-based email client, behaves more like its desktop cousins. Although it is server-based, Zend Framework's MVC system, which separates different layers of the application, helps make it easier to add Ajax functionality to your websites.

In this chapter, we will look at what Ajax is and how it is used in web applications. We'll also examine all the components that make up a simple example in both pure JavaScript and using prebuilt Ajax libraries. We will also integrate Ajax into a Zend Framework application so that we can investigate how Ajax interacts with the MVC system. First, let's look at exactly what Ajax is.

5.1   *Introducing Ajax*

As we have noted, Ajax-enabled applications are more user friendly because they are more responsive. Figure 5.1 shows Google Suggest (http://www.google.com/webhp?complete=1&hl=en), an Ajax application that provides a drop-down list of sorted search suggestions as you type your query into the search box. Another example of a good Ajax application is Google Calendar (http://calendar.google.com), with its ability to drag and drop calendar events in order to change their date and time.

There are advantages and disadvantages to using Ajax. The main advantages are that the UI is more intuitive, the user's workflow is interrupted much less, the application feels more responsive, and less bandwidth is used because only the required data is sent from the server. The main disadvantage is that Ajax applications tend to break well-known browser features, such as the back button and reliable URLs on the address bar for bookmarks or emailing to other people. There are additional UI issues for the web designer to be concerned about, such as providing notification of processing because Internet Explorer's (IE) "spinning globe" no longer performs this task. Websites that use Ajax can also have problems with adhering to the WAI accessibility guidelines, so a fall-back system is often required.

5.1.1   *Defining Ajax*

Ajax came into use in 2005 as a way of describing the suite of technologies used to build dynamic websites, and the official expansion is *Asynchronous JavaScript and XML.* So, let's look at each component technology in turn.

ASYNCHRONOUS

In order for an Ajax application to be an Ajax application, it needs to talk with the server without a page refresh. This is known as asynchronous data exchange, and it's

Figure 5.1   Google Suggest was developed in Google's labs incubator and uses Ajax to provide contextual auto-completion.

generally performed using the web browser's `XMLHttpRequest` object. A hidden `iframe` element can also be used. The `XMLHttpRequest` object is essentially a mini web browser built into the web browser that we use to talk to the web server without interrupting the user.

JAVASCRIPT

The key component in Ajax technologies is JavaScript and the browser's Document Object Model (DOM), which enables scripts to manipulate the web page. JavaScript is a proper programming language in its own right and has been implemented in mainstream browsers since 1995. The DOM is a standardized way of representing the elements of a web page as a tree of objects that can be manipulated by JavaScript. Within Ajax applications, this is the means by which the application dynamically changes the web page to show new information without the server's sending new data.

XML

To transfer the new data from the server to the web browser within an asynchronous request, XML is used to format the data. In general, the language used to write the server application is different from JavaScript as used in the web browser, so a language neutral data transfer format is used. XML is a well known standard for solving this type of problem, but other formats, notably structured HTML, plain text, and JSON (a JavaScript-based data transfer format) are also used in Ajax applications.

NOT JUST XML

JSON can be used as the data transfer format rather than XML, and the application is still known as an Ajax application (because it sounds better than "Ajaj"!). The term *Ajax* has taken on meaning beyond its original definition, and nowadays it represents a class of technologies that provide dynamic user interaction with the web server.

There are many uses of Ajax within a website to provide a better user experience. Let's look briefly at how Ajax is used in applications on the web to make users' lives easier.

5.1.2 Using Ajax in web applications

Ajax has many uses in all kinds of web applications. These are the main uses:

- Retrieving data without a page refresh
- Form validation
- Form helpers (auto-completion and drop-down lists)
- Dragging and dropping of items on the page

Let's look at each one in more detail.

RETRIEVING DATA WITHOUT A PAGE REFRESH

Web applications such as Google's Gmail and Calendar rely on Ajax in order to work. They retrieve data from the server directly, without forcing a page refresh. This allows for data to be updated in the relevant part of the page, such as when clicking on an email in the inbox, without the whole screen going white while it refreshes. Web applications also respond faster when using Ajax because less data needs to be transferred for each user interaction. The lack of a page refresh also makes the application more immersive for users because their workflow is not interrupted.

FORM VALIDATION

JavaScript has been used for form validation since Netscape first invented the language. Usually the validation is a piece of ad hoc code above the form that checks for the obvious errors, with the main validation being left to the server. Because your form is not the only way to post data to a given web page, it is vital that server-side validation remain. However, the more validation that can be done before the user has to wait for the full page to refresh, the better. There is nothing more frustrating than clicking the submit button, waiting 10 seconds, and then finding out that you didn't format your telephone number correctly!

FORM HELPERS: AUTO-COMPLETION AND DROP-DOWN LISTS

Forms are generally complicated, and anything that helps the user to complete one is welcome. Form field auto-completion is so useful that all the major web browsers offer this feature, remembering what you have typed into a given field. Ajax applications can take this idea one step further and help the user fill in text fields correctly all the time. Form drop-down lists of options that have too many choices can be replaced with text fields that are auto-complete enabled. Examples would include fields for choosing your country when completing your address.

Form field auto-completion is also useful when the user should either supply a new value or use an existing one, such as when assigning a task to a category within a project management application. Most of the time, the user would want to select an existing category (and not misspell it!), so the auto-complete drop-down will help them in this task. For those times when a new category needs to be created, the workflow is not interrupted as a new category can be entered straight into the field.

DRAGGING AND DROPPING

Dragging and dropping is very common in desktop computer tasks. For example, in a file manager you might select some files and drag them into another folder. Ajax enables this metaphor to work on the web as well. For instance, you could have a shopping basket in an e-commerce website that allows the user to drag items from the basket to a trash can to remove them from the order.

> **TIP**   One caveat with dragging and dropping is that most web applications don't allow for drag and drop, so users do not expect that it is possible on the web. You should, therefore, always allow for an alternative method of performing the action, or write very clear instructions!

Now that we have looked at what Ajax is and how it is used, we will write a simple example application that uses JavaScript to send a request back to the server and deals with the response.

5.2 *A simple Ajax example*

In this example application, we will use form validation and check that a given username is acceptable for use. To create the simplest of simple examples, we need three files:

- an HTML page for the form
- a JavaScript file to perform the XMLHTTPRequest
- a PHP file to do the server-side validation

As the user types each character into the form field, a message appears underneath it showing any errors in their choice of name. The application in action is shown in figure 5.2.

The flow of information in an Ajax request is a little more complicated than a straight web page request. It all starts with an HTML element containing a JavaScript callback function, such as `onclick`, which executes the JavaScript callback code. The JavaScript callback initiates a request to the web server using the XMLHt-

Registration:

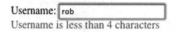

Username is less than 4 characters

Figure 5.2   A simple Ajax example showing an error message while the user types into the text field

tpRequest system, and the server-side code, such as PHP, performs the work. Once the PHP code has completed, it formats the response in either XML or JSON and sends it back to the browser, where it is processed by a JavaScript callback. Finally the JavaScript updates the HTML display to change the text, add new elements via the DOM, or change CSS styles. This process is shown in figure 5.3.

For this example, let's start with the server-side PHP validation code, in listing 5.1, which will check that the submitted username is at least four characters long and doesn't clash with an existing username.

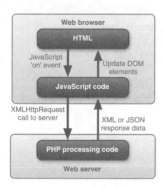

Figure 5.3   The application data flow in an Ajax request is controlled by the JavaScript code. A user does something, which triggers a request, and updates the web page when a response is received.

Listing 5.1   A simple server-side validation routine in PHP: ajax.php

```php
<?php
function checkUsername($username) {
    $existingUsers = array('rasmus', 'zeev', 'andi');
    // empty check
    if ($username == '') {              Returns an empty string if
        return '';                      there's no username
    } elseif (strlen($username) < 4) {        Checks that username
        return '<span class="error">          is long enough
            Username is less than 4 characters
            </span>';
    } elseif (in_array($username, $existingUsers)) {        Checks the
        return '<span class="error">                        username
            Username already exists                         doesn't exist
            </span>';
    } else {
        return '<span class="ok">
            Username is acceptable
            </span>';
    }
}

$name = isset($_GET['name']) ? $_GET['name'] : '';
echo checkUsername(trim($name));
```

Note that we put the actual validation code into a checkUsername() function so that it will be easy to test. We echo out the result of checkUsername() so that the browser can display it to the user. Although the list of existing users is an array in this example, it's more likely that the script would execute a database call to check the current list of users.

To access our validation script, we need a form where the user can type in the preferred username. The HTML is shown in listing 5.2.

Listing 5.2   HTML file with simple form that requires validation: index.html

```html
<!DOCTYPE html PUBLIC "-//W3C//DTD XHTML 1.0 Strict//EN"
    "http://www.w3.org/TR/xhtml1/DTD/xhtml1-strict.dtd">
<html xmlns="http://www.w3.org/1999/xhtml" lang="en" xml:lang="en">
<head>
<title>Simple Ajax Example</title>
<meta http-equiv="Content-Type" content="text/html;charset=utf-8" />
<style>
    .ok {color: green;}              Provides simple
    .error {color: red;}             styling
</style>
<script type="text/javascript" src="ajax.js" />
</head>
<body>

<h1>Registration:</h1>

<form action="#">
    <div>
```

```
        <label for="name">Username:</label>
        <input id="name" name="name" type="text"
            onkeyup="checkUsername(this.value)" />
        <div id="message"></div>
    </div>
  </form>
  </body>
  </html>
```

Calls checkUsername() on each keystroke

Specifies placeholder for message returned by server

This is a simple form that uses the onkeyup event on the input field to send the current text that the user has entered to the PHP file on the server. This is done in the JavaScript check() function, which is stored in a separate JavaScript file called ajax.js, shown in listing 5.3.

Listing 5.3   Hand-crafted JavaScript code to call back to the server for validation

```
var request;
if (navigator.appName ==
        "Microsoft Internet Explorer") {
    request = new ActiveXObject("Microsoft.XMLHTTP");
} else {
    request = new XMLHttpRequest();
}

function checkUsername(username)
{
    var success = 4;
    request.abort();
    request.open("GET", "ajax1.php?name="
        + username, true);

    request.onreadystatechange=function() {
    if (request.readyState == success) {
       document.getElementById('message').innerHTML
            = request.responseText;
    }
  }
  request.send(null);
}
```

Allows for IE's ActiveX control

Sends request back to server

Runs when the request object changes state

Displays returned text on success

To update the HTML page with the new data, we select an element on the page using document.getElementById() and change its attributes. In this case, we change it entirely by replacing its innerHTML property with the server's response. We could equally have changed its CSS style or built new child HTML elements, such as new li elements, based on the data received from the server.

You should now have an appreciation of what Ajax is and how the various components fit together. This example is necessarily simplistic, as this book is not about Ajax per se. To really understand what's going on and the full possibilities available with Ajax, we recommend *Ajax in Action* by Dave Crane and Eric Pascarello, published by Manning.

The JavaScript code we have presented here looks nice and simple and breaks pretty much every rule of defensive programming—there is no error checking at all! Other than the fact that it would clutter up the example, it is hard to get error checking right for all the browsers out there. We can abstract all the complications away into a client library though, and, fortunately, other people have already done this for us. We will examine Ajax client libraries next, and see how they can simplify the code we need to write.

5.3   *Using Ajax client libraries*

Adding the required JavaScript to create an Ajax application used to be quite painful. For example, the checkUsername() function in listing 5.1 mixes code dealing with the request with code that knows about how the HTML document is built. This is not good for long-term maintenance, as we have seen in chapter 2, where we used the MVC design pattern to separate business, control, and display code for our main application. We should be separating the responsibilities of our client-side Ajax code too, and rather than writing all the code ourselves, we can utilize an Ajax library to help us.

A JavaScript library will enable us to build upon the work of others. As PHP application developers, we are often more interested in solving our client's problems than worrying about the underlying technology. A JavaScript library will enable us to work with Ajax at a higher level, in much the same way that Zend Framework empowers us in our server-side application development.

There are many JavaScript libraries to choose from, and it is not obvious how to make the choice. In much the same way as we chose to use Zend Framework, the key considerations when choosing a JavaScript library are features, performance, documentation, and community.

The Yahoo! User Interface (YUI) provides a set of UI widgets along with core underlying classes to make the creation of Ajax applications easier. The attraction of the YUI is that a big company is supporting it, and it has great documentation, including examples. There is also a community of users who use the library, and they have produced extensions that enhance the standard components.

Let's convert our example from section 5.2 to use the YUI. To do this, we need to add the required YUI library files to the HTML file (yahoo.js and connection.js), then change the code in ajax.js as shown in listing 5.4.

Listing 5.4   Integrating YUI into our example Ajax application: ajax.js

```
var handleSuccess = function(o) {          ◁─────────┐  Displays results on success
    if(o.responseText !== undefined){
        document.getElementById('message').innerHTML = o.responseText;
    }
}                                                      ┐  Clears message
                                                       │  on failure
var handleFailure = function(o) {          ◁───────────┘
    document.getElementById('message').innerHTML = "";
}
```

```
function check(name)
{
    var sUrl = "ajax.php?name=" + name;
    var callback =
    {
        success: handleSuccess,
        failure: handleFailure
    };
    var request = YAHOO.util.Connect.asyncRequest('GET',
                sUrl, callback);    ◄───────────
}
```

Performs Ajax request with YUI's Connect object

As you can see, the code is pretty much the same. In this case, the class that wraps up XMLHttpRequest is called `YAHOO.util.Connect`, and we call the `asyncRequest` static method to initiate the connection to the server. Again, a configuration object is used to define which callback functions we want to use, though this time we have created the object, `callback`, first and then assigned it to the function.

Using YUI makes development of Ajax applications much easier and less prone to error than hand-coding from scratch. Obviously, there are a lot of other client libraries out there, such as JQuery, MooTools, Prototype, and Dojo, which are worth looking at before making a decision. For the remainder of this book, we will use the YUI library for no other reason than we quite like it!

Now that we have a library to make development easier, we can look at how Ajax fits with Zend Framework.

5.4   *Using Ajax with Zend Framework*

One thing to consider when using Ajax with Zend Framework is that Zend Framework version 1.5 does not provide an Ajax component per se, but does have various helper plug-ins. Also, the MVC system and other components such as `Zend_Json` make it easy to add Ajax features to your application. Throughout this book, maintenance of the application is a key design consideration, and Zend Framework's separation of the model and controller from the view makes it easy to replace the standard HTML-based view of most pages with another view, especially for Ajax requests.

NOTE   Zend Framework version 1.6 features integration with the Dojo JavaScript library, but it was not available at the time of writing. The Dojo support is provided as an optional extra, and all other JavaScript libraries, such as YUI, JQuery, and Prototype, can be used with Zend Framework 1.6. The online manual provides full details of how to use the new Dojo components.

Integrating Ajax into Zend Framework takes two forms: handling the Ajax request from the user within the controller, and providing the JavaScript elements to handle the response from the server back to the client.

From Zend Framework's point of view, an Ajax request looks remarkably like any other request that comes in to the application. The most significant difference is that the response back to the client is a snippet of HTML, XML, or JSON. Responding to an Ajax request is a matter of ensuring that we use a different view and turn off the layout if we are using one. This is done using the built-in `AjaxContext` action helper, which is supplied with the framework.

If `AjaxContext` detects an XMLHttpRequest, it will set an alternative view suffix based on the desired format, disable layouts if enabled, and send the correct response headers for the format if it isn't HTML. The advantage of the MVC design pattern becomes noticeable as the controller and model can be reused without any changes when adding Ajax to an application. The only part that has to change is the view, because we are sending data back rather than a nicely formatted web page. Let's look at the controller first.

5.4.1   *The controller*

When providing controller actions that respond to Ajax calls, the view must not send back full HTML pages, but must instead send HTML fragments, JSON, or XML data. The controller for our simple example application in section 5.3 will require two actions: one for displaying the page, and one for responding to the Ajax request. The action for displaying the page, shown in listing 5.5, should look familiar.

> **Listing 5.5   `IndexController` action to display the page**

```
public function indexAction()
{
    $this->view->baseUrl =
        $this->getRequest()->getBaseUrl();          ◁——————  Stores base URL
}                                                             to the view
```

The `indexAction()` method is very simple, as all we need to do is store the `baseUrl` value into the view. We need it so that we can reference the full path for the JavaScript files.

To respond to the Ajax call, we use a separate action, which we will call `checkAction()`. In order for `checkAction()` to respond to an Ajax call, we also need to set up the `AjaxContext` in `init()`, as shown in listing 5.6.

> **Listing 5.6   `IndexController::init()` sets up the `AjaxContext`**

```
public function init()
{                                                                     Creates HTML
    $ajaxContext = $this->_helper->getHelper('AjaxContext');          format
    $ajaxContext->addActionContext('check', 'html');    ◁——————       responses
    $ajaxContext->initContext();       ◁——————
}                                             ❶  Initializes context
                                                 object
```

The `AjaxContext` action helper is very simple to use. We call `addActionContext()` for each controller action that we want to respond to an Ajax call. We also have to define the type of response that the action will produce—in this case HTML. Finally, we initialize the action helper ❶ to register its `preDispatch()` hook, which will turn off the rendering of the layout and choose a different view script file based on the format of the incoming Ajax request.

The actual PHP server-side work that is done in response to the Ajax request has already been created. We will reuse the same ajax.php file that we have been using for all the examples in this chapter as it has a perfectly good checkUsername() function to do the actual validation. In keeping with the MVC separation, we have put this file in the models directory and included it for use in our action:

```
public function checkAction()
{
    include ('models/ajax.php');
    $name = trim($this->getRequest()->getParam('name'));
    $this->_view->result = checkUsername($name);
}
```

The associated view file, views/scripts/check.ajax.phtml, contains just one line of code to output the result:

```
<?php echo $this->result; ?>
```

The view script file has a different filename because it is an Ajax response, so the AjaxContext action helper has changed the filename to include "ajax" to differentiate it from the standard view script file that would be used. Other filename extensions are .json.phtml for JSON responses and .xml.phtml for XML ones. This is probably the simplest view file you'll ever see! Let's build the Ajax side now.

5.4.2   *The view*

In Zend Framework, the JavaScript part of an Ajax request is held within the view section, so the view script for the index action will manage the JavaScript side.

As we have come to expect, the view (application/views/scripts/index/index.phtml) contains the HTML code for the page. This is the same as before, except that we have to qualify where to find the JavaScript files using the baseUrl property that we created in indexAction():

```
<script type="text/javascript"
  src="<?php echo $this->baseUrl; ?>/js/yahoo.js"></script>
<script type="text/javascript"
  src="<?php echo $this->baseUrl; ?>/js/connection.js"></script>
<script type="text/javascript"
  src="<?php echo $this->baseUrl; ?>/js/ajax.js"></script>
```

We have chosen to continue with YUI for the Ajax request, but Prototype would work just as well. The remainder of the index.phtml file is the same as the code in listing 5.2, presented earlier. The JavaScript check() function also needs changing, because we need a fully qualified URL for the request back to the server. We therefore pass the base URL property to check() and rework the JavaScript sUrl variable to be in Zend Framework format (controller/action/param_name/param_value), as shown in listing 5.7.

Listing 5.7   YUI Ajax request to the controller action

```
function check(baseUrl, name)
{
   var sUrl = baseUrl +
           "/index/ajax/format/html/name/" + name;              ❶ Creates
                                                                     URL
   var callback =
   {
     success: handleSuccess,
     failure: handleFailure,                                   Sets  ❷
   };                                                X_REQUESTED_WITH
   YAHOO.util.Connect.initHeader('X_REQUESTED_WITH',      header
       'XMLHttpRequest');
   var request = YAHOO.util.Connect.asyncRequest('GET',
       sUrl, callback);
}
```

In addition to the controller and action, we need to tell the AjaxContext helper which format we want the results in. In this case, we want HTML, so we add the additional request parameter format with a value of html to the sUrl variable ❶. We also need to tell AjaxContext that the request is an XMLHttpRequest. This is done via the X_REQUESTED_WITH HTTP header. For YUI's Connect object, we use the initHeader() method ❷.

We now have a working Ajax example that uses Zend Framework's MVC structure. The only changes made to the basic example application were to ensure that the code was correctly separated according to its role. We can now do something more interesting and look at how to fully integrate Ajax into a typical Zend Framework application, such as the *Places* website.

5.5   *Integrating into a Zend Framework application*

When considering the use of Ajax in a Zend Framework application, it's not just the client-side JavaScript that needs to be written. We also have to ensure that the view doesn't try to display a full HTML page in response to an Ajax request and that our controller doesn't do work that our model should be doing. To look at these issues in context, we will write a feedback system into the *Places* example application.

Consider this use-case: We are hoping that *Places* becomes very popular and that we will get lots of reviews on each location. We would like to make it easy for users to let us know whether they thought any given review was helpful for them. We can then display the "helpfulness" of each listed review to users, which will guide them while reading the site. Also, as the number of reviews gets larger, we can display only the most helpful on the location's main page, and relegate the less-helpful reviews to a secondary page.

This is an ideal task for Ajax because we do not want to intrude upon users with a page refresh; an in-place update will allow them to continue looking at the other reviews once they have indicated whether a given review is helpful or not.

To provide feedback on a review, we need to ask the question "was this review helpful to you?" with the possible answers being yes or no. We keep a count of the number of people who have answered yes and the total number of respondents. This will then allow us to inform the user that "*N* of *M* people found this review helpful." At a later stage, as we get more and more reviews, we could even consider ordering the list by the "helpfulness" of the review.

The UI to our review feedback system is very simple, as shown in figure 5.4.

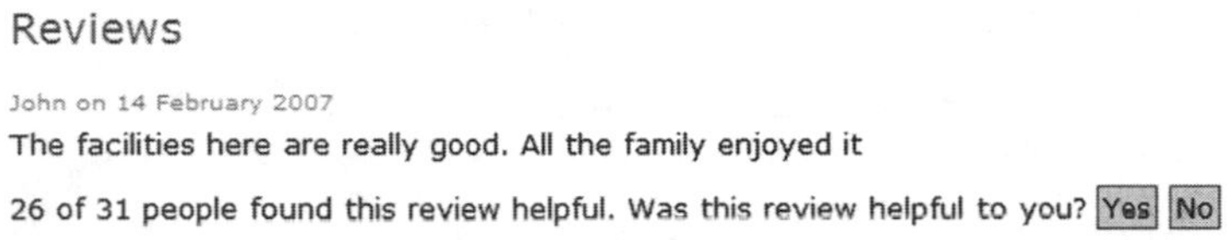

Reviews

John on 14 February 2007
The facilities here are really good. All the family enjoyed it

26 of 31 people found this review helpful. Was this review helpful to you? Yes No

Figure 5.4   The review feedback system has two buttons to provide feedback.

The review feedback system is a single line of text indicating the number of people who found the review helpful and the number of people who have provided feedback. The user is left to determine whether or not this ratio means that this review is "helpful." We also have two buttons to allow the user to provide feedback.

We will build this feature by starting with the view scripts and add HTML, then the JavaScript. We also need two database fields to hold the two count numbers: `helpful_yes` for the first one and `helpful_total` for the second. Let's look at the code necessary to build this system, starting with the controller.

5.5.1   The Place controller

First things first: we need a controller action to display the details of a location and its associated reviews. This is relatively straightforward. We just need an action within a controller. As this page displays a given place, we'll call the controller Place and use the index action. This means that we will have URLs of the form http://www.placesto-takethekids.com/place/index/id/{id}, which are easy to understand. Listing 5.8 shows this controller (with no error checking!).

> **Listing 5.8   The Place controller: application/controllers/PlaceController.php**

```
class PlaceController extends Zend_Controller_Action
{
    public function indexAction()
    {
        $placesFinder = new Places();
        $id = (int)$this->getRequest()->getParam('id');      Gets record from
        $place = $placesFinder->fetchRow('id='.$id);         database

        $this->view->place = $place;          Assigns
        $this->view->title = $place->name;    to view
    }
}
```

This simple action gets the place record from the database and assigns it to the view. The view file, application/views/scripts/place/index.phtml, shown in listing 5.9, is similar to the view scripts we've seen previously.

Listing 5.9   Place view script providing location details and a list of reviews

```php
<?php
$this->headScript()->appendFile($this->baseUrl().'/js/yahoo.js');
$this->headScript()->appendFile($this->baseUrl().'/js/connection.js');
$this->headScript()->appendFile($this->baseUrl().'/js/review_feedback.js');
?>
<h1><?php echo $this->escape($this->title);?></h1>
<div class="location">
<?php echo nl2br($this->escape(
    $this->displayAddress($this->place)));?>        ⊲—— Uses view helper
</div>                                                     to create

<h2>Reviews</h2>
<?php if(count($this->reviews)) : ?>
<ul id="reviews">
<?php echo $this->partialLoop(
        'place/_reviewItem.phtml',        Calls _reviewItem.phtml
        $this->reviews) ?>                for every review
</ul>
<?php endif; ?>
```

The first part of the view script adds the JavaScript files required to the headScript() view helper, which are then echoed into the <head> section of the layout file. The view script then displays information about the location itself. The displayAddress() view helper formats the location's address data for presentation and can be found in the accompanying source files if you want to inspect it. The reviews themselves are presented in an unsigned list and use a separate view script, views/scripts/place/_reviewItem.phtml, which is called by the partialLoop() view helper. This is shown in listing 5.10.

Listing 5.10   __reviewItem.phtml displays one review

```php
<li>
<div class="review-meta">
   <?php echo $this->escape($this->user_name); ?> on
   <?php echo $this->displayDate(
            $this->date_updated); ?>        ⊲—— Formats date with
</div>                                            displayDate() view
<div class="review-body">                        helper
   <?php echo $this->escape($this->body); ?>
</div>
</li>
```

Each review consists of the name of the reviewer and the date when they wrote the review, followed by the review body itself.

We are now ready to add the code required for the review rating system.

5.5.2   Adding review rating HTML to the view script

The view script that displays each review needs to have the count information and the Yes and No buttons added. We must also make sure that we can identify each HTML element that we want to change dynamically by giving it a unique ID. The easiest way to get a unique ID is to use a string followed by the review ID.

We do all this work in a separate partial view script that we integrate with the _reviewItem.phtml view script. The additional HTML for _reviewItem.phtml is shown in listing 5.11 and is added to the code in listing 5.10 just before the closing `</li>` tag.

Listing 5.11   The HTML for review feedback within _reviewItem.phtml

```
<div class="helpful">
<?php echo $this->partial('place/_reviewFeedback.phtml',
    array('id'=>$this->id,
        'helpful_yes'=>$this->helpful_yes,           Passes variables to
        'helpful_total'=>$this->helpful_total)) ?>   partial view script
</div>
```

We use a separate partial view script called _reviewFeedback.phtml to display the HTML for the feedback. This is stored in the same directory as the _reviewItem.phtml script, and is shown in listing 5.12.

Listing 5.12   The HTML for review feedback in _reviewFeedback.phtml

```
<?php
$id = $this->id;
$yesCount = $this->helpful_yes;
$totalCount = $this->helpful_total;
?>                                          ❶ Sets the id with the
                                               format {label}-{review_id}
<span id="counts-<?php echo $id ?>" >
    <?php echo $yesCount ?> of <?php echo $totalCount; ?>
</span>
people found this review helpful. Was this review
helpful to you?
<span id="yesno-<?php echo $id?>" >
    <a href="#" onclick="new ReviewFeedback(1,
        <?php echo $id; ?>,'              ❷ Instantiates a
        <?php echo $this->baseUrl(); ?>');   ReviewFeedback object for
        return false;">Yes</a>               Ajax calls and DOM updating
    <a href="#" onclick="new ReviewFeedback(0,
        <?php echo $id; ?>,'<?php echo $this->baseUrl(); ?>');
        return false;">No</a>
<span id="spinner-<?php echo $id ?>"></span></span>
<div id="message-<?php echo $id ?>"></div>
```

As you can see in listing 5.12, the HTML for the review feedback system consists of a message informing the user of the helpfulness of the review, two buttons for providing feedback (Yes or No), and two placeholders for providing interactive responses after clicking a link. To make this HTML code useful for an Ajax application, we have to make each part easily accessible from JavaScript. We do this by setting the id attribute to a unique value using the review's database id ❶.

The actual Ajax work is done in the ReviewFeedback JavaScript class ❷, which connects back to the web server within its constructor. Let's look in detail at this JavaScript, because it does all the real work.

5.5.3 Adding JavaScript to the view scripts

Using the YUI framework for the behind-the-scenes connection to the server gives us error checking and cross-browser compatibility for free. All our work will be done within a single JavaScript file, review_feedback.js, in the www/js directory. These were added to the view using the headScript() view helper within index.phtml in listing 5.9.

We can break down the client-side work into a number of distinct tasks:

1 Initiate request to server and start a spinner animation.
2 On success:
   – Update the count.
   – Stop the spinner animation.
   – Say thank you to the user.
3 On failure:
   – Inform the user.
   – Stop the spinner animation.

In order to prevent pollution of the global namespace, we put all the JavaScript code for the review feedback module into a class called ReviewFeedback. The constructor initializes everything and connects to the server, as shown in listing 5.13.

Listing 5.13 The ReviewFeedback class constructor

```
function ReviewFeedback(response, reviewId, baseUrl) {
    this.id = reviewId;
    this.baseUrl = baseUrl;

    this.startSpinner();            Turns on spinner and empties
    this.message("","");            information message

    var response = parseInt(response);    Uses parseInt() to avoid
    var reviewId = parseInt(reviewId);    encoding parameters

        var sUrl = baseUrl + "/review/feedback/format/json/id/"
                + reviewId + "/helpful/" + response;
                                                  Initiates Ajax call ❶
    // perform the request.                          back to server
    YAHOO.util.Connect.initHeader('X_REQUESTED_WITH', 'XMLHttpRequest');
    YAHOO.util.Connect.asyncRequest('GET', sUrl, this);
}
```

JavaScript's object model is a little different from PHP's, and to create a class, we don't need a class keyword; we need only a function that will act as the constructor. The rest of the class's methods are then added to the prototype property of the constructor function, which will make them available to all instances of the class. Appendix B of *Ajax in Action* (by Dave Crane and Eric Pascarello) has more details if you need to refresh your knowledge of the JavaScript object model.

As you can see in listing 5.13, when we initiate the Ajax call with `asyncRequest`, we pass in `this` as the callback object ❶. This means that we must define the member methods `success()` and `failure()` so that the YUI system can call them when appropriate. The advantage of using an instance is that we can store the `reviewId` and the `baseURL` into the instance, and they will be available in the member methods when we need them. We can also provide helper methods within the class to keep the main callback methods easier to read.

We need to provide a message on success and on failure, so it makes sense to write a method called `message()`:

```
ReviewFeedback.prototype.message = function(class, text) {
    document.getElementById('message-'+this.id).className = class;
    document.getElementById('message-'+this.id).innerHTML = text;
}
```

The thank-you message is displayed in the div with an ID of `message-{review_id}` and the message method just tucks away the verbosity of setting the CSS class and the text of the message that we need to display.

Two other helper methods, `startSpinner()` and `stopSpinner()`, are needed also. To create a spinner, we use an animated GIF image, which is added to the HTML in `startSpinner()` and removed in `stopSpinner()`:

```
ReviewFeedback.prototype.startSpinner = function() {
    var spinner = document.getElementById('spinner-'+this.id);
    var url = this.baseUrl+'/img/spinner.gif';
    spinner.innerHTML = '<img src="'+ url +' " border="0" />';
}

ReviewFeedback.prototype.stopSpinner = function() {
    document.getElementById('spinner-'+this.id).innerHTML = "";
}
```

We can now define the `success()` callback method that does the real work, as shown in listing 5.14.

Listing 5.14   The JavaScript success callback method

```
ReviewFeedback.prototype.success = function(o) {
    if(o.responseText !== undefined) {                         Checks if this is
        var json = eval("(" + o.responseText + ")") ;          the right review
        if(json.result && json.id == this.id) {        ◄───────┘

            document.getElementById(                   Updates count
                'counts-'+json.id).innerHTML            on web page
            = json.helpful_yes + ' of ' + json.helpful_total;

            this.message("success",                    Says thank you and
                'Thank you for your feedback.');        stops spinner
            this.stopSpinner();
```

```
        document.getElementById(
            'yesno-'+json.id).innerHTML = "";
    } else {
        this.failure(o);
    }
}
```

Removes buttons as feedback is given

Reuses failure() method

As we noted earlier, the `success` method has to do three different things: update the review count text, display a thank-you message, and stop the spinner. We also remove the Yes and No buttons, as they are no longer needed. To update the count, we deliberately placed a `<span>` with an ID of `helpful-{review_id}` around the two numbers that we needed to update. We then set the `innerHTML` property of the two spans to update the new number of "yes" and "total" counts. To update the message and stop the spinner, we use the helper methods that we previously created, which ensures that this method is easier to maintain.

The `failure()` callback method is very similar, except that we only need to display a message and stop the spinner:

```
ReviewFeedback.prototype.failure = function(o) {
    var text = "Sorry, please try later.";
    this.message("failed", text);
    this.stopSpinner();
}
```

This is all the JavaScript code required for our review feedback system. The server-side code is PHP and is similarly simple.

5.5.4 *The server code*

The client-side JavaScript calls into the feedback action of the Review controller. This is a standard action like any other in the system and so is a class method called `ReviewController::feedbackAction()` and stored in ReviewController.php. The most significant difference between an action that responds to an Ajax request and an action that displays HTML directly is the view code; we do not need any HTML. We use the `AjaxContext` action helper to turn off the layout rendering and to use a JSON-specific view script.

The output of the action is an array of JSON-encoded data that the `success()` method uses to set the HTML text appropriately. We set this up in the `init()` method of the `ReviewController` class, which is stored in application/controllers/Review-Controller.php, as showing in listing 5.15.

> **Listing 5.15**   `ReviewController::init()` **sets up the** `AjaxContext`

```
class ReviewController extends Zend_Controller_Action
{
    function init()
    {
        $ajaxContext = $this->_helper->getHelper('AjaxContext');
```

```
$ajaxContext->addActionContext('feedback',
    'json');
$ajaxContext->initContext();
}
```

> **Accepts JSON format for "feedback"**

The `init()` method is essentially the same as the one we examined earlier, in listing 5.6. The only difference is that this time we specify the format to be JSON.

The feedback action method is shown in listing 5.16.

Listing 5.16   The server-side Ajax response

```
public function feedbackAction()
{
    $id = (int)$this->getRequest()->getParam('id');
    if ($id == 0) {
        $this->view->result = false;
        return;
    }

    $helpful = (int)$this->getRequest()->getParam('helpful');
    $helpful = $helpful == 0 ? 0 : 1;

    $reviewsFinder = new Reviews();
    $review = $reviewsFinder->fetchRow('id='.$id);
    if ($review->id != $id) {
        $this->view->result = false;
        return;
    }

    if ($helpful) {
        $sql = "Update reviews SET helpful_yes = (helpful_yes+1),
            helpful_total = (helpful_total+1)
            WHERE id = $id";
    } else {
        $sql = "Update reviews SET helpful_total = (helpful_total+1)
            WHERE id = $id";
    }
    $reviewsFinder->getAdapter()->query($sql);

    $review = $reviewsFinder->fetchRow('id='.$id);

    $this->view->result = true;
    $this->view->id = $id;
    $this->view->helpful_yes = $review->helpful_yes;
    $this->view->helpful_total =
        $review->helpful_total;
}
```

> **Ensures ID is safe for SQL statements**

> **Ensures value is 0 or 1**

> **❶ Updates database**

> **Assigns to view**

The code in `feedbackAction()` is standard Zend Framework code that updates the counts of the database fields `helpful_yes` and `helpful_total` within the reviews table for the particular view in question. In this case, we construct the SQL directly and execute it using the `query()` method of the `Zend_Db_Adapter` object ❶. Note that as we use the review ID from the user within the SQL directly, the cast to an integer is vital to ensure that we don't accidentally introduce an SQL injection vulnerability. We then assign the result variable and all the other data we want the JavaScript to know about to the view, ready to be encoded in the view script.

The view script, views/scripts/review/feedback.json.phtml, is shown in listing 5.17.

Listing 5.17   Echoing the view's variables in feedback.json.phtml

```php
<?php
    echo get_object_vars($this);
?>
```

❶ **Converts public member variables to array**

The view script for the Ajax response is very simple, because the `AjaxContext` does the hard work of encoding to JSON for us. All we need to do is echo an array of all the data in the view. The simplest way to do this is to use `get_object_vars()` ❶.

We have now completed the full cycle of an Ajax request within the context of a proper Zend Framework application. There is a fair amount of detail to get right, but the hard bits of tying it all together are done for us by Zend Framework's `AjaxContext` action helper. Our users are now able to provide information on the usefulness of a review, which can be used for sorting if we want.

5.6   *Summary*

Within this chapter, we have looked at what Ajax is and where it fits within a Zend Framework application. While it is possible to handcraft all the Ajax code required, it is easier to use one of the many libraries available to simplify development and make the code more robust. We had a look at the Yahoo! YUI libraries and saw how easy it is to use. To place it all in context, we have also integrated a mechanism to allow users to provide feedback on the helpfulness of reviews in our *Places* website.

The `AjaxContext` action helper provides a mechanism to integrate Ajax calls within a Zend Framework application. This provides for multiple view scripts to be attached to an action—one for each format of response. The most common are JSON, XML, and plain HTML. The separation provided by the Model-View-Controller design pattern is very helpful when writing Ajax actions, as the controller and model are insulated from the view.

We have now covered all the basics of building a Zend Framework application and fitting out the front end with the latest technology. It is now time to look in detail at the database functionality provided by Zend Framework and how `Zend_Db_Table` can help us build models that are powerful, yet easy to maintain.

Managing the database

For most websites, a database is a vital part of their applications. Zend Framework acknowledges this with a comprehensive set of database-related components that provide varying levels of abstraction.

Two important levels of abstraction are databases and tables. The *database abstraction* keeps your PHP code independent from the underlying database server you use. This means that it is easier for your application to support multiple database servers. *Table abstraction* represents the database tables and rows as PHP objects. This allows the rest of your application to interact with PHP without knowing that there is an underlying database.

We'll start by looking at the `Zend_Db_Adapter` class, which provides a product-independent interface to the database server.

6.1   Database abstraction with Zend_Db_Adapter

The subject of database abstraction appears to be a religious one, with many developers claiming that such layers are a performance drain and that they serve no useful purpose. This belief comes from the fact that to get the best from a database engine, you have to understand how the engine works and use its specific interpretation of SQL to get the best from it. Other developers wouldn't dream of not using a database abstraction layer; they argue that it allows them to migrate easily from one database to another and to distribute their applications more widely. Also, a database abstraction layer allows the developer to learn one API for all databases that they use, which can speed up development time.

As always in such debates, it depends on what the task is. If you are developing an application that needs to extract the maximum performance out of the database, such as a search engine like Google, coding for one database is clearly the way forward. If you are writing an application that you intend to sell to customers, supporting multiple databases makes your product more desirable. There is no right answer. In Rob's current company, we have sold to customers who will only use SQL Server and will not countenance the use of MySQL or PostgreSQL, so we have found database abstraction layers very useful for making sales of the same software to multiple customers.

Zend Framework's interface to the database is via an abstraction layer. The standardized interface to the database that this creates ensures that the higher-level components will work with any database. It also means that the support for a given database is encapsulated at a single point, so supporting new database engines is easier.

Let's look at using Zend Framework's `Zend_Db_Adapter` to connect to a database and then interact with the data within it.

6.1.1   Creating a Zend_Db_Adapter

The heart of the database abstraction components within Zend Framework is `Zend_Db_Adapter_Abstract`. Each supported database engine has a specific adapter class that inherits from this class. For example, DB2's adapter is named `Zend_Db_Adapter_Db2`. The PDO extension is also used for some adapters, such as `Zend_Db_Adapter_Pdo_Pgsql` for PostgreSQL.

The Factory design pattern creates a database adapter using the `Zend_Db::factory()` method, as shown in listing 6.1.

Listing 6.1   Creating a `Zend_Db_Adapter` instance with `Zend_Db::factory()`

```
$params = array ('host'     => 'localhost',
                 'username' => 'rob',          Sets specific
                 'password' => 'password',     database engine
                 'dbname'   => 'places');      configuration
                                                              Specifies
$db = Zend_Db::factory('PDO_MYSQL', $params);   ◁────────    database
                                                              engine
```

As every adapter extends `Zend_Db_Adapter_Abstract`, only methods within the abstract class can be used if you want database independence. The list of supported databases is quite extensive and includes DB2, MySQL, Oracle, SQL Server, and PostgreSQL. We expect other databases to be supported over time too, especially PDO-based ones.

The database adapters use the lazy loading technique to avoid connecting to the database on creation of the object instance. This means that even though the adapter object is created using `Zend_Db::factory()`, the connection to the database doesn't happen until you do something with that object that requires a connection. Calling the `getConnection()` method will also create a connection if there isn't one already.

We've now connected to the database, so next we'll look at how to retrieve data from it using standard SQL queries or the `Zend_Db_Select` object, which can make it easier.

6.1.2 *Querying the database*

Running an SQL query directly against a database is very simple:

```
$date = $db->quote('1980-01-01')
$sql = 'SELECT * FROM users WHERE date_of_birth > ' . $date;
$result = $db->query($sql);
```

The `$result` variable contains a standard PHP `PDOStatement` object, so you can use the standard calls, such as `fetch()` or `fetchAll()`, to retrieve the data. In this case, we used a standard SQL string to specify the query.

The `query()` method also supports parameter binding to save having to `quote()` all strings. This system allows us to put placeholders into the SQL statement where we want our variables to be, then the adapter (or underlying core PHP) will ensure that our query is valid SQL and doesn't contain a string that isn't quoted properly. The preceding query could therefore be written like this:

```
$sql = 'SELECT * FROM users WHERE date_of_birth > ?';
$result = $db->query($sql, array('1980-01-01'));
```

As a rule of thumb, using parameter-based queries is a good habit to get into, because it removes the opportunity for accidentally forgetting to `quote()` data from the user and thereby possibly creating an SQL injection vulnerability in your application. It also has the side benefit that for some databases it is quicker to use bound data parameters.

Not everyone is comfortable creating complex SQL queries, though. Zend Framework's `Zend_Db_Select` classes provide a PHP-based object-oriented interface to generate SQL `SELECT` statements.

ZEND_DB_SELECT

`Zend_Db_Select` allows you to use PHP to build database query statements in the comfortable language of PHP, rather than SQL.

`Zend_Db_Select` provides a number of advantages. These are the most important ones:

- Metadata is automatically quoted (table and field names)
- Object-oriented interface provides for easier maintenance
- It helps to promote database-independent queries

- Quoting of values helps reduce SQL injection vulnerabilities

A simple query using `Zend_Db_Select` is shown in listing 6.2.

Listing 6.2 Creating a `Zend_Db_Adapter` instance using `Zend_Db::factory()`

```
$select = new Zend_Db_Select($db);
$select->from('users');
    ->where('date_of_birth > ?', '1980-01-01');
$result = $select->query();
```

Attaches `Zend_Db_Adapter` to select object

Executes query

One very useful feature of `Zend_Db_Select` is that you can build the query in any order. This differs from standard SQL in that you must have each section of your SQL string in the correct place. For a complex query, this simplifies the maintenance because `Zend_Db_Select` ensures that the SQL syntax generated is correct.

In addition to `Zend_Db_Select`, `Zend_Db_Adapter` provides functionality for interfacing directly with the database to allow you to insert, delete, and update data. Let's look at that now.

6.1.3 Inserting, updating, and deleting

To simplify the inserting, updating, and deleting of database rows, `Zend_Db_Adapter` provides the `insert()`, `update()`, and `delete()` methods.

Inserting and updating use the same basic premise, in that you provide an associative array of data and it does the rest. Listing 6.3 shows how to add a user to a table called users.

Listing 6.3 Inserting a row using `Zend_Db_Adapter`

```
// insert a user
$data = array(
        'date_created' => date('Y-m-d'),
        'date_updated' => date('Y-m-d'),
        'first_name' => 'Ben',
        'surname' => 'Ramsey'
);

$table = 'users';
$rows_affected = $db->insert($table, $data);
$last_insert_id = $db->lastInsertId();
```

Specifies an associative array of data

Stores ID of row just inserted

Note that `Zend_Db_Adapter`'s `insert()` method will automatically ensure that your data is quoted correctly because it creates an `insert` statement that uses parameter binding as discussed in section 6.1.2

Updating a record using the `update()` method works pretty much the same way, except that you need to pass in an SQL condition to limit the update to the rows that you are interested in. Typically, you would know the ID of the row you want to update, but `update()` is flexible enough to allow for updating multiple rows, as shown in listing 6.4.

Listing 6.4 Updating multiple rows using `Zend_Db_Adapter`

```
// update a user
$data = array(
        'country' => 'United Kingdom'        Specifies fields
);                                           to be updated

$table = 'users';                                          Quotes the
$where = $db->quoteInto('country = ?', 'UK');    ◄─────┘  string
$db->update($table, $data, $where);                        automatically
```

Again, `update()` automatically quotes the data in the `$data` array, but it does not automatically quote the data in the `$where` clause, so we use `quoteInto()` to ensure that the data is safe for use with the database.

Deleting from the database works in exactly the same manner, but we need the table and the `$where` clause, so the code for deleting a particular user would look like this:

```
$table = 'users';
$where = 'id = 1';

$rows_affected = $db->delete($table, $where);
```

Obviously, we need to quote strings in the `$where` clause again. In all cases `insert()`, `update()`, and `delete()` return the number of rows affected by the operation.

We'll now look at how to handle database-specific differences.

6.1.4 Handling database-specific differences

All databases are not equal, and this is especially true of their interpretation of SQL and the additional functions they provide to allow access to the more advanced features provided by the database. To call the specific SQL functions of your database server, the `Zend_Db_Select` class has a helper class called `Zend_Db_Expr`. `Zend_Db_Expr` is used for calling SQL functions or creating other expressions for use in SQL.

Let's consider an example where we want to concatenate the first and last names of our users. The code is in listing 6.5.

Listing 6.5 Using functions in SQL statements

```
$select = $db->select();
$columns = array(id,
        "CONCAT(first_name, ' ', last_name) as n";     Uses CONCAT(), which
$select->from('users', $columns);                       is MySQL-specific
$stmt = $db->query($select);
$result = $stmt->fetchAll();
```

The `from()` method realizes that a parenthesis has been used in the `columns` parameter and so converts it to a `Zend_Db_Expr` automatically. We can, however, use `Zend_Db_Expr` ourselves, by setting the `columns` statement explicitly:

```
$columns = array(id, "n"=>
new Zend_Db_Expr("CONCAT(first_name, ' ', last_name"));
```

Now that we have considered how to abstract away the differences between database engines by using adapters created by the factory method of `Zend_Db`, we can turn our attention to how we use a database within an application. Novice web programmers tend to put the database calls right where they need them, which leads to a maintenance nightmare, with SQL statements spread all through the application. We will consider ways to consolidate our SQL, and we'll look at how Zend Framework's `Zend_Db_Table` component helps to improve the architecture of our applications.

6.2   Table abstraction with Zend_Db_Table

When dealing with a database, it is useful to be able to abstract your thinking and consider the system at the domain level, rather than focusing on the nitty-gritty of the actual SQL statements. At the domain level, you can think about the problem in the language of the domain.

The easiest way to do this is to create classes that know how to load and save themselves to the database. A class that represents one row in a database table implements the Row Data Gateway pattern. This pattern provides for accessing a single row of the database and is closely related to the Active Record pattern.

> ### Differences between Active Record and Row Data Gateway
> The Active Record pattern is a close cousin of Row Data Gateway. The significant differences are that Row Data Gateway only contains database access functions while Active Record also contains domain logic. Active Record implementations also tend to have static finder functions included, but this is not a requirement of the pattern definition.
>
> In Zend Framework, `Zend_Db_Table_Row_Abstract` is extended to implement domain logic in the class, so we turn the provided Row Data Gateway into more of an Active Record in specific applications.

One area where the Row Data Gateway pattern doesn't work so well is when dealing with lists, such as when you are retrieving a list of products in an e-commerce application. This is because it works at the row level, and lists are generally dealt with at the table level. Zend Framework provides the `Zend_Db_Table` component to support database manipulation at the table level, and we'll look at what it provides and how table-level support differs from what we have already seen in `Zend_Db_Adapter`.

6.2.1   What is the Table Data Gateway pattern?

`Zend_Db_Table` has three main components: `Zend_Db_Table_Abstract`, `Zend_Db_Table_Rowset`, and `Zend_Db_Table_Row`. As indicated by its name, `Zend_Db_Table_Abstract` is an abstract class that has to be extended for each table that it acts as a gateway to.

When selecting multiple records from the table, an instance of `Zend_Db_Table_Rowset` is returned, which can then be iterated over to access each individual row.

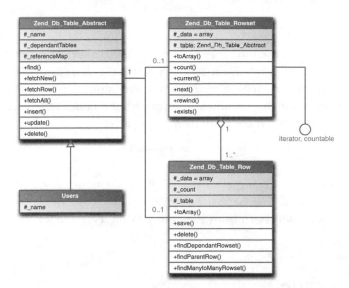

Figure 6.1 The `Zend_Db_Table` components provide a clean method of managing a database table and its associated rows.

Each row is an instance of `Zend_Db_Table_Row`, which is itself an implementation of the Row Data Gateway pattern. This is shown in figure 6.1.

`Zend_Db_Table_Abstract` is always extended, but `Zend_Db_Table_Rowset` is much less likely to be because it provides pretty much all you need for handling a set of database rows. In more complicated systems, extending `Zend_Db_Table_Row` into more of an Active Record by adding domain logic to it can help avoid duplicating code in multiple places, as we'll see when we look at how to use `Zend_Db_Table`.

6.2.2 Using Zend_Db_Table

In order to actually use the `Zend_Db_Table` components, you must create a class to represent your table, as shown in listing 6.6. This is usually named similarly to the database table that it accesses, but that is not a requirement.

Listing 6.6 Declaring a table class for use with `Zend_Db_Table`

```
class Users extends Zend_Db_Table_Abstract
{
    protected $_name = 'users';
}
```

As you can see in listing 6.6, we have explicitly set the name of the underlying table to users. If the $_name property is not set, the name of the class (preserving the case) will be used instead. However, because it is common practice to name the classes starting with an uppercase letter and to name the database tables entirely in lowercase, the database table name is usually explicitly declared.

Now that we have a Users class, we can fetch data from the table in exactly the same way as if we were collecting data from an instance of Zend_Db_Adapter:

```
$users = new Users();
$rows = $users->fetchAll();
```

While it performs the same function, the `Zend_Db_Table_Abstract`'s `fetchAll()` method is used completely differently from `Zend_Db_Adapter_Abstract`'s version of `fetchAll()`, which simply takes an SQL string parameter and returns an array of arrays. As we are working at a higher abstraction level with the table, `fetchAll()` also works at the higher level, as you can see from its signature:

```
public function fetchAll($where = null, $order = null,
    $count = null, $offset = null)
```

The `fetchAll()` method will create the SQL statement for us, using `Zend_Db_Table_Select` internally; we need to specify the parts we are interested in. For example, to select all female users born from 1980 on, we would use the following code:

```
$users = new Users();
$where = array('sex = ?' => 'F',
    'date_of_birth >= ?'=>'1980-01-01');
$rows = $users->fetchAll($where);
```

We can also use a `Zend_Db_Table_Select` object like this:

```
$users = new Users();
$select = $users->select();
$select ->where('sex = ?', 'F');
$select ->where('date_of_birth >= ?', '1980-01-01');
$rows = $users->fetchAll($select);
```

In this example, we build the query up in exactly the same way as we would with a `Zend_Db_Select` object, which allows us to create the query out of order if we need to. For instance, we could set the limit before we set the `$where` clauses.

Now that we know how to select data from the database using `Zend_Db_Table`, let's look at adding and editing the data using the `insert()` and `update()` methods.

6.2.3 *Inserting and updating with Zend_Db_Table*

Inserting and updating with `Zend_Db_Table` is very similar to the usage with `Zend_Db_Adapter`, except that this time we already know which database table to operate on. Table 6.1 shows exactly how similar inserting is with the two components. As you can see from table 6.1, exactly the same process is used in both cases, except that with `Zend_Db_Table` we already know the table's name, and we get the ID of the newly inserted record back directly.

Updating a database row is similar, as shown in table 6.2.

Note that you need to quote any values and identifiers in the SQL expression used for the `$where` clause. This is done by using the database adapter's `quote()`, `quoteInto()`, and `quoteIdentifier()` methods.

The similarities between inserting and updating lead to the conclusion that it might be worth having a single save method in `Zend_Db_Table`. This would be incorrect at the table level because you never know which record (or records) need updat-

Table 6.1   Inserting with `Zend_Db_Table` **and** `Zend_Db_Adapter` **compared**

Zend_Db_Adapter	Zend_Db_Table

<pre>// insert a user
$table = 'users';
 	
$data = array(
 'date_created' => date('Y-m-d'),
 'date_updated' => date('Y-m-d'),
 'first_name' => 'Ben',
 'surname' => 'Ramsey'
);
 	
$db->insert($table, $data);
$id = $db->lastInsertId();</pre>
	<pre>// insert a user
	$users = new Users();
	
	$data = array(
	 'date_created' => date('Y-m-d'),
	 'date_updated' => date('Y-m-d'),
	 'first_name' => 'Ben',
	 'surname' => 'Ramsey'
	);
	
	$id = $users->insert($data);</pre>

Table 6.2   Updating with `Zend_Db_Table` **and** `Zend_Db_Adapter` **compared**

Zend_Db_Adapter	Zend_Db_Table

<pre>// update a user
$table = 'users';
 	
$data = array(
 'date_updated' => date('Y-m-d'),
 'first_name' => 'Ben',
 'surname' => 'Ramsey'
);
 	
$where = 'id=2';
$db->update($table, $data,
$where);</pre>
	<pre>// update a user
	$users = new Users();
	
	$data = array(
	 'date_updated' => date('Y-m-d'),
	 'first_name' => 'Ben',
	 'surname' => 'Ramsey'
	);
	
	$where = 'id=2';
	$users->update($data, $where);</pre>

ing. At the `Zend_Db_Table_Row` level, it makes perfect sense. Looking at `Zend_Db_Table_Row`, we discover that this functionality is already written for us in a method called `save()`. Its use is shown in table 6.3.

Table 6.3   Saving data with `Zend_Db_Table_Row`**'s** `save()` **method**

Inserting a new record	Updating a record

<pre>$users = new Users();
$row = $users->fetchNew();
 	
$row->first_name = 'Chris';
$row->surname = 'Shiflett';
 	
$row->save();</pre>
	<pre>$users = new Users();
	$row = $users->fetchRow('id=2');
	
	$row->first_name = 'Chris';
	$row->surname = 'Shiflett';
	
	$row->save();</pre>

In this case, all of the differences between inserting a new record and updating a current one are hidden. This is because the Zend_Db_Table_Row object works at a higher level of abstraction.

6.2.4 *Deleting records with Zend_Db_Table*

As you would expect, deleting works exactly the same way as inserting and updating, only we use the delete() method. The delete() method is available in both Zend_Db and Zend_Db_Table, and as with insert() and update(), the usage is very similar between the two classes, as shown in table 6.4.

Table 6.4   Deleting rows with Zend_Db_Table **and** Zend_Db_Adapter **compared**

Zend_Db_Adapter	Zend_Db_Table
```// delete a user $table = 'users'; $where = 'id = 2'; $db->delete($table, $where);```	```// delete a user $users = new Users(); $where = 'id = 2'; $users->delete($where);```

The $where clause in delete() for both Zend_Db_Table and Zend_Db_Adapter does not quote the values for us, so if we were to delete based on anything other than an integer, we would have to use quote() or quoteInto(). For example, to delete all users who live in London, we would have to do the following:

```
$users = new Users();
$db = $users->getAdapter();
$where = $db->quoteInto('town = ?', 'London');
$users->delete($where);
```

We have now looked at all the major database operations that can be done using the Zend_Db_Adapter and Zend_Db_Table components. Database operations in a Model-View-Controller application usually are part of the model. This is because the model is where the business logic of the application is, and the data stored in a database is very much related to the business of the application.

We will now look at using Zend_Db_Table-based objects within a model and, possibly more importantly, at how to test such objects.

6.3 *Using Zend_Db_Table as a model*

Zend_Db_Table is usually where we integrate the Zend_Db component into a Zend Framework MVC application. One way to implement a model is to build a set of classes that extend Zend_Db_Table_Abstract and Zend_Db_Table_Row_Abstract.

Within our *Places* web application we use a model to represent the registered users of the website. The database table required is quite simple and is shown in figure 6.2.

As we want to make money from *Places*, we expect that advertisers will want to know the demographics of the membership, so we would like our members to tell us their age, sex, and location. Of course, this would be optional, but the username and password are mandatory. A more advanced model might even separate out the demographic information to a separate table.

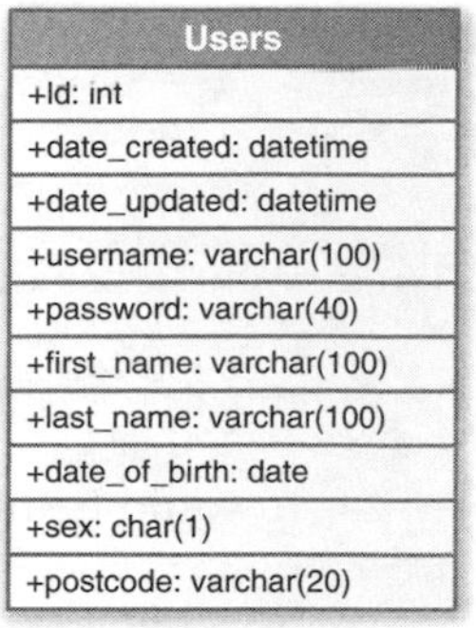

Users
+Id: int
+date_created: datetime
+date_updated: datetime
+username: varchar(100)
+password: varchar(40)
+first_name: varchar(100)
+last_name: varchar(100)
+date_of_birth: date
+sex: char(1)
+postcode: varchar(20)

Figure 6.2   The Users table for *Places* contains login information along with demographic information for advertisers.

We will need to access our database tables at two different levels: table and row. The table level is used when we need to display lists, and the row level is used when dealing with individual records. In order to deal with this in the code, we need two classes, Users and User, which are extensions of Zend_Db_Table_Abstract and Zend_Db_Table_Row_Abstract respectively. The class definitions are shown in listing 6.7. Note that you would usually use two files in the application/models directory for the two classes, Users.php and User.php, because it makes the application easier to maintain.

Listing 6.7   Creating a model using `Zend_Db_Table` components

```
class Users extends Zend_Db_Table_Abstract
{
    protected $_name = 'users';
    protected $_rowClass = 'User';          ❶ Sets generated row classes
}                                              to the User type

class User extends Zend_Db_Table_Row_Abstract
{
}
```

Linking the User class to the Users class is done through the $_rowClass property in the Users class ❶. This means that the Zend_Db_Table_Abstract class will create objects of type User whenever it would normally have created an object of type Zend_Db_Table_Row.

The implementation of the User class in listing 6.7 is no more useful than the standard Zend_Db_Table_Row, as no additional functionality is provided. To make our User class useful, we will add a new method called name. This will be used throughout the application to display the user's name. It will initially display the combination of first name and surname, but if they are not set, it will use the user's username.

Our initial implementation of the User::name() method is as follows:

```
Class User extends Zend_Db_Table_Row_Abstract
{
    public function name()
    {
        $name = trim($this->first_name . ' ' . $this->last_name);
        if (empty($name)) {
```

```
        $name = $this->username;
    }
    return $name;
    }
}
```

We can use our new `name()` method directly, like this:

```
$rob = $users->find(1)->current();
echo $rob->name();
```

It would be nicer to be able to treat the name as a read-only property of the record so that it is used in exactly the same way as, say, date_of_birth. This will increase the predictability of the class, because the programmer will not have to think about whether a given property is a field in the database or a function within the class. The easiest and most efficient way to do this is to override `__get()`, as shown in listing 6.8.

Listing 6.8 Overriding `__get()` to provide custom properties

```
class User extends Zend_Db_Table_Row_Abstract
{
//...
    function __get($key)
    {
        if(method_exists($this, $key))        ◁─┐  Checks if          Calls method
        {                                        │  class method       and returns
            return $this->$key();        ◁───────┘  exists            if method
        }                                ◁────────────                 exists
        return parent::__get($key);      ◁──────┐
    }                                           │  Calls parent's __get() if
//...                                           │  method doesn't exist
}
```

We have to call the parent's `__get()` method last, because it will throw an exception if `$key` does not exist in the database as a field. Note also that if one of the methods in the class is named the same as a field in the database, the method will be called rather than the value of the field being returned. This is handy if you want to do any processing on a given field before passing it through to the rest of the application, though such a use-case is rare.

We're now able to build our models, so we need to ensure that they work. The best way to do this is to test the code using a testing system.

6.3.1 Testing the model

As we have mentioned before, it is good practice to test your code, and it is even better practice to test it more than once! To test the `Users` model class, we'll use PHPUnit, because that's what Zend Framework itself uses. The tests will be stored in the tests/ models directory of the *Places* application.

We'll start our testing by ensuring the testing environment is consistent between tests, which, in testing circles, is known as *setup* and *teardown*.

SETUP AND TEARDOWN

One key thing about running tests automatically is that tests must not interfere with each other. Also, a given test must not depend upon a previous test having run. To achieve this separation, PHPUnit provides the setUp() and tearDown() methods, which are run just before and after each test.

In order to separate each database test, we use the setUp() method to recreate the database tables and populate them to a known state. This obviously means that we do not use the master database for testing! When testing, we use a different database that is configured in the main config.ini for the application. The ensures we can control the data within it. We use the [test] section to specify our test database, as shown in listing 6.9.

Listing 6.9   The [test] section overrides [general] in application/config.ini

```
[general]
db.adapter = PDO_MYSQL
db.config.host = localhost        Contains main
db.config.username = zfia         database connection
db.config.password = 123456       information
db.config.dbname = places
                                  Overrides      Overrides
[test : general]                  [general]      database
db.config.dbname = places_test                   name when
                                                 testing
```

In our case, we only need to change the database name from places to places_test; we can rely on the other settings in the general section to provide the other connection information.

We are now in a position to create the unit test class skeleton, as shown in listing 6.10.

Listing 6.10   Skeleton for unit test class: tests/models/UsersTests.php

```
<?php
require_once 'PHPUnit/Framework.php';

if(!defined('ROOT_DIR')) {
    define('ROOT_DIR',
        dirname(dirname(dirname(__FILE__))));          ❶ Sets up
                                                          path
    set_include_path('.'
    . PATH_SEPARATOR . ROOT_DIR . '/library'
    . PATH_SEPARATOR . ROOT_DIR .
        '/../../lib/zf/library'
    . PATH_SEPARATOR . ROOT_DIR . '/application/models'
    . PATH_SEPARATOR . get_include_path());
}

require_once 'Zend/Registry.php';
require_once 'Zend/Db/Table.php';
require_once 'Zend/Config/Ini.php';
require_once 'Users.php';   // Users: Table gateway
require_once 'User.php';    // User: Row gateway
```

```
class UsersTest extends PHPUnit_Framework_TestCase
{
    public function __construct($name = NULL)
    {
        parent::__construct($name);

        if(Zend_Registry::isRegistered('db')) {          Collects database adapter
            $this->db = Zend_Registry::get('db');        from registry
        } else {
            $configFile = ROOT_DIR .
                '/application/config.ini';               Loads test-specific
            $config = new Zend_Config_Ini($configFile,   configuration
                'test');                                 information
            Zend_Registry::set('config', $config);

            // set up database
            $dbConfig = $config->db->config->asArray();
            $db = Zend_Db::factory($config->db->adapter, Connects to
                $dbConfig);                              database and
            Zend_Db_Table::setDefaultAdapter($db);      stores adapter
            Zend_Registry::set('db', $db);              for later use
            $this->db = $db;
        }
    }
}
```

This section of the unit test file contains only the initialization code that is run once. As you can see at the top ❶, we have to ensure that we have set up our paths correctly so that the files can be found, and we also have to include all the files we are going to need. The definition of ROOT_DIR is checked to ensure that it hasn't already been defined. This will allow us to expand our tests in the future by placing this unit test file in a suite of files that can be tested all at the same time; when we are testing as part of a suite, we will not want to alter the path. We also include the files from the framework that we need for this test.

As the constructor is only called once, it is the ideal place to load the config.ini file and connect to the database. Again, if this class is part of a test suite, the database connection will already have been made. In that case, we just collect it from the registry. Otherwise, once we have connected, we set the database adapter as the default adapter for Zend_Db_Table and store to the registry. We also assign it as a class member variable, because it is going to be used in the setUp() method to set our database to a known state.

Initializing our database is just a case of using the database adapter to create the table and insert some rows. This is done in a method called _setupDatabase(), which is called by setUp(), as shown in listing 6.11.

Listing 6.11   Initializing the database in `setUp()`

```
public function setUp()           ◁───────────┐
{                                             Calls setUp() before
    // reset database to known state          every unit test
    $this->_setupDatabase();
```

```
}
protected function _setupDatabase()                               Drops
{                                                                  table if it
    $this->db->query('DROP TABLE IF EXISTS users;');    ←───────   exists

    $this->db->query(<<<EOT
        CREATE TABLE users (
        id INT NOT NULL AUTO_INCREMENT PRIMARY KEY,
        date_created DATETIME,
        date_updated DATETIME,
        username VARCHAR(100) NOT NULL,                 Creates
        password VARCHAR(40) NOT NULL,                  table
        first_name VARCHAR(100),
        last_name VARCHAR(100),
        email VARCHAR(150) NOT NULL,
        town VARCHAR(100),
        country VARCHAR(100),
        date_of_birth datetime,
        sex char(1),
        postcode VARCHAR(30)
        )
EOT
    );
    $row = array (          ←─────────       Inserts known
        'first_name' => 'Rob',               data
        'last_name'  => 'Allen',
        'username'   => 'rob',
        'password'   => 'rob',
        'email'  => 'rob@akrabat.com',
        'town'   => 'London',
        'country' => 'UK',
        'date_of_birth' => '1970-01-04',
        'sex' => 'M',
        'date_created' => '2007-02-14 00:00:00',
    );
    $this->db->insert('users', $row);
    // insert more rows and tables as required

}
```

This is very simple code that just ensures that our database is set up correctly for every test. It drops and recreates the table, then inserts the database rows, taking advantage of the database adapter's `insert()` method, which we discussed earlier.

NOTE   The DROP TABLE command in listing 6.11 is a MySQL-ism, which would need to be changed for other database engines.

We are now in a position to actually write some tests to ensure that our model works as expected!

TESTING THE USERS CLASS

The Users class overrides the `insert()` and `update()` methods to ensure that the date_created and date_updated fields are filled in, without the rest of the code having to worry about it. The unit tests that ensure that this code works are shown in listing 6.12. We have separated the tests into two separate methods: one to test inserting and one to test updating.

Listing 6.12   Initializing the database in `setUp()`

```php
public function testInsertShouldFillInDateCreatedAndUpdatedFields()
{
    $users = new Users();
    $newUser = $users->fetchNew();        // Creates new
                                          // empty row object

    $newUser->first_name = 'Nick';        // Fills in
    $newUser->last_name = 'Lo';           // some data
    $newUser->password = 'nick';
    $newUser->email = 'nick@example.com'; // Inserts data
                                          // into database
                                          // with save()
    $id = $newUser->save();

    $nick = $users->find($id)->current(); // Retrieves new row
    $this->assertSame(3, $nick->id);      // and checks its ID

    // check that the date_created has been filled in
    $this->assertNotNull($nick->date_created);   // ❶ Ensures date_created
                                                 //    is valid

    // check that the date_updated has been filled in
    $this->assertSame($nick->date_updated,
        $nick->date_created);             // ❷ Ensures date_update
}                                         //    equals date_created

public function testUpdateShouldUpdateDateUpdatedField()
{
    $users = new Users();
    $rob = $users->find(1)->current();    // Edits a row
    $rob->town = 'Worcester';             // to create a
    $rob->save();                         // change

    $rob2 = $users->find(1)->current();
    $this->assertTrue(                    // Checks date_updated
        ($rob2->date_updated > $rob2->date_created));  // is more recent than
}                                                      // date_created
```

Within `testInsertShouldFillInDateCreatedAndUpdatedFields()` there is a reasonable amount of setup code. Before we run the actual tests (❶, ❷) that we want to conduct, we need to have inserted a new record into the database. As you can see, `Zend_Db_Table`'s `fetchNew()` method returns an empty object of type `User` that represents a row in the database. We can then set the fields that we need and insert it into the database using the `save()` method. The row's `save()` method uses the associated `Zend_Db_Table_Abstract`'s `insert()` or `update()`, as appropriate, which then uses our overridden methods to ensure that the `date_created` and `date_updated` fields are correctly filled in.

The `testUpdateShouldUpdateDateUpdatedField()` method does a similar test, but here we simply edit one of the rows in the database that was created by the `setUp()` method to check that updating changes the `date_updated` field. It is important to get the row from the database again to ensure that the date_updated field has been changed in the database itself.

Now that we have explored the Zend_Db_Table class and its associated rowset and row classes, we can look at joining tables.

6.3.2 *Table relationships with Zend_Db_Table*

Table relationships are where Zend_Db_Table starts getting very interesting. This is the realm of linking tables together using SQL JOIN statements, and it's one area where it is nice to get the framework doing the legwork for us. We will look at how Zend_Db_Table can help us with one-to-many and many-to-many relationships.

ONE-TO-MANY RELATIONSHIPS

We have already come across one-to-many relationships in chapter 3, when we created the initial schema for the *Places* application. Each location can have many reviews. This is shown in figure 6.3.

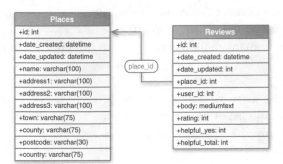

Figure 6.3 A one-to-many relationship is created via a foreign key (place_id) in the Reviews table.

To represent this using Zend_Db_Table, we'll create two new classes that extend from Zend_Db_Table_Abstract and then use the $_dependantTables and $_referenceMap properties to link them together. This is shown in listing 6.13.

Listing 6.13 One-to-many relationship using Zend_Db_Table

```
class Places extends Zend_Db_Table_Abstract
{
    protected $_name = 'places';              ◄—— Specifies the database table
    protected $_dependentTables = array('Reviews');   ◄—— Specifies the classname of dependency
}

class Reviews extends Zend_Db_Table_Abstract
{
    protected $_name = 'reviews';
    protected $_referenceMap = array(         ◄—— Lists relationships for table
        'Place' => array(
            'columns' => array('place_id'),
            'refTableClass' => 'Places',       ❶ Defines one-to-many relationship
            'refColumns  => array('id')
        )
    );
}
```

To define a one-to-many relationship, the $_referenceMap is used. Each relationship has its own subarray ❶, and to ensure maximum flexibility, you inform the class exactly which columns are used in each table. In our case, the Reviews table has a column called places_id, which is linked to the id column in the Places table.

NOTE Both columns' entries in the reference map are defined as arrays. This allows for composite keys containing more than one table field.

To actually retrieve the reviews for a given "place" record, the findDependent-Rowset() method is used:

```
$londonZoo = $places->fetchRow('id = 1');
$reviews = $londonZoo->findDependentRowset('Reviews');
```

The findDependentRowset() method takes two parameters: the name of the table class that you wish to receive the data from, and an optional rule name. The rule name must be a key in the $_referenceMap previously set up, but if you don't supply one, it will look for a rule with a refTableClass that is the same as the class name of the table from which the row was created ("Places" in our case).

We'll now turn our attention to many-to-many relationships, which use a joining or link table.

MANY-TO-MANY RELATIONSHIPS

By definition, each place can have many reviews written by different users. Therefore, for any given user, we can obtain the list of places that they have reviewed, and we can list the users who have reviewed any given place. This is known as a many-to-many relationship between places and users.

To map this relationship within a database, a third table, known as a *link table*, is required. In our case, the link table is the Reviews table, as shown in figure 6.4.

The Reviews table has two foreign keys, one to Places and one to Users, so there are two one-to-many relationships. We need to define three classes, as shown in listing 6.14.

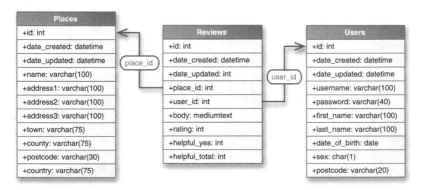

Figure 6.4   A many-to-many relationship between Places and Users is created via the Reviews table acting as a link.

Listing 6.14   A many-to-many relationship using `Zend_Db_Table`

```
class Places extends Zend_Db_Table_Abstract
{
    protected $_name = 'places';
    protected $_dependentTables = array('Reviews');
}

class Reviews extends Zend_Db_Table_Abstract
{
    protected $_name = 'reviews';
    protected $_referenceMap    = array(          Defines two rules to
        'Place' => array(                          create the relationship
            'columns' => array('place_id'),
            'refTableClass'  => 'Places',
            'refColumns'  => array('id')
        ),
        'User' => array(
            'columns' => array('user_id'),
            'refTableClass' => 'Users',
            'refColumns' => array('id')
        )
    );
}

class Users extends Zend_Db_Table_Abstract     Defines the directly
{                                               dependant class only
    protected $_name = 'users';
    protected $_dependentTables = array('Reviews');
}
```

As you can see in listing 6.14, the Users class follows the same pattern as the Places class and only defines the table classes that it directly depends on. This means that we don't explicitly state a many-to-many relationship in the code, and we let Zend_Db_Table work out that there is one.

To create a list of the places that a given user has reviewed, we can use the following code:

```
$users = new Users();
$robAllen = $users->fetchRow('id = 1');
$places = $robAllen->findManyToManyRowset('Places', 'Reviews');
```

As you can see, the function that does the work for us is called findManyToMany-Rowset(). The first parameter is the destination table class, and the second is the intersection table class containing the rules that will link the initial table class to the intersection table class. In both cases, the parameters can either be strings or instances of Zend_Db_Table, so the preceding snippet could be written as follows:

```
$users = new Users();
$places = new Places();
$reviews = new Reviews();

$robAllen = $users->fetchRow('id = 1');
$places = $robAllen->findManyToManyRowset($places, $reviews);
```

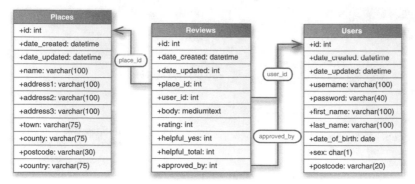

Figure 6.5   Multiple many-to-many relationships between Places and Users are created via two keys in the Reviews table.

This would produce exactly the same result. Note that if there is more than one rule in the $_referenceMap of the intersection table that would link the tables, you can specify which rule to use as an additional parameter to findManyToManyRowset().

Consider the situation where each review has to be approved by a moderator. The new table diagram would look like the one in figure 6.5.

In this case, we now have two foreign keys in the Reviews table that link to the Users table. To implement the second link, a new rule is required in the $_referenceMap for the Reviews table, as shown in listing 6.15.

Listing 6.15   Reviews class with updated $_referenceMap

```
class Reviews extends Zend_Db_Table_Abstract
{
    protected $_name = 'reviews';
    protected $_referenceMap = array(
        'Place' => array(
            'columns' => array('place_id'),
            'refTableClass' => 'Places',
            'refColumns' => array('id')
        ),
        'User' => array(
            'columns' => array('user_id'),
            'refTableClass' => 'Users',
            'refColumns' => array('id')
        ),
        'ApprovedBy' => array(
            'columns' => array('approved_by'),
            'refTableClass' => 'Users',
            'refColumns' => array('id')
        )
    );
}
```

> Defines second rule that also links to Users

> Defines linked field name in Users table

As you can see, we can have multiple rules in the reference map that refer to the same table, as long as they have different names (User and ApprovedBy, in this case). We then use the `columns` key in each map element to tell `Zend_Db_Table` the field name of the correct foreign key in the Reviews table.

Selecting the list of places that have been reviewed by a given user is done using `findManyToManyRowset()` again, but this time we pass in the name of the rule we want to use:

```
// find all places that John Smith has approved a review of.
$johnSmith = $users->fetchRow('id = 4');
$places = $johnSmith->findManyToManyRowset('Places', 'Reviews',
    'ApprovedBy');
```

`Zend_Db_Table`'s handling of one-to-many and many-to-many relationships is surprisingly powerful, although it requires us to manually set up the relationships in the intersection class.

6.4   *Summary*

Throughout this chapter, we have looked at the support for databases provided by Zend Framework. As nearly all web applications use databases to store their data, it comes as no surprise to find that rich database support is provided. The foundation is the database abstraction layer, `Zend_Db_Abstract`, which takes care of the differences between specific database engines and so provides a standardized interface for the rest of the components in the framework. `Zend_Db_Table` builds upon this foundation to provide a table-based interface to the data in the table, and so makes working with the database from within the model of an MVC application much easier. For those times when it is important to work with a specific row of data, `Zend_Db_Table_Row` provides simple access.

We have now covered the elements of the underlying structure of a Zend Framework application. We'll move on to look at authentication and authorization, which will allow us to restrict certain parts of our application to specific users and to ensure that those users can only perform actions appropriate to the trust that the application has in them.

User authentication and access control

This chapter covers

- The basics of authentication and access control
- Using `Zend_Auth` for logging into an application
- Using `Zend_Acl` to restrict access to certain web pages

Most websites restrict different areas to different people. For example, most e-commerce sites require that you're logged in before you can check out your order. Other sites have members-only pages that can only be accessed after logging in. In our *Places* application, only registered users can write or rate a review. This functionality is known as *authentication and access control*, and in this chapter we'll look at the support Zend Framework provides in the shape of the `Zend_Auth` and `Zend_Acl` components. We'll start by looking at the basics of authentication and access control, and we'll go on to integrating `Zend_Auth` and `Zend_Acl` into our *Places* application.

7.1 *Introducing authentication and access control*

There are two different processes involved when it comes to allowing a user acccess to specific pages on a website. *Authentication* is the process of identifying an individual based on her credentials (usually username and password), and *access control* is the process of deciding whether the user is allowed to do something. Zend Framework's `Zend_Auth` and `Zend_Acl` components provide comprehensive support for all aspects of authentication and access control for websites.

Because you must know who the user is before you decide if he or she can do something, it follows that the authentication process must occur before access control, so we'll look at authentication and `Zend_Auth` first, before looking at `Zend_Acl`.

7.1.1 *What is authentication?*

The goal of the authentication is deciding if someone is who they say they are. There are three ways to recognize a user, which are known as *factors*:

- Something they *know*, such as a password or PIN
- Something they *have*, such as a driver's license or credit card
- Something they *are*, such as fingerprints or typing patterns

When you buy something from a UK shop using a credit card, you authenticate the transaction with two of these factors: *have* (the credit card in your pocket) and *know* (the PIN). Elsewhere in the world, you may need to *know* the signature. For pretty much every website out there (including online banks) the *know* factor is the only mechanism used to identify a user. Generally this means a username and password, although banks tend to ask for multiple pieces of information, such as a memorable date or place, in addition to a password.

We will follow the standard web use of a username and password combination for authentication, but the choice of where to store the information still has to be made. For standalone websites, it's common to use a database table to hold the list of usernames and passwords, but there are other options. For sites that are part of a group, such as Yahoo!, a separate system to handle the authentication is necessary. One common system is LDAP, the Lightweight Directory Access Protocol, which stores information about users in a separate service, which can then be queried by other applications as required. OpenID and Six Apart's TypeKey are other systems that allow for authentication to be performed by another service. For *Places*, we will use a database table to hold the login details of our users.

7.1.2 *What is access control?*

Access control is the process of deciding whether or not to allow a user to access a resource or action. In web terms, this usually means we're deciding whether someone is allowed to view a certain page or perform an action, such as add a comment. One standard mechanism for doing this is to use an access control list (ACL), which is a list of permissions that are attached to a resource. The list specifies who is allowed access to the resource and what can be done with it. This means that the list will tell the system if a given user is allowed only to view a database record or to execute a controller action.

Whenever a user wishes to do something, the application checks the list to see if he's allowed to perform that action with that data item. For example, a user may be allowed to view a news article, but be denied permission to edit it.

Now that we have defined our terms, we can look at how to implement these features using Zend Framework components. First, we'll look at authentication with `Zend_Auth`.

7.2   *Implementing authentication*

Let's look at how to implement authentication with `Zend_Auth` using HTTP authentication, and then we'll look at how authentication is implemented within a real-world application using a database to hold the user information and sessions to store the information across multiple page views.

7.2.1   *Introducing Zend_Auth*

The `Zend_Auth` component is the part of the framework that deals with authentication. It's separated into the core component and a set of authentication adapters. The adapters contain the actual mechanisms for authorizing users, such as using HTTP with a file, or authorizing against a database table.

The authentication results are known as the *identity*, and the fields stored in the identity depend upon the adapter. For example, HTTP authentication will place only the username into the identity, but database authentication might also include the full name and email address. As it's common to display the name of the logged-in user, this feature is very useful.

To get at the identity information, `Zend_Auth` uses the Singleton design pattern, so that the identity results can be retrieved wherever they're required.

These are some of the authentication adapters that are provided out of the box for `Zend_Auth`:

- `Zend_Auth_Adapter_Http`
- `Zend_Auth_Adapter_Digest`
- `Zend_Auth_Adapter_DbTable`
- `Zend_Auth_Adapter_InfoCard`
- `Zend_Auth_Adapter_Ldap`
- `Zend_Auth_Adapter_OpenId`

The Http and Digest adapters authorize against a file on disk using the standard HTTP login mechanism built into all browsers. The DbTable adapter is used for authorizing against a list of users stored in a database table. The InfoCard, Ldap, and OpenId adapters authenticate against remote services and are not covered in this chapter. But due to the nature of `Zend_Auth`'s adapter system, changing from one authentication adapter to another is relatively easy. The system is flexible and designed so that you can also create your own adapters and integrate them into Zend_Auth. This makes it easy to integrate legacy systems or to authenticate against new systems for which an official Zend Framework adapter hasn't yet been written.

Let's start by looking at HTTP authentication.

7.2.2 *Logging in using HTTP authentication*

There must be very few people who have not seen the standard HTTP login box provided by web browsers, shown in figure 7.1. Using this login system within your web application has the benefit of being familiar to the user, at the expense of there being no easy way to log out. Also, you can't customize the look and feel of the login box.

Figure 7.1 The standard HTTP login box provided by a web browser

To authenticate someone using Zend_Auth, you create an instance of an auth adapter and authenticate using Zend_Auth's authenticate() function:

```
$authAdapter = new Zend_Auth_Adapter_Http();
// set up $authAdapter so that it knows what to do
$auth =  Zend_Auth::getInstance();
$result = $auth->authenticate($authAdapter);
```

The HTTP authentication protocol assumes that the pages that you want to protect are grouped into a realm, which is displayed to the user. For example, in figure 7.1, the realm is "My Protected Area". The name of the realm must be provided to the Zend_Auth_Adapter_Http adapter, and you must also create a resolver class to provide the password for a given username. The resolver class decouples the mechanism for authentication from the mechanics of retrieving the username and password from the user, and it generally reads the password from a database or file. Figure 7.2 shows a flowchart that describes the process.

To implement this, we first need to configure Zend_Auth_Adapter_Http, as shown in listing 7.1.

Listing 7.1 Configuration of Zend_Auth_Adapter_Http

```
// create a Zend_Auth_Adapter_Http instance
$config['accept_schemes'] = 'basic';
$config['realm'] = 'ZFiA Chapter 07';
$authAdapter = new Zend_Auth_Adapter_Http($config);

$resolver = new Zend_Auth_Adapter_Http_Resolver_File('passwords.txt');
$authAdapter->setBasicResolver($resolver);
$authAdapter->setRequest($request);
$authAdapter->setResponse($response);
```

❶ Creates the adapter

Sets up access to HTTP headers

As you can see, configuring a Zend_Auth_Adapter_Http object is a two-stage process, as some settings are configured within the $config array that is used on construction of the object ❶, and the setting of the resolver, request, and response objects is done

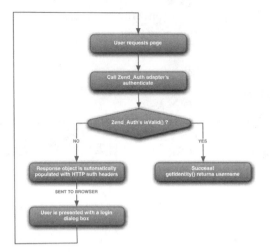

Figure 7.2   HTTP Authentication showing Zend_Auth methods

after creation. The request object is used to retrieve the username and password, and the response object is used to set the correct HTTP headers to indicate whether or not authentication was successful.

The `authenticate()` function performs the actual authentication, as shown in listing 7.2.

Listing 7.2   Authentication with `Zend_Auth_Adapter_Http`

```
$result = $authAdapter->authenticate();        ❶  Authenticates supplied
if (!$result->isValid()) {                          username and password
    // Failed to validate. The response contains the correct HTTP
    // headers for the browser to ask for a username/password.
    $response->appendBody('Sorry, you are not authorized');
} else {                                        ❷  Retrieves username
    // Successfully validated.                      and realm from result
    $identity = $result->getIdentity();        
    $username = $identity['username'];
    $response->appendBody('Welcome, '.$username);
}
```

When `authenticate()` is called, it looks for the username and password HTTP headers ❶. If they're not there, the validation has failed, and it'll set the WWW-Authenticate header in the response object. This will cause the browser to display a dialog box requesting a username and password. Upon successful validation, the username of the person who has just logged in can be retrieved using the `getIdentity()` function, which returns the identity ❷. The full source code to this mini-example is contained within one file and is provided in the accompanying source code zip file.

As you can see, HTTP authentication is easy with `Zend_Auth_Adapter_Http`. But most websites don't use it. Every public-facing, commercial website provides its own login form to identify the user, usually asking for a username and password. There are a number of reasons for this:

- There's no way to log out other than exiting the browser completely.
- It's not optional, so you can't display the page with different content for logged in users.
- You can't change the look and feel of the login dialog box or provide additional information in it. For example, you may want to use an email address rather than a username.
- It's not clear what users should do if they have forgotten their password or don't have an account.

Some of these problems can be worked around using cookies and JavaScript, but the user experience is still not good enough, which is why most sites use forms and sessions (or cookies).

We'll now integrate authentication using a login form and Zend_Auth into the *Places* application.

7.3 Using Zend_Auth in a real application

As *Places* is a community website, it is crucial to be able to identify members, and we have a users table ready to use. In order to implement authentication, we need a controller action to handle the display and processing of a form to allow the user to enter his username and password. We also need to ensure that we know the identity of the current user throughout the application, so we'll take advantage of Zend Framework's front controller plug-in system.

7.3.1 Logging in

To log in and out of our application, a separate controller, called AuthController is required. We use an action to display the form (auth/login) and a separate action (auth/identify) to perform the actual identification. The class skeleton, stored in controllers/AuthController.php, looks like this:

```
class AuthController extends Zend_Controller_Action
{
    public function indexAction()
    {
        $this->_forward('login');
    }

    public function loginAction()
    {
    }

    public function identifyAction()
    {
    }

}
```

Note that we set up `indexAction` to forward to the `loginAction` so that the /auth URL will work as expected. That is, we simply redirect to auth/login if someone goes to auth/ or auth/index.

The HTML for a login form is very simple, and it goes in the view script for the login action (scripts/auth/login.phtml), as shown in listing 7.3.

Listing 7.3   The login form: auth/login.phtml

```html
<h1>Log in</h1>
<p>Please log in here</p>

<form method="POST"
      action="<?php echo $this->url(array('controller'=>'auth',
              'action'=>'identify')); ?>">             Creates URL
                                                       ① for identify
                                                          action
   <div>
      <label>Username</label>
      <input type="text" name="username" value="" />
   </div>
   <div>
      <label>Password</label>
      <input type="password" name="password" value="" />
   </div>
   <div>
      <input type="submit" name="login" value="Login" />
   </div>
</form>
```

The HTML in listing 7.3 is very simple because we need the user to supply information in only two fields: username and password. As you can see, we use the built-in `url()` view helper ❶, to create the correct URL to the auth/identify controller action. The view script, itself, isn't interested in such details, which is why a view helper is the ideal solution. In chapter 8, after `Zend_Form` has been introduced, we will refactor this form to use the `Zend_Form` component instead of hand-coding it.

The identify action, shown in listing 7.4, handles the process of logging in. It uses `Zend_Auth` to check that the supplied username and password are valid.

Listing 7.4   The identify action validates the username and password

```php
public function identifyAction()
{                                              ❶ Checks for
  if ($this->getRequest()->isPost()) {            POST
    $formData = $this->_getFormData();         ❷ Retrieves
                                                  form data
    if (empty($formData['username'])
       || empty($formData['password'])) {      ❸ Stores error
      $this->_flashMessage('Empty username or password.');   message
    } else {
      // do the authentication               ❹ Sets up database
      $authAdapter = $this->_getAuthAdapter($formData);   adapter
      $auth = Zend_Auth::getInstance();
```

```
$result = $auth->authenticate($authAdapter);
if (!$result->isValid()) {                          ⑤  Checks
  $this->_flashMessage('Login failed');                 credentials
} else {
  $data = $authAdapter->getResultRowObject(null,'password');
  $auth->getStorage()->write($data);
                                                    ⑥  Stores in
                                                        the session
  $this->_redirect($this->_redirectUrl);
  return;
}
    }                             Redirects on
  }                               success      ⑦
}

  $this->_redirect('/auth/login');        ⑧   Redirects
}                                               on error

protected function _flashMessage($message) {
  $flashMessenger = $this->_helper->FlashMessenger;      ⑨  Stores message in
  $flashMessenger->setNamespace('actionErrors');             FlashMessenger
  $flashMessenger->addMessage($message);
}
```

We're only interested in this page request if it's a POST ❶. This is a minor security improvement to the code because it prevents the user from using a GET request. If a GET request is used, the username and password would be displayed on the address bar and could be bookmarked, which is obviously not good security.

We use a helper method, _getFormData(), to collect the data from the request and put it into an array ❷. The helper method filters the data to ensure that it's okay for use. In chapter 8, we'll refactor this form to use Zend_Form, which will handle filtering and validation for us.

When an error occurs, we use the FlashMessenger action helper to pass the message back to the auth/login action ❸. As we need to do this twice, a separate helper method, _flashMessage() is used.

Setting up the Zend_Auth_Adapter_DbTable instance is complicated enough that we factor it out to its own method called _getAuthAdapter() ❹. The authenticate() message does the authentication and returns a result object ❺. The result's isValid() method is used to test for successful log in. If we have successfully authenticated, we store the user's database record (*except* the password field) to the session ❻.

After successful authentication, we redirect to where the user wants to go ❼. If authentication has failed, we redirect back to the login form ❽.

The _flashMessage() method passes the supplied message to the next request, which is the login form ❾. The FlashMessenger action helper stores a one-time message that automatically deletes itself when it's read. This makes it ideal for sending validation messages from one screen to the next. In our case, it's read by the loginAction() controller action, and the message is assigned to the view using this code:

```
$flashMessenger = $this->_helper->FlashMessenger;
$flashMessenger->setNamespace('actionErrors');
$this->view->actionErrors = $flashMessenger->getMessages();
```

Listing 7.5 shows the _getAuthAdapter() method, which is the last part of the authentication puzzle. It creates an instance of Zend_Auth_Adapter_DbTable and assigns the supplied username and password to it, ready for authentication by Zend_Auth.

Listing 7.5   _getAuthAdapter() sets up the authentication adapter

```
protected function _getAuthAdapter($formData)
{
    $dbAdapter = Zend_Registry::get('db');          ❶ Retrieves database
                                                        adapter from registry

    $authAdapter = new Zend_Auth_Adapter_DbTable($dbAdapter);
    $authAdapter->setTableName('users')
            ->setIdentityColumn('username')         ❷ Sets up database-
            ->setCredentialColumn('password')          specific
            ->setCredentialTreatment('SHA1(?)');       information

    // get "salt" for better security
    $config = Zend_Registry::get('config');         ❸ Secures password
    $salt = $config->auth->salt;                       by adding salt
    $password = $salt.$formData['password'];           text

    $authAdapter->setIdentity($formData['username']);  ❹ Sets authentication
    $authAdapter->setCredential($password);               data

    return $authAdapter;
}
```

For a short method, quite a lot happens! The Zend_Auth_Adapter_DbTable object requires a connection to the database; fortunately, we stored one in the registry during the bootstrap start-up phase, ready for this sort of situation ❶. After creation, we need to tell the adapter the name of the database table to use, and which fields within that table contain the identity and credentials ❷. In our case, we need the username and password fields from the users table.

While you can store the password in the database in plain text, it's more secure to store a hash of the password. A hash can be thought of as a one-way encryption in that it's unique for a given source string, but if you know the hash, you still can't determine the original string. This is a common method of storing password data, so websites have sprung up containing thousands of hashes for the two common hash algorithms (MD5 and SHA1). To help prevent reverse engineering, should our data fall into the wrong hands, we further protect our users' passwords with a *salt* ❸. The salt is a private string, known only to the application, that we prepend to the user's password to create a word that won't be in an online dictionary. This makes the hash very difficult, if not impossible, to reverse engineer.

We use the database to perform the actual hashing of the salted password by called the auth adapter's setCredentialTreatment() function when setting up the database details for $authAdapter. ❹ Because we are using MySQL, we have specified that the SHA1() function is used, like this:

```
setCredentialTreatment('SHA1(?)');
```

The ? is a placeholder for the password string that is set using `setCredential()`. For other database servers, the appropriate function should be used.

We have now completed the logging-in section of our application, but it would be helpful if we provided links to help the user log in and out. A view helper is one way to do this, and it encapsulates the logic away from the view templates themselves.

7.3.2 *A view helper welcome message*

To provide a welcome message within a view helper, we can take advantage of the fact that `Zend_Auth` implements the Singleton pattern, so we don't need to pass an instance of `Zend_Auth` from the controller to the view. Listing 7.6 shows the Logged-InUser view helper.

Listing 7.6 The LoggedInUser view helper

```
class Zend_View_Helper_LoggedInUser
{
    protected $view;

    function setView($view)                        ❶ Saves view
    {                                                 object
        $this->view = $view;
    }

    function loggedInUser()
    {
        $auth = Zend_Auth::getInstance();          ❷ Checks if
        if($auth->hasIdentity())    <──────────       logged in
        {
            $logoutUrl = $this->view->url(
                    array('controller'=>'auth',
                    'action'=>'logout');          ❸ Gets user
            $user = $auth->getIdentity();   <───────  record
            $username = $this->view->escape(
              ➡   ucfirst($user->username));

            $string = 'Logged in as ' . $username . ' | <a href="' .
                    $logoutUrl . '">Log out</a>';
        } else {
            $loginUrl = $this->view-> url(
                    array('controller'=>'auth',
                    'action'=>'identify');   <──────  ❹ Creates
                                                         correct URL
            $string = '<a href="'. $loginUrl . '">Log in</a>';   <──
        }                                              ❺ Creates login
        return $string;                                   string
    }
}
```

The `setView()` method is automatically called by the view before calling the main helper function ❶. We use it to store a local reference to the view object so that we can reference other view helpers, such as `url()` ❹ and `escape()`.

The actual work is done within the `loggedInUser()` method. The `Zend_Auth` has-
Identity() method is used to check if there is a logged-in user ❷. If there is, the
user's record is retrieved using the `getIdentity()` method ❸. Because the user can
select her own username, we use the `escape()` method to ensure that we don't accidentally introduce an XSS vulnerability, then we create the string to be displayed. If
the current visitor isn't logged in, a string is created with a link to allow the user to log
in ❺.

We call the view helper in our main layout script to display the link in the main
menu bar using this code:

```
<p><?php echo $this->loggedInUser(); ?></p>
```

The final result looks like figure 7.3 and provides an easily discoverable logout link.

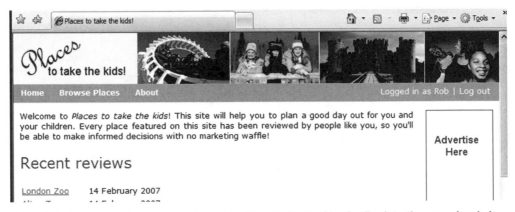

**Figure 7.3   The logged-in welcome message on the website provides feedback to the user when he's
logged in.**

Now we can implement the ability to log out.

7.3.3   Logging out

In comparison to logging in, logging out is very simple. All we need to do is call
`Zend_Auth`'s `clearIdentity()` function. Listing 7.7 shows the logout action in the
`AuthController` class.

Listing 7.7   The auth/logout controller action

```
public function logoutAction()
{
    $auth = Zend_Auth::getInstance();
    $auth->clearIdentity();          Unsets session
                                     variable
    $this->_redirect('/');           Redirects to
                                     home page
}
```

As you can see, logging out is very simple.

It's now time to move on and look at access control and giving logged-in users
more rights than visitors. This is handled by `Zend_Auth`'s sibling, `Zend_Acl`.

7.4 Implementing access control

As we discussed in section 7.1, access control is the process of allowing a logged-in user access to a specific resource. There are many ways of doing this, but a flexible and standard method is to employ role-based access control lists. Zend Framework provides Zend_Acl to take care of this for us.

> **Access control jargon**
> There is a lot of jargon when talking about access control. These are the key terms:
>
> - role: a grouping of users
> - resource: something to be protected, such as a controller action or a data record
> - privilege: the type of access required, such as *read* or *edit*

ACLs are a very flexible solution to access control. All you need to do is identify which items in your application relate to the role, resource, and privilege. Figure 7.4 shows how the three main pieces of the puzzle are related.

Figure 7.4   The relationship between the pieces of the ACL puzzle

This is just one way that ACL can be used to provide access to a resource, to controller actions in this case.

We'll start by looking at Zend_Acl and then move on to applying ACL to control access to different controller actions. Finally, we'll look at access control at the database level.

7.4.1   Introducing Zend_Acl

Using Zend_Acl is reasonably simple because the API is clear. You create some roles and resources, set up the required permissions, and call the isAllowed() function. Sounds easy enough! Let's look at that in a bit more detail, starting with Zend_Acl_Role.

ZEND_ACL_ROLE

A *role* is a responsibility that a user has within the system. A typical role would be "news editor" or "member." This is encapsulated with Zend_Acl_Role, which is a very simple class that just holds the name of the role. This is the code to create a role:

```
$roleMember = new Zend_Acl_Role('member');
```

Once a role is created, its name can't be changed. Note also that within the context of the ACL, each role name must be unique.

We can assign a role to the Zend_Acl instance using this code:

```
$acl = new Zend_Acl();
$acl->addRole($roleMember);
```

A given role may have a parent, which means that the new role can do everything the parent role can do.

A typical situation may be a forum moderator role, which would be coded like this:

```
$acl = new Zend_Acl();
$acl->addRole(new Zend_Acl_Role('member'));
$acl->addRole(new Zend_Acl_Role('moderator'), 'member');
```

In this situation, the moderator role has a parent of member, and so a moderator can do everything that a member can do, in addition to any other permissions that have been set for moderator. For a role to be useful, though, we need to have a resource to protect. This is the responsibility of Zend_Acl_Resource.

ZEND_ACL_RESOURCE

A *resource* is something you want to protect. A typical resource in a Zend Framework application may be a controller or action. You may want to protect access to the forums controller so that only those users belonging to the member role have access to the actions within it. Zend_Acl_Resource is as simple as Zend_Acl_Role and just holds the name of the resource, so you create one like this:

```
$forumResource = new Zend_Acl_Resource('comments');
```

A resource is attached to Zend_Acl like a role, using the add() method. Again, parents are supported:

```
$acl = new Zend_Acl();
$acl->addRole(new Zend_Acl_Role('member'));
$acl->addRole(new Zend_Acl_Role('moderator'), 'member');
$acl->add(new Zend_Acl_Resource('forum'));
$acl->add(new Zend_Acl_Resource('posts'), 'forum');
$acl->add(new Zend_Acl_Resource('threads'), 'forum');
```

Note that the method to add a resource is add(), and rather than a string, we pass in an instance of Zend_Acl_Resource. In this example, we have created resources called posts and threads that are children of the forum resource. If we're mapping resources to modules and controllers, the posts and threads resources represent controllers within the forum module.

To link resources and roles, we need to set up permissions. This is done directly within the Zend_Acl object.

SETTING UP ZEND_ACL'S PERMISSIONS

The final part of setting up a Zend_Acl object is telling the object which permissions a given role has for accessing a given resource. To do this, we need to look at the concept of *privileges*. A *privilege* is the type of access required. Typically, privileges are based on the operations that will be performed, so they have names like "view," "create," "update," and so on.

Zend_Acl has two methods for setting permissions: allow() and deny(). We start off with all roles being denied access to all resources. The allow() method then provides access to a resource for a role, and deny() removes a subset of the allowed access for a particular situation. Inheritance also comes into play here, as permissions set for a parent role will cascade to child roles.

Let's look at an example:

```
$acl->allow('member', 'forum', 'view');
$acl->allow('moderator', 'forum', array('moderate', 'blacklist'));
```

In this example, we have given view privileges to the member role for the forum resource and the additional privileges of moderate and blacklist to the moderator role, which also has view privileges because moderator is a child of member.

We have now looked at the building blocks of Zend_Acl and the key components of its API. Next, we will look at how to integrate it into a real Zend Framework application such as *Places*. The first approach we'll take is to protect specific controllers and actions for specific roles.

7.4.2 Configuring a Zend_Acl object

As we have discovered, a Zend_Acl object needs a fair amount of configuration before we can use it. This means we want to make the setting up as easy as possible, which we can do by storing the roles in our config.ini file.

For each role, we need to store its name and parent in the INI file. We can enter them into the INI file as shown in listing 7.8.

Listing 7.8 INI file entries to configure Zend_Acl roles

```
acl.roles.guest = null      ◁──────┐   Sets guest's
acl.roles.member = guest           │   parent to null
acl.roles.admin = member
```

To read the configuration file, we extend Zend_Acl to read the roles from a Zend_Config object and into itself. The code for this is in a class called Places_Acl that is stored in library/Places/Acl.php and it's shown in listing 7.9.

Listing 7.9 The extended Zend_Acl object

```
class Places_Acl extends Zend_Acl
{
    public function __construct()
    {
        $config = Zend_Registry::get('config');   ◁──┐  Retrieves config object
        $roles = $config->acl->roles;                 │  from registry
        $this->_addRoles($roles);
    }
```

```
    protected function _addRoles($roles)
    {
        foreach ($roles as $name=>$parents) {      ◁─── Iterates over
            if (!$this->hasRole($name)) {          ◁─── all roles
                if (empty($parents)) {              Adds role if it doesn't
                    $parents = null;                already exist
                } else {
                    $parents = explode(',', $parents);
                }
                $this->addRole(new Zend_Acl_Role($name), $parents);
            }
        }
    }
}
```

We have already explored `Zend_Config`, so it should come as no surprise how easy it is to retrieve the data from the config object using a `foreach()` loop. For each role, we check that it hasn't already been added, then we create a new `Zend_Acl_Role` and add it to this object. The `Acl` object will be used to check permissions for every action, so we can create it in the bootstrap.

7.4.3   *Checking the Zend_Acl object*

We must ensure that we don't load the `Acl` object with information about every controller and action. The main issues are maintenance and performance. Maintaining a list of controllers independently of the actual controller class files will result in inaccuracies. We also don't want to spend time and memory loading the ACL with rules that will never be required, because this is a needless performance hit.

With these requirements in mind, a good way to implement ACL checking is as an action helper. An action helper ties into the MVC dispatch system at the controller level and allows us to check the `Acl` rules before the controller's `preDispatch()` method is called. This happens before the action is executed and so is an ideal place for the check.

We need to populate the `Acl` object with the rules to be checked at `preDis-`

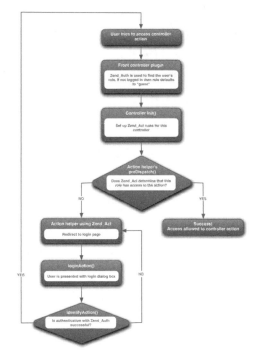

Figure 7.5   `Zend_Auth` and `Zend_Acl` work together to provide access to a controller action.

`patch()`. Because this needs to be done earlier in the process, the `init()` function is the place. In this case, the rules are controller-specific and so are written within each controller as required.

Figure 7.5 shows the complete flow from requesting access to a controller's action to gaining access.

The action controller is called `Places_Controller_Action_Helper_Acl`, and it handles two important functions: providing a controller-centric interface to the underlying `Acl` object and performing the authentication. The controller is too long to show completely here, so we'll look at the bits that do the real work (the full class is provided in the accompanying source code).

Listing 7.10 shows the class skeleton and the initial set up.

Listing 7.10　Setting up the ACL action helper

```
class Places_Controller_Action_Helper_Acl extends
        ⮕ Zend_Controller_Action_Helper_Abstract
{
    protected $_action;
    protected $_auth;
    protected $_acl;
    protected $_controllerName;

    public function __construct(Zend_View_Interface $view = null,
                       array $options = array())
    {
        $this->_auth = Zend_Auth::getInstance();        ❶ Stores auth and acl
        $this->_acl = $options['acl'];                     objects to member
    }                                                      variables

    /**
     * Hook into action controller initialization
     * @return void
     */
    public function init()
    {
        $this->_action = $this->getActionController();

        // add resource for this controller
        $controller = $this->_action->getRequest()
                ⮕ ->getControllerName();                ❷ Names resource
        if(!$this->_acl->has($controller)) {               after controller
            $this->_acl->add(
                new Zend_Acl_Resource($controller));
        }
    }
}
```

The constructor is used to pass in, via the options array, an instance of the `Acl` object that we'll use ❶. We have to use the options array because the constructor signature is already set in the parent `Zend_Controller_Action_Helper_Abstract` class. As the `Zend_Auth` class is a singleton, we can use its `getInstance()` function to collect a reference to it.

The init() method of an action helper is called before the call to the controller's init() method. This makes it an ideal place to set up the required resource for the controller ❷. We use the controller's name for the resource, because this will be unique within the *Places* application. We don't need any more resources than that. We'll use Zend_Acl's privileges as the actions so we don't have the performance hit of working out the names of the action methods dynamically here in order to add them as resources.

Listing 7.11 shows the controller-centric rule methods, allow() and deny(), which proxy through to the underlying Acl object.

Listing 7.11 The ACL action helper's rule methods

```
public function allow($roles = null, $actions = null)
{
    $resource = $this->_controllerName;          ❶ Sets resource name to
                                                     controller name
    $this->_acl->allow($roles, $resource, $actions);   ❷ Calls through to
    return $this;                                          an Acl's function
}

public function deny($roles = null, $actions = null)
{
    $resource = $this->_controllerName;
    $this->_acl->deny($roles, $resource, $actions);
    return $this;
}
```

The functions allow() and deny() are used to set up the authentication rules for the controller. Typically this is done in the controller's init() method. The view helper's versions of allow() and deny() simply fill in the resource parameter for us ❶ and change the terminology from privileges to actions. They then call the appropriate Zend_Acl method ❷. Although that doesn't seem like a lot, it makes much more sense when creating the rules in the controller, so maintenance is easier too.

The last part of the action helper is the preDispatch() hook method. This is called automatically by the front controller and is where we check that the use has sufficient rights to continue. This method is shown in listing 7.12.

Listing 7.12 The ACL action helper's preDispatch() method

```
public function preDispatch()
{
    $role = 'guest';                          ❶ Sets default
                                                 role to guest
    if ($this->_auth->hasIdentity()) {        ❷ Checks that user
        $user = $this->_auth->getIdentity();     is logged in
        if(is_object($user)) {
            $role =                           ❸ Retrieves
                $this->_auth->getIdentity()->role;   user's role
        }
    }

    $request = $this->_action->getRequest();
    $controller = $request->getControllerName();
```

```
$action = $request->getActionName();
$module = $request->getModuleName();
$this->_controllerName = $controller;

$resource = $controller;
$privilege = $action;
```
④ **Sets resource and privilege to test**

```
if (!$this->_acl->has($resource)) {
    $resource = null;
}
```
⑤ **Ensures that $resource is valid**

```
if (!$this->_acl->isAllowed($role, $resource,
            $privilege)) {
```
⑥ **Tests if role has permission to continue**

```
    $request->setModuleName('default');
    $request->setControllerName('auth');
    $request->setActionName('login');
    $request->setDispatched(false);
}
}
```
⑦ **Resets request to poin at login action**

First, we set the role to guest **❶**, then check that the user is logged in **❷**. If the user is logged in, we retrieve the role that has been assigned **❸**. Note that this means that we need to update our users table so that it contains a string column called role that contains a value from the list of available roles set up in the config.ini file in listing 7.8. Having determined the correct role to test, we look up the resource and privilege from the request **❹**. The resource is the controller name, and the privilege is the action name.

We then check to see if the resource has some ACL rules attached, and if not, set it to null **❺** in order to ensure that the isAllowed() check does not throw an exception. Finally we call isAllowed() to find out if this role is allowed access to this controller action **❻**. If not, we change the request's settings so that the front controller will dispatch to the auth controller's login action **❼** and so display the login form.

In order to test the resource, it must be set up before preDispatch() is called. We set up the resources and privileges required in the controller's init() method because this happens before preDispatch(). As you would expect, we have different rules depending on the controller in *Places*. For the index controller, we want to give everyone access, so the init() method is simply as follows:

```
class IndexController extends Zend_Controller_Action
{
    public function init()
    {
        $this->_helper->acl->allow(null);
    }

    //... class continues...
```

For other controllers, the rules will be more complex. For example, listing 7.13 shows what's needed to ensure that members can only view and not manage records within the `PlaceController`.

Listing 7.13   More complex ACL rules so only admins can manage place records

```
class PlaceController extends Zend_Controller_Action              Sets up      ❶
{                                                              member ACL
    function init()                                                  rules
    {
        $memberActions = array('index', 'details', 'report-error');
        $this->_helper->_acl->allow('member', $memberActions);

        $adminActions = array('add', 'edit', 'delete');
        $this->_helper->_acl->allow('admin', $adminActions);
    }                                                         Sets up admin  ❷
    //... class continues...                                   ACL rules
```

As you can see, we allow the `member` role access to one set of actions ❶ and administrators access to another set ❷. We don't need to explicitly tell the system to allow administrators access to the member actions because the `admin` role is a child of the `member` role and so inherits those permissions automatically.

This concludes our look at integrating `Zend_Auth` and `Zend_Acl` into the *Places* application. We used `Zend_Auth` to allow users to log into the website and `Zend_Acl` enables us to control exactly which controllers and actions a given user can access. This is achieved by setting each controller as an `Acl` resource, with the action as a privilege.

7.5   Summary

In this chapter, we have looked at the two related concepts of authentication and access control. Authentication ensures that we know the identity of the current user, and `Zend_Auth` is an intuitive and comprehensive component that allows for checking against different data sources. By leveraging `Zend_Session`, `Zend_Auth` provides a one-stop-shop solution and enables us to identify the currently logged on user very easily.

Choosing an authentication strategy to ensure that only users with the correct privileges are allowed access to certain parts of the application is an art in itself. Zend Framework provides `Zend_Acl` to manage this. We have explored a solution that uses an action helper to easily limit access to controller actions without having to do lots of setup independent of the controller being protected. One key benefit of the flexibility of Zend Framework is there is no need to force a particular application's requirements into one methodology; the framework can be molded to solve the problem in hand.

Forms are one of those aspects of building a website that developers either love or loathe due to the complexities of validation and ensuring that the user is informed about issues in the form in a friendly manner. In the next chapter, we'll look at how Zend Framework can help make building and validating online forms easier with `Zend_Form`.

Forms

8

This chapter covers

- An introduction to `Zend_Form`
- A step-by-step demonstration using `Zend_Form`
- Filtering and validating form data
- Form markup and styling

Anyone who has winced at the things toddlers unwittingly thrust into their mouths will understand the anxiety developers feel when building forms. Any opening into the application raises questions of security and stability. Just as a biological body must have its protective measures, so must our forms.

Having said that, protecting our forms isn't the only thing we need to take into consideration; they must also be usable. A form's usability is difficult to determine without a reasonable period of testing, which actually means that there is a hidden requirement of form design—flexibility. Discovered insecurities, usability issues, updates, and additions to the underlying architecture may all require forms to change. A flexible system allows these changes to be made promptly and inexpensively.

Zend Framework has many options for the design of forms, from its MVC architecture to its data filters and validators. Previous chapters have demonstrated various approaches to building forms; in this chapter we'll look at a component designed specifically for the job, `Zend_Form`.

8.1   Introducing Zend_Form

Because `Zend_Form` did not arrive until Zend Framework 1.5, early adopters had a lot of time to get along without it. That meant that one or two of us were a little suspicious of `Zend_Form` when it finally arrived and were going to need convincing as to its value. We're glad to say that while it isn't without a quirk or two, we've found that the more acquainted we get, the more we like it.

In a broader sense, the three main advantages of using `Zend_Form` are rapid application development, flexibility, and consistency. But you'll need to be comfortable enough with the component before those benefits become apparent. The aim of this chapter is, of course, to get you to that stage. Later in the chapter, we'll work on a login form for our *Places* application, but before we do so, we'll take a look at some `Zend_Form` features.

8.1.1   Integrated data filters and validators

If you're familiar with the security mantra "filter input—escape output," you'll also know that all forms need to validate and sanitize the user's input and escape the output that may be inserted into a database or displayed in a view script.

`Zend_Filter` and `Zend_Validate` are independent components used in `Zend_Form` and on their own, as we'll show. Table 8.1 lists the current filter classes that are available for use with any forms, including `Zend_Form` forms.

Table 8.1   Standard `Zend_Filter` classes available for use with `Zend_Form`

Standard `Zend_Filter` class	Function
Alnum	Removes all but alphabetic and digit characters.
Alpha	Removes all but alphabetic characters.
Digits	Removes all but digit characters.
HtmlEntities	Converts characters to their HTML entity equivalents where possible.
Int	Equivalent to `(int)`.
StringToLower	Converts alphabetic characters to lowercase.
StringToUpper	Converts alphabetic characters to uppercase.
StringTrim	Strips characters from the beginning and end; equivalent to `trim()`.
StripTags	Strips all HTML and PHP tags

You may question the benefit of some of the filters in table 8.1, such as `Int` or `StringTrim`. What could be more easy than casting to an integer using `(int)` or removing white space with `trim()`? Why would we need an extra class to do that? The answers lie in the ability to chain together and apply multiple filters to data, as demonstrated in listing 8.1.

Listing 8.1 Using `Zend_Filter` filter chains to apply multiple filters to input data

```
require_once 'Zend/Filter.php';
require_once 'Zend/Filter/StringTrim.php';
require_once 'Zend/Filter/Alnum.php';

$filterChain = new Zend_Filter();
$filterChain->addFilter(new Zend_Filter_Alnum())
        ->addFilter(new Zend_Filter_StringToLower());

$username = $filterChain->filter($_POST['password']);
```

Imagine that the user typed "MyPassword123\r". The filter chain in listing 8.1 would strip out nonalphabetic and nonnumeric characters and lowercase them, returning "mypassword123".

While this is certainly cleaner, it's a little troubling on its own, as we should not presume that the user hadn't intended that to be her password, even if our application doesn't approve of it. What we should have done is used `Zend_Validate` to check that the input matched our requirements and allowed the user a chance to change it if it did not pass. Table 8.2 shows the built-in validation classes we could have used to perform this check..

Table 8.2 Standard `Zend_Validate` classes available for use with `Zend_Form`

Standard `Zend_Validate` class	Function
Alnum	Data with only alphabetic and digit characters returns `true`
Alpha	Data with only alphabetic characters returns `true`
Barcode	Data that validates against the barcode validation algorithm returns `true`
Between	Data between the minimum and maximum values returns `true`
Ccnum	Data that follows the Luhn algorithm for credit card numbers returns `true`
Date	Data of a specified date format returns `true`
Digits	Data with only digit characters returns `true`
EmailAddress	Validates an email address
Float	Data that is a floating-point value returns `true`
GreaterThan	Data greater than a minimum returns `true`

Table 8.2 Standard `Zend_Validate` classes available for use with `Zend_Form` (continued)

Standard `Zend_Validate` class	Function
Hex	Data with only hexadecimal digit characters returns `true`
Hostname	Validates a hostname against specifications
InArray	Data with a "needle" value contained in a "haystack" array returns `true`
Int	Data that is a valid integer returns `true`
Ip	Data that is a valid IP address returns `true`
LessThan	Data less than a maximum returns `true`
NotEmpty	Data that isn't empty returns `true`
Regex	Data that matches against a regular expression pattern returns `true`
StringLength	Data with a string length at least a minimum and not greater than a maximum returns `true`

Using table 8.2 as a reference, we can see that `StringLength` and `Alnum` could be used to validate our password. Put through the validation chain in listing 8.2, our user's original password would fail the `isValid()` check, and we could return her to the form to make any corrections.

Listing 8.2   Using validation chains to apply multiple input data checks

```
require_once 'Zend/Validate.php';
require_once 'Zend/Validate/StringLength.php';
require_once 'Zend/Validate/Alnum.php';

$validatorChain = new Zend_Validate();
$validatorChain->addValidator(new Zend_Validate_StringLength(6, 15))
        ->addValidator(new Zend_Validate_Alnum());

if ($validatorChain->isValid($_POST['password'])) {
   // password meets our requirements
}
```

The examples in listings 8.1 and 8.2 demonstrated how data can be validated and filtered independently. Later in this chapter we'll look at how the integration of these components with `Zend_Form` makes the process a lot easier to manage.

8.1.2   *Integrated error handling*

In discussing listing 8.2, we mentioned having to return the user to his form to make changes to the input. This could be done with code something like the following:

```
$this->view->formMessages = $validatorChain->getMessages();
```

Those messages could then be shown to the user in our view script:

```
<?php if (!empty($this->formMessages): ?>
<ul>
<?php foreach ($this->formMessages as $message): ?>
    <li><?php echo $message; ?></li>
<?php endforeach; ?>
<ul>
<?php endif; ?>
```

Doing that for every element would clearly be a chore. Thankfully, `Zend_Form` has error handling built in, in the form of *decorators*, which reduce the amount of coding needed to achieve the same effect.

8.1.3 *Decorators to simplify markup*

The previous error-handling example partly illustrates the labor involved in form markup, from the form HTML itself, to showing the errors a user may have made in his submission. Picture all that markup for a long form, and you'll see that we have a lot of code to write and track.

Zend_Form decorators are based on their namesake Decorator design pattern, and they essentially allow layers of markup to be wrapped around form elements. Table 8.3 lists the standard decorators available in `Zend_Form`.

Table 8.3 `Zend_Form` **standard decorators used to add markup to form items**

`Zend_Form` decorator class	Function
Callback	Executes a callback to render content.
Captcha	Used with the Captcha form element to prevent unwanted automated form submission.
Description	Displays a description on items, such as for form hints.
DtDdWrapper	Wraps content in an HTML definition list.
Errors	Displays errors in an HTML unordered list.
Fieldset	Wraps content in an HTML fieldset element.
Form	Wraps content in an HTML form element.
FormElements	Iterates through all items, and renders and joins them.
HtmlTag	Wraps content in an HTML element you define.
Image	Inserts an HTML img element.
Label	Renders form element labels.
ViewHelper	Allows you to specify a view helper that will create an element.
ViewScript	Allows you to specify a view script that will create an element.

As with the filters and validators, these decorator classes are only the standard ones available in Zend Framework, and for many cases they're sufficient. If not, they can all be customized, and the next feature is particularly useful in that regard.

8.1.4 *Plug-in loaders for customization*

If your particular needs are not met by the standard validators, filters, and decorators, you'll be pleased to know that `Zend_Form` allows you to use `Zend_Loader_Plugin-Loader` to add your own alternatives. We could, for example, specify a location for our own filters like so:

```
$passwordElement->addPrefixPath(
    'Places_Filter', 'Places/Filter/', 'filter'
);
```

Or for validators:

```
$passwordElement->addPrefixPath(
    'Places_Validator', 'Places/Validator/', 'validate'
);
```

Or for decorators:

```
$passwordElement->addPrefixPath(
    'Places_Decorator', 'Places/Decorator/', 'decorator'
);
```

The great thing about the `PluginLoader` is that it gives your alternative locations priority over the standard locations. If we have, for example, a `Places_Form_Decorator_Errors` decorator class in library/Places/Validator/Errors.php, it'll be used instead of the standard Zend Framework `Zend_Form_Decorator_Errors` class just by using the same naming convention.

8.1.5 *Internationalization*

Somewhat surprisingly, `Zend_Form` was the first component to be fully integrated with the other Zend Framework internationalization components. We'll give a brief example of this in the coding examples that follow, but the subject itself is covered more fully in chapter 15 on internationalization and localization.

8.1.6 *Subforms and display groups*

Subforms and display groups are both ways of grouping form elements. Display groups are used in much the same way that the HTML fieldset is and in fact renders as a fieldset by default. Subforms are, as you may expect, `Zend_Form` or `Zend_Form_SubForm` objects that can be used within other forms.

To understand the distinction, we could consider a date-selector widget subform used for the birth date in a user registration form, like so:

```
$form->addSubForm($dateSelectorForm, 'birthdate');
```

The user's address details could be grouped within an address fieldset with a display group like so:

```
$form->addDisplayGroup(
    array('street', 'town', 'state','postcode'), 'address');
```

The form we're going to be building will have no need for display groups or subforms, but even these brief examples demonstrate their value in larger forms.

Subforms and display groups, in our opinion, are the key features that make Zend_Form an attractive option when building forms. The proof, though, is in the use, and so far we've not really demonstrated Zend_Form in any depth. In the next section, we'll take a step-by-step approach and show how these features work together by recreating the login form that was developed in chapter 7 on user authentication and authorization.

8.2 *Building a login form*

We have presented some of the options available when using Zend_Form, and there are clearly a lot of them. Using Zend_Form is very much about adding layers of functionality to form items, and this is best explained in a step-by-step way. For that reason, we're going to stick to the simple two-field login form discussed in the previous chapter. To get the full sense of the improvements that Zend_Form brings, please refer to the examples in chapter 7 as you work through this one.

We'll start by setting up the required files and the paths to their locations.

8.2.1 *Setting up paths*

To start, we need to add an application/forms directory in which we'll store our form classes and add that location to our include path in the bootstrap file:

```
set_include_path(get_include_path()
   . PATH_SEPARATOR . ROOT_DIR . '/library/'
   . PATH_SEPARATOR . ROOT_DIR . '/application/models/'
   . PATH_SEPARATOR . ROOT_DIR . '/application/forms/'
);
```

Next, we need to add the main files and start coding.

8.2.2 *Our form view script*

Once rendered our form is going to have to be displayed somewhere. We already have an auth/login.phtml view script from the previous chapter that we're going to leave for comparison. In listing 8.3 we've created a form.phtml file and added the code to show our Zend_Form version of the same authorization form from the previous chapter.

```
<h1>Log in</h1>
<p>Please log in here</p>
<?php echo $this->formResponse, ?>
<?php echo $this->form; ?>
```

Displays any feedback messages

Displays the rendered form

If, like us, you've read a lot of technical articles, you'll be forgiven for raising your eyebrows in suspicion at the cliché "all that in one line of code" which starts our discussion. Bear with us, as the updates to the controller action file are almost equally impressive.

8.2.3   Updating the AuthController controller action

Ruby on Rails has a useful idiom of "skinny controller—fat model," the basic premise of which is to keep your controller files lean and easy to understand by moving as much logic as possible to your model files. In chapter 7, we built some fairly complex controller files that we're now going to refactor using `Zend_Form`.

We'll start with a minor modification to our `indexAction()` method, as shown in listing 8.4. This checks whether the user has been identified, and, if not, he is forwarded to the `formAction()` method in listing 8.5, where he is shown the login form. In later development, this could allow us to add an `else` option to direct the user to his account page if he's already logged in.

Listing 8.4   Our refactored `indexAction()` controller action

```
public function indexAction()
{
    if (null === Zend_Auth::getInstance()->getIdentity()) {
        $this->_forward('form');
    }
}
```

Checks user authentication

Forwards to formAction()

Next we need to add a new action method, shown in listing 8.5, that will handle all aspects of our login form, from processing the POST request to setting up and rendering the form. Parts of it may seem unclear initially, but we'll cover them in more detail later in the chapter. We're showing it here because it remains unchanged throughout the process.

Listing 8.5   Our `formAction()` in our AuthController controller action class

```
public function formAction()
{
    $form = new LoginForm('/auth/form/');
    $this->view->formResponse = '';
    if ($this->_request->isPost()) {
        if ($form->isValid(
            $this->_request->isPost())
        ) {
```

❶ Instantiates subclassed Zend_Form object

❷ Checks if form has been submitted

❸ Checks validity of submission

```
        $authAdapter = $form->username          ◄──────┐    Gets authAdapter
                    ->getValidator('Authorise')       ❹    object from element
                    ->getAuthAdapter();
        $data = $authAdapter->getResultRowObject(  ◄──  ❺  Gets data row from
                    null, 'password');                      authAdapter
        $auth = Zend_Auth::getInstance();
        $auth->getStorage()->write($data);   ◄──────  ❻  Writes authorization
        $this->_redirect($this->_redirectUrl);             info to storage
    } else {                                        ◄────┐  Redirects
        $this->view->formResponse = '  ◄─┐  ❽ Sets form response  ❼  user
        Sorry, there was a problem with your submission.   message
        Please check the following:';
    }
}
$this->view->form = $form;   ◄──┐  ❾  Sets view variable
}                                     for form
```

The first thing our `formAction()` method does is instantiate the login `Zend_Form` object, passing it the URL to be used in the HTML form element's action attribute ❶. After checking whether the request is an HTTP POST ❷, and therefore a form submission, the submitted data is passed as a parameter to the `isValid()` method, which returns a Boolean from which we determine the next action ❸.

If it's valid, we retrieve the `authAdapter` object from our `Places_Validate_Authorise` custom validator via the username form element ❹, and from that we get the database row that includes the user's authorization information, excluding the password for security reasons ❺. We can then use `Zend_Auth` to store the database row to whatever storage method it's set to use (sessions, by default) ❻. Finally, we redirect the user to whatever page we decide ❼.

If the submitted data isn't valid, we set a message to let the user know there were problems ❽, which they'll see in the rendered form that has been sent to the view ❾.

At this point, it's worth mentioning that if we had wanted to, we could have used the following code to set the values of our form:

```
$form->populate($this->_request->isPost());
```

This would have been appropriate if we had wanted to set default values to fill the form with. Since this is a login form, we don't need to do that and, besides, the `isValid()` method automatically populates the form with the POST values.

With the controller action done, we can now move on to building our `LoginForm` class, which we'll do in a series of steps starting with the most basic version.

8.2.4 *The basic login form class*

We'll start by creating the most minimal elements needed to render a form consisting of a username field, password field, and submit button. The first step, shown in listing 8.6, is to create our LoginForm.php file in /application/forms/ and add a `loginForm` class that extends `Zend_Form`.

Listing 8.6   Our basic login form using `Zend_Form`

```
include_once 'Zend/Form.php';

class LoginForm extends Zend_Form
{
    public function init($action)
    {
        $this->setAction($action)          ← Creates HTML
            ->setMethod('post')              form element
            ->setAttrib('id', 'loginForm');

        $username = $this->addElement('text', 'username',   ← Creates username
            array('label' => 'Username'));                    text element

        $password = $this->addElement('password', 'password',  ←
            array('label' => 'Password'));               Creates
                                                         password
        $submit = $this->addElement('submit', 'Login');  ←  element

    }                                      Creates submit
}                                             button
```

The first thing to note with this code is that the form is being set up within the `init()` method, which is a convenience method that is called from within the constructor of `Zend_Form`. It adds components of the form, starting with the form element and its various attributes, followed by the other elements of the form.

The next point to note is that our elements are being created using the Factory Method design pattern for adding elements. The alternative is to instantiate the elements ourselves and pass them to the form, like this:

```
$username = new Zend_Form_Element_Text('username');
$this->addElement($username);
```

We've chosen the factory approach because it has the advantage of inheriting any settings we make in the form object.

Together with the controller action we created earlier, this form will work perfectly adequately as long as the submitted data always meets the requirements of our application. We all know that this isn't always the case, and users will often submit incorrect or empty fields that we need to account for by validating and filtering the data.

8.3   *Filtering and validation*

Earlier in this chapter, we mentioned that `Zend_Filter` and `Zend_Validate` are integrated into `Zend_Form`, and here we get a chance to show how that simplifies their use.

8.3.1   *Basic filtering and validation*

In listing 8.7 the username and password elements have been expanded to include filtering and validation, using the fluent interface of the `addValidator()` and `addFilter()` methods.

Listing 8.7   Adding filtering and validation to our login form elements

```
$this->addElement('text', 'username',
    array('label' => 'Username'));
$username = $this->getElement('username')
        ->addValidator('alnum')
        ->setRequired(true)
        ->addFilter('StringTrim');

$this->addElement('password', 'password',
    array('label' => 'Password'));
$password = $this->getElement('password')
        ->addValidator('stringLength', true, array(6))
        ->setRequired(true)
        ->addFilter('StringTrim');
```

All of these additions rely on their namesake `Zend_Filter` or `Zend_Validate` components; even `setRequired()` uses the `NotEmpty` validator. The role of the validator is to highlight any data submitted that does not pass validation. This can then be used by the error decorator to indicate fields that need correction when the form is rendered. Figure 8.1 shows the error messages in the rendered form after an empty form is submitted.

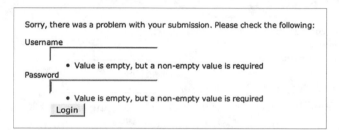

Figure 8.1   The results of an empty form submission

Beyond the required setting, which ensures the element has a value when submitted, we've insisted that usernames be alphanumeric with any whitespace trimmed, and that passwords be no shorter than six characters with whitespace trimmed. If we then submit the form with information that doesn't meet those requirements, we're returned to the form with the messages shown in figure 8.2.

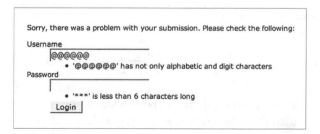

Figure 8.2   The results of submitting invalid data

Error messages like "'@@@@@' has not only alphabetic and digit characters" and "'***' is less than 6 characters long" may not suit the kind of application you're building. Luckily it's quite easy to add your own custom messages.

8.3.2   *Custom error messages*

Adding our own messages to validators is simply a case of getting the validator by name and using its setMessage() method to change the message to one that suits our needs. These further additions to our form elements are shown in listing 8.8.

Listing 8.8   Adding custom messages to our login form elements

```
$this->addElement('text', 'username',
   array('label' => 'Username'));
$username = $this->getElement('username')
      ->addValidator('alnum')
      ->setRequired(true)
      ->addFilter('StringTrim');
$username->getValidator('alnum')->setMessage(
   'Your username should include letters and numbers only');

$this->addElement('password', 'password',
   array('label' => 'Password'));
$password = $this->getElement('password')
      ->addValidator('stringLength', true, array(6))
      ->setRequired(true)
      ->addFilter('StringTrim');
$password->getValidator('stringLength')->setMessage(
   'Your password is too short');
```

If we now submit the same information we did before changing the messages, we get feedback that is much more suitable for our *Places* site, as shown in figure 8.3. We should note that while it may be helpful to our users, our form may be providing a little too much feedback information that could help those trying to break into our site. You should obviously consider this when building your own forms.

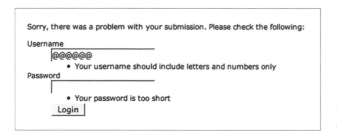

Figure 8.3   Our login form with custom error messages

Places is currently focused on entertainment for families in the United Kingdom, so the only thing we needed to do was make the messages more friendly. Once it becomes popular enough to move into other European countries, we'd need to start looking at internationalizing the forms and other content.

8.3.3 *Internationalizing the form*

It's interesting that Zend_Form is the first component in Zend Framework to be incorporated with its internationalization components. The benefit for our use is the ease with which we can change the form to show error messages in another language, such as the German version shown in listing 8.9.

Listing 8.9 Our login form with translated error messages

```
public function init()
{                                                          Includes
    include ROOT_DIR .                                     translation file
        '/application/configuration/translations/de_DE.php';  <───
    $translate = new Zend_Translate(
        'array', $translationStrings, 'de');  <───
    $this->setTranslator($translate);         <───          Instantiates
                                                            Zend_Translate
    $this->setAction('/auth/index/')          Passes translate  object
        ->setMethod('post')                   object to form
        ->setAttrib('id', 'loginForm');

    $username = $this->addElement('text', 'username',
        array('label' => 'Username'));
    $username = $this->getElement('username')
            ->addValidator('alnum')
            ->setRequired(true)
            ->addFilter('StringTrim');

    $password = $this->addElement('password', 'password',
        array('label' => 'Password'));
    $password = $this->getElement('password')
            ->addValidator('stringLength', true, array(6))
            ->setRequired(true)
            ->addFilter('StringTrim');

    $submit = $this->addElement('submit', 'Login');
}
```

The translations for each element are based on the value for the constants contained in each validator class, so for Zend_Validate_StringLength, the constant is

```
const TOO_SHORT = 'stringLengthTooShort';
```

The stringLengthTooShort value is the one we use as the key in our translation array:

```
'stringLengthTooShort' => 'Ihr Kennwort ist zu kurz'
```

Once we've added all the translation data, our error messages will now be automatically translated to the language we specify, as shown in figure 8.4.

You may notice that while our messages are in German, the submit button is still in English, which means our translation is incomplete. We'll look at internationalization in more detail in chapter 15. For now we have to move on to making a custom validator.

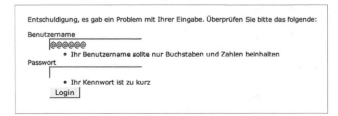

Figure 8.4   Our login form translated into German

8.3.4   *Adding a custom validator*

The last thing we need for our login form is a way to check whether or not the user is registered. We could do that as an added step in the formAction() controller action method, but earlier in this chapter we described how plug-in loaders allow us to add our own filters, validators, and decorators to forms. In listing 8.10 we do just that with our Authorise validator.

Listing 8.10   Our username element with custom Authorise validator added

```
$username = $this->addElement('text', 'username',
    array('label' => 'Username'));
$username = $this->getElement('username')
        ->addValidator('alnum')
        ->setRequired(true)
        ->addFilter('StringTrim')
        ->addPrefixPath('Places_Validate',          Specifies custom
          'Places/Validate/', 'validate')           validator location
        ->addValidator('Authorise');                Adds custom
$username->getValidator('alnum')                    validator
        ->setMessage(
'Your username should include letters and numbers only');
```

Our Authorise validator, shown in listing 8.11, is going to check the contents of both the username and password fields and only validate the form if both pass. We're attaching it to the username field, which means its error messages will be displayed under the username field. To allow for that, we have kept the message suitably vague, so it isn't really an issue.

Listing 8.11   Our custom Authorise validator

```
class Places_Validate_Authorise          ❶ Defines class name using
    extends Zend_Validate_Abstract          correct naming convention
{
    const NOT_AUTHORISED = 'notAuthorised';

    protected $_authAdapter;
    protected $_messageTemplates = array(
        self::NOT_AUTHORISED => 'No users with those details exist'
    );

    public function getAuthAdapter()
    {
```

```
        return $this->_authAdapter;
    }
    public function isValid($value, $context = null)
    {
        $value = (string) $value;
        $this->_setValue($value);

        if (is_array($context)) {
            if (!isset($context['password'])) {
                return false;
            }
        }

        $dbAdapter = Zend_Registry::get('db');
        $this->_authAdapter = new Zend_Auth_Adapter_DbTable($dbAdapter);
        $this->_authAdapter->setTableName('users')
                ->setIdentityColumn('username')
                ->setCredentialColumn('password');
        $config = Zend_Registry::get('config');
        $salt = $config->auth->salt;
        $password = sha1($salt.$context['password']);

        $this->_authAdapter->setIdentity($value);
        $this->_authAdapter->setCredential($password);
        $auth = Zend_Auth::getInstance();
        $result = $auth->authenticate($this->_authAdapter);
        if (!$result->isValid()) {
            $this->_error(self::NOT_AUTHORISED);
            return false;
        }
        return true;
    }
}
```

❷ Adds required IsValid() method

❸ Checks for needed $context array

Our Authorise custom validation class should feel familiar to readers of the previous chapter, so we'll stick to pointing out the additions we have made to make it a validator.

First, it must extend Zend_Validate_Abstract, use the Places_Validate name prefix we gave to our plug-in loader in the loginForm class ❶, and be placed in Places/Validate/Authorise.php. It must also contain an isValid() method ❷, which will have the value of the attached element, username in this case, automatically passed through it, as well as the $context array of all the other form values.

Since we need both the username and password to determine whether our user is registered, we first check whether the $context array is available and whether it includes a password item ❸. If all information is present and the user is found to be a valid user, our validator will return a true response; otherwise it'll return false together with any error messages that can be shown to the user.

Now that we've added the custom validators, the backend functionality of the form is complete and we can turn our attention to the frontend with decorators.

8.4   *Decorating our login form*

As mentioned earlier in this chapter, decorators are a way to add layers of markup to forms and form elements. In this section, we'll use them to change the HTML markup of our form.

8.4.1   *Zend_Form default decorators*

Up to now, we've been using the default decorators that are loaded in `Zend_Form_Element`, like so:

```
$this->addDecorator('ViewHelper')
    ->addDecorator('Errors')
    ->addDecorator('HtmlTag', array('tag' => 'dd'))
    ->addDecorator('Label', array('tag' => 'dt'));
```

We've also used the ones in `Zend_Form`, like so:

```
$this->addDecorator('FormElements')
    ->addDecorator('HtmlTag',
      array('tag' => 'dl', 'class' => 'zend_form'))
    ->addDecorator('Form');
```

For our login form, these default settings produce the markup shown in listing 8.12, which essentially displays our form elements wrapped within an HTML definition list.

> **Listing 8.12   Our login form HTML produced by the default decorators**
>
> ```
> <form id="loginForm" enctype="application/x-www-form-urlencoded"
>                       action="/auth/index/" method="post">
> <dl class="zend_form">
>    <dt><label for="username" class="required">Username</label></dt>
>    <dd> <input type="text" name="username" id="username" value=""></dd>
>    <dt><label for="password" class="required">Password</label></dt>
>    <dd><input type="password" name="password" id="password" value=""></dd>
>    <dt></dt>
>    <dd><input type="submit" name="Login" id="Login" value="Login"></dd>
> </dl>
> </form>
> ```

With the addition of some CSS, a definition list can be styled very effectively, but for our needs, we'd rather our form was wrapped in a slightly simpler HTML unordered list. This is what we'll do next.

8.4.2   *Setting our own decorators*

When using Zend Framework, you'll find there are often several ways to write your code. This is the case with decorators, so bear in mind that the way we add our decorator settings in listing 8.13 isn't the only way to do it. We'll try to point out our reasoning as we go.

Listing 8.13 Our login form with decorator settings

```php
public function init()
{
    $this->setAction('/auth/index/')
        ->setMethod('post')
        ->setAttrib('id', 'loginForm');

    $this->addElementPrefixPath('Places_Validate',
        'Places/Validate/', 'validate');

    $this->clearDecorators();                              ❶ Disables default
                                                              decorators
    $decorators = array(
        array('ViewHelper'),                               ❷ Sets up
        array('Errors'),                                      decorators as
        array('Label', array(                                 array
            'requiredSuffix' => ' *',
            'class' => 'leftalign'
        )),
        array('HtmlTag', array('tag' => 'li')),
    );

    $this->addElement('text', 'username',
        array('label' => 'Username'));
    $username = $this->getElement('username')
            ->addValidator('alnum')
            ->setRequired(true)
            ->addFilter('StringTrim')
            ->addValidator('Authorise');
    $username->getValidator('alnum')
            ->setMessage(
            'Your username should include letters and numbers only'
            );
    $username->setDecorators($decorators);

    $this->addElement('password', 'password',
        array('label' => 'Password'));
    $password = $this->getElement('password')       ❸ Sets
            ->addValidator('stringLength', true, array(4))   decorators
            ->setRequired(true)                              per element
            ->addFilter('StringTrim');
    $password->getValidator('stringLength')
            ->setMessage('Your password is too short');
    $password->setDecorators($decorators);

    $this->addElement('submit', 'Login');
    $submit = $this->getElement('Login')          ❹ Sets submit button
            ->setDecorators(array(                   decorators
            array('ViewHelper'),
            array('HtmlTag', array(
            'tag' => 'li',
            'class' => 'submit')),
    ));
    $this->setDecorators(array(          ❺ Sets form
        'FormElements',                     decorators
        array('HtmlTag', array('tag' => 'ul')),
        array(
```

```
            array(
                'DivTag' => 'HtmlTag'
            ),
            array(
                'tag' => 'div',
                'class' => 'loginDiv'                    ❻  Sets a decorator
            )                                  ◁──────        alias
        ),
        'Form'
    ));
}
```

Before adding our own decorator settings, we first must disable the default decorators using the clearDecorators() method ❶. Having done that, we can set up a default array of element decorators ❷. Our settings aren't too dissimilar from the default decorators, aside from the addition of a leftalign class name for the HTML label, an asterisk suffix for all required elements (not strictly necessary in this case, but included here for illustration), and wrapping that all in an HTML list tag. The resulting HTML looks like so:

```
<li><label for="username" class="leftalign required">Username *</label>
<input type="text" name="username" id="username" value=""></li>
```

One advantage of using the factory method to add form elements is that we could set all element decorators at once, and they would inherit our decorator settings like so:

```
$this->setElementDecorators($decorators);
```

With only two form fields, we won't benefit from this convenience, so we're setting our decorators on a per-element basis ❸, except for the submit button, which is set individually because it doesn't require a label or error messages ❹.

To finish up, we set the overall form decorator ❺. The order in which decorators are added is important, and in this case we add the form elements first followed by a ul HTML tag and, sounding a little like a cookery lesson, we wrap all that in an HTML div tag.

Notice that because we're wrapping with one HtmlTag followed by another, we need to give the second one an "alias"; otherwise, multiple decorators of the same type will overwrite one another. In this case, our second HtmlTag decorator is given the alias DivTag, which uniquely identifies it ❻. Admittedly, for our form, this last div tag isn't necessary, but for the sake of the demonstration, let's imagine it's a request from our designer.

In listing 8.14, we can see that the full HTML generated by our changes is notably different from the original default HTML in listing 8.12.

Listing 8.14 Our login form HTML produced by our custom decorator settings

```
<form id="loginForm" enctype="application/x-www-form-urlencoded"
    action="/auth/index/" method="post">
<div class="loginDiv">
  <ul>
    <li>
      <label for="username" class="leftalign required">
        Username *
      </label>
      <input type="text" name="username" id="username" value="">
    </li>
    <li>
      <label for="password" class="leftalign required">
        Password *
      </label>
      <input type="password" name="password" id="password" value="">
    </li>
    <li class="submit">
      <input type="submit" name="Login" id="Login" value="Login">
    </li>
  </ul>
</div>
</form>
```

Although we have been able to customize the markup considerably, Zend_Form does allow for even more complex customization. Whether you do that by building your own custom decorators, which extend Zend_Decorator_Abstract, or with custom view helper scripts, or even just using your own view scripts, is dependent on your particular needs. We do suggest that you look at keeping your HTML as simple as possible and do as much styling as possible using CSS.

STYLING WITH CSS

For the sake of completeness, we'll finish building our form by demonstrating the changes that even the small amount of CSS shown in listing 8.15 can make to the simple HTML our new decorator settings produce.

Listing 8.15 The form.css CSS styles used to style our login form

```
form div#loginDiv {width: 400px; }

form ul {
   list-style: none;
   margin: 0;
   padding: 0;
}

form ul li {
   margin: 0;
   clear: both;
   border-top: 1px dotted #666;
   padding: 0.5em 0;
}

label.leftalign {
```

```
        display: block;
        float: left;
        font-weight: bold;
        padding-right: 10px;
        line-height: 1.6em;
        text-align: right;
        width: 100px;
    }

    form li.submit {padding-left: 110px; }
```

In figure 8.5, we can see how these CSS styles improve our login form by aligning the labels to the left and adding borders to differentiate the form fields. We could clearly have gone further, had styling forms with CSS been the focus of this book.

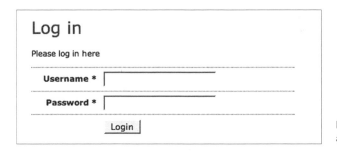

Figure 8.5   Our login redecorated and styled with CSS

Our basic login form now not only is translatable and filters, validates, and produces custom error messages, but it can be styled to suit the requirements of our application too.

8.5   *Summary*

We hope you're confident about using `Zend_Form` and more aware of the flexibility it provides. The benefits of using `Zend_Form` become more apparent as you build up a library of components that can be used in various applications. Separating out your forms into subclasses of `Zend_Form` as we have done also improves the structure of your application and makes testing easier.

Unfortunately, there is much that we could not cover, such as using subforms and exploring the customization options, but `Zend_Form` has enough functionality to fill several chapters, and we need to move on. A great place to get more information on `Zend_Form` is from the blog of our technical proofreader, Matthew Weier O'Phinney, at http://weierophinney.net/matthew/.

Searching

9

This chapter covers

- The Zend_Search_Lucene component
- How to add a search page to a real-world application
- The Observer pattern and how it helps code separation

One feature that separates an excellent website from a mediocre one is *search*. It doesn't matter how good your navigation system is, your users are used to Google and expect that they can search your website to find what they're looking for. If they can't search, or if the search doesn't return useful results, they'll try another site and another until they find one that does. A good search system is hard to write, but Zend Framework provides the Zend_Search_Lucene component to make it easier.

In this chapter, we'll look at how search should work for the user and at how the Zend_Search_Lucene component works. We'll then integrate search into our *Places* website, looking at how to index a model and how to present results to the user.

9.1   *Benefits of search*

For most of us, we get the best from a website when we successfully read the information we came for. For an e-commerce site, this generally means finding the item and purchasing it. For other sites, we're generally looking for relevant articles on the topics that interest us. Searching is one way to help a user to quickly find the results they're looking for. A good search system will provide the most relevant results at the top.

9.1.1   *Key usability issue for users*

Users want only one thing from their search: to find the right thing with the minimum amount of effort. Obviously, this isn't easy, and it's a major reason why Google is the number one search engine. Generally, a single text field is all that is required. The user enters his search term, presses the submit button, and gets a list of relevant answers.

9.1.2   *Ranking results is important*

For a search system to be any good, it's important that relevant results are displayed, which requires ranking each result in order of relevance to the search query. To do this, a full-text search engine is used. Full-text search engines work by creating a list of keywords, an *index*, for each page of the site. Along with the list of keywords, other relevant data is also stored, such as a title, the date of the document, the author, and information on how to retrieve the page, such as the URL. When the user runs a query, each document in the index is ranked based on how many of the requested keywords are in the document. The results are then displayed in order, with the most relevant pages at the top.

Providing a simple search system using a simple database query is quite easy using PHP. The difficultly lies in ranking the results with the most relevant coming first. `Zend_Search_Lucene` is designed to solve this problem.

9.2   *Introducing Zend_Search_Lucene*

Zend Framework's search component, `Zend_Search_Lucene`, is a very powerful tool. It's a full-text search engine based on the popular Apache Lucene project, which is a search engine for Java. The index files created by `Zend_Search_Lucene` are compatible with Apache Lucene, so any of the index-management utilities written for Apache Lucene will work with `Zend_Search_Lucene` too.

`Zend_Search_Lucene` creates an index that consists of documents. The documents are each instances of `Zend_Search_Lucene_Document`, and they each contain `Zend_Search_Lucene_Field` objects that contain the actual data. A visual representation is shown in figure 9.1.

Queries can then be issued against the index, and an ordered array of results (each of type `Zend_Search_Lucene_Search_QueryHit`) is returned.

The first part of implementing a solution using Zend_Search_Lucene is to create an index.

Figure 9.1 A `Zend_Search_Lucene` index consists of multiple documents, each containing multiple fields. The data in some fields is not stored, and some fields may contain data for display rather than searching.

What's a full-text search engine?

A full-text search engine searches through a separate index file of the contents of the website to find what the user is looking for. This means that the content information can be stored very efficiently, because it's only used for finding the URL (or the means to work out the URL) of the page required. The search engine can also order the search results based on more complex algorithms than are available when using a simple database query. Hopefully, this means that the user is presented with more-relevant results at the top.

One consequence is that all of the content that is to be searched needs to be in the index file, or it won't be found. If your website contains static HTML as well as database content, this needs to be added to the search engine's index file.

9.2.1 Creating a separate search index for your website

Creating an index for `Zend_Search_Lucene` is a matter of calling the `create()` method:

```
$index = Zend_Search_Lucene::create('path/to/index');
```

The index created is actually a directory that contains a few files in a format that is compatible with the main Apache Lucene project. This means that if you want to, you could create index files using the Java or .Net applications, or conversely, create indexes with `Zend_Search_Lucene` and search them using Java.

Having created the index, the next thing to do is put data into it for searching on. This is where it gets complicated and we have to pay attention! Adding data is easily done using the `addDocument()` method, but you need to set up the fields within the document, and each field has a type. Here's an example:

```
$doc = new Zend_Search_Lucene_Document();
$doc->addField(Zend_Search_Lucene_Field::UnIndexed('url', $url));
$doc->addField(Zend_Search_Lucene_Field::UnStored('contents', $contents));
$doc->addField(Zend_Search_Lucene_Field::Text('desc', $desc));
```

```
$index->addDocument($doc);
```

As you can see in this example, the URL data is of field type UnIndexed, contents are UnStored, and the description is Text. Each field type is treated differently by the search engine to determine whether it needs to store the data or use it for creating the index file. Table 9.1 shows the key field types and what the differences are.

Table 9.1 Lucene field types for adding fields to an index

Name	Indexed	Stored	Tokenized	Description
Keyword	Yes	Yes	No	Use for storing and indexing data that is already split into separate words for searching.
UnIndexed	No	Yes	No	Use for data that isn't searched on, but is displayed in the search results, such as dates or database ID fields.
Text	Yes	Yes	Yes	Use for storing data that is both indexed and used in the search results display. This data is split into separate words for indexing.
Unstored	Yes	No	Yes	Use for indexing the main content of the document. The actual data isn't stored because you won't be using it for search results display.
Binary	No	Yes	No	Use for storing binary data that is associated with the document, such as a thumbnail.

There are two reasons for adding a field to the search index: providing search data and providing content to be displayed with the results. The data field types identified in table 9.1 cover both these operations, and choosing the correct field type for a given piece of information is crucial for the correct operation of the search engine.

Let's first look at storing the data for searching. This is known as *indexing*, and the Keyword, Text, and Unstored fields are relevant. The main difference between Keyword and Text/Unstored is the concept of *tokenizing*, which is when the indexing engine analyzes the data to determine the actual words in use. The Keyword field isn't tokenized, which means that each word is used exactly as spelled for the purposes of search matching. The Text and Unstored fields are tokenized, which means that each word is analyzed and the underlying base word is used for search matching. For example, punctuation and plurals are removed for each word.

When using a search engine, the list of results needs to provide enough information for users to determine whether a given result is the one they're looking for. The field types that are stored can help with this, because they are returned by the search engine. These are the Keyword, UnIndexed, Text, and Binary field types. The Unindexed and Binary field types exist solely for storing data used in the display of results. Typically, the Binary field type would be used for storing a thumbnail image that relates to the record, and the UnIndexed field type is used to store items such as a summary of the result or data related to finding the result, such as its database table, ID, or URL.

Zend_Search_Lucene will automatically optimize the search index as new documents are added. You can also force optimization by calling the optimize() method if required.

Now that we have created an index file, we can perform searches on the index. As you'd expect, Zend_Search_Lucene provides a variety of powerful mechanisms for building queries that produce the desired results, and we'll explore them next.

9.2.2 *Powerful queries*

Searching a Zend_Search_Lucene index is as simple as this:

```
$index = Zend_Search_Lucene::open('path/to/index');
$index->find($query);
```

The $query parameter may be a string or you can build a query using Zend_Search_Lucene objects and pass in an instance of Zend_Search_Lucene_Search_Query.

Clearly, passing in a string is easier, but for maximum flexibility, using the Zend_Search_Lucene_Search_Query object can be very useful. The string is converted to a search query object using a query parser, and a good rule of thumb is that you should use the query parser for data from users and the query objects directly when programmatically creating queries. This implies that for an advanced search system, which most websites provide, a hybrid approach would be used. We'll explore that later.

Let's look first at the query parser for strings.

STRING QUERIES

All search engines provide a very simple search interface for their users: a single text field. This makes them very easy to use, but at first glance this approach seems to make it harder to provide a complex query. Like Google, Zend_Search_Lucene has a query parser that can convert what's typed into a single text field into a powerful query. When you pass a string to the find() method, the Zend_Search_Lucene_Search_QueryParser::parse() method is called behind the scenes. This class implements the Lucene query parser syntax, as supported by Apache Lucene 2.0.

To do its work, the parser breaks down the query into *terms*, *phrases*, and *operators*. A *term* is a single word, and a *phrase* is multiple words grouped using quotation marks, such as "hello world". An *operator* is a Boolean word (such as AND) or symbol used to provide more complex queries. Wildcards are also supported using the asterisk (*) and question mark (?) symbols. A question mark represents a single character, and the asterisk represents several characters. For instance, searching for frame* will find frame, framework, frameset, and so on. Table 9.2 lists the key modifier symbols that can be applied to a search term.

Table 9.2   Search-term modifiers for controlling how the parser uses the search term

Modifier	Symbol	Example	Description
Wildcards	`?` and `*`	`H?t h*t`	`?` is a single character place-holder, and `*` represents multiple characters.
Proximity	`~x`	`"php power"~10`	Terms must be within a certain number of words apart (10 in the example).
Inclusive range	`fieldname:[x TO y]`	`category:[skiing TO surfing]`	Finds all documents whose field values are between the upper and lower bounds specified.
Exclusive range	`fieldname:{x To y}`	`published:[20070101 TO 20080101]`	Finds all documents whose field values are greater than the specified lower bound and less than the upper bound; the field values found don't include the bounds.
Term boost	`^x`	`"Rob Allen"^3`	Increases the relevance of a document containing this term; the number determines how much of an increase in relevance is given.

Each modifier in table 9.2 affects only the term to which it's attached. Operators, on the other hand, affect the makeup of the query. The key operators are listed in table 9.3.

Table 9.3   Boolean operators for refining the search

Operator	Symbol	Example	Description
Required	`+`	`+php power`	The term after the `+` symbol must exist in the document.
Prohibit	`–`	`php -html`	Documents containing the term after the `–` symbol are excluded from the search results.
AND	`AND` or `&&`	`php and power`	Both terms must exist somewhere in the document.
OR	`OR` or `||`	`php or html`	Either term must be present in all returned documents.
NOT	`NOT` or `!`	`php not java`	Only includes documents that contain the first term but not the second term.

Careful use of the Boolean operators can create very complex queries, but few users in the real world will use more than one or two operators in any given query. The supported Boolean operators are pretty much the same as those used by major search engines, such as Google, so your users will have a degree of familiarity. We'll now look at the other way to create a search query: programmatic creation.

PROGRAMMATICALLY CREATING SEARCH QUERIES

A programmatic query involves instantiating the correct objects and putting them together. There are a lot of different objects available that can be combined to make up a query. Table 9.4 lists search query objects that can be used.

Table 9.4 Search query objects

Type	Example and description
Term query	A term query is used to search for a single term. Example search: category:php ```$term = new Zend_Search_Lucene_Index_Term('php', 'category'); $query = new Zend_Search_Lucene_Search_Query_Term($term); $hits = $index->find($query);``` Finds the term "php" within the category field. If the second term of the `Zend_Search_Lucene_Index_Term` constructor is omitted, all fields will be searched.
Multiterm query	Multiterm queries allow for searching through many terms. For each term, you can optionally apply the required or prohibited modifier. All terms are applied to each document when searching. Example search: +php power -java ```$query = new Zend_Search_Lucene_Search_Query_MultiTerm(); $query->addTerm(new Zend_Search_Lucene_Index_Term('php'), true); $query->addTerm(new Zend_Search_Lucene_Index_Term('power'), null); $query->addTerm(new Zend_Search_Lucene_Index_Term('java'), false); $hits = $index->find($query);``` The second parameter controls the modifier: `true` for required, `false` for prohibited, and `null` for no modifier. In this example, the query will find all documents that contain the word "php" and may contain the word "power" but don't contain the word "java".

Table 9.4   Search query objects *(continued)*

Type	Example and description
Wildcard query	Wildcard queries are used for searching for a set of terms where only some of the letters are known. Example search: super* ``` $term = new Zend_Search_Lucene_Index_Term('super*'); $query = new Zend_Search_Lucene_Search_Query_Wildcard($term); $hits = $index->find($query); ``` As you can see, the standard Zend_Search_Lucene_Index_Term object is used, then passed to a Zend_Search_Lucene_Search_Query_Wildcard object to ensure that the * (or ?) modifier is interpreted correctly. If you pass a wildcard term into an instance of Zend_Search_Lucene_Search_Query_Term, it'll be treated as a literal.

Phrase query	Phrase queries allow for searching for a specific multiword phrase.
	Example search: "php is powerful"
	
	``
	$query = new
	Zend_Search_Lucene_Search_Query_Phrase(array('php', 'is',
	            'powerful'));
	$hits = $index->find($query);
	``
	
	or
	
	``
	// separate Index_Term objects
	$query = new Zend_Search_Lucene_Search_Query_Phrase();
	$query->addTerm(new Zend_Search_Lucene_Index_Term('php'));
	$query->addTerm(new Zend_Search_Lucene_Index_Term('is'));
	$query->addTerm(new
	Zend_Search_Lucene_Index_Term('powerful'));
	$hits = $index->find($query);
	``
	
	The words that make up the query can be either specified in the constructor of the Zend_Search_Lucene_Search_Query_Phrase object, or each term can be added separately. You can also search with *word* wildcards:
	
	``
	$query = new
	Zend_Search_Lucene_Search_Query_Phrase(array('php',
	'powerful'), array(0, 2));
	$hits = $index->find($query);
	``
	
	This example will find all three word phrases that have "php" as the first word and "powerful" as the last. This is known as "slop," and you can also use the setSlop() method to achieve the same effect, like this:
	
	``
	$query = new
	Zend_Search_Lucene_Search_Query_Phrase(array('php',
	'powerful'));
	$query->setSlop(2);
	$hits = $index->find($query);
	``

Table 9.4 Search query objects *(continued)*

Type	Example and description
Range query	Range queries find all records within a particular range—usually a date range, but it can be anything. Example search: published_date:[20070101 to 20080101] ```$from = new Zend_Search_Lucene_Index_Term('20070101', 'published_date'); $to = new Zend_Search_Lucene_Index_Term('20080101', 'published_date'); $query = new Zend_Search_Lucene_Search_Query_Range($from, $to, true /* inclusive */); $hits = $index->find($query);``` Either boundary may be `null` to imply "from the beginning" or "until the end," as appropriate.

The benefit of using the programmatic interface to `Zend_Search_Lucene` over the string parser is that it's easier to express search criteria exactly, and you can allow the user to access an advanced search web form to refine his search.

This covers our look at what you can do with `Zend_Search_Lucene`, and as you can see, it's a very powerful tool. Before we look at how to implement searching within a website, let's look at how to get the best out of `Zend_Search_Lucene`.

9.2.3 Best practices

We have covered all you need to know about using `Zend_Search_Lucene`, but it's useful to look at a few best practices for using `Zend_Search_Lucene`.

First, don't use `id` or `score` as document field names, because this will make them harder to retrieve. For other field names, you can do this:

```
$hits = $index->find($query);
foreach ($hits as $hit) {
   // Get 'title' document field
   $title = $hit->title;
}
```

But to retrieve a field called `id`, you would have to do this:

```
$id = $hit->getDocument()->id;
```

This is only required for the fieldnames called `id` and `score`, so it's best to use different names, such as `doc_id` and `doc_score`.

Second, you need to be aware of memory usage. `Zend_Search_Lucene` uses a lot of memory! The memory usage increases if you have a lot of unique terms, which occurs if you have a lot of untokenized phases as field values. This means that you're indexing a lot of non-text data. From a practical point of view, this means that `Zend_Search_Lucene` works best for searching text, which isn't a problem for most websites. Note that indexing uses a bit more memory too, and this can be controlled with the `MaxBufferedDocs` parameter. You'll find further details in the Zend Framework manual.

Last, `Zend_Search_Lucene` uses UTF-8 character coding internally, and if you're indexing non-ASCII data, it's wise to specify the encoding of the data fields when adding to the index. This is done using the optional third parameter of the field-creation methods. Here's an example:

```
$doc = new Zend_Search_Lucene_Document();
$doc->addField(Zend_Search_Lucene_Field::Text('body', $body, 'iso-8859-1'));
```

Now let's do something interesting with `Zend_Search_Lucene` and integrate searching into the *Places* website.

9.3   Adding search to Places

As *Places* is a community site, a search facility will be expected by its members. We'll implement a simple one-field search on every page in the sidebar so that it's very easy for users to find what they want. The search results will be displayed as in figure 9.2.

To achieve this, we're first going to create the index files used by the search, then we'll write the simple form and search the results page, finishing with the advanced search form.

9.3.1   Updating the index as new content is added

We have two choices about when we create index files: we can do it when data is added to the database or as a scheduled task using cron or another scheduler. The traffic

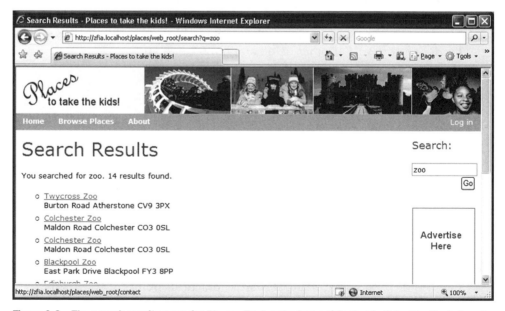

Figure 9.2   The search results page for *Places*. Each entry has a title that is linked to the indexed page, followed by a summary. The results are ranked with the most relevant at the top.

that the site receives largely determines how much additional stress these two methods cause.

For *Places*, we want to use both methods. Adding entries to the index as new data is added to the site is vital for a useful website. We also want the ability to re-index all the data in one hit so we can optimize the search index files as the amount of data on the site gets larger.

We'll start by looking at adding to the index as we go along because we can leverage that work for the full re-indexing later.

DESIGNING THE INDEX

We need to consider the fields that we're going to create in our index. The search index is going to contain records with different content types, such as places, reviews, or user profile data, but the results will be presented to the user as a list of web pages to view. We need to unify the set of fields in the index so that the results will make sense to the user. Table 9.5 shows the set of fields we'll use.

The basic code for creating the Zend_Search_Lucene_Document to be indexed is the same no matter what type of data we're going to be indexing. It looks something like the code in listing 9.1.

Table 9.5 Lucene field types for adding fields to an index

Field name	Type	Notes
class	UnIndexed	The class name of the stored data. We need this on retrieval to create a URL to the correct page in the results list.
key	UnIndexed	The key of the stored data. Usually this is the ID of the data record. We need this on retrieval to create a URL to the correct page in the results list.
docRef	Keyword	A unique identifier for this record. We need this to find the record for updates or deletions.
title	Text	The title of the data. We'll search on and display this within the results.
contents	UnStored	The main content for searching. This isn't displayed.
summary	UnIndexed	The summary, which contains information about the search result to display within the results. It isn't used for searching.
createdBy	Text	The author of the record. This is used for searching and display. We use the Keyword type to preserve the author's name exactly when searching.
dateCreated	Keyword	The date created. This is used for searching and display. We use the Keyword type because we don't want Lucene to parse the data.

Listing 9.1   Adding a document to the search index

```
function addToIndex($index, $class, $key, $title, $contents,
    $summary, $createdBy, $dateCreated)
{                                                          ⌐ Creates search
    $doc = new Zend_Search_Lucene_Document();    ◁─┘      document

    $doc->addField(
        Zend_Search_Lucene_Field::UnIndexed('class',
        $class));
    $doc->addField(
        Zend_Search_Lucene_Field::UnIndexed('key',
        $key));
    $this->addField(Zend_Search_Lucene_Field::Keyword(     ❶ Adds
        'docRef', "$class:$key"));                            each
    $doc->addField(Zend_Search_Lucene_Field::Text(           field
        'title', $title));
    $doc->addField(Zend_Search_Lucene_Field::UnStored(
        'contents', $contents));
    $doc->addField(
        Zend_Search_Lucene_Field::UnIndexed('summary',
        $summary));
    $doc->addField(Zend_Search_Lucene_Field::Keyword(
        'createdBy', $createdBy));
    $doc->addField(Zend_Search_Lucene_Field::Keyword(
        'dateCreated', $dateCreated));

    $index->addDocument($doc);    ◁─   Adds document
}                                  ❷  to index
```

This method creates a Zend_Search_Lucene document, called $doc, then we add each field's data to the document, specifying its type and name ❶, before calling addDocument() ❷.

Because we're going to be adding documents for every page on the website, we should make the creation of the document as easy as possible. We'll extend Zend_Search_Lucene_Document so we can instantiate the object with the right data in one line of code. This is shown in listing 9.2.

Listing 9.2   Extending Zend_Search_Lucene_Document for easier creation

```
class Places_Search_Lucene_Document extends Zend_Search_Lucene_Document
{
    public function __construct($class, $key, $title,
        $contents, $summary, $createdBy, $dateCreated)
    {
        $this->addField(Zend_Search_Lucene_Field::Keyword(
            'docRef', "$class:$key"));
        $this->addField(Zend_Search_Lucene_Field::UnIndexed(
            'class', $class));
        $this->addField(Zend_Search_Lucene_Field::UnIndexed(
            'key', $key));
        $this->addField(Zend_Search_Lucene_Field::Text(
            'title', $title));
```

```
$this->addField(Zend_Search_Lucene_Field::UnStored(
        'contents', $contents));
$this->addField(Zend_Search_Lucene_Field::UnIndexed(
        'summary', $summary));
$this->addField(Zend_Search_Lucene_Field::Keyword(
        'createdBy', $createdBy));
$this->addField(Zend_Search_Lucene_Field::Keyword(
        'dateCreated', $dateCreated));

    }

}
```

This class has a constructor that simply adds all the data to the fields we want to create. Using the new `Places_Search_Lucene_Document` class is extremely easy, as shown in listing 9.3.

Listing 9.3 Adding to the index

```
$index = Zend_Search_Lucene::open($path);          ◁──────┐         Create the document
                                                           │         in one line of code
$doc = new Places_Search_Lucene_Document(                  │
    $class, $key, $title, $contents,       Open the        │
    $summary, $createdBy, $dateCreated);   index           │
                                                           │         Add to
$index->addDocument($doc);            ◁────────────────────┘         the index
```

We now need to write this code within each model class that is to be searched over, and we immediately hit a design brick wall. The model clearly knows all about the data to be searched, but it should not know how to add that data to the search index. If it did, it would be tightly coupled to the search system, which would make our lives much harder if we ever want to change the search engine to another one. Fortunately, programmers before us have had the same basic problem, and it turns out that it's so common that there's a design pattern named after the solution: the Observer pattern.

USING THE OBSERVER PATTERN TO DECOUPLE INDEXING FROM THE MODEL

The Observer design pattern describes a solution that uses the concept of notifications. An *observer* object registers interest in an *observable* object, and when something happens to the *observable*, the *observer* is notified and can take appropriate action. In our case, this is shown in figure 9.3.

Our observable classes are our models, so we want to allow observers to register themselves with the models. The data we're interested in are instances of `Zend_Db_Table_Row_Abstract`, so we'll create an extension class called `Places_Db_Table_Row_Observable` that will contain the methods that allow us to register and notify observers. Listing 9.4 shows the class skeleton.

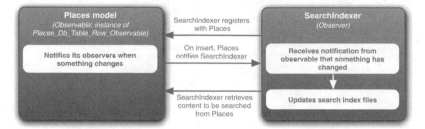

Figure 9.3   The Observer design pattern allows us to decouple the search indexing from the model data, making it easy to add new models to be searched or to change the way we index for searching.

Listing 9.4   The `Places_Db_Table_Row_Observable` class

```
class Places_Db_Table_Row_Observable extends Zend_Db_Table_Row_Abstract
{
    protected static $_observers = array();          ⟵  Creates array of
                                                          registered observers
    public static function attachObserver($class)
    {
        if (!is_string($class)
            || !class_exists($class)
            || !is_callable(array($class,              Ensures observer contains
                'observeTableRow'))) {                 observeTableRow()
            return false;                              function
        }

        if (!isset(self::$_observers[$class])) {       Adds observer to
            self::$_observers[$class] = true;          list if it's not there
        }

        return true;
    }

    protected function _notifyObservers($event)
    {
        if (!empty(self::$_observers)) {
            foreach (array_keys(self::$_observers) as $observer) {      ❶
                call_user_func(array($observer , 'observeTableRow'),
                    $event, $this);
            }
        }
        parent::_postInsert();
    }
}
```

The first two methods we need are the core of the Observer pattern. The `attach-Observer()` method allows an observer to attach itself. We use a static method because the list of observers is independent of a specific model class. Similarly, the array of observers is static because it needs to be accessible from every model class.

The `_notifyObservers()` method notifies all observers that have been attached to the class. This method iterates over the list and calls a static method, `observerTable-`

Row() within the observer class ❶. The observer can then use the information about what the event is and the data from the model to perform whatever action is necessary. In this case, we'll update the search index.

Zend_Db_Table_Row_Abstract provides a number of hook methods that allow us to perform processing before and after the database row is inserted, updated, or deleted. We use the _postInsert(), _postUpdate(), and _postDelete() methods to call _notifyObservers(), in order to update the search index. Each method is the same; _postInsert() is shown in listing 9.5 (except for the notification string).

Listing 9.5   Notifying the observer after an insert

```
class Places_Db_Table_Row_Observable extends Zend_Db_Table_Row_Abstract
{
    protected function _postInsert()
    {
        $this->_notifyObservers('post-insert');   ⟵——  Passes event type to
    }                                                  observer as a string
}
```

Let's look now at the observer class. This class is called SearchIndexer and, because it's a model, it's stored in application/models. The code to register it with the observable class is in the Bootstrap class in application/boostrap.php, and it looks like this:

```
SearchIndexer::setIndexDirectory(ROOT_DIR . '/var/search_index');
Places_Db_Table_Row_Observable::attachObserver('SearchIndexer');
```

As you can see, it's simply a case of setting the directory to store the search index files and attaching the class to the list of observers in Places_Db_Table_Row_Observable using the name of the class. The three main methods in SearchIndexer are shown in listings 9.6, 9.7, and 9.8.

Listing 9.6   The notification hook method: `SearchIndexer::observeTableRow()`

```
class SearchIndexer
{
    public static function observeTableRow($event, $row)
    {
        switch ($event) {
            case 'post-insert':              Adds to index only
            case 'post-update':              for certain events
                $doc = self::getDocument($row);   ⟵
                if ($doc !== false) {                          Retrieves data
                    self::_addToIndex($doc);   ⟵          ❶  from model
                }
                break;                         ❷ Updates
        }                                         search index
    }
}
```

The notification hook method, observeTableRow(), checks the event type, and if the event indicates that new data has been written to the database, it retrieves the data from the model ❶ and updates the search index files ❷. All that's left to do is retrieve the data from the model.

ADDING THE MODEL'S DATA TO THE INDEX

The process of retrieving the data from the model is a separate method, because it'll be used when re-indexing the entire database. This method is shown in listing 9.7.

Listing 9.7   Retrieving the field information: `SearchIndexer::getDocument()`

```
class SearchIndexer
{
    // ...
    public static function getDocument($row)
    {
        if(method_exists($row,                          ❶ Ensures that data-
                'getSearchIndexFields')) {                  retrieval method exists
            $fields = $row->getSearchIndexFields($row);
            $doc = new Places_Search_Lucene_Document(    ❷ Gets data
                $fields['class'], $fields['key'],            from model
                $fields['title'], $fields['contents'],
                $fields['summary'], $fields['createdBy'],
                $fields['dateCreated']);
            return $doc;                     Creates new
        }                                Zend_Search_Lucene
        return false;                         document ❸

    }
    // ...
```

The `SearchIndexer` is only interested in models that need to be searched. As the observation system can be used for many observers, it's possible that some models may be sending out notifications that are not relevant to the `SearchIndexer`. To test for this, `getDocument()` checks that the model implements the `getSearchIndexFields()` method ❶. If it does, we call the method to retrieve the data from the model in a format that is suitable for our search index ❷, and then we create the document ready to be added to the index ❸.

We now need to add a document to the search index. This is done in `_addToIndex()` as shown in listing 9.8.

Listing 9.8   Adding to the search index: `SearchIndexer::_addToIndex()`

```
class SearchIndexer
{
    // ...
    protected static function _addToIndex($doc)
    {
        $dir = self::$_indexDirectory;                Opens the
        $index = Zend_Search_Lucene::open($dir);    ❶ search index

        $index->addDocument($doc);    ❷ Adds document
        $index->commit();                and stores to disk
    }
```

Adding the search document to the index in `_addToIndex()` is really easy. All we need to do is open the index using the directory that was set up in the bootstrap ❶, then add the document ❷. Note that we need to commit the index to ensure that it's saved for searching on. This isn't necessary if you add lots of documents, because there is an automatic commit system that will sort it out for you.

One problem is that `Zend_Search_Lucene` doesn't handle updating a document. If you want to update a document, you need to delete it and re-add it. We don't want to ever end up with the same document in the index twice, so we'll create a class, `Places_Search_Lucene`, as an extension of `Zend_Search_Lucene` and override `addDocument()` to do a delete first if required. The code for `Places_Search_Lucene` is shown in listing 9.9.

Listing 9.9   Deleting a document before adding it

```
class Places_Search_Lucene extends Zend_Search_Lucene
{
    public function addDocument(Zend_Search_Lucene_Document $document)
    {
        $docRef = $document->docRef;                          ⟵  Retrieves unique docRef
                                                                  from document
        $term = new Zend_Search_Lucene_Index_Term(
                $docRef, 'docRef');
        $query = new Zend_Search_Lucene_Search_Query_Term($term);
        $results = $this->find($query);                      ⟵  Finds the
                                                                 document
        if(count($results) > 0) {
          foreach($results as $result)
          {
              $this->delete($result->id);                    Deletes current
          }                                                  documents
        }                                                    from index

        return parent::addDocument($document);               ⟵  Adds new document
    }                                                           to index
}
```

This method does exactly what we need, but it doesn't work! This is because the static method `Zend_Search_Lucene::open()` creates an instance of `Zend_Search_Lucene`, not `Places_Search_Lucene`. We need to override the `open()` and `create()` methods, as shown in listing 9.10.

Listing 9.10   Overriding `open()` so that it all works

```
class Places_Search_Lucene extends Zend_Search_Lucene
{
  public static function create($directory)
  {
    return new Zend_Search_Lucene_Proxy(
      new Places_Search_Lucene($directory, true));           ⟵
  }
                                                             Instantiates an instance
  public static function open($directory)                    of Places_Search_Lucene
```

```
  {
    return new Zend_Search_Lucene_Proxy(
      new Places_Search_Lucene($directory, false));
  }
// continue class...
```

The create() and open() methods in listing 9.10 are very simple but also very necessary. We need to update SearchIndexer::_addToIndex() to reference Places_Search_Lucene, as shown in listing 9.11, and everything will work as expected.

Listing 9.11 Correcting `SearchIndexer::_addToIndex()`

```
protected static function _addToIndex($doc)
{
    $dir = self::$_indexDirectory;                       ❶ Opens index using
    $index = Places_Search_Lucene::open($dir);              Places_Search_Lucene

    $index->addDocument($doc);             ❷ Adds document,
    $index->commit();                        removing duplicates
}
```

The method in listing 9.11 is the same as that in listing 9.8, with the exception of calling Places_Search_Lucene::open() ❶. This means that the call to addDocument() ❷ now calls our newly written method so we can be sure that there are no duplicate pages in the search index.

We now have a working system for adding updated content to our search index. We need only to implement the search system on the frontend so our users can find what they're looking for.

RE-INDEXING THE ENTIRE SITE

Now that we have the ability to update the index as new content is added, we can utilize all the code we have written to easily re-index all the data in the site. This is useful for supporting bulk inserting of data and also as a recovery strategy if the index is damaged or accidentally deleted.

The easiest way to support re-indexing is to create a controller action, search/reindex, which is shown in listing 9.12.

Listing 9.12 The re-indexing controller

```
public function reindexAction()
{                                                   Creates a new index,
    $index = Places_Search_Lucene::create(          deleting old one
        SearchIndexer::getIndexDirectory());

    $places = new Places();
    $allPlaces = $places->fetchAll();
    foreach($allPlaces as $place) {                 Adds each
        $doc = SearchIndexer::getDocument($place);  document
        $index->addDocument($doc);                  in turn
    }
}
```

The `reindex` action is very simple. It uses `Zend_Search_Lucene`'s `create()` method to start a new index, effectively overwriting any current index. To add each document, we take advantage of the `SearchIndexer`'s `getDocument()` method, which creates a document using the model's `getSearchIndexFields()` method, reusing the code and making this method very simple.

TIP   The re-indexing action should be protected using `Zend_Acl` if deployed on a live server. This is because a malicious user could repeatedly call this action, which would result in significant CPU usage and probably cause the website to slow to a halt.

We now have complete control over creating search indexes within the *Places* website, and we can look at creating a search form to allow the user to search and then view the results.

9.3.2 *Creating the search form and displaying the results*

The search form for *Places* is very simple. It consists only of a single input text field and a Go button. The form is available on every page, so the HTML for it is contained in views/layouts/_search.phtml as shown in listing 9.13.

Listing 9.13   A simple search form in HTML

```html
<h3>Search:</h3>
<form method="get" action="<?php echo $this->baseUrl;?>/search">
    <input type="text" name="q" value="">          <--  Creates text field
    <input type="submit" name="search" value="Go">  <--  for search terms
</form>
</div>
                        Creates Go button to
                           initiate search
```

The search form's action attribute points to the index action in the search controller, which is where the searching takes places. Because *Places* follows the MVC pattern, the searching takes place in the `SearchController::indexAction()` method, and the display of the search results is separated into the associated view file, views/scripts/search/index.phtml.

    Let's look at the controller first.

PROCESSING A SEARCH REQUEST IN THE CONTROLLER

This method performs the search and assigns the results to the view. It also validates and filters the user's input to ensure that we don't accidentally introduce XSS security holes. The controller action is shown in listing 9.14.

Listing 9.14   Filtering and validating for the search form

```php
public function indexAction()
{                                          Doesn't trust  ❶
    $this->view->title = 'Search Results';  user input

    $filters = array('q' => array('StringTrim' ,
      'StripTags'));
```

```
    $validators = array('q' => array('presence' =>
        'required'));
    $input = new Zend_Filter_Input($filters, $validators, $_GET);
    if ($input->isValid()) {
        $this->view->messages = '';
        $q = $input->getEscaped('q');
        $this->view->q = $q;

        // do search
        $index = Places_Search_Lucene::open(
            SearchIndexer::getIndexDirectory());

        $results = $index->find($q);
        $this->view->results = $results;
    } else {
        $this->view->messages = $input->getMessages();
    }
}
```

③ Validates

Ensures search query exists ②

④ Opens search index

⑤ Finds results

⑥ Assigns error messages to view

To use data provided by a user, we first have to ensure that it's safe to do so. The Zend_Filter_Input component provides both filtering and validation functionality. We use filtering to remove any whitespace padding on the search term and also to remove any HTML with the StripTags filter ❶. The only validation we do on the search term is to ensure that the user has provided it ❷, because searching for an empty string won't return useful results! Zend_Filter_Input's isValid() method filters the data and checks that the validation passes ❸. On success, we collect the search query text and reassign it to the view to display.

Having checked that the data provided by the user is okay to use, we can now perform the search. As usual, with Zend_Search_Lucene, we first open the index ❹, then call the find() method to do the work ❺. In this case, we can use the built-in string query parser, because the user can provide a very simple search query (such as "zoo" to find all zoos, or a more complicated one such as "warwickshire -zoo" to find all attractions in Warwickshire except zoos).

If the validation fails, we collect the reason from Zend_Filter_Input by assigning the return value of getMessages() ❻ to the view. Now that we have generated either a result set or failed validation, we need to display this information to the user in the view.

DISPLAYING THE SEARCH RESULTS IN THE VIEW

The view has two responsibilities: to display any failure messages to the user and display the search results. To display the error messages, we simply iterate over the list and echo within a list. This is shown in listing 9.15.

Listing 9.15 Displaying error messages from Zend_Filter_Input

```php
<?php if ($this->messages) : ?>
<div id="error">
  There was a problem:
  <ul>
    <?php foreach ($this->messages['q'] as $msg) : ?>
```

Sets id for styling output using CSS

Iterates over all messages for 'q'

```
      <li><?php echo $msg; ?></li>
    <?php endforeach; ?>
  </ul>
</div>
```

This is very straightforward, and the sole thing to note is that we iterate over only the 'q' array within messages because we know that there is only one form field in this form. For a more complicated search form, we'd have to iterate over all the form fields.

The second half of the view script displays the search results. The fields we have available are limited to those we set up in Places_Search_Lucene_Document, back in listing 9.2 and we use these fields in the output as shown in listing 9.16.

Listing 9.16 Displaying error messages from Zend_Filter_Input

```
<p>You searched for <?php echo $this->escape($this->q); ?>.      ◁──────
<?php echo count($this->results);?> results found.
</p>                                                        Uses escape() to handle
                                                              special characters

<ul>
<?php foreach ($this->results as $result) : ?>
<li><a href="<?php echo $this->getSearchResultUrl(        Retrieves
$result->class, $result->id); ?>">                        the URL
   <?php echo $this->escape($result->title);?></a>
   <div class="summary">
      <?php echo $this->escape($result->summary);?>     Displays the score
      <!-- (<?php echo $result->score;?>) -->  ◁──────  as a comment
   </div>
</li>
<?php endforeach; ?>
```

As with any response to a user action, we provide important feedback about what the user searched for and how many results were found. We then iterate over the results array, displaying each item's information within an unsigned list. The search results don't contain the URL to the page containing the result, so we need to work it out from the class and key fields that we do have in the search index. This is outsourced to a view helper, getSearchResultUrl() (shown in listing 9.17), to keep the code contained. The results are ordered by the score field, which shows the weighting of each result. The user isn't interested in this, but we may be; it's included as a comment so it can be inspected using the view source command when investigating search queries. Obviously, this can be omitted from a production application.

Listing 9.17 View helper to retrieve the search result's URL

```
function getSearchResultUrl($class, $id)
{
    $id = (int)$id;                        Ensures parameters
    $class = strtolower($class);           are "sane"

    $url = $this->_view->url(array('controller'=>$class,
            'action'=>'index', 'id'=>$id));
```

```
        return $url;

    }
```

The initial version of `getSearchResultUrl()` is very simple because there is a one-to-one mapping from the model's class name to the controller action. That is, for a model called `Places`, the controller used is places/index. It's likely that this would change when more models are introduced into the application. As this happens, the complexity of mapping from the model to the URL will increase and be completely contained within the view helper. This will help make long-term maintenance that much easier.

9.4   *Summary*

This chapter has introduced one of the exceptional components of Zend Framework. `Zend_Search_Lucene` is a very comprehensive full-text search engine written entirely in PHP, and it easily enables a developer to add a search facility to a website. We have looked in detail at the way `Zend_Search_Lucene` works and at how queries can be either a simple string like a Google search or programmatically constructed using the rich API to allow for very complex queries.

To put `Zend_Search_Lucene` in context, we have also integrated search into the *Places* community website. The search in *Places* is relatively simplistic, as it only has one model that requires indexing. However, we have future-proofed our code using the Observer pattern to separate the search indexing from the models where the data is stored. The result is a search engine that performs a ranked search algorithm and helps your users find the information they're looking for quickly, with all the benefits that this brings to your website.

10 *Email*

This chapter covers

- Introducing `Zend_Mail`
- Sending emails using sendmail and SMTP
- Integrating `Zend_Mail` into a Zend Framework application
- Creating HTML emails
- Reading email

PHP has a reasonably diverse range of functions for dealing with mail, from its `mail()` function, which most PHP programmers of any level will be familiar with, to its IMAP, POP3, and NNTP functions. Unfortunately, the latter need to be specifically compiled into the PHP installation, which means they may not be available for some users. In contrast, `Zend_Mail` is a fairly complete mail implementation that does not require any specific PHP configuration aside from the general requirements of Zend Framework itself.

We'll start this chapter with general information about how email works, then we'll go into more detail about the construction of an email message with `Zend_Mail`. From there, we'll expand on your practical knowledge by building a simple support tracker that we'll use while developing our *Places* application.

189

10.1   *The basics of email*

Whenever we need to describe technology to clients, we start by looking for comparable real-world examples, particularly appropriate when explaining email, because it's actually modeled on physical mail. Let's look at how email works and see what part `Zend_Mail` plays in the process.

10.1.1 *Email simplified*

Just as the complex routing process of physical mail can be reduced to simply dropping a letter in the mailbox and waiting for it to arrive in the addressee's letterbox, so it is with email, albeit many times faster. In the following example, illustrated in figure 10.1, we'll look at a fairly typical use of email in a web application, where our user, Bert, sends a message inviting his friend, Ernie, to sign up on this fantastic new website he has just found.

Bert starts by writing his message in the website's form and, once satisfied, clicks Submit, which sends the contents to the server in a POST, or occasionally a GET, HTTP request method. `Zend_Mail` then composes this information into email format and forwards it to the mail transfer agent (MTA). Since `Zend_Mail` defaults to using `Zend_Mail_Transport_Sendmail`, which is a wrapper for PHP's own `mail()` function, the expected mail transfer agent is sendmail.

Having accepted the email, the MTA routes any local mail to local mailboxes (that is, mail for domains with a DNS entry on the same machine) or, in the case of this email for Ernie, places it in the queue to be forwarded on. Once it clears the queue and is sent, the email will be bounced from server to server before finally landing in the receiving mail server where it awaits collection. From there, all that is needed is for Ernie to click Get New Mail, and his mail client (mail user agent, or MUA) will collect the mail using a protocol like the Post Office Protocol (POP3).

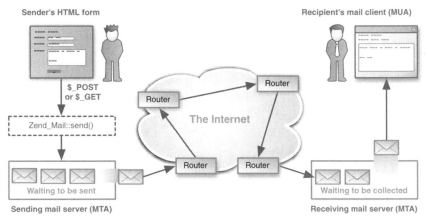

Figure 10.1   A simplified illustration of the processes involved in sending an email from an HTML form to its recipient's email client

10.1.2 Dissecting an email address

To go into a bit more detail about the routing of email messages, we need to look at the key component, the email address. The simplest way is to compare it to a physical address. Table 10.1 shows how the two compare. While Bert's physical location is indicated by an increasingly widening, or narrowing, depending on how you read it, geographic description, his email address similarly uses a series of suffixes to identify his network location.

Table 10.1 Comparing a physical address with an email address

Physical Address		Email Address	
Addressee name:	Bert	**Account name:**	`bert@`
Street address	10 Some Street, Sydney, NSW 2000	**Account domain:**	`bertsblog`
		Generic top-level domain	`.com`
		Country code top-level domain (additional and optional)	`.au`
Country	Australia		

Just as the responsibility for relaying physical mail lies with the sending parts of the various postal mechanisms and postal workers, so to do the sending MTAs handle the transfer of email. By constant referrals to the Domain Name System (DNS), the mail transfer agents work backward through the email address until the message arrives at the local domain. At each stage, the path taken is determined by the availability of servers, successfully passing firewalls, spam, and virus filters.

There's much more to the workings of email, but this is a good time to start looking at the main reason we're here: Zend_Mail. As well as going into some of its features, we'll focus on some of the details of email that Zend_Mail can take care of.

10.2 Introducing Zend_Mail

While the previous discussion portrayed Zend_Mail as having a fairly minor role in the overall process, it's nonetheless a pivotal one. Not only can Zend_Mail be used to send mail via sendmail or SMTP, it can also enable you to compose messages, add attachments, send HTML-formatted email, and even read mail messages.

10.2.1 Creating emails with Zend_Mail

An email needs at least three things before Zend_Mail can send it:

- a sender
- a recipient
- a message body

In listing 10.1, we can see how that bare minimum, plus a subject header, is perfectly adequate for Bert to send his invite to Ernie. All those familiar with PHP's own `mail()` function will immediately appreciate the way `Zend_Mail` encapsulates the mail composition in a much more pleasing interface.

Listing 10.1   A simple `Zend_Mail` example

```php
<?php
require_once 'Zend/Mail.php';
$mail = new Zend_Mail();
$mail->setFrom('welcome@greatnewsite.com', 'Support');
$mail->addTo('bert@bertsblog.com.au', 'Bert');
$mail->setSubject('An Invite to a great new site!');
$mail->setBodyText(
    'Hi Bert, Here is an invitation to a great new web site.'
);
$mail->send();
```

Now that we're looking at the composition of our email, the first thing worth mentioning is that the email produced by listing 10.1 is simple enough that it sits comfortably within the specification for email, otherwise known as RFC 2822. The specifications for email are handled by the official internet body, the Internet Engineering Task Force (IETF), and it's worth being familiar with some of this information because you'll see references to it elsewhere. For example, the Zend Framework manual states that one of the validation classes, `Zend_Validate_EmailAddress`, "will match any valid email address according to RFC 2822."

Unfortunately RFC 2822 is a fairly limited specification, and had Bert wanted to send an invite to his friends in non-English-speaking countries, he would have had problems without the Multipurpose Internet Mail Extensions (MIME). MIME is a collective name for a series of RFC documents that add additional functionality to the basic email specification, such as character encoding, attachments, and more. `Zend_Mime` provides the MIME functionality in `Zend_Mail`; it can also be used as a component on its own.

All that the code in listing 10.1 really does is define a few headers followed by the body, then it sends the email. Table 10.2 compares the role of that email content to the parts of a physical letter.

Table 10.2   Comparing a physical letter with an email

Physical mail		Email	
Envelope	Recipient and address	**Headers**	Sender name, recipient name, and more
Letter	The written contents	**Body**	The text of the message being sent

Just as you may want to send a picture of your kids in a physical letter, you can add images as attachments with `Zend_Mail` by using a line like this:

```
$mail->createAttachment($pictureOfKids);
```

Having dropped that important picture into your physical envelope, you could then write a warning on the envelope: "Photographs—Do NOT Bend." With `Zend_Mail`, we could theoretically do the same thing by adding additional headers:

```
$mail->addHeader('PhotoWarningNote', 'Photographs - Do NOT Bend');
```

Of course, just as the note on the envelope will likely be ignored, so too will that header, because `PhotoWarningNote` isn't a header recognized by any mail user agents.

Adding headers with PHP's `mail()` function is something a developer needs to take care with, because it's possible for a malicious user to add headers, such as further recipient addresses. This is known as *email header injection,* and you'll be relieved to know that `Zend_Mail` does filter all headers to prevent such an attack.

Now that we know how to create our email, it's time to look at the options available when sending it.

10.2.2 Sending emails with Zend_Mail

In `Zend_Mail` there are two ways to send mail: using sendmail or SMTP. Let's look at why you would choose one over another and what options are available with each.

SENDING VIA SENDMAIL

It was mentioned earlier in this chapter that `Zend_Mail` defaults to using `Zend_Mail_ Transport_Sendmail`, which itself uses PHP's `mail()` function. What that means is that, unless you decide otherwise, your emails are simply being composed and passed on to PHP's `mail()` function, and from there to the local sendmail (or equivalent) mail server, which handles the actual transfer of the email.

To illustrate more clearly how this works, we'll make use of PHP `mail()`'s option of passing additional parameters in the command sent to the mail server. In this case, we'll use it to set a header in the constructor of `Zend_Mail_Transport_Sendmail`, like so:

```
$transportWithHeader = new Zend_Mail_Transport_Sendmail(
                '-fwelcome@greatnewsite.com'
);
Zend_Mail::setDefaultTransport($transportWithHeader);
```

What that does is pass on `-fwelcome@greatnewsite.com` as the fourth parameter in the `mail()` function. `mail()` then sends that parameter in the following sendmail command, which sets the sender address of the email:

```
sendmail -f welcome@greatnewsite.com
```

Since all we're doing is sending a command, this method should be fast and incur little latency, but that is dependant on the setup of the machines it's being called and run from.

NOTE Because `sendmail` is a *nix command, it isn't even an option on Windows-based servers, which will default to using SMTP anyway.

SENDING VIA SMTP

There are occasions when you don't want to burden the local mail server with sending your mail. A good example would be when sending large volumes of mail in an environment where there may be restrictions on the amount of mail your local mail server can send. Another example would be ensuring mail sent from a web cluster has the same originating server, helping prevent your email being categorized as spam when it hits recipients' inboxes. In this case, it's possible to pass on the mail via SMTP (Simple Mail Transfer Protocol) to another service provider.

Because SMTP is the standard by which all mail is sent across the internet, our email is ultimately sent using SMTP even if we use sendmail. In this case, when we say "send via SMTP," we mean setting up `Zend_Mail` to send email through a specified outgoing SMTP server in much the same way that we set up our email clients to send our mail. In listing 10.2 we're setting up `Zend_Mail` to send via SMTP using the authentication required by the service provider and through a secure connection.

Listing 10.2   Setting up `Zend_Mail` to use an SMTP connection

```php
<?php
require_once 'Zend/Mail/Transport/Smtp.php';
$authDetails = array(
        'ssl' => 'tls',              Sets optional settings for
        'port' => 25,               secure transport layer
        'auth' => 'login',               Sets optional
        'username' => 'myusername',      authentication details
        'password' => 'mypassword'       for SMTP server
);
$transport = new Zend_Mail_Transport_Smtp(       Passes server and
        'mail.our-smtp-server.com', $authDetails  authentication details
);                                                to the constructor
Zend_Mail::setDefaultTransport($transport);   ◁⎯⎯
                                                 Sets SMTP as the default
                                                 transport method
```

Having set up `Zend_Mail` to use the SMTP connection, we're ready to use it, and since we mentioned sending large volumes of email, we'll start with sending multiple emails.

SENDING MULTIPLE EMAILS VIA SMTP

There are occasions when you may need to send several emails out in one go, such as when sending a newsletter to multiple users. However, in the PHP manual, the `mail()` function has the following note:

> It is worth noting that the `mail()` function is not suitable for larger volumes of email in a loop. This function opens and closes an SMTP socket for each email, which is not very efficient.
>
> —http://www.php.net/manual/en/function.mail.php

In contrast, when using `Zend_Mail_Transport_Smtp`, the SMTP connection is maintained by default until the object stops being used. Therefore, it's more suitable than `mail()` for sending larger volumes of email. Here's an example:

```
foreach ($users as $user) {
    $mail->addTo($user->email, $user->full_name);
    $mail->setBodyText('Hi ' . $user->first_name . ',
        Welcome to our first newsletter.');
    $mail->send();
}
```

If you're wondering why anyone would want to send such an uninteresting newsletter, you're ready for the next section, where we'll begin to use `Zend_Mail` in an actual application and make better use of the email body.

10.3 Building a support tracker for Places

The more you work on a project, the more you build up lists of bugs, issues, and feature ideas. These lists tend to end up all over the place—spread across emails, jotted down after phone conversations, scribbled illegibly in meetings. There are existing options for maintaining such lists, like bug trackers and project management applications, but they're often overkill for clients to use and, besides, that would be too easy! Instead we're going to build a solution, and since the key to good support is communication, our support tracker will do a lot of mailing. Our support tracker will also demonstrate `Zend_Mail`'s options for reading mail.

10.3.1 Designing the application

Our support tracker must:

- Be simple enough that we'll want to use it rather than a regular email client.
- Allow updates to bug statuses.
- Integrate with current user data and not require new usernames and passwords.
- Allow notification by email to all concerned.
- Have the ability to add attachments, such as screenshots, and send them with notification emails.
- Permit optional formatted emails for quick scanning.

The second requirement makes it clear that we're going to need to store this data, and figure 10.2 shows the initial table structure of our application. Since we could have many support issues for a single user, this is reflected in the one-to-many relationship of the schema.

If you've read chapter 5, you should be familiar with the use of `Zend_Db_Table` relationships and recognize the model in listing 10.3. By specifying the `$_dependent Tables` and `$_referenceMap`, we're defining the relationship between the existing `Users` class from our *Places* application and our new `Support_Table` class.

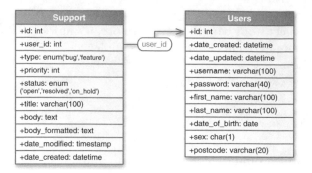

Figure 10.2 The initial database structure of our support tracker, requiring the addition of a single Support table alongside our existing Users table

---

Listing 10.3   One-to-many relationship using `Zend_Db_Table`

```php
class Users extends Zend_Db_Table_Abstract
{
    protected $_name = 'users';
    protected $_dependentTables = array('Support_Table');
}

class Support_Table extends Zend_Db_Table_Abstract
{
    protected $_name = 'support';
    protected $_rowClass = 'Support_Row';
    protected $_referenceMap = array(
        'Support' => array(
            'columns' => array('user_id'),
            'refTableClass' => 'Users',
            'refColumns' => array('id')
        )
    );
}
```

Linking these two classes fulfills the third requirement of integrating the current *Places* user data with the support tracker. Users will be able to submit support tickets without having to log in to a separate system.

In order to add support tickets, the least we're going to need is a submission form and the functionality to create an entry in the database. We'll start by creating a Support model class, as shown in listing 10.4, which will be responsible for the data handling.

Listing 10.4   Our Support model class

```php
include_once 'Support/Table.php';

class Support
{
    public function __construct()
    {
        $this->_supportTable = new Support_Table;
    }

    public function getIssues()
```

```
    {
        return $this->_supportTable->fetchAll();
    }

    public function getIssue($id)
    {
        $where  = $this->_supportTable->getAdapter()
                    ->quoteInto('id = ?', $id);
        return $this->_supportTable->fetchRow($where);
    }

    public function saveIssue(array $data, $id = null)
    {
        $filterStripTags = new Zend_Filter_StripTags;
        $filterFormat = new Zend_Filter;
        $filterFormat->addFilter(new Zend_Filter_StripTags)
                ->addFilter(new ThirdParty_Filter_Markdown);

        if (null === $id) {
            $row = $this->_supportTable->createRow();
            $row->date_created   = date('Y-m-d H:i:s');
        } else {
            $row = $this->getIssue($id);
        }

        $row->user_id = Zend_Auth::getInstance()->
            getIdentity()->id;
        $row->type = $filterStripTags->
            filter($data['type']);
        $row->priority = (int) $data['priority'];
        $row->status = $filterStripTags->
            filter($data['status']);
        $row->title = $filterStripTags->
            filter($data['title']);
        $row->body = $filterStripTags->
            filter($data['body']);
        $row->body_formatted = $filterFormat->
            filter($data['body']);

        $id = $row->save();
        return $id;
    }
}
```

Annotations:
- Passes support ticket data plus optional ID
- Sets up data filters
- Creates new Zend_Db_Table_Row object if no ID
- Uses existing database row data if ID exists
- Sets up row data
- Saves row and returns row ID

To provide some context, listing 10.5 includes other methods that are contained in our Support class. Since we're focusing on email in this chapter, the key method in our Support class is saveIssue(), because it's that action that will trigger the notification emails.

Until we add mail code, saveIssue() takes the support ticket data, decides whether this is a new ticket or an update to an existing one, filters the data, and saves it to the database. Listing 10.5 shows how saveIssue() will be called after a valid support-ticket form is submitted in our SupportController controller action class.

Listing 10.5   The addAction() method in our SupportController action class

```
public function addAction()
{
    $form - new SupportForm('/support/create/');
    $this->view->formResponse = '';
    if ($this->getRequest()->isPost()) {
        if ($form->isValid(
            $this->getRequest()->getPost()
        )) {
            $id = $this->_support->saveIssue(
                $form->getValues()
            );
            return $this->_redirect('/support/edit/id/' . $id . '/');
        } else {
            $this->view->formResponse =
            'Sorry, there was a problem with your submission.
            Please check the following:';
        }
    }
    $this->view->form = $form;
}
```

Calls saveIssue() after valid form submission

If you read chapter 8, you'll recognize that we're making use of Zend_Form to generate our support-ticket submission form in listing 10.5. There would be little value in
going through that code here, but for the sake of completeness and for a visual reference, figure 10.3 shows the final rendered form.

We can now move on to the fourth requirement, which is to notify support team
members when support tickets are added and updated. This also brings us back on to
the topic of this chapter: email.

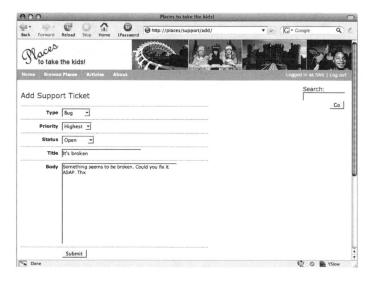

Figure 10.3   The support-tracker submission form used to send bug or feature requests to the development team

10.3.2 *Integrating Zend_Mail into the application*

You'll have noticed that there is no mail functionality in any of our code so far, and all saveIssue() currently does is filter the input and create the database row. The first question that arises is where to add the mailing code.

We know that the Support::saveIssue() method uses Zend_Db_Table_Abstract, which ultimately uses the Zend_Db_Table_Row::save() method for updating existing rows as well as creating new ones. This is a possible place to trigger the mail to the support team members.

In listing 10.6, you can see the contents of an example Zend_Db_Table_Row subclass, and how our save() method could override the parent class's save() method and add the notification email to the support team.

Listing 10.6 Overriding `save()` in our `Support_Row` subclass to trigger an email

```
class Support_Row extends Zend_Db_Table_Row_Abstract
{
    public function save()                        Calls the parent
    {                                             class's save() method
        parent::save();
        $mail = new Zend_Mail();                         Instantiates
        $mail->setBodyText($this->body);                 Zend_Mail, sets
        $mail->setFrom('system@example.com', 'The System');   up headers, and
        $mail->addTo('support@example.com', 'Support Team');  sends mail
        $mail->setSubject(strtoupper(
            $this->type) . ': ' . $this->title
        );
        $mail->send();
    }
}
```

In listing 10.6, whenever a call is made to the save() method, an email is sent to the support team with the support ticket information in the body of the email.

It isn't hard to see that this code is far from optimal. For example, when we later want to send a copy to the submitter, add an attachment, or perhaps format the body text, our save() method would have bloated beyond its purpose. With that in mind, let's refactor out the mailing code from the save() method and create a Support_Mailer class, shown in listing 10.7, which can focus on that task.

Listing 10.7 Our `Support_Mailer` class, which will send out notification mail

```
include_once 'Table.php';

class Support_Mailer
{
    public $supportId;

    public function __construct($supportId)        Passes support ticket
    {                                              ID to constructor
        $this->supportId = intval($supportId);
    }
```

```
function sendMail($html=false)
{
    $supportTable = new Support_Table;
    $supportIssue = $supportTable->find($this->supportId);
    $mail = new Zend_Mail();

    if ($html) {
        $mail->setBodyHtml(
            $supportIssue->current()->body_formatted
        );
    }
    $mail->setBodyText($supportIssue->current()->body);


    $mail->setFrom('system@example.com', 'The System');
    $mail->addTo('support@example.com', 'Support Team');
    $mail->addHeader(
        'X-Priority', $supportIssue->current()->priority, true
    );
    $mail->send();
}
}
```

Annotations pointing to code:
- Retrieves issue database row → `$supportTable->find($this->supportId);`
- Sets HTML body if required → `if ($html) {`

The `Support_Row::save()` method in listing 10.6 could now call our new mailing class and pass its `id` as a parameter, like so:

```
$id = parent::save();
$mailer = new Support_Mailer ($id);
$mailer->sendMail();
```

There is something dissatisfying about that, because we now have mail code embedded in a fairly low-level data-handling object. Ideally, we'd want to decouple the mailing function entirely from the data objects, and a good way to do this would be to use the Observer pattern that we discussed in chapter 9. Trying to do that in this chapter would distract from the main subject, email, so we're going to go part way by moving the `Support_Mailer::sendMail()` call to the last lines of the `saveIssue()` method in our more general `Support` class in listing 10.4:

```
$id = $row->save();
$mailer = new Support_Mailer ($id);
$mailer->sendMail();
return $id;
```

That puts it in an easier place to refactor out at a later date, and it allows us to move on to looking at the functionality of the mail class itself.

10.3.3 *Adding headers to the support email*

The fourth requirement in our application specification was that notification emails be sent to "all concerned." It turns out that this does not mean just to the support team at support@example.com. In fact, all admin users of the system are to be emailed, and the submitter is to be sent a copy as well. We also need to add a priority indication that email clients like Microsoft's Outlook and Apple's Mail can recognize.

Luckily, both of these are relatively easy to do and simply require working with email headers.

ADDING RECIPIENTS

For the sake of simplicity, our application stores the roles of users as a single field in the Users table, so to retrieve all admin users we need to use the following query:

```
$users = new Users;
$where = array(
        'role = ?' => 'admin',
        'user_id <> ?' => Zend_Auth::getInstance()->getIdentity()->id
);
$rows = $users->fetchAll($where);
```

You'll notice the additional term in the argument to `fetchAll()`, which filters out cases where the submitter is also an admin user. This prevents them from receiving an additional unnecessary admin email on top of the CC version they'll receive as a submitter. In some cases, you may actually prefer to send a different version to the submitter from the one sent to the support team, so this is largely an implementation preference.

Having retrieved all admin users, we can now loop over them and add them to the mail with a To header:

```
foreach ($rows as $adminUser) {
    $mail->addTo($adminUser->email, $adminUser->name);
}
```

Next, we'll retrieve the email details for the submitter by using her ID from `Zend_Auth`, and we'll add them to the mail with a CC header:

```
$users->find(Zend_Auth::getInstance()->getIdentity()->id);
$submitter = $users->current();
$mail->addCC($submitter->email, $submitter->name);
```

We also have the option of adding users with a BCC header by using `Zend_Mail::addBcc()`, but we don't need it in this case.

ADDING HEADERS

The `addHeader()` method can be used to set additional headers, with its first two arguments being the name and value pair of the header. A third Boolean argument indicates whether there will be multiple values for the header. The requested priority indication is an additional header that appears in the email as a `name:value` pair:

```
X-Priority: 2
```

We were clever enough to have preempted this requirement and designed our database field to contain an integer that corresponds to the value of the priority. Adding this value as a header is now simple enough, and you may have noticed the following line in our `Support_Mailer` code in listing 10.7:

```
$mail->addHeader('X-Priority', $supportIssue->current()->priority, false);
```

The arguments now specify that we're adding a header with the name X-Priority, that it's the priority value chosen for the current support ticket, and that it's a single value. The received email should have an at-a-glance indication of its priority if the recipient's email client recognizes the priority header.

We mentioned before that one reason to create our Support_Mailer class was to allow for expansion. One such example is the need to add attachments to the email, which we'll cover next.

10.3.4 *Adding attachments to the support email*

It would be a safe bet to say that there won't be a single developer reading this book who hasn't had bug reports with descriptions as vague as "it's broken" or "it's not working." Narrowing down the actual problem can occasionally be more frustrating than fixing it. In such cases, a screenshot of the offending page can be a great help, and that's why adding attachments to the support email is the fifth requirement of our application.

Once we add a file input field to the support-ticket submission form, the user will be able to browse for her screenshot file and have it upload when she submits the form. The process of dealing with the uploaded file isn't something we can do justice to in this chapter, but let's imagine it works something like this:

```
move_uploaded_file(
    $_FILES['attachment']['tmp_name'],
    realpath(getcwd()) . '/support/' . $id . '/'
);
```

This moves the uploaded file, which we'll call error-screenshot.jpg, to a subdirectory of /support/, using the support-ticket ID as its directory name.

Now that we have the file in place, we can attach it to the email with the code shown in listing 10.8.

Listing 10.8   Attaching the screenshot file to the support email

```
$file = "/home/places/public_html/support/67/err.jpg";      Gets general
$fileBody = file_get_contents($file);                        information
$fileName = basename($file);                                 about the file
$fileType = mime_content_type($file);

$at = $mail->addAttachment($fileBody);      Adds attachment
$at->filename    = $fileName;               to the email
$at->type        = $fileType;                        Sets optional
$at->disposition = Zend_Mime::DISPOSITION_INLINE;    settings for the
$at->encoding    = Zend_Mime::ENCODING_BASE64;       attachment
```

The optional settings in listing 10.8 are only needed if your attachment deviates from the default, which is a binary object transferred with Base64 encoding and handled as an attachment. In our case, we've specified that the attachment be displayed inline in the email just so we don't have to open the file separately to view it. As mentioned early in the chapter, settings like this are handled by Zend_Mime, so you'll need to look at its section of the Zend Framework manual for more information.

With the fifth requirement taken care of, that leaves the sixth and final one, which is to format the emails so they can be quickly and easily read by the busy admin team.

10.3.5 *Formatting the email*

The choice of whether to send text or HTML email is a contentious issue that is debated at almost every opportunity. Whatever your personal preference, as a developer you still need to know how to send either one, though, ironically, Zend_Mail makes the process easier than the choice.

SENDING HTML FORMATTED MAIL

As part of the input filtering in the saveIssue() method of our Support class, the body text is formatted as HTML using the PHP Markdown conversion tool written by Michel Fortin and based on John Gruber's original code. The formatted body is then saved in a separate field alongside the original, giving us two versions of the body to use in our email. You may have noticed in our Support_Mailer class in listing 10.7 that we allowed for this in the following code:

```
if ($html) {
    $mail->setBodyHtml($supportIssue->current()->body_formatted);
}
$mail->setBodyText($supportIssue->current()->body)
```

When we first introduced this code in listing 10.7, we made no mention of where it would be set. Since it is a personal preference, we could recover it from the current authorized user's information like so:

```
$mailer->sendMail(
    Zend_Auth::getInstance()->getIdentity()->mail_format
);
```

Even if your user has opted to receive an HTML version of your email, you also send a plain text version for those who find they can't or don't want to view the HTML version, as shown here.

FORMATTING WITH ZEND_VIEW

We now know how to send preformatted mail in plain text or HTML versions, but what if we want to do some formatting to the email body before it's sent? Earlier, while adding recipients, we mentioned that you may prefer to send a different email to the support-ticket submitter than you sent to the support team. This submitter email is the example we'll use to demonstrate how Zend_View can be used to render an email from the same kind of view script as used in our HTML pages.

What we have decided to do is send an email to the submitter that notifies them of the support ticket number, includes the body of the submission, gives a brief description of what will happen next, and thanks them. Listing 10.9 shows the plain text version.

Listing 10.9   Plain text version of support-ticket submitter email in text-email.phtml

```
Hello <?php echo $this->user->name; ?>,

Your support ticket number is <?php echo $this->supportTicket->id; ?>
Your message was:

<?php echo $this->supportTicket->body; ?>

We will attend to this issue as soon as possible and if we have any further
    questions will contact you. You will be sent a notification email when this
    issue is updated.

Thanks for helping us improve Places,

The Places Support team.
```

Unless you've jumped straight into this chapter, that should look very familiar, because it's much the same as the view scripts you saw in previous chapters. The HTML version in listing 10.10 is probably even more familiar.

Listing 10.10   HTML version of support-ticket submitter email in html-email.phtml

```
<p>Hello <?php echo $this->user->name; ?>,</p>

<p>Your support ticket number is <b><?php echo $this->supportTicket->id; ?></
    b></p>

<p>Your message was:</p>

<?php echo $this->supportTicket->body_formatted; ?>

<p>We will attend to this issue as soon as possible and if we have any further
    questions will contact you. You will be sent a notification email when this
    issue is updated.</p>

<p>Thanks for helping us improve Places,</p>
<p><b>The Places Support team.</b></p>
```

All that is needed to turn those view scripts into something we can use in our email is to have Zend_View render them, like so:

```
$mail->setBodyText($this->view->render('support/text-email.phtml'));
$mail->setBodyHtml($this->view->render('support/html-email.phtml'));
```

Figure 10.4 shows the resulting emails.

Clearly this is incredibly useful and simple, largely because it's the same process used for any view script, which makes it flexible enough to be used for anything from a lost password email to a more involved HTML newsletter.

Having completed the final requirement of our support tracker, we have now also covered the composition and sending features of Zend_Mail. This leaves us with the final link in the email chain: reading mail. Zend_Mail has thoughtfully provided functionality to do that.

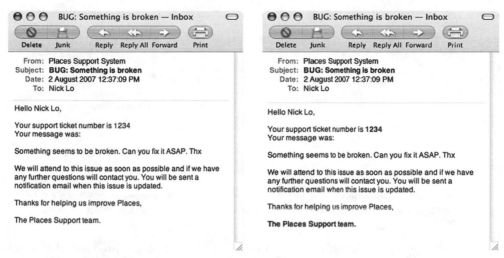

Figure 10.4 **Side-by-side comparison of the output of our plain text (left) and HTML (right) support-ticket notification emails**

10.4 *Reading email*

Our support tracker now has a web form that allows issues to be recorded and the support team to be notified, but it's very likely that issues will be coming from other sources, such as being sent or forwarded in an email. In order to deal with this, we're going to take advantage of Zend_Mail's ability to read mail messages. We're going to monitor a support email account and add issues from those messages to the support tracker.

Before we look at the requirements for this new feature in our application, let's look at some of the components for collecting and storing email.

10.4.1 *Collecting and storing email*

Earlier in the chapter, we noted that Ernie collected his invite from Bert using POP3, but he could have just as likely used the other main email collection protocol, IMAP. Since Zend_Mail can work with both, we'll take a look at the differences between the two.

POP3 AND IMAP

Our two characters, Bert and Ernie, make use of these two protocols to access their mail, and figure 10.5 shows the basic difference between Bert's use of IMAP and Ernie's use of POP3. As Ernie works out of a home office and rarely needs to access his mail from anywhere else, he uses POP3; Bert, who is always on the move, needs his mail to be available wherever he is, so he uses IMAP.

POP3 could be seen as the older and dumber of the two protocols, and it works on a connect, collect, and disconnect relationship, with the mail user agent (email client) having most of the responsibility. On the other hand, the fact that it's so simple, is

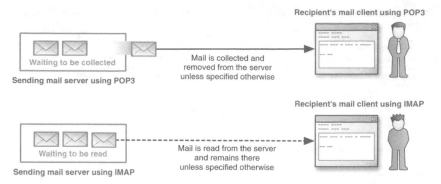

Figure 10.5 Comparing the main difference in email collection between POP3, which works on a simple connect, collect, and disconnect relationship, and the more capable IMAP

widely supported, and makes minimal use of server resources is the reason it's so widely used.

IMAP, in comparison, is a more capable protocol, and it has more responsibility in the relationship with the email client. Mail is kept on the server, and the email client requests a copy, which it will cache locally. Unlike POP3, IMAP allows an ongoing connection with the server, multiple client access to the same mailbox, email folders, server-side searches, partial mail retrieval, and more.

If you, like Bert, need to access your mail from multiple locations or multiple devices, such as a PDA, mobile phone, and laptop, IMAP would be a better solution, because each device would simply be accessing the mail rather than collecting it.

EMAIL STORAGE

In contrast to the official internet standards we have described so far, such as MIME, SMTP, POP3, IMAP, and the email format outlined in RFC 2822, the file format for email storage isn't standardized. Instead it's left to the developers of email clients.

`Zend_Mail` currently supports the Mbox and Maildir formats, and the key difference between the two is that the former requires application-level file locking to maintain the integrity of the message. There isn't much benefit going into great detail about the formats, so we can get back to working on our application.

10.4.2 *Reading email with our application*

We'll first jot down a few requirements for this additional work before we start. This list will make it easier to see exactly what we're trying to achieve and how `Zend_Mail` can help us accomplish it. So far, these are the requirements we've put together:

- It should periodically read mail from a designated mail account and store it in the support table.
- It should recover and store some details about the reporter.
- It should save the original email as a file attachment.

Before we can do anything with the stored mail, we first need to open a connection to it.

OPENING A CONNECTION

For the production version of our support tracker, it's most likely that we'd connect to a local storage location with either `Zend_Mail_Storage_Maildir` or, as in the following example, with `Zend_Mail_Storage_Mbox`:

```
$mail = new Zend_Mail_Storage_Mbox(
    array('filename' => '/home/places/mail/inbox')
);
```

For our example, we'll use remote storage because it's the one most readers will have access to and can start using right away with minimal setup. We could do so using `Zend_Mail_Storage_Imap` or `Zend_Mail_Storage_Pop3`. We'll choose the latter for its ubiquitousness, and connect using this code:

```
$mail = new Zend_Mail_Storage_Pop3(array('host'     => 'example.com'
                                    'user'     => 'support',
                                    'password' => 'support123'));
```

Our mail object now has a connection open, and we can start fetching messages.

FETCHING AND STORING THE SUPPORT MESSAGES

Because `Zend_Mail_Storage_Abstract` implements one of the standard PHP library iterator classes, it can be iterated over easily, so let's start with the first requirement of our application and look at storing the messages in our support table. Listing 10.11 shows the first implementation without filtering.

> **Listing 10.11 Turning the support email into a row in the support table**

```
foreach ($mail as $messageNum => $message) {              Uses x-priority header
    $data['priority'] = isset($message->xPriority)?       as priority setting
                  ➥ $message->xPriority : 3;
    $data['status']   = 'open';               Uses email subject
    $data['title']    = $message->subject;    as issue title
    $data['body']     = $message->getContent();      Uses email body
    $id = $this->saveIssue($data);                   as issue body
}
```

Combine this code with some way to run it periodically, such as with cron, and we've pretty well covered the first requirement. There are a few points to mention, the first being that we've not done anything about the `body_formatted` field of our support table.

When we entered the body information with the web form, it was put through the Markdown text-to-HTML markup filter. In this case, the body of the email could be plain text or HTML or both, which is referred to as *multipart*. If we enter an HTML or multipart email body directly into the body field, it's going to be a mess, so in listing 10.12 we'll check for that and reduce the body to the plain text content.

> **Listing 10.12 Reducing a multipart email to its plain text component**

```
$part = $message;                             Loops while Content-Type header
while ($part->isMultipart()) {                of $part contains multipart
```

```
    $part = $message->getPart(1);
}
```
> **Reassigns first part of multipart message to $part**

```
if (strtok($part->contentType, ';') == 'text/plain') {
    $plainTextContent - $part->getContent();
}
```
> **Checks that first part is plain text**

> **Assigns plain text content to a variable**

In theory, we could also insert any HTML part into the body_formatted field of our support table, but we'd then need to do some careful filtering of the data, and even after doing so we'd have to deal with all the varieties of HTML markup from the various email clients. Instead, we'll just pass the plain-text version to the text-to-html Markdown filter in Support::saveIssue() to give it basic but clean formatting.

This leaves us with the following adjustment and addition to the code in listing 10.12:

```
$data['body'] = $plainTextContent;
```

Even if we store a well-formatted version of the support email body text, there is the possibility that the issue, itself, may not provide us with all the information we need. For that reason, we'll also store the sender of the email so we can contact her for any further clarification.

In figure 10.6, we've added a reported_by field in our support table to hold this information and we'll need to add the following code to our Support::saveIssue() method in listing 10.4:

```
$row->reported_by = $filterStripTags->filter($data['from']);
```

We'll also need to add the sender to the code in listing 10.12 with this addition:

```
$data['reported_by'] = $message->from;
```

We could spend a bit more time breaking up that sender string into the sender's name and email address if we needed to, but for now it's sufficient for our needs.

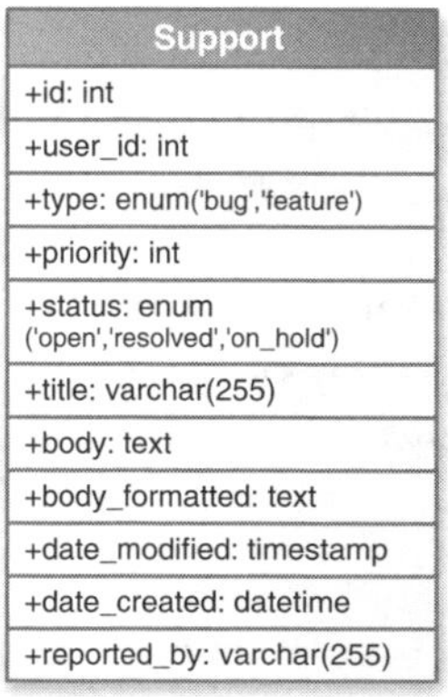

Support
+id: int
+user_id: int
+type: enum('bug','feature')
+priority: int
+status: enum ('open','resolved','on_hold')
+title: varchar(255)
+body: text
+body_formatted: text
+date_modified: timestamp
+date_created: datetime
+reported_by: varchar(255)

Figure 10.6   The support table with the new reported_by field which allows us to record the details of the sender of the support email

Our support table can now include tickets sent via email, but, as one last measure, we're going to save the email as a file attachment just in case we need to refer to it for whatever reason.

SAVING THE FETCHED MAIL TO FILE

When we loop through the support mail messages in listing 10.12, we recover all the text from the email we need and store it in the $message variable, ready to write out to a file. Listing 10.13 shows the code to do that, fulfilling the third requirement.

> **Listing 10.13　Writing the message out to a file**

```
$messageString = '';
foreach ($message->getHeaders() as $name => $value) {     ◁────  Loops over headers and
   $messageString .= $name . ': ' . $value . "\n";              appends to $messageString
}
$messageString .= "\n" . $message->getContent();    ◁───  Appends message content
file_put_contents(                                            to $messageString
   getcwd() . '/support/' . $id . '/email.txt',    ◁───┐ Stores in file in a
   $messageString                                          directory named with
);                                                         support ticket ID
```

This final addition means that not only are these stored text files a useful backup in case there are problems with the database insert, but they're also useful to pass around to other team members if needed. Let's now take a look at the full code.

THE FINAL READMAIL() METHOD

Just to wrap up properly, listing 10.14 brings together all the code we've written so far, so you can see how it all fits together. While you're looking over it, note that the filtering that occurs in Support::saveIssue() provides a level of security against any malicious code that could be included in the emails. We also use type hinting to ensure that the method is passed the mail connection we established at the beginning of this section, most likely by way of a controller action.

> **Listing 10.14　Adding read mail functionality to our Support class**

```
public function readMail(Zend_Mail_Storage_Abstract $mail)
{
   foreach ($mail as $messageNum => $message) {
      $part = $message;

      while ($part->isMultipart()) {
         $part = $message->getPart(1);
      }

      if (strtok($part->contentType, ';') == 'text/plain') {
         $plainTextContent = $part->getContent();
      }

      $data['priority'] = isset(
         $message->xPriority) ?
         $message->xPriority :
         3;
```

```
        $data['status']   = 'open';
        $data['title']    = $message->subject;
        $data['body']     = $plainTextContent;
        $data['reported_by'] = $message->from;
        $id = $this->saveIssue($data);

        $messageString = '';
        foreach ($message->getHeaders() as $name => $value) {
            $messageString .= $name . ': ' . $value . "\n";
        }
        $messageString .= "\n" . $message->getContent();
        file_put_contents(getcwd() . '/support/' . $id . '/email.txt',
                $messageString
        );
    }
}
```

We have satisfied all three requirements of our support tracker feature addition, and we've also given a short practical demonstration of some of Zend_Mail's read functionality.

10.5   *Summary*

Having read this chapter, you may well have discovered that email is a much deeper subject than you had anticipated. Since almost all web applications use email to one degree or another, we've attempted to give enough background so that you'll come away with not only a better understanding of Zend_Mail itself, but of how it fits into the bigger picture.

Adding Zend_Mail to the components we've covered in previous chapters also provides us with a good basic toolset we can use to build web applications. Before we continue adding to our arsenal, our next chapter on deployment will take a detour into some practices that will improve the way we develop such applications.

11 *Deployment*

This chapter covers
- Setting up a server for multiple websites
- Using Subversions to control versions
- Functional testing strategies with Selenium IDE and Zend_Http_Client

PHP and Zend Framework allow you to develop web applications rapidly, but they also present the temptation to cut corners while developing. Many readers will have experienced that sudden cold sweat after having accidentally deleted an important piece of code and frantically tried to fix a live site before anyone noticed! In this chapter, we'll run through development and deployment methods that can be used to ensure quality work without curbing enthusiasm. By providing a kind of safety net, the practices we'll discuss allow more freedom and confidence in the way you approach your work.

11.1 Setting up the server

We'll kick off this chapter by looking at the environment under which development will progress to final deployment. Just as the rehearsal stages of any theatrical performance are intended to prevent problems occurring in the live production, careful preparation through the proper setup of our server environment can avoid problems in our live implementations.

The typical development, staging, and production environments are set up as follows, whether on the same physical machine or spread across several:

- *Development*—This is the rehearsal stage, in which the application is developed, changes are made and tested, and the final production is shaped. Depending on the preferences of the individual developers, this may include one or several machines. Different configurations of development machines may also have the advantage of showing up bugs that might otherwise have been missed.

- *Staging*—Like a dress rehearsal, this stage should mimic the final production environment as closely as possible. No development takes place on this server, so any changes still need to be made on the development server and moved across to staging. This version is accessible only by the development team and anyone else concerned with moderating the release of the application.

- *Production*—This is the live public performance, accessible via the internet. No development takes place on this server, because it would not only potentially break a live site but also the chain of quality control.

For single developers and very small teams, using a development server to make local changes before committing to a production server would be a minimal requirement. Changes made and tested on the development server are only uploaded to the production server when all tests have been passed. Larger teams needing to coordinate local changes made by several developers before moving to a live production server would likely require a staging server.

It's worth stressing that what is "best practice" depends on the requirements of the team and the project. Each stage in the process adds administration requirements and costs that could stretch the resources of small teams and add to the complexity of low-budget projects. An ideal development environment is of little use if it introduces administrative delays that result in projects being late. We'll work through an example based on how we worked with some of the code for this book, and we urge you to take from it what's relevant to your particular needs.

11.1.1 *Designing for different environments*

One of the development goals for any kind of application is to be able to be deployed in different environments and work with minimal reconfiguration. Other than requiring PHP 5.1.4 or greater, Zend Framework itself has few specific requirements, so application portability is largely a matter of careful design.

Most of the differences between one implementation of an application and another occur during initialization where the configuration settings are read in. In a Zend Framework application, this differentiation most commonly occurs in the bootstrap file. In our *Places* application, we've separated the bootstrapping into its own class, to which we can pass the deployment environment as a parameter from the index.php file in the web root, as shown in listing 11.1.

Listing 11.1   The contents of our index.php file

```php
<?php

set_include_path(get_include_path() . PATH_SEPARATOR
    . '/path/to/zf-working-copy/trunk/incubator/library/'
    . '/path/to/zf-working-copy/trunk/library/' );
include '../application/bootstrap.php';
$bootstrap = new Bootstrap('nick-dev');
$bootstrap->run();
```

> **Sets paths specific to application environment**

> **Includes bootstrap file and instantiates with configuration section**

> **Runs application**

You'll notice that an additional benefit of this approach is that it allows us to set any environment-specific paths—in this case, to a local working copy of the latest Zend Framework core components as well as the "incubator" components.

In listing 11.1, we specified using the `nick-dev` configuration section by passing it as a parameter to the `Bootstrap` constructor before the call to `run`. Listing 11.2 shows a stripped-down version of bootstrap.php that highlights how the deployment environment is set and used when calling the configuration settings.

Listing 11.2   A stripped-down version of the `Bootstrap` class in bootstrap.php

```php
<?php
class Bootstrap
{
    protected $_deploymentEnv;

    public function __construct($deploymentEnv)
    {
        $this->_deploymentEnv = $deploymentEnv;
    }
    public function run()
    {
        $config = new Zend_Config_Ini(
            'config/config.ini',
            $this->_deploymentEnv);
```

> **Receives environment parameter from index.php**

> **Initializes and starts our application**

> **Sets Zend_Config_Ini to use the section nick-dev**

The second parameter passed to `Zend_Config_Ini` in listing 11.2 specifies that the section to be read from our config.ini file, which is the one passed from index.php (nick-dev). `Zend_Config_Ini` not only supports INI sections but also implements inheritance from one section to another. An inheriting section can also override values inherited from its parents.

In listing 11.3, we can see that the `nick-dev` section in our config file inherits from the general settings, as indicated by the `[child : parent]` syntax of the INI file. Therefore, the database settings are being reset to those of a local development database.

Listing 11.3   The contents of our config.ini file

```
[general]          ◁─────────
database.type = PDO_MYSQL           Specifies general INI section from
database.host = localhost           which all other sections inherit

[production : general]     ◁─────────
database.username = production           Specifies settings for final
database.password = production123        production server
database.dbname = production_main

[rob-dev : general]        ◁─────────
database.username = rob                  Specifies settings for Rob's
database.password = roballen123          development server
database.dbname = robs_dev

[nick-dev : general]       ◁─────────
database.username = nick                 Specifies nick-dev
database.password = nicklo123            settings
database.dbname = nicks_dev
```

What we've managed to do so far is to contain the implementation changes within the index.php file and the configuration file. Even better, we've managed to do it in a way that allows us to move those files around without having to change the files themselves. To demonstrate this a little further, let's take a look at Rob's index.php file, which never needs to move from his local machine:

```
$bootstrap = new Bootstrap('rob-dev');
$bootstrap->run();
```

Finally, on the production server is the untouched index.php file with its own setting:

```
$bootstrap = new Bootstrap('production');
$bootstrap->run();
```

Having set all that up, the only file that needs to move between environments is config.ini, which, because it contains the varying sections, can be the same file in use by all stages. Containing our application in this way simplifies the moving of files between hosts, whether you're synchronizing using your favorite FTP client or through a scripted deployment.

While we're on the subject of hosts, let's look at ways of setting up hosts for our development machines.

11.1.2   *Using virtual hosts for development*

Having outlined the use of separated hosting environments for the different stages of development, it's worth going through an example of how the hosting itself can be set up to accommodate this. In this section, we'll look at a brief example that uses the Apache web server on a Unix-based machine on a small local network.

Virtual hosting is a method of serving multiple websites from a single machine. The use of a single machine reduces not only the cost of hardware but also the time required to support and maintain that machine. The two main variations of virtual hosts are name-based virtual hosts that share the same IP address, and IP-based virtual hosts, in which each virtual host has its own IP address. For the sake of simplicity, we're using name-based hosting. Once it's set up, we should be able to access our separate development stages with URLs like http://places-dev/ and http://places-stage/.

TIP Zend Framework uses `mod_rewrite` to direct all requests via the front controller file. Combine that with its routing functionality, and you increase the possibilities of errors resulting from path issues. Setting up virtual hosts is one way to reduce the time wasted on path problems, because http://127.0.0.1/~places-dev can become http://places-dev/.

SETTING UP THE HOSTS FILE

The hosts file stores the information that maps the hostname to an IP address. Name-based hosting uses a single address for multiple names, so if we look at the hosts file in /etc/hosts we'll see the following entry:

```
127.0.0.1 places-dev
127.0.0.1 places-stage
```

The names `places-dev` and `places-stage` are both being mapped to the localhost IP address 127.0.0.1, meaning that any requests this machine gets for those names will be directed to its own web server. Rather than attempt to configure a full DNS, we're also going to configure the hosts file of one of the networked machines to point the same names to the IP address of the host machine:

```
192.168.1.110 places-dev
192.168.1.110 places-stage
```

Those settings in each network machine will ensure that requests to `places-dev` and `places-stage` will be directed to the IP of the machine acting as our web server. Remember that the IP address of the machine you're working with may not be the same as this example. That also applies to many of the settings in this chapter, including those in the following Apache configuration settings.

CONFIGURING APACHE

Having set up the hosts file, we now need to configure the virtual hosts in Apache's httpd.conf configuration file, as shown in listing 11.4.

Listing 11.4 Our virtual host settings in Apache's httpd.conf file

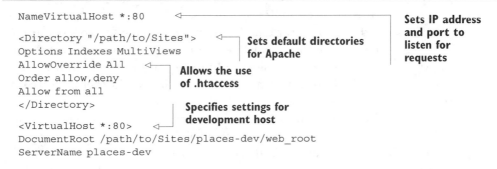

```
NameVirtualHost *:80                          Sets IP address
                                              and port to
<Directory "/path/to/Sites">      Sets default directories   listen for
Options Indexes MultiViews        for Apache                 requests
AllowOverride All          Allows the use
Order allow,deny           of .htaccess
Allow from all
</Directory>
                           Specifies settings for
                           development host
<VirtualHost *:80>
DocumentRoot /path/to/Sites/places-dev/web_root
ServerName places-dev
```

```
</VirtualHost>
                              Specifies settings
<VirtualHost *:80>            for staging host
DocumentRoot /path/to/Sites/places-stage/web_root
ServerName places-stage
</VirtualHost>
```

In listing 11.4, we can see that the NameVirtualHost directive specifies that anything coming in on port 80 will receive requests for the name-based virtual hosts.

The directory section defines a few general settings for all virtual host directories. One to note in particular is the AllowOverride setting, which allows directories to override certain server settings using .htaccess files. This is a requirement for Zend Framework-based sites because mod_rewrite is used to direct all incoming requests through the index.php file.

Each VirtualHost section defines the full path to the web root and the name of the server.

Having specified the DocumentRoot in httpd.conf, we need to create those directories:

```
$ cd Sites/
$ mkdir -p places-dev/web-root
$ mkdir -p places-stage/web-root
```

Now, when we restart Apache, it will pick up the new settings:

```
$ sudo apachectl graceful
```

If all went well, pointing our web browser at http://places-dev from either of the two machines whose host files we edited should take us to whatever files are located in /path/to/Sites/places-dev/web_root on the hosting machine. Of course, at this point there are no files in the hosting space. To get those files, we'll need to check them out of the version control repository.

11.2   *Version control with Subversion*

With Rob being in the United Kingdom and Nick and Steven being in Australia, working collaboratively on the code for this book wasn't as simple as shouting across a desk. In order to keep up with our changes, we needed to have some kind of version control system. There are many different version control systems with varying functionality, and the one we'll use for *Places* is the same one used in the development of Zend Framework: Subversion.

Subversion is an open source system that can sort, store, and record changes to your files and directories over time, whilst also managing the collaborative use of that data over a network. Getting acquainted with the process of version control, and with Subversion in particular, will allow you to work more closely with the framework's repository and also introduce you to a workflow that will further improve your deployment practices.

We're going to run through some of the day-to-day uses of version control using Subversion. Our intention is to give you an overview of the process and leave you with the confidence to investigate further.

To try some of the examples out for yourself you'll need to have access to a Subversion host. This is admittedly a bit of a chicken and egg situation; setting up a Subversion server is beyond the scope of this chapter. We'll therefore presume you have access, and we'll focus on setting up and working with a project in Subversion. (You can find information on Subversion online, or in books such as the *Subversion in Action* ebook by Jeffrey Machols (www.manning.com/machols).

11.2.1 *Creating the Subversion repository*

To store projects in Subversion, we first need to create a repository. Because creating a repository on a network drive isn't supported, this must be done locally using a drive on the same machine. To create the repository for *Places*, we need to enter the following command:

```
svnadmin create /path/to/repository/places/
```

The Subversion project officially recommends setting up three directories, trunk/, tags/, and branches/, under any number of project roots. The trunk is fairly obviously the main directory where the bulk of the action takes place. The tags directory holds meaningfully *tagged* copies; for example, we might decide to mark a stage in the development of *Places* in the context of writing this book:

```
$ svn copy http://svn.example.com/svn/places/trunk \
http://svn.example.com/svn/places/tags/chapter-04 \
-m "Tagging places as snapshot of development at chapter 4."
```

The branches/ directory holds *branched* copies of the filesystem, such as those we'd create if we needed to experiment with a significant change to the architecture of *Places*. We'll cover branching in a little more detail further on in this chapter.

Since we're setting up these directories locally and we want them to be under version control, we'll do so using the svn mkdir command:

```
$ cd /path/to/svn/places/
$ svn mkdir trunk
$ svn mkdir tags
$ svn mkdir branches
```

Having created the relevant directories, we can import the partial project we have started:

```
$ svn import /path/to/places file:////path/to/svn/places/trunk/ \
-m "Initial import"
Adding places/web_root/index.php
Adding places/web_root/.htaccess
Adding places/application

Committed revision 1
```

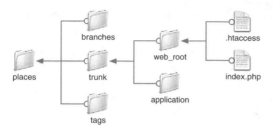

Figure 11.1   The *Places* Subversion repository after the first commit

Having created those directories and imported the start of our project into the Subversion repository, we're ready to start using it for development. Figure 11.1 shows the Subversion directory structure after the first commit.

With the basic structure in place, we now need to create a working copy on our local machines, which means checking it out from the repository.

11.2.2 Checking out code from the repository

Having set up the project repository to this stage, those of us on one side of the world can finish up for the day and leave the others, whose day has just begun, to add their work. By the time our morning comes, the repository is bursting at the seams with new files, which we check out as a working copy into our local development machine, as shown in condensed form in listing 11.5.

Listing 11.5   Checking out the latest work from the repository

```
$ svn checkout \
http://www.example.com/svn/places/trunk/ places/    ◁──┐   Specifies local
A places/web_root                                        │   Places directory
A places/web_root/css
...
A places/db
A places/db/test_data.sql
Checked out revision 2.
```

Once we've checked out a working copy of the files and made some changes, the next step is committing those changes back to the repository.

11.2.3 Committing changes to the repository

A commit sends changes from your working copy to the Subversion repository, usually accompanied by a short, descriptive message. At this point, it's worth developing some good *commit* habits, the main one being to keep the purpose of your changes as focused as possible. Just think of the other members of your team having to check out one big set of changes that could be scattered across multiple files and you'll realize how much additional work you have just given them, especially if your changes clash with any of theirs. You'll also notice any lack of focus when your commit messages start becoming unclear and difficult to write. Most teams will have at least a few basic commit guidelines, such as including issue-tracker reference numbers in the commit message.

Going through our new working copy of *Places*, the first thing we notice is that the database settings in the config.ini file are different from those needed for our local database server, so we will need to change them. For now, we can make a copy, which we'll call config.ini.default, and use the original to get the local application working. Ultimately, we'll set the config file up more consistently, but for now let's commit config.ini.default, as shown in listing 11.6, so that any further commits won't write over our individual config files.

Listing 11.6   Committing our changes to the repository

```
$ cd ~/Sites/places
$ svn status |                                              Gets feedback on the status
? application/configuration/config.ini.default             of the working copy
$ svn add application/configuration/config.ini.default
A application/configuration/config.ini.default
$ svn status
A application/configuration/config.ini.default             Commits working copy
$ svn commit -m "Added .default config file."        ⟵    to the repository
Adding application/configuration/config.ini.default
Transmitting file data ......
Committed revision 3.
```

In listing 11.6, you may have noticed the repeated status checks. To be sure that your working copy is as you expect, it's good to get into the habit of checking its status before performing any further action.

Since each user of our repository will also be committing changes, we're going to need to keep up to date with those changes by using the svn update command.

11.2.4   *Updating a local working copy*

At each stage of development, we need to check on the status of our working copy and make sure it's up to date with the repository. Not surprisingly, the svn update command takes care of updating a local working copy with the latest changes, and those changes are indicated by the output of the command. In listing 11.7 we perform an update of our working copy.

Listing 11.7   Updating our working copy from the repository

```
$ cd ~/Sites/places              Checks status of working
$ svn status      ⟵              copy before proceeding
$ svn update      ⟵
A application/classes                        Initiates the
A application/classes/Places                 update action
A application/classes/Places/Controller
A application/classes/Places/Controller/Action
A application/classes/Places/Controller/Action/Helper
A application/classes/Places/Controller/Action/Helper/ViewRenderer.php
Updated to revision 4.
```

As indicated by the letter *A* preceding each output line in listing 11.7, the ViewRenderer.php file has been added, together with its parent directories. This has been a simple update, and no changes conflict with our working copy. Sometimes, though, conflicts do occur, and we need to be able to deal with them.

11.2.5 Dealing with conflicts

Subversion is able to manage changes even when two people have edited the same file at the same time by simply combining changes as needed. Conflicts may arise, though, if changes have been made to the same lines of a file. For example, this is what you'd see when a later update results in a conflict with the file bootstrap.php, indicated by the letter *C* preceding the following file information:

```
$ svn update
C application/bootstrap.php
Updated to revision 5.
```

In figure 11.2, we can see that the update produced four variations of the conflicting file:

- bootstrap.php.r1110 is the original before our local modification. The "r1110" is the revision number of the file at the previous update
- bootstrap.php.r1112 is the most recent revision that someone else committed to the repository
- bootstrap.php.mine is our modified local working copy
- bootstrap.php contains the difference between the files, otherwise known as the *diff*, of both versions

Taking a look inside bootstrap.php, we can see the following conflicting lines:

```
<<<<<<< .mine
Zend_Controller_Action_HelperBroker::addPrefix(
   'Places_Controller_Action_Helper'
);
=======
Zend_Controller_Action_HelperBroker::addPrefix(
   'Zend_Controller_Action_Helper_'
);
>>>>>>> .r1112
```

This is roughly equivalent to the output generated if we were to run this command:

```
diff bootstrap.php.mine bootstrap.php.r1112
```

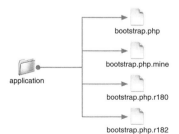

bootstrap.php

bootstrap.php.mine

application

bootstrap.php.r180

bootstrap.php.r182

Figure 11.2   The four conflicting variations of the bootstrap.php file after `svn update`

From this, we can see that our edit, .mine, removed the underscore from the end of the parameter string `Places_Controller_Action_Helper`, while the other edit changed the start of the parameter name to `Zend_` instead of `Places_`. After a quick discussion, we decide that neither of our changes is needed and we should revert to the version before either of our changes. This is a simple fix—we could either edit bootstrap.php or copy bootstrap.php.r1110 over bootstrap.php. For the sake of the example, let's edit bootstrap.php to contain only this line:

```
Zend_Controller_Action_HelperBroker::addPrefix(
    'Places_Controller_Action_Helper_'
);
```

Having done that, a quick status check indicates that while we've corrected the file, the Subversion conflict still exists:

```
$ svn status
C application/bootstrap.php
```

Since we've decided that, out of the four variations, bootstrap.php is now the file we want to use, we need to tell Subversion that the issue has been resolved and which file to go with:

```
$ svn resolved application/bootstrap.php
Resolved conflicted state of 'application/bootstrap.php'
```

Having done that, another `svn status` check indicates that the file is now marked as modified:

```
$ svn status
M application/bootstrap.php
```

The other three files have also been removed as part of the resolution process, leaving only the bootstrap.php file:

```
$ ls
bootstrap.php config.ini controllers views
classes configuration models
```

The final step is to commit the changes back to the repository and to add a message noting the resolution:

```
$ svn commit -m "Resolved change conflict with bootstrap.php"
Sending application/bootstrap.php
Transmitting file data .
Committed revision 6.
```

We've now taken a quick look at some of the common day-to-day tasks involved in using Subversion. There remain just a few topics that are worthy of mention, starting with getting a clean copy of our code from the repository.

11.2.6 *Getting a clean copy from the repository*

Subversion stores its information in its own .svn directories inside each directory in the repository. Those .svn directories are necessary while the content is under version control, but you may not want them in the final release, such as when you're going to FTP the contents to a server. Listing 11.8 shows how you can use the export command to get a copy from the repository, without all those hidden directories. (The output has been abbreviated.)

Listing 11.8   Using the export command to get a clean working copy

```
$ svn export \
http://www.example.com/svn/places/trunk/ places_export/    ◁──┐  Specifies source
A places_export                                                 and destination
A places_export/web_root                                        directories
...
A places_export/db
A places_export/db/test_data.sql
Exported revision 7.
```

Note that having performed the export in listing 11.8, we're left with the same files we would have had if we had done a checkout, but since they don't contain the .svn directories, they're not under version control.

One reason to export a clean copy of our code is so we can work it into another project or take it in a different direction. There is another way to take our code in a different direction though, by using separate branches.

11.2.7 *Using branches*

We gave an example of how tagging could be used to mark specific points in the progress of this book, but what about a bigger occasion, such as when we actually finish it? That would be an occasion to use the branching capabilities of Subversion:

```
$ svn copy http://www.example.com/svn/places/trunk/ \
http://svn.example.com/places/branches/its-finished \
-m "Woohoo, we've finished the book!"

Committed revision 200.
```

As the name suggests and figure 11.3 illustrates, branching creates a line of history independent of the main trunk. There are numerous reasons why we might decide to branch our code. Zend Framework branches on each official minor and major release, but we could equally decide to branch for a custom version of the main code or for an experimental version.

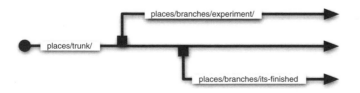

Figure 11.3   Branches in a Subversion repository

The subject of branching could fill a whole chapter, so this brief mention is really just to indicate its use, so you can look into it further on your own; again, the *Subversion in Action* ebook by Jeffrey Machols (www.manning.com/machols) has information on this topic.

The last topic to mention is how to include external code that your own code relies on.

11.2.8 Externals

While we're moving files between working copies and the repository, there is one element that has not been accounted for—our *Places* application is reliant on the Zend Framework code, which is external to our *Places* code. How do we make sure that the revisions in our code are matched with any external code dependencies? We can avoid having to deal with that by mapping one of our local directories to the external URL of Zend Framework's repository:

```
svn propedit svn:externals .
application/library/Zend \
http://framework.zend.com/svn/framework/standard/branches/
    ➥ release-1.5/library/Zend/
```

Now any checkout of the repository that includes that local directory will also check out the Zend Framework code. Notice that in order to avoid issues with mismatched code versions, we pointed to a stable release branch rather than a branch that changed too frequently, such as trunk.

One of the adages of version control is never to commit broken code, and one way we can assure that this doesn't happen is to thoroughly test our code before committing. In the next section, we'll look at one of the ways to test the systems we're developing.

11.3 Functional testing

Throughout this book, we've made a point of unit testing the code we've been working on. The combination of the thorough code coverage of Zend Framework's unit tests with application-specific unit tests should, from the programmer's perspective, provide ongoing feedback that the code is performing as expected. But even a system that successfully passes all unit tests may fall short in other areas, such as how the system functions in actual use. To test this, we need to move on to what can be somewhat broadly referred to as *functional testing*.

While the functionality of the system can be narrowed into more specific testing areas, such as its usability, security, and performance, we're going to outline more general methods of testing the system from the perspective of the end user. We'll attempt to test what the user can do with the system. For example, in security testing we could test whether a user that isn't logged in can access a restricted area.

Because we're most often developing web applications with Zend Framework, testing from the perspective of the end user is most closely mimicked via a web browser. The Selenium IDE testing tool does exactly this.

11.3.1 *Functional testing with Selenium IDE*

Selenium IDE is a tool for testing web applications the same way you use them: with a web browser. The Selenium IDE is a tool for recording, editing, and playing back actions. Once actions are recorded, you can run, walk, or step through them with or without start points and breakpoints.

What makes Selenium IDE particularly useful is that the PHPUnit unit-testing tool used by Zend Framework has a Selenium RC extension, which means we can integrate the Selenium IDE tests into our overall testing procedure. Hopefully you already have PHPUnit installed, so let's look at the installation of Selenium IDE.

NOTE   The installation of PHPUnit was discussed in chapter 3.

INSTALLING SELENIUM IDE

Since Selenium IDE is an add-on for the Firefox web browser, you need to have Firefox installed (available at http://www.mozilla.com/firefox/) before you can install the extension.

Selenium IDE can be downloaded from the Firefox add-ons page (https://addons.mozilla.org/firefox) or from the project's own download page (http://www.openqa.org/selenium-ide/download.action). The easiest method of installing the extension is to click the link to the .xpi file from within Firefox, and allow Firefox to handle the download and install.

RECORDING A SELENIUM IDE TEST

To record a test, select Selenium IDE from the Firefox tools menu, which automatically sets it in recording mode. Next, simply interact with the web pages as usual.

Let's record a very simple test that queries Google for "zend framework", then follows the links to Zend Framework's manual page. Follow these steps:

1 Navigate to google.com.au.
2 Enter "zend framework" in the search field, and click the "Google Search" button.
3 After the list of results appears, click the link to http://framework.zend.com.
4 On Zend Framework's home page, click the Documentation link and choose Reference Guide from the drop-down list to get to the manual.

Once you've finished performing those steps, you can stop recording by clicking the red button at the top right of the window. If all went well, Selenium IDE will have the recorded actions visible in its Table tab, shown in figure 11.4.

If all did not go well, you can either repeat the process, altering the steps as needed, or you can edit the steps you have already recorded.

EDITING THE TEST

If you're following along, you'll probably notice in figure 11.4 that we accidentally clicked the Downloads link on Zend Framework's home page. Since this was not the

Figure 11.4   Selenium IDE in Table tab with the results of the recording

aim of our test, we want to edit out that step. We can do so by switching to the Source tab of the Selenium IDE window, which will display the HTML shown in figure 11.5.

The lines that we need to remove from the source in figure 11.5 are these:

```
<tr>
    <td>clickAndWait</td>
    <td>link=Download</td>
    <td></td>
</tr>
```

They can be edited directly in the Source tab.

Having removed those lines, we can give it a quick run through by clicking the Play button.

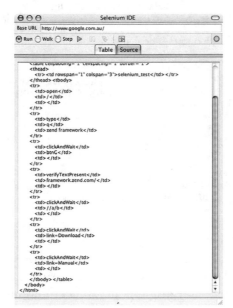

Figure 11.5   Selenium IDE in Source view with the results of our recording

SAVING THE TEST

If the test performs as expected, we can save it for future use. With Selenium IDE active, choosing File from the menu bar presents several options for saving tests. In this instance, we'll choose Save Test As, which will save the test in the default HTML format we saw in figure 11.5. It can be opened later and the test repeated as needed, ideally in an automated way.

11.3.2 *Automating Selenium IDE tests*

In the previous example, we recorded a single test and ran it completely inside the browser under what's called Selenium IDE's *test runner* mode. This is fine for single tests, but to make ourselves truly productive, we need to use Selenium RC, which allows us to run multiple Selenium IDE tests written in a programming language.

One of the supported languages is, of course, PHP, which is available as "PHP— Selenium RC" when saving the test via Export Test As. Unfortunately, at the time of writing, the resulting exported file contains code that is not only wordy but does not make use of the newer PHPUnit_Extensions_SeleniumTestCase PHPUnit extension. Listing 11.9 shows the exported Selenium IDE test as a PHPUnit test case, which we chose to rewrite to be more efficient. Whether you will need to rewrite your own tests will depend on updates to the Selenium IDE and personal preference.

Listing 11.9   Our Selenium IDE test as a PHPUnit test case

```php
<?php
require_once 'PHPUnit/Extensions/SeleniumTestCase.php';

class seleniumExampleTest extends PHPUnit_Extensions_SeleniumTestCase
{
    protected function setUp()          ◁──────────┐  Sets up default settings
    {                                               │  for every test
        $this->setBrowser('*firefox');
        $this->setBrowserUrl('http://www.google.com.au/');
    }

    function testMyTestCase()          ◁──────────┐  Replicates the test we
    {                                              │  did in Selenium IDE
        $this->open('http://www.google.com.au/');
        $this->type('q', 'zend framework');
        $this->click('btnG');
        $this->waitForPageToLoad('30000');
        try {
            $this->assertTrue($this->isTextPresent('framework.zend.com/'));
        } catch (PHPUnit_Framework_AssertionFailedError $e) {
            array_push($this->verificationErrors, $e->toString());
        }
    }
}
```

Notice that our test case is actually missing the part of the test we made with Selenium IDE that operates within the zend.com domain. Because Selenium RC runs partly outside the browser, we ran into issues with the same-origin policy, which prevents a doc-

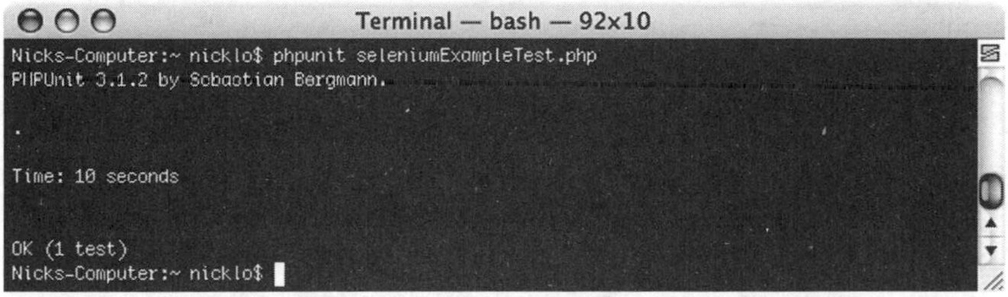

Figure 11.6 Running our Selenium IDE example unit test using PHPUnit through the Selenium RC Server

ument or script "loaded from one origin from getting or setting properties of a document from a different origin." The original test we recorded with Selenium IDE worked because it was running completely inside the browser as an extension. Selenium RC runs pages through a proxy, which partly circumvents the same-origin issue, but support for switching domains is currently experimental.

Having written our test, we're almost ready to run it, but because it relies on the Selenium RC Server, we need to downloaded that from http://www.openqa.org/selenium-rc/download.action and start it with this command:

```
java -jar /path/to/server/selenium-server.jar
```

Once the server is running, we're ready to run our test, as shown in figure 11.6.

Great! It passed. Now that our Selenium IDE test is written as a PHPUnit unit test, we can continue adding tests and incorporating them as part of an overall test suite that can be run from a single command.

11.3.3 *Functional testing with Zend_Http_Client*

As the manual states, "Zend_Http_Client provides an easy interface for performing Hyper-Text Transfer Protocol (HTTP) requests." At its most basic level, that is what a web browser like Firefox is. With that in mind, let's look at listing 11.10, which shows an example of the tests we ran with Selenium IDE rewritten to use Zend_Http_Client.

Listing 11.10 Our Selenium IDE test rewritten to use Zend_Http_Client

```php
<?php

set_include_path(get_include_path() . PATH_SEPARATOR . '/path/to/zend/
   library/');
include_once 'Zend/Http/Client.php';

class ZendHttpTest extends PHPUnit_Framework_TestCase
{
   public function testLoadGoogle()
   {
      $client = new Zend_Http_Client(
         'http://www.google.com.au/'
```

```
        );
        $response = $client->request();           |——      Asserts request to
        $this->assertContains(                     |        Google contains HTML
            '</from>', $response->getBody()
        );                                     <——
    }

    public function testQueryGoogle()
    {
        $client = new Zend_Http_Client(
        'http://www.google.com.au/search?q=zend+framework'
        );                                         |——     Asserts Google
        $response = $client->request();            |       search query
        $this->assertContains('framework.zend.com/',|      contains a string
        $response->getBody());                 <——
    }
}
```

The similarities between the code for this and the previous Selenium IDE test are pretty evident, so there isn't any need to do much more than run the test. The results are shown in figure 11.7.

We had one failure due to the typo </from> instead of </form>. After correcting that, let's check the results of running the test again in figure 11.8.

Great! That passed, and just like the Selenium IDE-based tests, it can be easily incorporated into a test suite. Zend_Http_Client does not currently have all the capa-

Figure 11.7   One failure, due to a typo, on the first run of our unit test

Figure 11.8   The final unit test is successful

bilities that Selenium IDE has, such as the ability to test JavaScript, but it is a relatively simple way to make functional tests.

We're almost at the end of this chapter, but we'll briefly cover an aspect of deployment that will appeal to the inner laziness of all developers: scripting the deployment process.

11.4 Scripting the deployment

We briefly mentioned using the `svn export` command to get a clean version of a Subversion repository, which we could transfer via FTP to a production server. That solution would be useful if, for example, we're working with a client's production server over which we have no control. If we did have control over the server, there's no reason why the production server could not also be under version control and be updated with the `svn update` command. Since we've already spent a lot of time discussing methods of automating tests, the natural extension would be to automate the testing and deployment of our code between the different environments.

Unfortunately, scripting deployments is too deep a topic for a few paragraphs in this chapter, and it's also quite specific to each team's work requirements. We can, however, point you to Zend Framework's build-tools directory for inspiration. This is available at http://framework.zend.com/svn/framework/build-tools/ and contains a series of shell scripts that export from the repository, generate the documentation, and generate the zip and tarball archives that can be downloaded from Zend Framework's download page.

Another option would be to run all automated tests and only continue with the deployment if all tests pass. The running of these deployment scripts can also be automated, perhaps on a scheduled basis, resulting in a form of "continuous integration."

11.5 Summary

This chapter's tour of deployment practices is admittedly more a taste than a full meal, but hopefully it has whetted your appetite for more information. Our reason for including a chapter on the topic of deployment was to illustrate that producing a quality product does not stop with just writing quality code and to give you a grounding in some of the approaches and practices.

We also wanted to demonstrate how some of the current Zend Framework components, like `Zend_Http` and `Zend_Config`, can be involved in the process. You can be sure that there will be an increase in the number of components specifically targeted at the deployment aspect of development.

Which of these practices you decide to implement will depend not only on your working environment but also on the needs of the projects you're working on. Ultimately, if this chapter has given you a clearer overview of the process and has inspired you to investigate any part of the topic further, it will have done its job.

Part 3

More power to your application

Chapters 12-16 cover the components that can be used to add depth to your applications, from integrating applications with XML-RPC and REST technologies to incorporating the wide variety of public web services available using the Zend_Service components. Web services introduce network availability issues that can be significantly decreased by caching—we'll cover this, along with the use of caching in improving overall performance.

Increasing the reach of your application will often include its international exposure, so we'll also look at the features within Zend Framework that help translate a web site into multiple languages. Finally, we'll round off the book by moving from web to print, using the Zend Framework components that create PDF files.

Following part 3 are three appendices.

Appendix A provides a short tour of the PHP syntax, for those coming from another language.

Appendix B describes the PHP5 object model, providing a leg up for those who have mainly programmed procedurally before using Zend Framework.

Appendix C provides tips and tricks to develop Zend Framework applications more easily.

Talking with other applications

This chapter will cover the use of various components of Zend Framework that can be loosely lumped together under the term "web services," which the World Wide Web Consortium (W3C) defines as "a software system designed to support interoperable machine-to-machine interaction over a network." For the sake of simplicity, we'll base our use of the term "web services" in this chapter on that definition, rather than on the more specific W3C focus on it being a combination of SOAP and WSDL (Web Services Description Language).

Part of that interoperation includes the use of XML, but one of the benefits of using these components is that we don't need to focus on XML itself. Zend Framework provides a series of tools that takes care of the formatting and protocol of the interaction, leaving you to focus on the logic using only PHP. If you take a moment to list all the formats available just for web newsfeeds, the benefits of not having to deal with that range of formats and their rate of change will be obvious.

Before we get into using the Zend Framework components, we'll take a look at how we can and why we would integrate applications using web services.

12.1   *Integrating applications*

It's interesting just how much web services have become a part of our offline and online existence. Every time Nick starts up his computer, a newsreader fires up and digests a list of XML-formatted news from sites that he could never keep up with otherwise. Recently his wife sold some of the clutter from their garage using GarageSale, a Mac OS X desktop application that talks to eBay using its XML-based API over HTTP. The key to all of these actions is the exchange of information across a network, and the distribution of the computing.

12.1.1 *Exchanging structured data*

XML stands for Extensible Markup Language and originates from Standard Generalized Markup Language (SGML), which is one of the many markup languages whose role is simply to describe text. Probably the best known is HTML (Hypertext Markup Language), which describes text documents that are intended to be transmitted by HTTP.

Data does not need to be marked up to be exchanged, but in most cases it does need to have some kind of structure. Here are some examples:

- comma- or tab-separated values (CSV or TSV)
- structured text that bases its structure on a regular sequence of data separated by consistent delimiters
- serialized data such as that created by PHP's own `serialize()` function
- other formats like JavaScript Object Notation (JSON), which can be used as an alternative to XML in AJAX (and which is accommodated for in Zend Framework by `Zend_Json`)

Little of this information should be new to readers of this book, but the point is we're trying to pass information from one system to another such that the recipient system knows how to handle that data.

If we take a look at the GarageSale application in figure 12.1, it's clearly a fairly complex application whose data could not be exchanged unless it were suitably structured so that eBay could process it and carry out whatever requests it makes, such as creating a new item for auction.

Having looked at the formatting of the data involved in this discussion between applications, the next question is how the applications talk to each other.

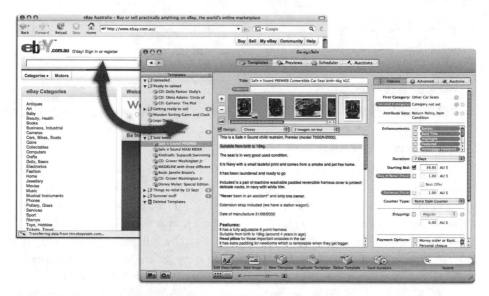

Figure 12.1   The GarageSale Mac OS X desktop application, which converses with eBay's XML-based API using web services

12.1.2 *Producing and consuming structured data*

Email serves as a good example of how applications talk to each other using a structured data format (internet email format) that is produced at one end, sent by a mail server (MTA), and consumed by the receiving email client (MUA) at the other end. The application conversations we're looking at in this chapter take that basic concept a step further by using that exchange to trigger actions at either end through what's known as a remote procedure call (RPC).

Later in this chapter, we'll be covering `Zend_XmlRpc`, which uses `Zend_XmlRpc_Server` to send and receive XML-encoded RPCs over HTTP. Originally created by Dave Winer, XML-RPC is a surprisingly simple and flexible specification, which allows it to be used in numerous situations.

As functionality was added, XML-RPC evolved into SOAP (originally an acronym, but now just a word in itself) and has been adopted by the W3C. You don't need to look too far to find complaints about how this added functionality has also added a lot more complexity, which partly explains why XML-RPC is still in use despite the official W3C adoption of SOAP. In some ways, SOAP is itself being superseded by other protocols like Atom. You can see the status of these protocols reflected in Zend Framework itself; `Zend_Soap` lingered in the incubator for over two years before being finalized, due in large part to lack of interest by users, while XML-RPC and Atom are both included in the core.

We'll look at Zend Framework's components shortly, but first we need to cover how web services work and why we would use them.

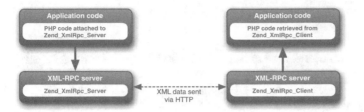

Figure 12.2 The basic web service transaction between two systems using XML-RPC

12.1.3 How web services work

The fastest way to present the simplicity of web services is with an illustration like figure 12.2. At their most basic, web services work like many other data-transmission methods, formatting some data (such as into XML format with XML-RPC) at one end, passing it via some protocol (HTTP, in this case), and using it at the other end.

Of course, that explanation is so generic as to be fairly worthless, so to further illustrate how web services work, let's follow the steps of an XML-RPC example in which a desktop application needs to get updated prices from an online service:

1 A desktop application gathers the data required to make a procedure call (including the ID of the requested item and the remote procedure that gets the prices for items). The XML-RPC client component of the desktop application encodes this remote procedure call into XML format and sends it to the online service like so:

```
<?xml version="1.0"?>
<methodCall>
    <methodName>onlineStore.getPriceForItem</methodName>
    <params>
       <param>
          <value><i4>123</i4></value>
       </param>
    </params>
</methodCall>
```

2 The XML-RPC server of the online service receives the XML-encoded procedure call and decodes it into a format that the system code can process, such as `$store->getPriceForItem(123)`. The system code returns the requested price to its XML-RPC server, which encodes that as an XML response and sends it back to the requesting desktop application:

```
<?xml version="1.0"?>
<methodResponse>
   <params>
     <param>
       <value><double>19.95</double></value>
     </param>
   </params>
</methodResponse>
```

3 The desktop application receives the response, decodes it into a format it can process, and updates the price for item 123 to $19.95.

That should give you an idea of how web services work, but the question remains as to why we need to use them.

12.1.4 Why we need web services

So why do we need web services? The simple answer is also the most ironic: we need web services so that applications running on different platforms or frameworks can talk to each other in a standard way. This chapter has already started to point out the irony in that concept by, in all likelihood, confusing you with a small selection of the varied protocols that make up these "standards."

Pushing this cynicism aside, and returning to the example of our desktop application fetching updated prices from the online service, you'll notice that there was little detail about how each end of the transaction actually performed its procedure calls. The reason is it doesn't matter, because as long as each application is able to convert its internal processes into a standard form of communication—the XML-RPC protocol—the transaction can be completed.

Clearly this can lead to very powerful interactions, such as the one between GarageSale and eBay. In this chapter and the next, we'll look at examples of how Zend Framework components can bypass some of the complexities of web services to take advantage of such interactions.

We'll start with an example that most readers are probably familiar with: web feeds and the benefits of using `Zend_Feed` to produce and consume them.

12.2 Producing and consuming feeds with Zend_Feed

Zend Framework's online manual describes `Zend_Feed` as providing "functionality for consuming RSS and Atom feeds." We're going to start from the opposite end of that transaction by showing how it can also be used to produce RSS and Atom feeds. We'll then look at examples of consuming web feeds.

12.2.1 Producing a feed

If you took up the challenge mentioned at the start of this chapter to list all the formats available for web feeds, you'd have started with the RDF or RSS 1.* branch, which includes RSS 0.9, 1.0, and 1.1. You'd then have moved to RSS 2.*, which includes RSS 0.91, 0.92, and 2.0.1. From there you'd have followed on to the Atom syndication format. If you did that while working under the pressure of a deadline, and then discovered that all these formats are currently in use across millions of syndicated sites, you'd have probably sat down in a cold sweat!

Fortunately, all you need to do is pick the latest and greatest formats and concentrate on outputting those. But even that isn't needed, because `Zend_Feed` can take care of the format for you; you just need to pass it the data for your feed. Listing 12.1

demonstrates a very simple controller action that produces an RSS (2.0) or Atom feed from the articles in our *Places* application.

Listing 12.1   A feed-producing controller action

```
require_once 'Zend/Feed.php';
require_once 'models/ArticleTable.php';

class FeedController extends Zend_Controller_Action
{
    public function indexAction()
    {
        $format = $this->_request->getParam('format');        ❶ Defaults format
        $format = in_array($format,                              to RSS if
            array('rss', 'atom')) ? $format : 'rss';            unspecified

        $articlesTable = new ArticleTable();                  ❷ Gets feed data
        $rowset = $articlesTable->fetchAll();                   from database

        $channel = array(                          ❸ Builds <channel>
            'title'       => 'Places',                element
            'link'        => 'http://places/',
            'description' => 'All the latest articles',
            'charset'     => 'UTF-8',
            'entries'     => array()
        );                                      ❹ Builds <item>
                                                   elements
        foreach ($rowset as $item) {                         ❻ Generates
            $channel['entries'][] = array(                      output
                'title'       => $item->title,
                'link'        => 'http://places/article/index/id/'
                                 . $item->id . '/',
                'description' => $item->body         ❺ Imports array
                );                                     into Zend_Feed
        }
        $feed = Zend_Feed::importArray($channel, $format);
        $feed->send();
        $this->_helper->viewRenderer->setNoRender();      Disables view and
        $this->_helper->layout()->disableLayout();      ❼ layout rendering
    }
}
```

In listing 12.1, we begin by determining the feed format, and if neither RSS or Atom feed format is requested, we default to RSS ❶. Next, we grab a selection of articles from the database to insert into the feed (this would likely be limited, but it is simplified for this example) ❷. A multidimensional array consisting of the <channel> element is then constructed ❸, with each <item> being added by looping over the rowset retrieved from the Articles table ❹. That array is then imported into Zend_Feed, along with the format in which it is to be encoded ❺, then it is outputted as an XML string ready to be digested by a newsfeed reader or aggregator ❻.

Note that we use the send() method, which sets the content type of the HTTP header string to something like this:

```
Content-Type: text/xml; charset=UTF-8
```

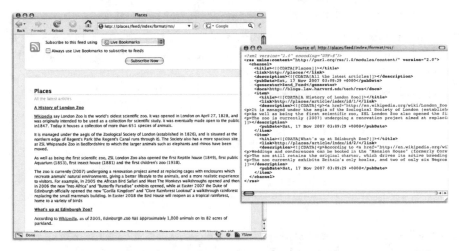

Figure 12.3   The feed we produced as it appears in the Firefox web browser, together with the XML source

If we were using the feed in some other way, we could just use the following line to get the XML string without the HTTP headers:

```
$feed->saveXml()
```

Finally, because we're generating an XML string and using this in a controller action, we disable the automatic view and layout rendering ❼.

In figure 12.3, we can see that Firefox recognizes this as a web feed, shows its parsed content, and asks if we'd like to subscribe to it through its Live Bookmarks. It should be noted, that the feed we've produced is a little too minimal, and we'd likely need to add further elements for it to work with other readers and aggregators. We've kept it simple for the sake of clarity.

Now that we've produced a feed with Zend_Feed, we can move on to consuming that feed.

12.2.2 Consuming a feed

While working on this chapter, Nick mentioned using web feeds to supplement a directory site with news retrieved from the websites of its listings. In that particular case, each listing had the URL of its feed stored along with its other data. If that site had been built using Zend Framework, storing the specific feed URL would have been unnecessary, because Zend_Feed is able to parse any HTML page and search for the same link elements that modern browsers use to indicate the presence of a feed, like these:

```
<link rel="alternate" type="application/rss+xml"
      title="Places RSS Feed" href="/feed/index/format/rss/" />
<link rel="alternate" type="application/atom+xml"
      title="Places Atom Feed" href="/feed/index/format/atom/" />
```

All that is required is a single line of code:

```
$feedArray = Zend_Feed::findFeeds('http://places/');
```

Since we are using the feed from the example we produced earlier, we already know the URL, and the code to consume that feed is straightforward because it imports directly from that URL:

```
$this->view->feed = Zend_Fed::import(
                'http://places/feed/index/format/rss/'
            );
```

The elements of that feed could then be presented in a view, like so:

```
<h1>
    <a href="<?php echo $this->feed->link(); ?>">
        <?php echo $this->feed->title(); ?>
    </a>
</h1>
<div class="channeldesc"><?php echo $this->feed->description(); ?></div>
<?php foreach ($this->feed as $item): ?>
    <h2>
        <a href="<?php echo $item->link; ?>">
            <?php echo $item->title(); ?>
        </a>
    </h2>
    <div class="itemdesc"><?php echo $item->description(); ?></div>
<?php endif; ?>
```

While we're covering the methods of consuming feeds, it would be remiss of us not to mention the remaining methods, such as importing from a text file:

```
$cachedFeed = Zend_Feed::importFile('cache/feed.xml');
```

And here's an example of importing from a PHP string variable:

```
$placesFeed = Zend_Feed::importString($placesFeedString);
```

While we've not covered all the features of Zend_Feed, we have covered those you are likely to use most of the time. Having done so let's move on to the next section on Zend_XmlRpc.

12.3   *Making RPCs with Zend_XmlRpc*

We already described how XML-RPC makes XML-encoded RPCs through HTTP requests and responses. The relative youth of XML might suggest this is yet another new technology being thrust upon us by marketing departments, but RPCs are not a new concept. Written over thirty years ago, RFC 707, "A High-Level Framework for Network-Based Resource Sharing," describes the RPC protocol in a slightly quaint way:

> *Given such a protocol, the various remote resources upon which a user might wish to draw can indeed be made to appear as a single, coherent workshop by interposing between him and them a command language interpreter that transforms his commands into the appropriate protocol utterances.*
>
> —RFC 707, "A High-Level Framework for Network-Based Resource Sharing," January 14, 1976

The start of RFC 707 makes an interesting challenge to ARPANET, the predecessor to today's internet: "This paper outlines an alternative to the approach that ARPANET system builders have been taking". While it is interesting to consider how the internet might look now had that alternative approach been taken, the key point is that RPC is one solution among many, including the internet itself, for allowing disparate applications to talk to each other.

Just as a further note, because RPC mediates between one application and another, it can be classified as *middleware*, which isn't particularly interesting until you notice that amongst the others in that classification is SQL.

Clearly XML-RPC has enough credentials to add to any proposal: it's based on technology established over thirty years ago, which was partly proposed as an alternative to today's internet, and it shares the same problem-solving area as the language through which we converse with databases.

Having determined that XML-RPC has a suitable lineage and, with the addition of XML, enough youth to keep it vibrant, we can move on to using Zend Framework's implementation. The example we're going to work through is an implementation of the various blog APIs that allow blog editors an alternative method of adding, editing, and deleting blog entries via desktop or other remote applications. We'll start by setting up an XML-RPC server using `Zend_XmlRpc_Server`.

12.3.1 Using Zend_XmlRpc_Server

`Zend_XmlRpc_Server` is used to implement the single point of entry for XML-RPC requests, and in that respect it acts much like Zend Framework's front controller does. In fact, you can make your XML-RPC server a controller action that receives its request via the front controller, but that would involve a lot of unnecessary processing overhead. Instead, we're going to separate out parts of the bootstrapping process and build our server capabilities on top of that.

SETTING UP THE BOOTSTRAPPING

If you've read previous chapters, you'll already be aware that the Zend Framework MVC structure relies on `mod_rewrite` settings in a .htaccess file to pass all requests via a front controller file like index.php. Since our XML-RPC server has its own single point of entry, we need to exclude it from that rewrite rule. In listing 12.2 we do that by adding a rewrite condition that excludes any requests for /xmlrpc from the final rewrite rule that passes requests to index.php.

> **Listing 12.2 Rewrite rules modified to allow requests through to the XML-RPC server**

```
RewriteEngine on
RewriteCond %{REQUEST_URI} !^/css
RewriteCond %{REQUEST_URI} !^/img
RewriteCond %{REQUEST_URI} !^/js
RewriteCond %{REQUEST_URI} !^/xmlrpc        ⟵──┐ Excludes /xmlrpc/ directory
RewriteCond %{REQUEST_FILENAME} !-f              from final rewrite rule
RewriteCond %{REQUEST_FILENAME} !-d
RewriteRule ^(.*)$ index.php/$1
```

Alternatively, figure 12.4 illustrates a solution you'll appreciate if, like Nick, you're a coward when it comes to the mystical arts of mod_rewrite.

What we've done in figure 12.4 is added a .htaccess file with one line within our xmlrpc directory:

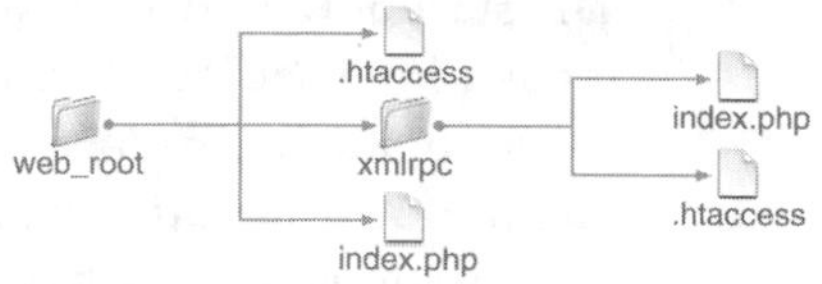

Figure 12.4   The directory structure with our xmlrpc controller file

```
RewriteEngine off
```

This means we can drop our xmlrpc directory into any of the applications we're working on, and any requests to /xmlrpc/ will go to our xmlrpc/index.php file. This means that we don't have to tamper with what could be a finely tuned .htaccess file belonging to the main application or several applications, each with potentially varying rewrite settings.

Now that requests are successfully getting to index.php, we can add the code to forward those requests on to the bootstrap file in our application directory. Readers of the previous chapter will be familiar with this setup. Note the call to a new method, runXmlRpc(), shown in listing 12.3.

Listing 12.3   The contents of our xmlrpc/index.php file

```
include '../../application/bootstrap.php';      Sets configuration
$bootstrap = new Bootstrap('general');          section to use
$bootstrap->runXmlRpc();                         Runs xmlrpc function
                                                 in the bootstrap
```

Having got all that together, we're now finally able to get to the main topic of this section: using Zend_XmlRpc_Server. Listing 12.4 shows a stripped-down version of the bootstrap file, which includes the runXmlRpc() method that was called from our index.php file.

Listing 12.4   Using Zend_XmlRpc_Server in our bootstrap file

```
class Bootstrap
{
    public function __construct($deploymentEnvironment)
    {                                                        Initializes the
        // Set up any configuration settings here            application
    }

    public function runXmlRpc()
    {                                                    Initializes XML-
        $server = new Zend_XmlRpc_Server();              RPC server
                                                                        Attaches
        require_once 'Blogger.php';                                     class
        require_once 'Metaweblog.php';      Includes class files        methods as
        require_once 'MovableType.php';     that attach to server       XML-RPC
                                                                        method
        $server->setClass('Blogger', 'blogger');                       handlers
        $server->setClass('Metaweblog', 'metaWeblog');
        $server->setClass('MovableType', 'mt');
```

```
$response = $server->handle();
$response->setEncoding('UTF-8');
header(
    'Content-Type: text/xml; charset=UTF-8'
);
echo $response;
    }
}
```

Handles RPCs

Sets response character encoding

Sets HTTP header

Outputs the response

We've intentionally left out the contents of the constructor in listing 12.4, but we've included the method to show where we would introduce configuration settings, set include paths, establish a database connection, and perform any other application-specific initialization. Setting up the server is then a fairly straightforward process of instantiating the server object, supplying that server with the class methods that will become its method handlers, handling the XML RPC, and echoing back the response.

One thing you might notice is that when we set the method handlers we also passed in a namespace string. The example classes that we're working with demonstrate exactly why this is important—both the `Blogger` and `Metaweblog` classes contain `editPost()` methods that would clash without the ability to namespace them as `metaWeblog.editPost` and `blogger.editPost`.

With the server set up and ready to go, we can now elaborate on the class methods that the server will be using.

CREATING THE XML-RPC METHOD HANDLERS

Since the purpose of our XML-RPC server is to receive RPCs, our next step is to create those procedures. As already mentioned, we'll be implementing some of the APIs for several of the blog applications so that a desktop application can work with articles on our *Places* application.

First, let's take a look at the Ecto application we'll be working with, which describes itself as "a feature-rich desktop blogging client for Mac OS X and Windows, supporting a wide range of weblog systems." The main reason we chose Ecto was it has a console, which makes it very useful when debugging our XML-RPC transactions, but most of what we discuss in this section is applicable to other similar applications. In figure 12.5, we can see Ecto's main window on the left, with a list of *Places* articles, and its editing window on the right.

After we set up the connection details and select the API we want to connect to, Ecto runs through a series of method calls to establish the account. We've chosen to use the MovableType API, but doing so still involves calls to methods that belong to other APIs, such as `blogger.getUsersBlogs` and `blogger.getUserInfo`, which belong to the Blogger API, or `metaWeblog.editPost`, which belongs to the MetaWeblog API. For this reason, we're obliged to provide those methods for our XML-RPC server, and that obligation is an indication that we need to create interfaces.

CREATING THE INTERFACES

In order to work with any of the APIs already mentioned, our application must implement the methods required by those APIs. If we pick an example method like

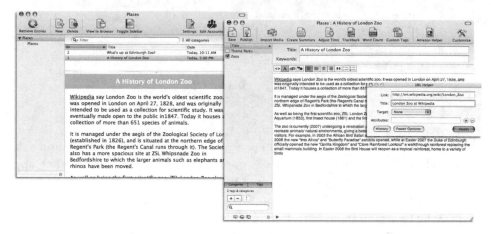

Figure 12.5   Ecto, the desktop blogging client we'll be using to make XML-RPC requests, shown editing some *Places* content.

`metaWeblog.editPost`, the requirement is that it returns a Boolean value and consumes the following parameters:

```
metaWeblog.editPost (postid, username, password, struct, publish)
```

How our application carries out the processing of this request depends on the application itself, but the fact that it must implement the required methods clearly calls for object interfaces. According to the PHP manual, "object interfaces allow you to create code which specifies which methods a class must implement, without having to define how these methods are handled." Listing 12.5 shows one of our interfaces establishing all the methods of the MetaWeblog API.

Listing 12.5   Our interface for the MetaWeblog API

```
interface Places_Service_Metaweblog_Interface
{
    public function newPost(
                $blogid, $username, $password, $content, $publish
                );
    public function editPost(
                $postid, $username, $password, $content, $publish
                );
    public function getPost($postid, $username, $password);
    public function newMediaObject(
                $blogid, $username, $password, $struct
                );
    public function getCategories(
                $blogid, $username, $password
                );
    public function getRecentPosts(
                $blogid, $username, $password, $numposts
                );
}
```

This interface was quite straightforward to set up, because it's clearly detailed in the MetaWeblog spec. The XML-RPC Blogger API and MovableType APIs are a bit more fiddly because they have actually been deprecated, despite still being used in many current web and desktop applications.

Having set up an example interface, we can use it in our concrete classes, where it'll ensure that those classes will adhere to the requirements of the original API.

CREATING THE CONCRETE CLASSES

Since our original shot of Ecto in figure 12.5 showed us editing an article on *Places*, we'll continue that theme and use the MetaWeblog editPost() method to demonstrate both the use of our interface and how methods need to be set up so Zend_XmlRpc_Server can use them.

Listing 12.6 shows a stripped-down version of the Metaweblog class that resides in our models/ directory.

Listing 12.6   Our MetaWeblog model implementing the interface from listing 12.5

```
include_once 'ArticleTable.php';
include_once 'ServiceAuth.php';                                    ❶ Implements
                                                                      Metaweblog
class Metaweblog                                                      interface
    implements Places_Service_Metaweblog_Interface      ◁┘
{
    protected $_auth;
    protected $_articleTable;
    public function __construct()              ❷ Instantiates
                                                 objects needed
    {                                            by editPost
        $this->_auth = new ServiceAuth;     ◁┘
        $this->_articleTable = new ArticleTable();
        // Full version would have further code here...
    }
    /**

    * Changes the articles of a given post
    * Optionally, publishes after changing the post
    *
    * @param string $postid
    * Unique identifier of the post to be changed
    * @param string $username                          ❸ Defines
    * Login for a user who has permission to edit the     required
    * given post (either the original creator or an       method
    * admin of the blog)                                  parameters
    * @param string $password Password for said
    * username
    * @param struct $struct New content of the post
    * @param boolean $publish
    * If true, the blog will be published
    * immediately after the post is made         ❹ Defines method
    * @return boolean                       ◁┘      return value
    */
    public function editPost($postid, $username,   ❺ Defines parameters which
            $password, $struct, $publish              must match DocBlocks
```

```
        )
    {
        $identity = $this->_auth->authenticate(
                    $username, $password);
        if(false === $identity) {
            throw new Exception('Authentication Failed');
        }

        $filterStripTags = new Zend_Filter_StripTags;
        $data = array(
            'publish' => (int)$struct['publish'],
            'title'   => $filterStripTags->filter($struct['title']),
            'body'    => $struct['description']
        );
        $where = $this->_articleTable->getAdapter()

                    ->quoteInto('id = ?', (int)$postid);
        $rows_affected = $this->_articleTable
                        ->update($data, $where);
        if(0 == $rows_affected) {
            throw new Exception('Your post failed to be updated');
        }
        return true;
    }
    // Add all the other required methods here...
}
```

6 Checks authorization

7 Builds array used in update query

8 Updates post

9 Returns Boolean on success

This model class implements our Metaweblog interface ❶, so the final version would have to include all the methods in the interface, but for the sake of space they have not been included here. Similarly, only the objects needed for our `editPost()` method have been instantiated in our constructor ❷, but the full version would need more.

DocBlocks are the key to getting methods working with `Zend_XmlRpc_Server`. We'll go into more detail about their importance in this section, but their key role is to determine the method help text and method signatures. In our example, you can see that they indicate the type, variable name, and description of each parameter ❸ and the return value ❹. The parameters of our method must then match those in the DocBlock ❺, though our interface will also enforce the parameters.

For security, we do a rudimentary authorization check using the username and password passed in the parameters with a custom auth class ❻, and we throw an exception upon failure. Data used to build the array used in the update query is also filtered where necessary ❼. If all is well, we update the database row that corresponds to the provided ID ❽, and, as specified in the return value of the DocBlock, we return a Boolean.

After a simple authentication check using the username and password passed in the parameters, this `editPost()` method filters and formats an array from the received data and updates the database row that corresponds to the provided ID on success ❾, or raises an exception that will be handled by `Zend_XmlRpc_Server` on failure.

You'll notice that the `editPost()` method is only minimally different from any standard method in that it has the DocBlock parameter data type `struct`, which isn't a native PHP data type. When you use `Zend_XmlRpc_Server::setClass()` or `Zend_XmlRpc_Server::addFunction()`, `Zend_Server_Reflection` checks all methods or functions and determines their method help text and signatures using the DocBlocks.

In table 12.1, we can see that in the case of `@param $struct`, the data type has been set to the `struct` XML-RPC type that corresponds to the associative array PHP type, which is processed using the `Zend_XmlRpc_Value_Struct` object.

Table 12.1   Mapping PHP types to their XML-RPC types and `Zend_XmlRpc_Value` objects

PHP native type	XML-RPC type	`Zend_XmlRpc_Value` object
Boolean	`<boolean>`	`Zend_XmlRpc_Value_Boolean`
Integer	`<int>` or `<i4>`	`Zend_XmlRpc_Value_Integer`
Double	`<double>`	`Zend_XmlRpc_Value_Double`
String	`<string>` (the default type)	`Zend_XmlRpc_Value_String`
dateTime.iso8601	`<dateTime.iso8601>`	`Zend_XmlRpc_Value_DateTime`
Base64	`<base64>`	`Zend_XmlRpc_Value_Base64`
Array	`<array>`	`Zend_XmlRpc_Value_Array`
Associative array	`<struct>`	`Zend_XmlRpc_Value_Struct`

Using these mappings, we can, at any time, call on a `Zend_XmlRpc_Value` object to prepare values for XML-RPC. This is often needed when preparing values in an array, for example:

```
array('dateCreated' => new Zend_XmlRpc_Value_DateTime(
    $row->date_created, Zend_XmlRpc_Value::XMLRPC_TYPE_DATETIME);
```

The preceding example formats a date from a database table row into the ISO8601 format required by XML-RPC. The second parameter refers to the class constant `XMLRPC_TYPE_DATETIME`, which is unsurprisingly defined as `dateTime.iso8601`.

If you're thinking that all this introspection by `Zend_Server_Reflection` must come at a price, you'd be right, particularly when a lot of classes or functions are attached to the server. Thankfully, there is a solution in the form of `Zend_XmlRpc_Server_Cache`, which, as the name implies, can be used to cache the information gathered by `Zend_Server_Reflection`. We don't need to change too much from the example given in the Zend Framework manual, because `Zend_XmlRpc_Server_Cache` is very simple to use, as shown in listing 12.7.

Listing 12.7   Our `Zend_XmlRpc_Server` with caching implemented

```
$cacheFile = ROOT_DIR . '/cache/xmlrpc.cache';        ◁──┐ Sets file path for
$server = new Zend_XmlRpc_Server();                        cached information

if (!Zend_XmlRpc_Server_Cache::get(        Checks for cache before
    $cacheFile, $server)                   attaching classes
  ) {
  require_once 'Blogger.php';
  require_once 'Metaweblog.php';
  require_once 'MovableType.php';

  $server->setClass('Blogger', 'blogger');
  $server->setClass('Metaweblog', 'metaWeblog');
  $server->setClass('MovableType', 'mt');

  Zend_XmlRpc_Server_Cache::save(          Saves introspection
                 $cacheFile, $server);     information in cache
}
```

With `Zend_XmlRpc_Server_Cache` in place, we can cut out all that resource-intensive introspection. If we need to change the code in any of the attached classes, we need only delete the cache file so that a new version that reflects the changes can be rewritten.

Now that we've set up our XML-RPC server, we can look at the client side of the exchange with `Zend_XmlRpc_Client`.

12.3.2   Using Zend_XmlRpc_Client

For our *Places* application, our intention was to set up an XML-RPC server so that we could remotely edit articles with any of the desktop applications that support the blog APIs. In doing so, we've covered a lot of the functionality of `Zend_XmlRpc`. In this section, we'll demonstrate those functions a little further by using `Zend_XmlRpc_Client` to simulate a client request to the `editPost()` method we demonstrated in listing 12.6.

Unlike `Zend_XmlRpc_Server`, which was used within its own front controller, we're using `Zend_XmlRpc_Client` within a controller action, as shown in listing 12.8.

Listing 12.8   Using `Zend_XmlRpc_Client` within a controller action

```
public function editPostAction()
{                                                       Assigns server URL
  $xmlRpcServer = 'http://places/xmlrpc/';      ◁──┐   to XML-RPC server
  $client = new Zend_XmlRpc_Client($xmlRpcServer);  ◁──┐
                                                         Instantiates
  $filterStripTags = new Zend_Filter_StripTags;        client object
                                                         with server URL
  $id = (int) $_POST['id'];
  $publish = (bool) $_POST['publish'];         Sets up and filters data
                                               for XML-RPC struct
  $structData = array(   ◁───────────────┘
```

```
        'title' => $filterStripTags->filter($_POST['title']),
        'dateCreated' => new Zend_XmlRpc_Value_DateTime(time(),
                Zend_XmlRpc_Value::XMLRPC_TYPE_DATETIME),
        'description' => $filterStripTags->filter($_POST['body']
    );
    $server = $client->getProxy();              ◁──────────────    Sets up server
    $server->metaWeblog->editPost(                                 proxy object
        array($id,'myusername','mypassword',      Makes RPC
            $structData,$publish));               with data
}
```

In this example, we're filtering the data from an HTML form and preparing it for use by the client, which has been set up with the URL of the XML-RPC server we'll be sending requests to. The `Zend_XmlRpc_Client` server proxy object then handles the rest by compiling the XML-encoded request and sending it via HTTP to the XML-RPC server it was instantiated with.

Borrowing Ecto's console window, we can illustrate the process more thoroughly in figure 12.6. There we can see the XML-encoded request in the left console window, which is processed by the XML-RPC server. If it's successful, it will update the article in the middle and return an XML-encoded response with the Boolean value `true` back to the client.

Not all XML-RPC requests are successful, of course, and for that reason `Zend_XmlRpc_Client` has the ability to handle HTTP and XML-RPC errors through exceptions. In listing 12.9 we add error handling to the `editPost()` procedure call from listing 12.8.

Figure 12.6 Demonstrating the `editPost()` method call with the request on the left, the updated article in the middle, and the response returned from the XML-RPC server on the right.

Listing 12.9 Adding error handling to our XML-RPC client

```
try {
    client->call('metaWeblog.editPost',          ◁—— Attempts RPC
        array($id,'myusername','mypassword', $structData, $publish));
} catch (Zend_XmlRpc_HttpException $e) {          ◁
    // echo $e->getCode() . ': ' . $e->getMessage() . "\n";    Handles HTTP request
} catch (Zend_XmlRpc_FaultException $e) {         ◁           error if call fails
    // echo $e->getCode() . ': ' . $e->getMessage() . "\n";    Handles any
}                                                              XML-RPC error
                                                               if not HTTP
```

Our client now attempts to make the RPC and on failure can handle HTTP and XML-RPC errors. Note that because we're not actually using the client in our *Places* application, we've not gone into any detail about what we'd do with those error messages.

As we've demonstrated in this section, XML-RPC is quite straightforward to set up and use, and `Zend_XmlRpc` makes it even easier. However, like any technology, XML-RPC has its critics, and in the next section we'll look at another approach to web services using `Zend_Rest`.

12.4   *Using REST web services with Zend_Rest*

At the start of this chapter, we mentioned that the various Zend Framework components we'd be working with would include XML but that we wouldn't be needing to deal with it directly. The `Zend_Rest` section of the manual opens by stating that "REST Web Services use service-specific XML formats," which is true, but it needs a little clarification because REST web services don't care whether or not they use XML. `Zend_Rest` does use XML as its format of choice, but it's possible to circumvent this if you dig around a bit, which we'll do after looking at REST in a bit more detail.

12.4.1 *What is REST?*

REST stands for Representational State Transfer and was originally outlined in "Architectural Styles and the Design of Network-based Software Architectures" by Roy Fielding, whose role as "primary architect of the current Hypertext Transfer Protocol" explains some of the background to REST. As Fielding states in the document, "REST ignores the details of component implementation and protocol syntax in order to focus on the roles of components, the constraints upon their interaction with other components, and their interpretation of significant data elements." He also states that "the motivation for developing REST was to create an architectural model for how the Web should work, such that it could serve as the guiding framework for the Web protocol standards." In other words, every time we make an HTTP request, we're using a transfer protocol based on the REST concept.

While the key element of RPC is the command, usually accessed via a single point of entry, the key element in REST is the resource, an example of which could be the *Places* login page, whose resource identifier is the URL http://places/auth/login/.

Resources can change over time (for example, our login page could have interface updates), but the resource identifiers should remain valid.

Of course, having a lot of resources doesn't hold a great deal of value unless we can do something with them, and in the case of web services we have the HTTP methods. To illustrate the value that such apparently simple operations have, Table 12.2 compares the HTTP methods POST, GET, PUT, and DELETE with the common generic database operations: create, read, update, and delete (CRUD).

All readers of this book will likely be familiar with the POST and GET HTTP request methods, whereas PUT and DELETE are less well known, partly because they're not often implemented by all HTTP servers. This limitation is reflected in Zend_Rest, because Zend_Rest_Client is able to send all of these request methods but Zend_Rest_Server will only respond to GET and POST.

Table 12.2 Comparing HTTP methods used in REST with common generic database operations

HTTP methods	Database operations
POST	Create
GET	Read
PUT	Update
DELETE	Delete

Presuming that readers will already know enough HTTP to be able to join the dots on the fundamentals, we've kept this introduction to REST intentionally brief. Hopefully, as we start to explore some of the REST components of Zend Framework, things will become clearer. We'll start with Zend_Rest_Client.

12.4.2 Using Zend_Rest_Client

As we mentioned at the start of this section, Zend_Rest uses XML to serialize the data it processes in the body of the HTTP request or response, but not all RESTful web services use XML. One example is the Akismet spam-filtering service, which we'll use to demonstrate the various ways of accessing REST-based web services. Figure 12.7 shows where we could use the service to check the reviews submitted by users of our *Places* application to make sure spam replies are kept out.

Another reason we've chosen Akismet is that Zend Framework has a Zend_Service_Akismet component, which means you won't be left with a partially implemented solution and will hopefully be able to understand how that component works.

The Akismet API provides a small choice of resources, shown in table 12.3, from which we'll choose the resource to verify that the API key, which is required to use Akismet and is obtained from Wordpress.com, is valid.

The first thing we'll do is attempt to use Zend_Rest to access this resource in the method demonstrated in the manual. You can see this in listing 12.10.

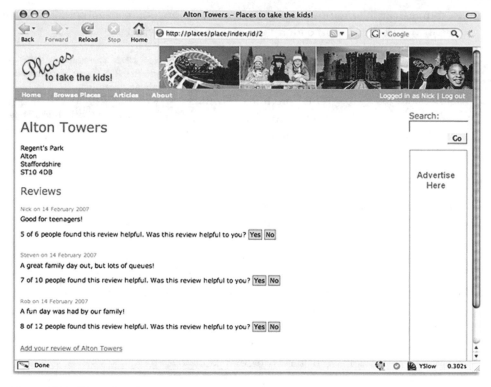

Figure 12.7   The reviews in our *Places* application, which we could filter using the Akismet spam-filtering service

Table 12.3   The resources provided by the Akismet API

Resource identifier	Description
`rest.akismet.com/1.1/verify-key`	Verifies the required API key.
`api-key.rest.akismet.com/1.1/comment-check`	Identifies whether or not the submitted comment is spam.
`api-key.rest.akismet.com/1.1/submit-spam`	Submits missed spam.
`api-key.rest.akismet.com/1.1/submit-ham`	Submits content incorrectly marked as spam.

Listing 12.10   Sending a REST request to Akismet using `Zend_Rest_Client`

```
$client = new Zend_Rest_Client(              ◁——  Instantiates client with
        'http://rest.akismet.com/1.1/verify-key'      URL of the resource
    );
echo $client->key('f6k3apik3y')              ◁——  Sets key to
        ->blog('http://places/')       ◁——        value of API
        ->post();       ◁——                        key
                    Sends request    Sets blog to
                    as HTTP POST     URL of blog
```

In this example, we construct our client with the URL of the verify key resource, then, using the fluent interface that is common in many Zend Framework components, we set the two required variables key and blog using the built-in magic methods. Finally, we send them via an HTTP POST request. Unfortunately, despite the pleasing simplicity of this code, the resulting request will fail because Akismet doesn't return the XML response that is expected by Zend_Rest_Client when used this way.

Since all Akismet needs is a simple HTTP request, and Zend_Rest itself uses Zend_Http_Client, why can't we just use Zend_Http_Client in the first place? The answer, as demonstrated in listing 12.11, is that we can.

Listing 12.11   Sending a REST request to Akismet using `Zend_Http_Client`

```
$client = new Zend_Http_Client(               ◁——  Instantiates client
        'http://rest.akismet.com/1.1/verify-key'      with resource URL
    );
$data = array(              ◁——  Builds array with required
   'key' => 'f6k3apik3y',          data for verify request
   'blog' => 'http://places/'
);

$client->setParameterPost($data);   ◁——  Formats data into
                                          an HTTP POST
try {
   $response = $client->request(              ◁——  Makes
            Zend_Http_Client::POST                  request
        );
} catch (Zend_Http_Client_Exception $e) {
   echo $e->getCode() . ': ' . $e->getMessage() . "\n";
}
```

Zend_Http_Client won't attempt to parse the returned response from Akismet as if it were XML, and we'll receive the plain text response valid or invalid depending on whether or not our data is verified successfully.

If Zend_Http_Client can successfully make the request, surely there is a way that Zend_Rest can do the same? Of course there is, and in listing 12.12, which should be looking familiar by now, we bypass having Akismet's plain text response parsed as XML by calling the restPost() method directly. Unlike our first attempt, this method returns the body of the HTTP response rather than sending it through Zend_Rest_Client_Result.

Listing 12.12   Sending a REST request to Akismet using `Zend_Rest`

```
$client = new Zend_Rest_Client(          ◁──── Instantiates client
            'http://rest.akismet.com'              with request URL
        );
$data = array(                     ◁──── Builds array with required
    'key'  => 'f6k3apik3y',                 data for verify request
    'blog' => 'http://places/'
);
try {
    $response = $client->restPost(      ◁──── Makes HTTP
                '/1.1/verify-key', $data        POST request
            );
    var_dump($response);
} catch (Zend_Rest_Client_Exception $e) {
    echo $e->getCode() . ': ' . $e->getMessage() . "\n";
}
```

Having solved our problem with Akismet's service, we now know we can use `Zend_Rest_Client` with plain-text-based and XML-based RESTful web services. If we wanted to work with the rest of Akismet's resources, it would obviously make more sense to use `Zend_Service_Akismet`, but if there weren't a prebuilt Zend Framework component we'd have several options. One of those is to use `Zend_Rest_Server` to interact with REST-based web services provided by our own application server.

12.4.3 Using Zend_Rest_Server

Let's imagine that we've convinced one of the advertisers on *Places*, Edinburgh Zoo, to take part in a joint promotion that will be hosted separately from both of our sites. The idea is to make a short lifespan mashup site based on content from *Places*, Edinburgh Zoo, and other interested sites.

   As we did with our XML-RPC server earlier, we'll start by making a simple interface called `Places_Service_Place_Interface` to make sure our server has a consistent API. Listing 12.13 shows our interface with two methods: one to get a place and one to get the reviews for a place.

Listing 12.13   Our *Places* service application interface

```
interface Places_Service_Place_Interface
{
    public function getPlace($id);
    public function getReviews($id);
}
```

In listing 12.14, we make a concrete implementation of our interface using queries similar to those from chapter 6. Note that the database results are returned as an array rather than as the default objects, which would have failed when processed by `Zend_Rest_Server`. Another thing you may notice is that unlike `Zend_XmlRpc_Server`, `Zend_Rest_Server` does not require parameters and return values specified in DocBlocks even though it will use them if provided.

```
class ServicePlaces implements Places_Service_Place_Interface
{
   public function getPlace($id)
   {
      $placesFinder = new Places();
      $place = $placesFinder->find($id);
      return $place->current()->toArray();
   }
   public function getReviews($id)
   {
      $reviewsFinder = new Reviews();
      $rowset = $reviewsFinder->fetchByPlaceId($id);
      return $rowset->toArray();
   }
}
```

Returns query results as array

Now that we have the concrete class, we can attach it to Zend_Rest_Server with the same approach that we covered with Zend_XmlRpc_Server. Listing 12.15 shows our REST server set up within an action controller and accessible via an HTTP GET or POST that must supply the name of the service method you wish to invoke.

```
class RestController extends Zend_Controller_Action
{
   protected $_server;

   public function init()
   {
      $this->_server = new Zend_Rest_Server();
      $this->_helper->viewRenderer->setNoRender();
   }

   public function indexAction()
   {
      require_once 'ServicePlaces.php';
      $this->_server->setClass('ServicePlaces');
      $this->_server->handle();
   }
}
```

Figure 12.8 shows the XML-formatted results of some example GET requests to the resources http://places/rest/?method=getPlace&id=6 (on the left) and http://places/rest/?method=getReviews&id=6 (on the right) using Firefox.

All our mashup site needs to do is use Zend_Rest_Client to make requests like the following:

```
$client = new Zend_Rest_Client('http://places/rest/?method=getPlace');
$response = $client->id('6')->get();
```

This will return a Zend_Rest_Client_Result object that allows us to access the elements of the response as properties that can be used in our site like so:

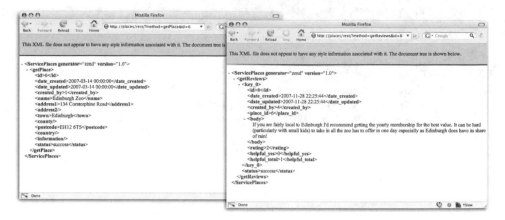

Figure 12.8   The results of our REST server query: `getPlace` on the left and `getReviews` on the right

```
echo $response->name; // Outputs "Edinburgh Zoo"
```

Having worked through the implementation of Zend_XmlRpc_Server, itself relatively simple when compared to, say, SOAP, you'll have found Zend_Rest_Server very easy to follow. As with any brief introduction, there is a lot that has not been covered, such as PUT and DELETE HTTP requests, which are not handled by Zend_Rest_Server, and authentication. However, what we've set up is a REST server whose strength lies in the relationship between Zend_Rest_Server and Zend_Rest_Client and the simplicity of implementation.

12.5   *Summary*

This chapter has taken quite a concentrated look at some of the web service components of Zend Framework. The emphasis has been on the client/server relationships that we set up first by using Zend_Feed to generate a newsfeed of our *Places* articles and then by consuming that newsfeed. Next, we set up Zend_XmlRpc_Server to allow remote editing of *Places* articles through the blog APIs, and we followed that with an example of how Zend_XmlRpc_Client can make the RPCs to that server. Finally, we covered Zend_Rest, first filtering comments through Akismet's REST-based spam-filtering service using Zend_Rest_Client and then providing our own API to *Places* content with Zend_Rest_Server.

Hopefully you'll leave this chapter with a decent understanding of how web services work and be able to implement useful services using the various Zend Framework components. You should also be well prepared for the next chapter, where we'll use the more specific components with some of the publicly available web services.

Mashups with public web services

13

This chapter covers

- Integrating `Zend_Service_Amazon` into a Zend Framework application
- Displaying images from Flickr
- Presenting YouTube videos on your own website

In the previous chapter, we looked at some of the more general web service components of Zend Framework and explored both client and server roles. In this chapter, we're going to take on the client role and use some of the publicly available web services to make significant additions to our *Places* site. It would also be fair to say that this chapter should be easier and, if it's possible, even a bit more exciting than the last. Chapter 12 demonstrated the use of one such public web service, the Akismet spam-filtering service, using the more general components `Zend_Http_Client` and `Zend_Rest`. While doing so, we also mentioned that Zend Framework has a pre-built component for doing this: `Zend_Service_Akismet`. Of course, this chapter wouldn't exist if there weren't more of these components, and we'll start off with an overview of many of the currently available web service components.

We'll then demonstrate some of those components. Our aim in doing so is not only to show how they can be used but also how they can be integrated into a Zend Framework-based application. In the process, we'll also give you an early introduction to the use of Zend_Cache to cache the results and avoid the inevitable slowness of including content from remote web services.

13.1 Accessing public web services

Constructing our own API to allow desktop blog editors to access our *Places* web application in the last chapter should have left you quite comfortable with the concept of APIs. That knowledge will be very useful when dealing with the public web service APIs. However, one of the great things about the Zend_Service_* components is that you don't always need to get too involved in the APIs to get them working.

The number of Zend_Service_* components is growing at quite a rate, attesting to the importance and attention given to including web services in Zend Framework. Aside from the components we'll shortly introduce, there are many in various stages of proposal as the number of web services increase. The following list includes those in the Zend Framework core at the time of writing and some that were in development and which may be in a public offering as you read this. It's inspiring to see that the variety of companies offering web services ranges from the very large to the comparatively small:

- Zend_Gdata
- Zend_Service_Akismet
- Zend_Service_Amazon
- Zend_Service_Audioscrobbler
- Zend_Service_Delicious
- Zend_Service_Flickr
- Zend_Service_Gravatar
- Zend_Service_Nirvanix
- Zend_Service_RememberTheMilk
- Zend_Service_Simpy
- Zend_Service_SlideShare
- Zend_Service_StrikeIron
- Zend_Service_Technorati
- Zend_Service_Yahoo

Before we get into demonstrating the use of some of some of these components, we'll describe each briefly and give some indication of its possible uses in relation to the *Places* application we have been building, in the hope that this will help indicate the potential of these services.

13.1.1 Zend_Gdata

While you'd expect this Google Data client to be called Zend_Service_Gdata, Zend_Gdata breaks the naming scheme of the other components for historical reasons. Google's own team of developers was responsible for putting together what has become the official PHP5 client for the Google Data APIs. The fact that it's available as a separate standalone download indicates the standing the `Gdata` component has as part of the framework.

Later in this chapter, we'll give an example of the use of `Zend_Gdata` with one of Google's services, but before we do, let's take a quick look at Google's mission statement:

> *Google's mission is to organize the world's information and make it universally accessible and useful.*
>
> —http://www.google.com/corporate/index.html

That doesn't really tell us, the potential users of Google's APIs, much about what the services might provide. If we look at table 13.1, we can see that this is because Google provides a large number of services accessible via the Google Data API.

Table 13.1   The services available via Google's Data API

Service	Purpose
Google Calendar	Manages an online calendar application
Google Spreadsheets	Manages an online spreadsheet application
Google Documents List	Manages word-processing documents, spreadsheets, and presentations; otherwise known as Google Docs
Google Provisioning	Manages user accounts, nicknames, and email lists on a Google Apps-hosted domain
Google Base	Manages an online database application
YouTube	Manages an online video application
Picasa Web Albums	Manages an online photo application
Google Blogger	Manages a blogging application; the current incarnation of the Blogger API that we covered in chapter 12
Google CodeSearch	Searches the source code of public projects
Google Notebook	Views public notes and clippings

The Google Data API is a collective name for the services based on the Atom syndication format and publishing protocol (APP). This explains why services like Google Maps, which embeds maps in your web application using JavaScript, are not included in this selection.

NOTE   Because the `Zend_Gdata` components are extended versions of Atom, they could theoretically also be used as generic Atom components to access services not provided by Google.

13.1.2 *Zend_Service_Akismet*

We're already familiar with this service from Akismet because we used it in chapter 12 to filter user reviews for potential spam:

> *Automatic Kismet (Akismet for short) is a collaborative effort to make comment and trackback spam a nonissue and restore innocence to blogging, so you never have to worry about spam again.*
>
> —http://akismet.com/

The service, which originated with the WordPress blogging system, provided a spam-filtering service for reader comments, but it can be used for any kind of data. Zend_Service_Akismet also allows you to send back to Akismet spam that gets through the filter, as well as false positives. Of course, having covered the use of Akismet in   chapter 12, we have to demonstrate how we could have done it with Zend_Service_Akismet. Listing 13.1 does just that.

Listing 13.1 Using `Zend_Service_Akismet` to filter a review for possible spam

```
require_once 'Zend/Service/Akismet.php';
$apiKey = 'f6k3apik3y';
$akismet = new Zend_Service_Akismet(          ◁──┐  Sets up connection
    $apiKey, 'http://places/'                      │  with API key
  );
                                    ┌─── Requires only user_ip
$data = array(          ◁───────────┘     and user_agent
   'user_ip' => $_SERVER['REMOTE_ADDR'],
   'user_agent' => $_SERVER['HTTP_USER_AGENT'],
   'comment_type' => 'comment',
   'comment_author' => $_POST['author'],
   'comment_author_email' => $_POST['email'],
   'comment_content' => $_POST['message']
);
if ($akismet->isSpam($data)) {          ◁──┐  Checks data
   // Mark as spam to be reviewed by admin  │  for spam
} else {
   // Continue
}
```

We start by setting up our connection with Akismet and our required API key. We then compile an array of data to be checked, including the required `user_ip` and `user_agent` and also some other information that may be useful in determining the nature of the content. Finally, we send the data to Akismet to check whether it's spam and then act accordingly.

13.1.3 *Zend_Service_Amazon*

Amazon is probably the largest and most well-known store on the internet. As Google is to search, so Amazon is to e-commerce, and its vision is only slightly less broad:

Our vision is to be earth's most customer-centric company; to build a place where people can come to find and discover anything they might want to buy online.
>   —http://phx.corporate-ir.net/phoenix.zhtml?c=97664&p=irol-faq)

`Zend_Service_Amazon` gives developers access to store item information, including images, prices, descriptions, reviews, and related products via the Amazon web services API. We'll demonstrate its capabilities later when we use it to find a selection of books that may be useful to users of our *Places* web application.

13.1.4 *Zend_Service_Audioscrobbler*

Audioscrobbler is the engine behind the social music site last.fm, which tracks and learns your musical tastes and connects you to new music. The engine is described like so:

The Audioscrobbler system is a massive database that tracks listening habits and calculates relationships and recommendations based on the music people listen to.
>   —http://www.audioscrobbler.net/

The Audioscrobbler web service API allows access to user, artist, album, track, tag, group, and forum data. For our *Places* application, we could use this service to find music the kids might like to take on trips.

13.1.5 *Zend_Service_Delicious*

Along with a fairly recent update to its previously unpronounceable Web 2.0 name, Yahoo!-owned Delicious's description of itself has also been simplified:

Delicious is a social bookmarking service that allows users to tag, save, manage and share web pages from a centralized source.
>   —http://delicious.com/about

`Zend_Service_Delicious` provides read-write access to Delicious posts as well as read-only access to public data. Aside from the obvious personal uses for such an application API, we could use it for accessing statistical information about users bookmarking our *Places* website.

13.1.6 *Zend_Service_Flickr*

Flickr, owned by Yahoo!, has an equally simple and self-confident description:

Flickr—almost certainly the best online photo management and sharing application in the world
>   —http://www.flickr.com/about/

In section 13.3, we'll use the Flickr data API's read-only access to lists of images matching specific tags, user information, and more, to display a selection of images that match keywords in our *Places* articles.

13.1.7 *Zend_Service_Gravatar*

Gravatar is now owned by Automattic, which is responsible for the Akismet service. This may partly explain the grand description for what is currently a way to centralize users' identification icons, otherwise known as avatars:

> *Gravatar aims to put a face behind the name. This is the beginning of trust. In the future, Gravatar will be a way to establish trust between producers and consumers on the internet.*
>
> —http://site.gravatar.com/about

The component is currently in the incubator, but it looks to provide access to users' avatars and could be used to put a face to the name in our *Places* reviews.

13.1.8 *Zend_Service_Nirvanix*

Nirvanix provides read-write access to its online storage service:

> *Nirvanix is the premier "Cloud Storage" platform provider. Nirvanix has built a global cluster of storage nodes collectively referred to as the Storage Delivery Network (SDN), powered by the Nirvanix Internet Media File System (IMFS).*
>
> —http://www.nirvanix.com/company.aspx

Places could use this exactly as described for online storage of media that we may not want to store and serve from our own hosting service, such as video or other large files.

13.1.9 *Zend_Service_RememberTheMilk*

Remember The Milk, is, as the name suggests,

> *The best way to manage your tasks. Never forget the milk (or anything else) again.*
>
> —http://www.rememberthemilk.com/

The *Places* developers could use this with the support tracker we put together in chapter 10 to track tasks we have to do. Another idea would be to use it to help parents organize their trips on *Places*.

13.1.10 *Zend_Service_Simpy*

Like Delicious, Simpy is a social bookmarking service:

> *Simpy is a social bookmarking service that lets you save, tag, search and share your bookmarks, notes, groups and more.*
>
> —http://www.simpy.com/

Choosing whether to use this or the Delicious service is largely a matter of taste, but either way its potential use is similar.

13.1.11 *Zend_Service_SlideShare*

SlideShare hosts and displays PowerPoint, Open Office, and PDF presentations for worldwide distribution, or as the company puts it,

> *SlideShare is the best way to share your presentations with the world.*
>
> —http://www.slideshare.net/

Using `Zend_Service_SlideShare`, we could embed SlideShare-hosted slideshows in *Places* and also upload our own presentations for potential *Places* investors or presentations of our great web application for the next developers conference!

13.1.12 *Zend_Service_StrikeIron*

StrikeIron's service is a little harder to describe because it's actually a collection of smaller services:

> *StrikeIron's Data Services give you access to live data to use now, integrate into applications or build into websites.*
>
> —http://www.strikeiron.com/

Three out of the hundreds of available services—ZIP Code Information, U.S. Address Verification, and Sales & Use Tax Basic—have supported wrappers in `Zend_Service_StrikeIron`, but the API can be used with many of the other services too. Most, if not all, of the services are subscription-based, with costs being relative to the number of hits to the service.

13.1.13 *Zend_Service_Technorati*

WordPress users may already be familiar with the integration of Technorati in WordPress's dashboard to show incoming links, but Technorati's own description suggests greater things:

> *Technorati is the recognized authority on what's happening on the World Live Web, right now. The Live Web is the dynamic and always-updating portion of the Web. We search, surface, and organize blogs and the other forms of independent, user-generated content (photos, videos, voting, etc.) increasingly referred to as "citizen media."*
>
> —http://technorati.com/about/)

We can use `Zend_Service_Technorati` to search and retrieve blog information, and for *Places* we'd likely use it the same way WordPress does—to track incoming links and find out what people are saying about us. Listing 13.2 shows an example of how this could be done.

Listing 13.2   Checking incoming links to Places!

```
require_once 'Zend/Service/Technorati.php';
$technorati = new Zend_Service_Technorati('PLACES_API_KEY');
$results = $technorati->cosmos('http://www.placestotakethekids.com/');
```

This quick but effective example fetches the results of a search of blogs linking to our *Places* URL.

13.1.14 Zend_Service_Yahoo

Yahoo! is another company whose scale and ubiquity make it hard to define:

> *Yahoo! powers and delights our communities of users, advertisers, and publishers—all of us united in creating indispensable experiences, and fueled by trust.*
>   —http://yahoo.client.shareholder.com/press/overview.cfm)

`Zend_Service_Yahoo` focuses on search through Yahoo! Web Search, Yahoo! News, Yahoo! Local, and Yahoo! Images. A useful feature for our *Places* application would be checking the indexing of our site with the kind of code that listing 13.3 demonstrates.

Listing 13.3   Checking indexing of our site

```
require_once 'Zend/Service/Yahoo.php';
$yahoo = new Zend_Service_Yahoo('PLACES_YAHOO_APPLICATION_ID');
$results = $yahoo->pageDataSearch('http://www.placestotakethekids.com/');
```

You may have noticed how similar the code in this Yahoo! example is to the previous Technorati one. While that is somewhat coincidental, it does begin to demonstrate how the web services components simplify and make available a broad range of services with a relatively simple approach.

With that in mind, and having completed our overview of some of the web services available in Zend Framework, it's time to go a little deeper with some more detailed examples of the components in use. We'll start by retrieving some items from Amazon using Amazon's web services API.

13.2   Displaying ads with Amazon web services

You may have noticed in previous chapters that we've left a noticeable blank space on the right side of our *Places* application, waiting for some advertising. Having gone through the available web services, it is obvious that we have a candidate for that space with `Zend_Service_Amazon`.

Since that space is in the layout file, we're going to make use of a view helper whose purpose, as stated in the manual, is to "perform certain complex functions over and over." This is well-suited to our need to show the same view data repeatedly from outside of any controller. Dealing with the data retrieval, however, is a job for a model class, and we'll do that first.

13.2.1 *The Amazon model class*

The first thing we need to do is establish some settings before querying Amazon. The model class we're setting up here is quite specific to the needs of our *Places* application but it could, if needed, be made more generic. The point of our examples is to demonstrate the separation of responsibilities, with the model class being responsible for the data retrieval, which will be used by the view helper.

We've decided that all we really need in order to fill our advertising space is a small selection of books matching some keywords that will be passed to the view helper in the layout file. A thumbnail image of the cover and a title linked back to its parent page on Amazon UK is all we need for each book.

After having provided the required Amazon API key, our code in listing 13.4 uses the fluent interface of Zend_Service_Amazon_Query to pass in some of our requirements. Information about obtaining an API key and more is available through the Amazon Web Services website at http://www.amazon.com/gp/aws/landing.html.

Listing 13.4 The Amazon model class that will be used for data retrieval

```php
require_once 'Zend/Service/Amazon/Query.php';

class Amazon
{
    protected $apiKey;

    public function __construct()
    {
        $this->apiKey = Zend_Registry::get('config')      ❶ Recovers
                            ->amazon_api_key;                  Amazon API key
    }

    public function search($keywords)
    {                                          ❷ Stops if no API
        if(empty($this->apiKey)) {                 key available
            return null;
        }                          ❸ Wraps query in a
        try {                          try-catch block
            $query = new Zend_Service_Amazon_Query(
                            $this->apiKey, 'UK'
                            );
            $query->category('Books')       ❺ Searches only
                ->Keywords($keywords)           for books
                ->ResponseGroup('Small,Images');
            $results = $query->search();
            if ($results->totalResults() > 0) {
                return $results;
            }
        } catch (Zend_Service_Exception $e) {
            return null;
        }                          ❽ Returns null
        return null;                   if no service
    }
}
```

❹ Instantiates Zend_Service_Amazon_Query

❻ Passes keywords that we want to search for

❼ Specifies the response group

Our API key is stored in a `Zend_Config` object that is itself stored in a `Zend_Registry` object and is recovered in the constructor of our class ❶. If no API key is available, our search method will immediately halt and return a `null` value ❷. Because we have no control over the availability of public web services, or over the network connections, our code needs to allow for that. PHP5's new exception model is particularly valuable in such circumstances, and in this case we've wrapped the query in a try-catch block and allowed it to fail silently because its availability isn't crucial to the operation of our website ❸.

   If all is well, we first set up our `Zend_Service_Amazon_Query` object with our API key and specify Amazon UK as the service ❹. Then we set options for the search, starting by specifying that we want only books to be searched ❺. Next, we set the keywords ❻ and the response group ❼, which "controls the data returned by the operation." In this case, we have specified the `Small` group, which "provides global, item-level data (no pricing or availability), including the ASIN, product title, creator (author, artist, composer, directory, manufacturer, etc.), product group, URL, and manufacturer," and the `Images` group, so that we have some thumbnail images of the covers to show. If all isn't well, we return a `null` value ❽, but we could do something more adventurous if needed.

   With our model class now ready to accept query requests, we can move on to the view helper that will prepare the view data.

13.2.2 *The Amazon ads view helper*

Our view helper will take the data retrieved by our Amazon model class in listing 13.4 and format it into an unordered HTML list. It can then be included in the site layout file, like so:

```
<?php echo $this->amazonAds('kids,travel', 2); ?>
```

Here we're specifying that the keywords to search for are "kids, travel" and that the number of books we want to show is 3 (when the `foreach` loop hits key 2). In listing 13.5, we can see that the `amazonAds()` method in our view helper code also takes a third parameter, which is an optional `UL` element ID. As with all view helpers, the naming of this method is important and must match the class name (aside from the lowercase first character) so that it can be automatically called when the object is used in view files.

Listing 13.5 Our `AmazonAds` view helper that composes the HTML for our view

```
require_once 'Amazon.php';

class Zend_View_Helper_AmazonAds
{
    public function amazonAds($keywords, $amount=3, $elementId='amazonads')
    {
        $amazon = new Amazon;              ⟵┐ Instantiates our
        $results = $amazon->search($keywords);   ⟵┘ Amazon model object
                                                      Makes query
                                                      with keywords
```

```
        if(null === $results) {
           return null;              ⟵─────────────┐
        }                                          │    Returns null
                                                   │    if no results              Sets up HTML
        $xhtml = '<ul id=' . $elementId . '>';      ⟵──────────────────────────   to return
        foreach ($results as $key => $result) {
           $xhtml .= '<li>';
           $xhtml .= '<a href="' . $result->DetailPageURL . '">';
           $xhtml .= '<img src="' . $result->SmallImage->Url
              . '" width="' . $result->SmallImage->Width
              . '" height="' . $result->SmallImage->Height
              . '" alt="Cover for ' . $result->Title . '" />';
           $xhtml .= '</a>';
           $xhtml .= '<a href="' . $result->DetailPageURL
              . '" title="Details for ' . $result->Title . '">'
              . $result->Title . '</a>';
           $xhtml .= '</li>';
           if(intval($amount) == $key) {
              break;
           }
        }
        $xhtml .= '</ul>';              ───────┐    Returns
        return $xhtml;                  ⟵──────   HTML
     }
  }
```

Our method starts by instantiating our Amazon model object from listing 13.4. Then we use it to make the query with the requested keywords. If the search gives no results, we return a null value; otherwise we set up the HTML, which will be returned and displayed in our view file.

Since you're reading this book, you're obviously sharp-witted enough to have noticed, even without trying out this code, that it has a few notable flaws. The first problem is that if it fails, it returns a null value, which will leave a blank space on our page. The second problem is that if it succeeds, it may still cause a noticeable delay, because the information is retrieved from Amazon every time a page on our site is requested.

The first problem isn't too hard to deal with. We could, for example, simply call another view helper to show a banner ad if our Amazon query fails. The second problem is not only out of our control, but is also more important, because annoying page delays can turn users away from our site. What we need is a way to reduce our vulnerability to network delays.

The way to do this is to cache the view helper result, which we'll do using the Zend_Cache component.

13.2.3 Caching the view helper

This section will introduce the use of caching to reduce the number of query calls we need make to Amazon, but it isn't intended as a detailed introduction to caching, because that's the subject of the next chapter. Nevertheless, we'll take a bit of time to explain the example shown in listing 13.6.

Listing 13.6   Our `AmazonAds` view helper with added caching using `Zend_Cache`

```php
require_once 'Amazon.php';

class Zend_View_Helper_AmazonAds
{
    protected $cache;
    protected $cacheDir;

    public function __construct()
    {
        $this->cacheDir = ROOT_DIR .                    ← Sets cache storage directory
                      '/application/cache';
        $frontendOptions = array(                       ← Sets 2 hour lifetime
            'lifetime' => 7200,
            'automatic_serialization' => true
        );
        $backendOptions = array(                         ← Sets cache directory
            'cache_dir' => $this->cacheDir
        );
        $this->cache = Zend_Cache::factory(              ← Gets Zend_Cache_Core object with options
                'Core','File', $frontendOptions,$backendOptions);
    }

    public function amazonAds($keywords, $amount=3,
                    $elementId='amazonads')
    {
        if(!$xhtml = $this->cache->load('amazon')) {     ← Tries loading cached version
            $amazon = new Amazon;                        ← Continues with query if no cached version
            $results = $amazon->search($keywords);
            if(null === $results) {
                return null;
            }

            $xhtml = '<ul id=' . $elementId . '>';
            foreach ($results as $key => $result) {
                $xhtml .= '<li>';
                $xhtml .= '<a href="' . $result->DetailPageURL . '">';
                $xhtml .= '<img src="' . $result->SmallImage->Url
                    . '" width="' . $result->SmallImage->Width
                    . '" height="' . $result->SmallImage->Height
                    . '" alt="Cover for ' . $result->Title . '" />';
                $xhtml .= '</a>';
                $xhtml .= '<a href="' . $result->DetailPageURL
                    . '" title="Details for ' . $result->Title . '">'
                    . $result->Title . '</a>';
                $xhtml .= '</li>';
                if(intval($amount) == $key) {
                    break;
                }
            }
            $xhtml .= '</ul>';
            $this->cache->save($xhtml, 'amazon');         ← Saves output as cached version
        }
        return $xhtml;
```

```
    }
}
```

Our cached version of our view helper will store a copy of the HTML output in a file that is set to update every two hours. Each view helper call is preceded by a check to see if there is an up-to-date cache file that can be used as the output of the view helper. If a current cache file isn't available, we make the request to Amazon and, before outputting, save the HTML to the cache file to be used in the next request.

The benefit of all this is that we need to make a request to Amazon only every two hours, at most, rather than on every page request. Because we're only showing a selection of books we think might interest our readers, the two-hour delay between data refreshment is insignificant. If we needed more recent data, we'd just reduce the lifetime in the frontend options.

In figure 13.1, you can see that what was previously a blank space is now filled with a selection of books linked back to Amazon, from which we could earn a percentage of sales through the Amazon affiliate program. It is cached to avoid unnecessary delays in page loading, but it isn't perfect because the images themselves still need to be retrieved from Amazon. For our needs, this is acceptable. The HTML will allow the page to render, and users are generally accepting of some delay in image loading. If demand got high enough, we could cache the images as well, but we'd need to check the Amazon Web Services terms of use before doing so.

An unfortunate side effect of adding the Amazon thumbnail images is that our site content, particularly the article content, now looks quite bare. In the next section, we'll remedy that by using images from Flickr to complement the articles.

Figure 13.1   Our new Amazon ads shown on the right, and a similar search on Amazon on the left

13.3   *Displaying pictures from Flickr*

Before we get into our example, it's important to note that what we'll be showing here is for demonstration purposes only. For actual use, we'd need to be careful that our use of images from Flickr complied with its terms of use, which includes licensing limitations on individual images as well as limitations on what Flickr considers commercial use.

Our intention is to display relevant images from Flickr within our articles, but the main purpose of our example is to demonstrate the use of a public web service within an action controller rather than to suggest a particular use of Flickr's service. With that disclaimer in mind, we can move on to our example.

The methods available in `Zend_Service_Flickr` are a relatively small set of those available in Flickr's API, limited basically to finding images by tag, user information, or specific image details. While this could be used to retrieve a specific user's images from Flickr for use in an article submitted by that user, we're going to use the more general tag search for our example. Our starting point will be the same as for our Amazon example—a model class responsible for retrieving the data from Flickr.

13.3.1   *The Flickr model class*

The model class we're about to cover for Flickr is very similar to the one we developed for our Amazon example. Like Amazon, Flickr also requires an API key, available via the API documentation page at http://www.flickr.com/services/api/, which is used for tracking use of the API. Listing 13.7 shows that once again we're developing a model responsible for data retrieval, but this time it will be used within the article action controller.

Listing 13.7   Our Flickr model class

```
require_once 'Zend/Service/Flickr.php';

class Flickr
{
    protected $apiKey;

    public function __construct()
    {
        $this->apiKey = Zend_Registry::get('config')
                ->flickr_api_key;          ◁──┐  Gets API key from
    }                                          │  Zend_Config object
    public function search($keywords, $amount=6)
    {
        if(empty($this->apiKey)) {    ◁──┐  Stops if no
            return null;                 │  API key
        }
                                                     ┌─ Uses try-catch block
        try {                               ◁────────┘  to handle errors
            $flickr = new Zend_Service_Flickr(   ◁──┐  Instantiates
                        $this->apiKey);            │  Zend_Service_Flickr
                                                   │  with API key
```

```
$results = $flickr->tagSearch($keywords,
    array(
        'per_page' => $amount,
        'tag_mode' => 'all',
        'license'  => 3
    ));

    if ($results->totalResults() > 0) {
        return $results;
    }
} catch (Zend_Service_Exception $e) {
    return null;
}
    return null;
    }
}
```

Searches with keywords and options

Returns null on failure

In listing 13.7 our API key is recovered from the config object and passed to the Zend_Service_Flickr object. Next, we use the tagSearch() method, which is a wrapper for the flickr.photos.search Flickr method, passing it a few option settings.

It's worth checking out the API documentation, because the list of available options is huge and allows a great variation in the type of results returned. We could limit our search to different date settings, a specific user, a geographical area, a group and more. In our case, we're specifying a per-page limit, that the search uses all the tags we specify when searching, and that the license for images returned is suitable for our use. In this case, the license value 3 indicates the No Derivative Works Creative Commons license, which is defined like so:

> *No Derivative Works. You let others copy, distribute, display, and perform only verbatim copies of your work, not derivative works based upon it.*
>
> —http://creativecommons.org/about/license/

Limiting the results by group would be particularly useful, as it would allow us to work with groups of images that we had some control over, but for the sake of our example we've kept things simple.

On that note, our example model class is now complete enough to move on to its integration in the action controller.

13.3.2 *Using Flickr in an action controller*

Our Amazon example used a view helper, because we were going to use it repeatedly across pages and it wasn't specific to any single page. In this case, we're only going to use the Flickr images with articles, so calling our model from the article controller action is quite sufficient.

Since we're doing a search for images based on their tags, we're going to need a way of getting words to search for. We'll do this by adding a keywords column to the articles table in our *Places* database, and as shown in listing 13.8, passing those keywords to the Flickr object from the previous section.

Listing 13.8   Using our Flickr model class in our article controller action

```php
public function indexAction()
{
  $id - (int)$this->_request->getParam('id');
  if ($id == 0) {
    $this->_redirect('/');
    return;
  }

  $articlesTable = new ArticleTable();              ◁─────────┤ Gets the
  $article = $articlesTable->fetchRow('id='.$id);             │ article
  if ($article->id != $id) {
    $this->_redirect('/');
    return;
  }
  $this->view->article = $article;

  include_once 'Flickr.php';  │ Sets up Flickr                   ┤ Uses article
  $flickr = new Flickr;       │ object                          │ keywords in
  $results = $flickr->search($article->keywords);   ◁──────────┤ search
  $this->view->flickr = $results;    ◁────────┐
}                                             │ Passes results
                                              ┘ to view
```

In listing 13.8, we can see the original code for retrieving a requested article inside the
`ArticleController::indexAction()` method, and underneath that our code to get
the complementary images from Flickr. Having retrieved the article based on the ID
passed to the action controller, we then pass that article's keywords to our Flickr class.
Finally, we pass the results to the view, which is shown in listing 13.9.

Listing 13.9   The article view with the added Flickr images

```php
<h1><?php echo $this->escape($this->article->title); ?></h1>
<?php echo $this->article->body; ?>
<h2>Reviews</h2>
<?php if(count($this->reviews)) : ?>
<ul id="reviews">
<?php foreach($this->reviews as $review) : ?>
<li>
   <p class="review-meta">
      <?php echo $this->escape($review->user_name); ?> on
      <?php echo $this->displayDate($review->date_updated); ?>
   </p>
   <p class="review-body">
      <?php echo $this->escape($review->body); ?>
   </p>
</li>
<?php endforeach; ?>
</ul>
<?php endif; ?>

<?php if ($this->flickr->totalResults() > 0): ?>    ◁─────┤ Checks that we
<h3>Images from Flickr</h3>                                 have results
<ul id="flickr">
```

```php
<?php foreach ($this->flickr as $key => $result): ?>     ◁── Loops over
    <li>                                                         results
        <a href="<?php echo $result->Small->clickUri; ?>">
            <img src="<?php echo $result->Small->uri; ?>"
            width="<?php echo $result->Small->width; ?>"
            height="<?php echo $result->Small->height; ?>"
            alt="<?php echo $result->title; ?>" />
        </a>
        <a href="<?php echo $result->Small->clickUri; ?>"
        title="<?php echo $result->title; ?>">
            <?php echo $result->title; ?>
        </a>
    </li>
<?php endforeach; ?>
</ul>
<?php endif; ?>
```

The additional code in the view is quite straightforward. It comprises a simple test to make sure we have some results before looping over them and setting up a linked image element and image title within an unordered list. With a little bit of CSS magic, we can float those images and achieve a gallery effect, as shown in figure 13.2. You can see the original images from the tag search in Flickr now appearing with our article on Edinburgh Zoo.

You may have noticed that we didn't use any caching in this example. That was partly to keep the focus on the web service component, but, also, as we mentioned in the Amazon section, the presence of the HTML means that the whole page won't be overly delayed by network delays. In practice, it would probably be a good idea to implement some caching, taking note that the Flickr API terms warn us not to "cache

Figure 13.2 On the right, Flickr images based on article keywords displayed with the article; on the left, the original images on the Flickr site

or store any Flickr user photos other than for reasonable periods in order to provide the service you are providing to Flickr users."

Having seen the improvement that the Amazon ads made to that blank right side of our site and now how the addition of images from Flickr have improved our articles, we're up for a bigger and more visually dynamic challenge: adding video. In the next section, we'll do that using what's undoubtedly the biggest web service component in Zend Framework: `Zend_Gdata`.

13.4   Using Zend_Gdata for Google access

In our earlier introduction to Gdata, we gave a brief overview of the different services available through the Google Data API. Our site, *Places to take the kids*, is one that would clearly benefit from some videos from one of those services: the YouTube API.

Adding video to your site isn't an easy undertaking. Not only does it require proper preparation of the video for internet delivery; it can also stress your hosting space and bandwidth requirements. The success of YouTube and, in particular, its embedded video, is clearly a reflection of the benefits of outsourcing your video.

Of course, any video you add and use from YouTube is going to be carrying the YouTube branding, which makes it unsuitable for some needs. In such cases, solutions like `Zend_Service_Nirvanix` could be a possible option for dealing with hosting and bandwidth demands. We aren't worried about the YouTube connection on *Places*, and in fact could use it as a way to draw traffic to our site.

As when using any public services, the first step is to find out what the terms of use allow you to do. Our intention is to add a video section to *Places* that will first show a list of video categories, then a list of videos in a selected category, and finally a selected video, and this seems to comply with the YouTube terms of service. With that check out of the way, we can start building the video categories page. As with the Flickr example in section 13.3, we'll use an action controller.

13.4.1   The YouTube API in an action controller

What's interesting about the example in this section is just how little actual coding is needed to achieve a significant addition to the *Places* site. We're going to cover each page of our video section in detail shortly, but let's pause and look at how concise our controller action in listing 13.10 is. After all, we can't leave all the gloating over code brevity to the Ruby on Rails developers!

Listing 13.10   Our videos controller action

```
include_once 'Zend/Gdata/YouTube.php';

class VideosController extends Zend_Controller_Action
{
    protected $_youTube;

    function init()
    {
        $this->_youTube = new Zend_Gdata_YouTube;    ◁──┐ Sets up
                                                          Zend_Gdata_Youtube
                                                          object
```

```
    }
    public function indexAction()              Gets
    {                                          playlists
        $this->view->playlistListFeed =
            $this->_youTube->getPlaylistListFeed('ZFinAction');
    }
                                               Gets playlist
    public function listAction()               videos
    {
        $playlistId = $this->_request->getParam('id');
        $query = $this->_youTube->newVideoQuery(
            'http://gdata.youtube.com/feeds/playlists/' . $playlistId);
        $this->view->videoFeed = $this->_youTube->getVideoFeed($query);
    }
                                               Gets
    public function viewAction()               video
    {
        $videoId = $this->_request->getParam('id');
        $this->view->videoId = $videoId;
        $this->view->videoEntry = $this->_youTube->getVideoEntry($videoId);
    }

}
```

In the interest of full disclosure, there is a bit of logic that takes place in the view files, so before we get too self indulgent, we should take a look through them, starting with the video categories page.

Note that because we have only read-only access, the YouTube API does not require an API key, but we have established a YouTube user account to work with.

13.4.2 *The video categories page*

This page is a selection of video categories. Our users can click on one to see the list of videos that it contains. Our controller action file in listing 13.10 has an index-Action() method, which is responsible for this page. It simply gets a playlist feed for our "ZFinAction" user account and passes it to the view:

```
public function indexAction()
{
    $this->view->playlistListFeed =
        $this->_youTube->getPlaylistListFeed('ZFinAction');
}
```

YouTube refers to playlists as "collections of videos that can be watched on YouTube, shared with other people, or embedded into websites or blogs." In figure 13.3, you can see the YouTube account page, which we used to set up the playlists. Those playlists then appear in the view file shown in listing 13.11 as our video categories. Notice that we can also set a description for each one that we can use on our page.

Figure 13.3   Our video category page on the right, and the YouTube playlist management page on the left

---

Listing 13.11   Our video categories view code

```
<h1>Videos</h1>                                          Loops over playlist feed
<dl>
<?php foreach ($this->playlistListFeed as $playlistEntry): ?>
<?php $id = substr(strrchr(
   $playlistEntry->getPlaylistVideoFeedUrl(), '/'          Gets playlist entry
), 1); ?>                                                   ID from URL
   <dt>
      <a href="/videos/list/id/<?php echo $id; ?>/">        Shows linked
         <?php echo $playlistEntry->title->text; ?>         title and
      </a>                                                   description
   </dt>
   <dd><?php echo $playlistEntry->description->text; ?></dd>
<?php endforeach; ?>
</dl>
```

The view file simply loops over the playlist feed, filters out the playlist entry feed ID from its URL, then uses that ID and a description in a link to our next page—the video list page.

13.4.3 *The video list page*

The video list page shows the videos in the playlist that the user selected. Figure 13.4 shows the YouTube account we used to add video selections to each playlist and their appearance on our video list page.

Looking at the `listAction()` action controller method in listing 13.10, we can see that it takes the ID that we previously filtered out of the playlist entry URL and uses it in a query that gets the video feed for the chosen playlist:

Figure 13.4 Our video list page on the right, and the YouTube video list management page on the left

```php
public function listAction()
{
    $playlistId = $this->_request->getParam('id');
    $query = $this->_youTube->newVideoQuery(
        'http://gdata.youtube.com/feeds/playlists/' . $playlistId);
    $this->view->videoFeed = $this->_youTube->getVideoFeed($query);
}
```

That video feed is then passed to the view file in listing 13.12.

Listing 13.12 Our video list view file

```php
<h1>Videos in <?php echo $this->videoFeed->title->text; ?></h1>    ◁── Loops over video feed
<dl>
<?php foreach ($this->videoFeed as $videoEntry): ?>
<?php $id = substr(strrchr(          ◁── Filters out video ID from the URL
  $videoEntry->getFlashPlayerUrl(), '/'),
1); ?>
    <dt>
        <a href="/videos/view/id/<?php echo $id; ?>/">    ◁── Shows linked title and description
            <?php echo $videoEntry->mediaGroup->title->text; ?>
        </a>
    </dt>
    <dd><?php echo $videoEntry->mediaGroup->description->text; ?></dd>
<?php endforeach; ?>
</dl>
```

This view file is much the same as the video categories page. It loops over the video feed, filters out the video ID from its URL, and uses that ID along with a description in a link to our next page, the video page. Note that there are further options available, such as thumbnail images, which you could also display. You can find more information about these options on Google's YouTube API pages at http://code.google.com/apis/youtube/overview.html.

13.4.4 *The video page*

The video page is the simplest of them all because it just needs to show the video itself. In figure 13.5, you can see the selected video from YouTube now showing on our video page.

The controller action code in the `viewAction()` method that does this is equally simple. It uses the video ID passed to it to get the video from YouTube and sets that up as a view variable.

```
public function viewAction()
{
    $videoId = $this->_request->getParam('id');
    $this->view->videoId = $videoId;
    $this->view->videoEntry = $this->_youTube->getVideoEntry($videoId);
}
```

Note that we also pass that video ID as a view variable of its own, because this will be used in the view, shown in listing 13.13, to construct the URLs needed to retrieve the data from YouTube.

Figure 13.5   Our video page on the right, and the original video on YouTube on the left

Listing 13.13 Our video view file

```
<h1><?php echo $this->videoEntry->mediaGroup->title->text; ?></h1>
<object width="425" height="355">
   <param name="movie"
      value="http://www.youtube.com/v/
         <?php echo $this->videoId; ?>&rel=0">     ◁─────── Uses video ID
   </param>                                                  to retrieve
   <param name="wmode" value="transparent"></param>         video data
   <embed src="http://www.youtube.com/v/
         <?php echo $this->videoId; ?>&rel=0"      ◁───────
      type="application/x-shockwave-flash"
      wmode="transparent" width="425" height="355">
   </embed>
</object>
```

In our view file in listing 13.13, the videoEntry data is used to get the title and the video ID, included in the URL, which allows our video to appear on the final page.

The end result of what's actually very little work is that you can add quite a considerable amount of value to your site with a video section that can be fully controlled through your YouTube account. That means that you can not only use public video but also upload and feature your own video. Anyone who has been doing internet work for a while or who has ever wished he could control his own TV station will recognize that this has quite exciting possibilities.

13.5 *Summary*

In the previous chapter, we covered a lot of the theory and practice of working with web services using Zend Framework from both the client and server sides. This chapter should have felt a lot easier, not only because it worked only with the client side, but also because the Zend_Service_* and Zend_Gdata components wrap a lot of the complexities of each service in a more digestible form. This was evident in how little we needed to mention any of the technologies behind the services.

You now should have a good idea of some of the Zend Framework web service components that are available and are aware that more are on their way. Even better, you may be inspired to add some of your own.

Our brief examples were meant to give an idea of how you could use the components in your own projects, and our more detailed examples should have provided some indication of how the components can work within the MVC structure of Zend Framework. In a chapter that had to cover so many components, there were clearly limits to how much detail we could go into. Nevertheless, we hope that we did cover the main points, including checking the service's terms of use, taking care to code defensively, particularly in dealing with the very real issue of network delays, and using caching to reduce the number of service requests.

Caching is a topic that requires its own chapter, and it's the topic of our next chapter.

Caching: making it faster

14

This chapter covers

- How caching works
- Introducing the `Zend_Cache` component
- Using `Zend_Cache` frontend classes
- Choosing what to cache and for how long

Caching refers to taking a computationally expensive task, such as a database query or intense mathematical calculation, and storing the result so that next time the result can be quickly retrieved from the cache instead of repeating the task. This chapter will explain the benefits of caching, show you how to take advantage of these benefits using Zend Framework's `Zend_Cache`, and guide you through the process for choosing appropriate cache settings for your application.

On one project, Steven's client was told that the shared hosting account they were using was consuming too many resources and that, if the issue wasn't resolved, the account would be suspended. The site served over 40,000 members, many of whom visited the site on a daily basis. Having the account suspended would have been a disaster. The site was also slowing to a crawl, and database and memory errors had started to appear.

On analyzing the site's load, Steven discovered that the database was causing the load issues and slowness. He investigated further and found that one query was causing the problem. A piece of code on the site added together one field from all rows in a table and returned the result. At first, the task ran fine, but as the number of rows increased, first into the thousands, then tens of thousands, this query became slower and slower. This code was on every page, and it was obvious just how the load issue had come about.

Assuming there were 1,000 visitors per day, and each visitor went to 10 pages, the query was being run 10,000 times per day. As most visitors would hit the site around the same time each morning, most of the 10,000 queries would be performed in a short period of time, say over an hour or two. No wonder the site was falling over!

The solution was simple. The result of the query was stored in cache, and the cache was set to refresh hourly. The query was now running only once per hour instead of several thousand times per hour. Instantly the server load was reduced to almost nothing, and the site performed better than ever. Ultimately, caching saved the cost of upgrading the hosting account (or of losing it, for that matter).

14.1   Benefits of caching

The core benefit of caching is to reduce resource usage and deliver content more quickly. Reducing resource usage means you can serve more users from a lower-cost hosting account, and delivering content more quickly results in a much better user experience.

Caching a database request means that your application spends less time connecting to the database, which translates into more resources available for database operations that can't be cached. It also reduces page-rendering time, which frees up your web server resources to deliver more pages.

Caching gives you great leverage. Where normally an increase in traffic would mean an increase in load-intensive tasks such as database requests, the only increase with caching is in checking and retrieving the cached data. The number of database requests (or other computationally intensive tasks) will stay the same regardless of the increase in traffic.

Caching doesn't only apply to database queries. Zend_Cache is very flexible and can be used for everything from database queries to function calls. You can apply it to any load-intensive operation in your application, but it's important to understand how caching operates so that you know when and how to apply it.

14.2   How caching works

Caching is an economical way to increase the speed of your application and reduce server load. For most PHP applications, the most resource-intensive and time-consuming task is performing database operations.

Listing 14.1 shows typical code that might be used to retrieve information from a database using Zend_Db_Table.

Listing 14.1   Retrieving database data without caching

```
Zend_Loader::loadClass('Products');
$productTable = new Products();
$products = $productTable->fetchAll();
```

This is standard Zend Framework code, where we load the `Product` model and call `fetchAll()` to retrieve a list of all products in the database. A flow diagram showing the overall process is shown in figure 14.1.

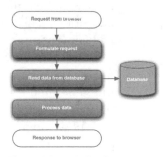

In most applications, there will be multiple database queries—tens or even hundreds. Every request to the database uses processor time and memory. If you have many visitors on your site at a time, your server resources can very quickly be consumed. This is common in high-traffic situations or on low-budget servers where resources are minimal.

Figure 14.1   A database request without caching

Listing 14.2 shows how `Zend_Cache`'s caching abilities can be added to the previous code example.

Listing 14.2   Retrieving database data with caching

```
Zend_Loader::loadClass('Zend_Cache');
$frontendOptions = array(
   // set frontend options
);                                          Sets
$backendOptions = array(                    cache
   // set backend options                   options
);

$query_cache = Zend_Cache::factory('Core', 'File',    Creates      ❶ Sets the
    $frontendOptions, $backendOptions);               cache object    unique
                                                                      identifier
$cacheName = 'allproducts';
if(!($result = $query_cache->load($cacheName))) {                    Loads
    Zend_Loader::loadClass('Product');                              from
    $productTable = new Product();          ❸ Performs resource-    cache if
    $result = $productTable->fetchAll();       intensive operation ❷ possible

    $query_cache->save($result, $cacheName);         Stores to
}                                               ❹  cache
```

A `Zend_Cache` cache object is created using the `factory()` method, which returns a frontend cache object that is attached to a backend. In this case, we use the "core" frontend class (`Zend_Cache_Core`) and the "file" backend (`Zend_Cache_Backend_File`), which means that the cached data is stored to files on disk.

To store data to a cache, we need a unique name ❶, and we use the `load()` method to retrieve the data from the cache ❷. If the data isn't in the cache (or has expired), we can perform our resource-intensive operation ❸ and use `save()` to store the results to the cache ❹.

A flow diagram showing the overall process with caching in place is shown in figure 14.2.

In this way, the query is run once (depending on how long your cache is set to last), and the cache is able to serve out the data hundreds, thousands, or millions of times without having to interact with the database again until the cache expires.

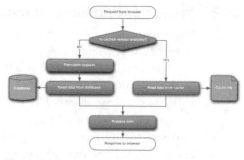

Figure 14.2 A database request using caching

Caching relies on two principles:

- *The unique identifier*—When the cache system checks to see if a cache result already exists, it uses the unique identifier to check. It's very important to ensure that your unique identifiers are indeed unique; otherwise you'll have two separate items using the same cache and conflicting with each other. The best way to ensure this is to have the caching code for that identifier only once in your code, such as in a function or method, and call it from multiple places if necessary.

- *The expiry time*—This is the expiry time for a cache, after which its contents are regenerated. If the cached data changes infrequently, you might set the expiry time to 30 days. If something changes frequently but you have a high-traffic site, you'd choose to set the expiry time to 5 minutes, 30 minutes, or an hour. Choosing the right expiry time is discussed in section 14.4.

Figure 14.3 shows how a caching system determines whether or not to run the intensive task or to load the result from cache.

A caching system uses the unique identifier to check for an existing cache result. If a result does exist, it will check to see if the result has expired. If it hasn't expired, the cached result is returned—this is known as a *cache hit*. If there is no existing cache result or the existing cache result has expired, this is known as a *cache miss*.

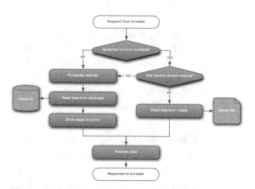

Figure 14.3 The decision-making process of a caching system

Now that we've looked at how caching works, let's look at how to add caching to an application using Zend_Cache.

14.3   *Implementing Zend_Cache*

Implementing Zend_Cache is very simple. Once you discover how easy it is, you'll want to use it everywhere!

The Zend_Cache options are divided into two main parts, the frontend and the backend. The frontend refers to the operation that you're caching, such as a function call or a database query. The backend refers to how the cache result is stored.

As we saw in listing 14.2, implementing Zend_Cache involves instantiating the object and setting the frontend and backend options. Once this is done, you perform the cache check. Each frontend does this in a different way, but essentially you ask if there is an existing cache; if there isn't you'll proceed into the code required to generate the result to be stored in cache. You then command Zend_Cache to store the result.

Listing 14.3 shows an example of using Zend_Cache to cache a database query using a model.

Listing 14.3   Example usage of Zend_Cache

```
Zend_Loader::loadClass('Zend_Cache');
$frontendOptions = array(
    'lifetime' => 60 * 5, // 5 minutes
    'automatic_serialization' => true,
);
$backendOptions = array(
    'cache_dir' => BASE_PATH . '/application/cache/',
    'file_name_prefix' => 'zend_cache_query',
    'hashed_directory_level' => 2,
);
$query_cache = Zend_Cache::factory('Core', 'File', $frontendOptions,
    $backendOptions);

$cacheName = 'product_id_' . $id;
if(!($result = $query_cache->load($cacheName))) {
    Zend_Loader::loadClass('Product');
    $productTable = new Product();
    $result = $productTable->fetchRow(array('id = ?' => $id));
    $query_cache->save($result, $cacheName);
}
```

The frontend options control how the cache operates. For example, the lifetime key determines how long the cached data is to be used before it's expired. The backend options are specific to the type of cache storage that is used. For Zend_Cache_Backend_File, information about the directory (cache_dir) and how many directory levels to use (hashed_directory_level) are important.

The rest of the code is similar to that in listing 14.2, only this time the cache name is specific to the product ID, and the cached data is only related to a single product. Let's look in detail at the Zend_Cache frontends and the configuration options available.

14.3.1   *Zend_Cache frontends*

All of the frontends extend Zend_Cache_Core, but you don't instantiate Zend_Cache_Core or any of the frontends. Instead, you use the Zend_Cache::factory()

static method. The four arguments for this method are $frontendName (string), $backendName (string), $frontendOptions (associative array), and $backendOptions (associative array). The command is as follows:

```
$cache = Zend_Cache::factory(
    $frontendName,
    $backendName,
    $frontendOptions,
    $backendOptions
);
```

Each frontend and backend has its own options that affect its operation. The core frontend options are shown in table 14.1.

Table 14.1   Core frontend options of `Zend_Cache`

Option	Description
caching	By default this is set to `true`, so you likely won't have to change it, but you can set it to `false` if you want to temporarily turn off caching for testing. This is an alternative to commenting out the cache test.
lifetime	This is the amount of time in seconds before the cache expires and the result is regenerated. By default, it's set to 1 hour (`3600` seconds). You can set it to `null` if you want the cache to last forever.
logging	If you set this to true, the caching will be logged using `Zend_Log`. By default it's set to `false`. If set to true, there will be a performance hit.
write_control	By default, this is set to `true`, and the cache will be read after it's written to check that it hasn't become corrupted. You can disable this, but it's good to have some extra protection against corruption, so we recommend leaving it on.
automatic_serialization	If set to `true`, this will serialize the cache data (refer to the PHP manual for the serialize function). This allows you to store complex data types such as arrays or objects. If you're only storing a simple data type such as a string or integer, you do not need to serialize the data and can leave this as the default value of `false`.
automatic_cleaning_factor	The automatic cleaning facility will clean up expired caches when a new cache result is stored. If you set it to `0`, it won't clean up expired caches. If set to `1`, it will clean up on every cache write. If you set it to a number higher than `1`, it will clean up randomly 1 in *x* times, where *x* is the number you enter. By default, it's set to `10`, so it will randomly clean up 1 in 10 times a new cache result is stored.

Each frontend is designed to give you caching capability at various levels of your application. The following subsections describe the individual frontends and their remaining options. Please note that all examples assume that $backendName, $frontendOptions, and $backendOptions have already been defined. This will allow you to interchange your own options with each frontend.

The frontends are listed in table 14.2

Table 14.2   The cache frontends

Name	Description
Core	The core of all frontends but can also be used on its own. This uses the `Zend_Cache_Core` class.
Output	This uses an output buffer to capture output from your code and store it in the cache. It uses the `Zend_Cache_Frontend_Output` class.
Function	This stores the result of procedural functions. It uses the `Zend_Cache_Frontend_Function` class.
Class	This stores the result of static class or object methods. It uses the `Zend_Cache_Frontend_Class` class.
File	This stores the result of loading and parsing a file. It uses the `Zend_Cache_Frontend_File` class.
Page	This stores the result of a page request. It uses the `Zend_Cache_Frontend_Page` class.

The most basic frontend you'll use is Zend_Cache_Core.

ZEND_CACHE_CORE

This is the base class for all frontends, but we can access it directly if needed. This is most useful for storing variables, such as strings, arrays, or objects. All of the frontends convert the cache result into a variable for storing in this way. The simplest use of Zend_Cache_Core is shown in listing 14.4.

Listing 14.4   Simple use of `Zend_Cache_Core`

```
$frontendName = 'Core';
$cache = Zend_Cache::factory(
    $frontendName, $backendName, $frontendOptions, $backendOptions
);
if (!($data = $cache->load('test'))) {
    // perform computationally intensive task here
    $cache->save($data, 'test');
}
```

One great use of `Zend_Cache_Core` is for storing the result of database calls, because there is no specific `Zend_Cache_Frontend_*` class to do so. An example of this is shown in listing 14.5.

> **Listing 14.5   Using `Zend_Cache_Core` to store database results**

```
$cacheName = 'product_' . $productId;
if(!$result = $cache->load($cacheName)) {
    Zend_Loader::loadClass('Product');
    $productTable = new Product();
    $result = $productTable->fetchRow(array('id = ?' => $productId));
    $cache->save($result, $cacheName);
}
```

As you can see, we've added `$cacheName`. This allows you to set the unique identifier using variables and use it for loading and saving the cache. Be aware that the identifier used in this example is very simple because we are only fetching the row based on one condition. If you were performing a query with multiple conditions, you'd need to devise a means of generating a unique identifier to suit the purpose. If the identifier you choose is not unique enough, you might accidentally use the same identifier for two different queries, which could cause errors.

Setting a unique identifier

In many cases, you can generate a unique identifier using this code:

```
md5(serialize($conditions));
```

This converts the conditions, which may be an array, into a single unique string. You can join all of your conditions into one array for this. The `serialize()` function produces a single string that can be passed to `md5()`. The `md5()` function implements the MD5 algorithm, which produces a 32-character string representation of the serialized data.

The MD5 algorithm creates what's called a one-way hash. The same input will result in the same hash value, and the chance of two different input values producing the same hash is extremely slim. This makes it a pretty good means of reducing a long string to a smaller, unique value.

The `sha1()` function is an alternative that uses the SHA1 algorithm. It's similar to MD5 in that it produces a one-way hash, but the result is 40 characters, meaning the chances of two different values resulting in the same hash is even slimmer.

When setting your own unique identifier, it's important to follow the rules for what characters it can contain. The identifier can't start with "internal-", because this is reserved by `Zend_Cache`. Identifiers can only contain a–z, A–Z, 0–9, and _. Any other characters will throw an exception and abort your script.

As you can see in listing 14.5, if there is a cache hit, the `$result` variable is filled with the cached result and can be treated as if it were directly returned by the database query. If there is a cache miss, the database query is performed and populates the $result value again before saving the result to the cache. Either way, the $result value can be treated exactly the same from here on in.

NOTE   When storing objects in a cache (such as database query results), you'll need to ensure you have loaded the appropriate class (such as Zend_Db_Table_Row) before reading the object from the cache. Otherwise the object can't be properly reconstructed, and your application will most probably fail because the properties and methods you expect won't be there. If you are using autoloading, the class will be automatically loaded for you when it is needed. See section 3.2.2 in chapter 3 for more information on autoloading.

You might find it useful to place the caching code inside a method of a model, as shown in listing 14.6.

Listing 14.6   Using cache code inside a model

```
class Product extends Zend_Db_Table_Abstract {

    protected $_name = 'product';
    protected $_primary = 'id';

    public function fetchRowById($id) {
        Zend_Loader::loadClass('Zend_Cache');
        $frontendOptions = array (
            //...
        );
        $backendOptions = array (
            //...
        );
        $queryCache = Zend_Cache::factory(
            'Core', 'File', $frontendOptions, $backendOptions
        );
        $cacheName = 'product_id_' . $id;
        if (!($result = $queryCache->load($cacheName))) {
            $result = $this->fetchRow(array('id = ?' => $id));
            $queryCache->save($result, $cacheName);
        }
        return $result;
    }
}
```

By moving the cache code to the fetchRowById() method, we now have a central place to manage our cache options. For example, we could change the lifetime in one place rather than many, fix a bug with the unique identifier, disable caching for debugging, or clear the cache.

If you need to get a row from the Product table with a specific ID, you can now use this code:

```
$productTable->fetchRowById($id);
```

You can place this code at multiple points and not have to worry about caching every time, because it's handled for you.

Although you could use `Zend_Cache_Core` to cache output from your code, Zend Framework comes with a class called `Zend_Cache_Frontend_Output` designed just for that.

ZEND_CACHE_FRONTEND_OUTPUT

This frontend uses output buffering to cache output from your code. It captures all output, such as echo and print statements, between the start and end methods. It uses a simple identifier to determine whether a cache result exists. If not, it will execute the code and store the output.

There are no additional frontend options for `Zend_Cache_Frontend_Output`, as you can see in listing 14.7.

Listing 14.7 Usage of `Zend_Cache_Frontend_Output`

```
if (!($cache->start('test'))) {
    echo 'Cached output';
    $cache->end();
}
```

As you can see, if the `start()` method returns `false` (no valid cache was found), it will cache the output. If `start()` returned `true`, `Zend_Cache_Frontend_Output` will output whatever was stored in the cache. You'll have to be careful that you don't use the same unique identifier for different output in separate areas of your code.

If you want to store the result of a function, you can use the `Zend_Cache_Frontend_Function` class.

ZEND_CACHE_FRONTEND_FUNCTION

This frontend stores the result of a function call. It's able to distinguish one function call from another by comparing the input values. If the input values match an existing cache result, it's able to return that rather than performing the function operation again.

The frontend options for `Zend_Cache_Frontend_Function` allow you to control the caching of individual functions from one point. The main benefit of this is that if you decide you don't want to cache a particular function, you don't have to change every call to that function; you simply change the option.

This may seem a little bit confusing, but we'll explain it in more detail shortly. Table 14.3 shows the additional frontend options for `Zend_Cache_Frontend_Function`.

Table 14.3 Additional frontend options for `Zend_Cache_Frontend_Function`

Option	Description
`cacheByDefault`	By default this is `true`, meaning all functions passed through `Zend_Cache_Frontend_Function` will be cached and you'll need to set `nonCachedFunctions` to turn off individual functions. If set to `false` you'll need to set `cachedFunctions` to enable caching for particular functions.

Table 14.3   Additional frontend options for `Zend_Cache_Frontend_Function`

Option	Description
cachedFunctions	If cacheByDefault is turned off, you can define the functions you'd like to cache here, as an array.
nonCachedFunctions	If cacheByDefault is turned on (the default setting) you can disable caching of functions by adding them here as an array.

Listing 14.8 shows an example of a normal call to a computationally intensive function without using caching.

Listing 14.8   Example function call without caching

```
function intensiveFunction($name, $animal, $times)
{
    $result = '';
    for ($i = 0; $i < $times; $i++) {
        $result .= $name;
        $result = str_rot13($result);
        $result .= $animal;
        $result = md5($result);
    }
    return $result;
}
$result = yourFunction('bob', 'cat', 3000);
```

To cache this function, you'd use `Zend_Cache_Frontend_Function`'s `call()` method. Listing 14.9 shows `Zend_Cache_Frontend_Function` applied to listing 14.8.

Listing 14.9   Example function call with caching

```
function intensiveFunction($name, $animal, $times)
{
    $result = '';
    for ($i = 0; $i < $times; $i++) {
        $result .= $name;
        $result = str_rot13($result);
        $result .= $animal;
        $result = md5($result);
    }
    return $result;
}

Zend_Loader::loadClass('Zend_Cache');
$frontendOptions = array (
    ...
);
$backendOptions = array (
    ...
);
$queryCache = Zend_Cache::factory(
```

```
    'Function', 'File', $frontendOptions, $backendOptions
);
$result = $cache->call('intensiveFunction', array('bob', 'cat', 3000));
```

This is exactly the same as calling `call_user_func_array()` except that the result will be cached. If you decided you no longer wanted to cache this function, you could set it in the options rather than having to change all of your code back to the original `intensiveFunction()` call:

```
$nonCachedFunctions = array('intensiveFunction');
```

If you want to enable caching again, just remove it from the array.

If you change the input for your function, `Zend_Cache_Frontend_Function` will treat this as a unique identifier:

```
$result = $cache->call('yourFunction', array('alice,' 'dog', 7));
```

`Zend_Cache_Frontend_Function` will cache this separately from the previous function call. This means you don't have to create your own unique identifier.

Please note that you can't use `Zend_Cache_Frontend_Function` for calling static methods of classes. Instead, you'll need to use `Zend_Cache_Frontend_Class`.

ZEND_CACHE_FRONTEND_CLASS

This frontend is similar to `Zend_Cache_Frontend_Function`, but it's able to store the result of the static methods of a class, or the result of non-static methods of an object.

The additional frontend options for `Zend_Cache_Frontend_Class` are shown in table 14.4.

Table 14.4   The additional frontend options for `Zend_Cache_Frontend_Class`

Option	Description
cachedEntity	Set this to either the class (for static methods) or the object (for non-static methods). This is required for each cache call.
cacheByDefault	By default this is `true`, meaning all methods passed through `Zend_Cache_Class_Function` will be cached and you'll need to set `nonCachedMethods` to turn off individual functions. If set to `false`, you'll need to set `cachedMethods` to enable caching for particular functions.
cachedMethods	If `cacheByDefault` is turned off, you can define the methods you'd like to cache here, as an array.
nonCachedMethods	If `cacheByDefault` is turned on (the default) you can disable caching of methods by adding them here as an array.

When calling the method through the cache, treat the cache object as if it were the original class or method you were calling. For example,

```
$result = $someObject->someMethod(73);
```

becomes

```
$result = $cache->someMethod(73);
```

Or for a static method,

```
$result = someClass::someStaticMethod('bob');
```

becomes

```
$result = $cache->someStaticMethod('bob');
```

The `Zend_Cache_Frontend_Class` frontend uses the class or object and the method input as a unique identifier, so you don't have to create one.

The next useful frontend is `Zend_Cache_Frontend_File`.

ZEND_CACHE_FRONTEND_FILE

This frontend caches the result of parsing a particular file. Essentially, it's able to determine whether the file has changed and uses that to determine whether or not it needs to be reparsed. Parsing can be anything really; what you're caching is the code that is dependent upon the contents of a particular file. This is essentially the same as `Zend_Cache_Core` except that the cache expires if the file changes rather than after a fixed time period.

There is one additional frontend option for `Zend_Cache_Frontend_File`, which is shown in table 14.5.

Table 14.5   The additional frontend option for `Zend_Cache_Frontend_File`

Option	Description
`master_file`	This is required and must contain the complete path and filename of the file you're caching.

Once you have defined the master file, you can use `Zend_Cache_Frontend_File` as shown in listing 14.10.

Listing 14.10   Example usage of `Zend_Cache_Frontend_File`

```
$filename = 'somefile.txt';
$cacheName = md5($filename);
if (!($result = $cache->load($cacheName))) {
    $data = file_get_contents($filename);
    $result = unserialize($data);
    $cache->save($result, $cacheName);
}
```

The `$filename` value here is fed into the frontend options. We then use an MD5 digest of `$filename` as the unique identifier. You may want to cache different operations on a file; for example, you may load in an XML file and search the contents in one area, while directly outputting the contents in another area. In order to cache both operations, you'll need to use a different unique identifier for each area.

If the file somefile.txt ever changes, `Zend_Cache_Frontend_File` will notice (based on the modification time) and the code will be run again. Otherwise the result of the code (not the data from the file itself) will be returned.

ZEND_CACHE_FRONTEND_PAGE

The `Zend_Cache_Frontend_Page` frontend is like `Zend_Cache_Frontend_Output`, except that it caches the output based on the `$_SERVER['REQUEST_URI']` variable and optionally the user-submitted data contained with the `$_GET`, `$_POST`, `$_SESSION`, `$_COOKIE`, and `$_FILES` variables. You initiate it by calling the `start()` method, and it will self-store when the page has been rendered. You can save all page-code execution if the input variables match an existing cache result.

The additional frontend options for `Zend_Cache_Frontend_Page` are shown in table 14.6.

Table 14.6   The additional frontend options for `Zend_Cache_Frontend_Page`

Option	Description
`debug_header`	This is set to `false` by default, but if you set it to `true`, it will output "DEBUG HEADER : This is a cached page !" Unfortunately, you can't change this message, but it will at least let you check to be sure the output is the cached page rather than the original.

`default_options`	This can get really complex, but thankfully in most situations you can leave the default settings alone. If you really must dig deeper, you can set the associative array with the following options.
	
	`cache`
	  By default, this is `true` and the page will be cached if all other conditions are met. If you set it to `false`, the page won't be cached.
	
	`cache_with_get_variables`
	  By default, this is `false`, which means that if there are any variables in `$_GET`, the page will be rerendered. If you set it to `true`, the page will still be loaded from cache. Be careful setting this to `true` if the `$_GET` variables change the contents of the page.
	
	`cache_with_post_variables`
	  Same as `cache_with_get_variables`, but with `$_POST`.
	
	`cache_with_session_variables`
	  Same as `cache_with_get_variables`, but with `$_SESSION`.
	
	`cache_with_files_variables`
	  Same as `cache_with_get_variables`, but with `$_FILES`.
	
	`cache_with_cookie_variables`
	  Same as `cache_with_get_variables`, but with `$_COOKIE`.
	
	`make_id_with_get_variables`
	  This is set to `true` by default, which includes `$_GET` in the automatic unique identifier generator. If you set it to `false`, the generator will use the other variables. Be careful with this one; if the `$_GET` variables change the output of the page, you may have cache conflicts if you don't set it to `true`.

Table 14.6 The additional frontend options for `Zend_Cache_Frontend_Page` (continued)

Option	Description

default_options
(continued)
	`make_id_with_post_variables`
	   Same as `make_id_with_get_variables`, but with `$_POST`.
	
	`make_id_with_session_variables`
	   Same as `make_id_with_get_variables`, but with `$_SESSION`.
	
	`make_id_with_files_variables`
	   Same as `make_id_with_get_variables`, but with `$_FILES`.
	
	`make_id_with_cookie_variables`
	   Same as `make_id_with_get_variables`, but with `$_COOKIE`.

regexps	This is a very powerful feature. Since you'll most likely only have one instance of the frontend handling all of your pages, you may want to treat some pages differently than others. This option is an associative array, the key is the regular expression you use to define the page to apply the options to, and the value is an array just like `default_options` above. The regular expression is run on `$_SERVER['REQUEST_URI']`, so you can use whatever you like, but in most cases it will be a simple expression to match controllers or controller and action combinations.

The most basic implementation of `Zend_Cache_Frontend_Page` looks like this:

```
$cache = Zend_Cache::factory('Page', 'File', $frontendOptions,
    $backendOptions);
$cache->start();
```

Note that once `$cache->start()` is called and a valid cache exists, your application will end once the cached page has been output.

If we wanted to turn off caching for a particular controller, we'd add the following in the `$frontendOptions`:

```
'regexps' => array(
    '^/admin/' => array(
        'cache' => false,
    ),
),
```

This turns off page caching for the entire admin section of the site. If you don't know much about regular expressions, you should be able to get by with putting ^ at the beginning of each entry. If you need to know more, research regular expressions or "regex."

If we wanted to turn off caching for admin, but keep the products action cached, we'd do this:

```
'regexps' => array(
    '^/admin/' => array(
        'cache' => false,
    ),
    '^/admin/products/' => array(
        'cache' => true;
    ),
),
```

The last rule will always be followed if in conflict with previous rules, so this will work as expected. If the `^/admin/products/` line was above the `^/admin/` line, the products action wouldn't be cached because the `^/admin/` line would overrule it.

Now you know about all of the frontends, so let's look at the `Zend_Cache` backend classes.

14.3.2 Zend_Cache backends

The backends define the way in which the cache data is stored. In most cases, `Zend_Cache_Backend_File` is the best and easiest backend to use. It uses simple files to store the data. Simple file operations are generally much faster than accessing a database, or in some cases performing resource-intensive tasks. This makes files perfect for cache storage.

The additional options for `Zend_Cache_Backend_File` are shown in table 14.7.

Table 14.7   The additional options for `Zend_Cache_Backend_File`

Option	Description
cache_dir	This is the full path where the cache files are stored. By default, it's set to `/tmp/` but we prefer to set it to a path within our application so that we can easily view and manage cache files manually if we need to.
file_locking	This will use an exclusive lock to offer some protection against cache corruption. It's turned on by default, and there is little reason to turn it off, although there may be a very minor performance improvement in situations where file locking isn't supported.
read_control	By default this is turned on, and it adds a control key (digest or length) that is used to compare the data that is read from cache to ensure it matches the data that was stored.
read_control_type	This sets the read control type. By default, it uses `crc32()`, but it can be set to use `md5()` or `strlen()`.
hashed_directory_level	Some file systems struggle when there is a large number of files in one directory. This can be a hassle when you're listing files or accessing via FTP and so on. Also, it can bog down statistics and similar applications. In order to protect against this, you can set the `hashed_directory_level`, which causes the backend to create multiple directories and subdirectories for the cache files to be stored in, so that there are fewer files in each directory. By default, it's set to `0`, which means all files are in the one directory, but you can set it to `1` or `2` (or more) levels of subdirectories, depending on how many files you expect. `1` or `2` are probably the safest options.
hashed_directory_umask	This uses `chmod()` to set the permissions for the directories it creates. By default, it's set to `0700`.

Table 14.7 The additional options for `Zend_Cache_Backend_File` (continued)

Option	Description
`file_name_prefix`	This sets a prefix for all cache files that are created. By default, it's set to `zend_cache`, which is good if you're using a generic /tmp/ directory for storage, but we prefer to use a prefix that describes the items that will be cached with this backend, such as "query" or "function". This allows us to know which files are related to which cache activity.

There are a few other backends, listed in table 14.8, but explaining them is beyond the scope of this book because they're much more specialized and only change the system that stores the cache data. If you're experienced with some of these other systems, you should be able to easily adapt your knowledge of Zend_Cache_Backend_File to suit. Please note that you may lose some functionality in choosing alternative backends.

Table 14.8 The additional `Zend_Cache_Backend` classes

Option	Description
`Zend_Cache_Backend_Sqlite`	This uses an SQLite database for storage.
`Zend_Cache_Backend_Memcached`	This uses a Memcached server for storage.
`Zend_Cache_Backend_Apc`	This uses Alternative PHP Cache.
`Zend_Cache_Backend_ZendPlatform`	This uses the Zend Platform.

Once you have your head around how to add caching to your code, you have to decide where you'll add caching to get the optimal results.

14.4 Caching at different application levels

While caching is an amazingly powerful tool, it can be used incorrectly. The most important decisions you'll have to make are deciding what to cache and how long the cache should last for.

14.4.1 Choosing what to cache

You have to be very careful when caching to be sure you're not caching something that must be run each time. For example, if you have `rand()`, `time()`, or database inserts or updates in the cache code, these won't be executed if there is valid cache data. This can be very unfortunate if you rely on these occurring further down in your code.

When you're using `Zend_Cache_Frontend_Page`, for example, and you're storing request details in the database for statistical purposes, you'll need to perform the database operations before calling `$cache->start()`. Otherwise, only one entry will be made for each expiry period, invalidating your statistics.

But there are some times when you'll want to cache things like `rand()`. For example, if you're displaying three random products on your home page as product highlights, you can probably cache it for five minutes or so without it affecting the user experience. In fact, you might want to cache it for 24 hours so that each day there are three new "products of the day."

14.4.2 *Optimal cache expiry*

One of the trickiest parts of caching is choosing the expiry time for the items you're caching. You can set up multiple cache objects anywhere in your code for various uses and assign different expiry times to each. It's a good idea to put these into a common place if possible, so that the caching is applied automatically for you, as described previously, with `$productTable->fetchRowById()`. This will ensure that all of your cache options, such as the expiry time, are consistent, and it allows you to easily change the options if you need.

When you're choosing an expiry time, it comes down to the type of data you're caching and how often it's likely to change, as well as how much traffic you expect. If the data changes often, such as users' comments, you may have to set the cache to five minutes. At most, the data will only be five minutes old. If you have a high-traffic web site, this will still offer a considerable performance improvement because you may receive a few hundred requests in five minutes.

If you have data that does not change frequently, such as product details, you may want to set the cache to seven days. You will, however, have to clear the cache using `Zend_Cache_Core`'s `clean()` or `remove()` methods when the price changes.

In some situations, where your load-intensive task takes a long time, there may be a second request for the information before the first request has completed and stored the result in cache. In this case, the load-intensive task will run again for the second request and for any additional requests until a result is stored in the cache. In high-traffic situations, this can bring your site to a grinding halt each time the cache expires. To avoid this, you should run the load-intensive task and replace the data in the cache when the data changes, and set the cache's `lifetime` to `null` so that it is always valid. This will ensure that the data is always read from the cache when it is needed, and the load-intensive task runs only when you want it to.

There is some data you can cache for a long period of time, such as the output of an intensive mathematical function, where the same input will always produce the same output. In this case, you could set the expiry to 365 days, or longer.

If you make a change to the expiry of a cache at any time, it will take effect immediately.

14.5   *Cache tags*

When you save data to cache, you can attach an array of tags. These tags can then be used to clear out caches containing a specific tag. The code for this is as follows:

```
$cache->save($result, 'product_56', array('jim', 'dog', 'tea'));
```

If you ever need to, you can clear the cache programmatically; for instance, if you cache a product for seven days and wish to force a cache refresh to reflect an immediate price change. Cache cleaning can be very specific, down to a unique identifier:

```
$cache->remove('product_73');
```

Or it can be very broad:

```
$cache->clean(Zend_Cache::CLEANING_MODE_OLD);
$cache->clean(Zend_Cache::CLEANING_MODE_ALL);
```

These two commands clean out old caches, or all caches (every cache will then need to be recreated).

You can also clean out caches that have specific tags attached:

```
$cache->clean(
   Zend_Cache::CLEANING_MODE_MATCHING_TAG,
   array('dog', 'salami')
);
```

Remember to use the same configuration options for the cache object when cleaning that you did when you created the cache data.

14.6   *Summary*

In this chapter, we covered how to implement caching in your application using frontends and backends. We covered the details of each frontend so that you can make the best decision about which frontend is most appropriate for each part of your application. We covered one backend option, but you might like to explore some of the other backends to see if they are more appropriate for your needs.

Caching can be a powerful way to improve the performance of your application, and Zend_Cache is an excellent tool for the job, but it can take some thought to ensure that information is cached properly. As your application evolves and your traffic patterns change, you may find that you need to add to or adjust your cache settings to resolve new performance issues.

If you are lucky enough to deal with an extremely high-traffic application, you will be able to combine your use of Zend_Cache with other performance-improving technology, such as static content servers and load-balancing server clusters.

Now that we know how to ensure our application performs well as traffic grows, it's time to turn our attention to the rest of the world, which represents a very large market. There are many languages other than English, so we'll look at how Zend Framework's internationalization and localization features can be used to broaden the appeal of your application worldwide.

Internationalization and localization

Most websites are written in a single language for a single country, and this makes life easier for both the designers and developers. Some projects, however, require more than this. Some countries have more than one language (in Wales, both English and Welsh are used) and some websites are intended to target all the countries that the company operates in. To create a website targeted at different countries and cultures, significant changes to the application are required to support multiple languages and the different formats for dates, times, currency, and so on, that each country uses.

We're going to look at what needs to be done to make a multilingual website, then look at how the `Zend_Locale` and `Zend_Translate` components of Zend Framework help to make the process easier. Finally, we'll implement a second language into the *Places* website to show how to create a localized application.

15.1 Translating languages and idioms

Before making a multilingual website, we first need to consider how language and customs affect a website. Intuitively, most people think about changing the language when they consider supporting another country on their website. Clearly, we need to display all the text in the correct language, but for some locales, there are cultural issues to consider too. The most common are the formatting of dates and currency.

For dates, the most infamous issue is that the U.S. uses mm/dd/yy whereas the UK uses dd/mm/yy, so it gets tricky determining what date 02/03/08 actually is. Is it the second of March or the third of February? Similarly, for currency. In France they use the comma where the UK uses a decimal place, and they use a space where the UK would use a comma. To make a French user feel at home, €1,234.56 should be displayed as €1 234,56.

The key control on a computer system for this is called the *locale*. The locale is a string that defines the current language and region used by the user. For example, the locale "en_GB" means English language in the Great Britain region. Similarly, "es_PR" is Spanish language in Puerto Rico. Generally, for language localization, only the first part of the locale is used, because it's rare to find a website that provides both U.S. and UK English.

Let's look first at what's involved in translating languages in web applications, and then we'll look at handling idioms.

15.1.1 Translating languages

Translating languages involves making changes to both the HTML design and build of the website and to the PHP code that runs it. The most obvious change that's required is that every string displayed to the user has to be in the correct language, so correct sizing of areas for text is required in the design. This also includes any text that is embedded in a graphical image, so to provide for multiple languages, the image files need to be separated out into generic and language-specific ones if text is used in images.

There are multiple methods of doing the actual translation, but they all boil down to the same thing. Every string displayed on the site needs to be mapped to a string in the target language. It follows that it's important that the strings are rewritten using a professional translator, because there is rarely a one-to-one mapping from one language to another. Industry-standard systems, such as `gettext()`, have many tools dedicated to making it simple for a translator to perform the translation of phrases used in the application without having to know anything about programming.

15.1.2 Translating idioms

The most obvious idioms that need translation are the formatting of currency and dates. PHP has locale support built in that is set using the `setlocale()` function. Once the locale is set, all the locale-aware functions will use it. This means that `strftime()` will use the correct language for the months of the year and `money_format()` will use the comma and period characters in the right places for the language involved. One gotcha is that `setlocale()` isn't thread-safe, and the strings you need to set are inconsistent across operating systems, so care must be taken using it. Also, some functions like `money_format()` aren't available on all operating systems, such as Windows. The `Zend_Locale` component is intended to mitigate these issues, and it also provides additional functionality, like normalization.

Now that we know a little about what localization and internationalization is, let's look at what Zend Framework provides to make the process of creating an international website easier. We'll start by looking at `Zend_Locale`'s ability to convert numbers and dates before moving on to investigate `Zend_Translate`'s functionality for providing translated text.

15.2 Using Zend_Locale and Zend_Translate

`Zend_Locale` and `Zend_Translate` are the key components of Zend Framework for providing a multilingual, worldwide website. Other components that are locale-aware are `Zend_Date` and `Zend_Currency`. Let's look at `Zend_Locale` first.

15.2.1 Setting the locale with Zend_Locale

Selecting the correct locale is as easy as this:

```
$locale = new Zend_Locale('en_GB');
```

This will create a locale object for the English language, Great Britain region. This means that a locale always contains two parts: the language and the region. We need to know both before we can specify the locale string when creating an instance of `Zend_Locale`. We can also create a `Zend_Locale` object for the locale of the user's browser, like this:

```
$locale = new Zend_Locale();
```

The `locale` object can then be used for translating lists of common strings, such as countries, units of measurement, and time information, such as month names and days of the week. We can also retrieve the language and region using this code:

```
$language = $locale->getLanguage();
$region = $locale->getRegion();
```

Clearly, we can then use this information to provide websites in the correct language with the right formatting of dates, times, and currencies, which will make our user feel right at home. Let's look at numbers first.

DEALING WITH NUMBERS

The most significant regional problem with numbers is that some countries use the comma to separate the decimal places from the whole number, and some countries use the period character. If your website allows the user to enter a number, you may have to convert it appropriately. This is known as *normalization*.

Consider a form that asks someone to enter her monthly insurance costs in order to try to provide a cheaper quotation. A German user might type in the number 3.637,34 (three thousand, six hundred, and thirty-seven euros, and thirty-four cents), which you need normalize to 3637.34. This is achieved using the code shown in listing 15.1.

Listing 15.1   Number normalization with `Zend_Locale`

```
$locale = new Zend_Locale('de_DE');                    ◁──  Specifies the
$number = Zend_Locale_Format::getNumber('3.637,34',         German locale
    'locale' => $locale));
                              ┌──── Prints the number
                              │     "3637.34"
print $number;         ◁──────┘
```

We can then process the number as appropriate, and we may need to display a number to the user. In this case, we again need to format the number appropriately for the user's location, and we can use `Zend_Locale`'s `toNumber()` function to do this, as shown in listing 15.2.

Listing 15.2   Number localization with `Zend_Locale`

```
$locale = new Zend_Locale('de_DE');                ◁──  Specifies the
$number = Zend_Locale_Format::toNumber(2435.837,        German locale
        array('precision' => 2,          ◁──
        'locale' => $locale));                Rounds to two
                                              decimal places
print $number;    ◁──┐  Prints the number
                     └─ "2.435,84"
```

The `precision` parameter is optional and is used to round the provided number to the given number of decimal places.

This covers the basics of what `Zend_Locale` can do with numbers, but `Zend_Locale` provides complete number handling, including translation of numbers between different numeral systems, such as from Arabic to Latin. There is also support for integer and floating-point number normalization and localization. The manual gives full information on these functions.

DATE AND TIME WITH ZEND_LOCALE

Handling the formatting of dates and times is also within the province of `Zend_Locale`. This class operates in conjunction with `Zend_Date` to provide comprehensive support for reading and writing dates. Let's start by looking at normalizing dates because, like numbers, different regions of the world write dates in different formats, and residents obviously use their local language for the names of the months and days of the week.

Consider, the date 2 March 2007. In the UK, this may be written as 2/3/2007; in the U.S. it would be written as 3/2/2007. To use the date supplied by our users, we need to normalize it, and getDate() is the function to use, as shown in listing 15.3.

Listing 15.3   Date normalization with Zend_Locale

```
$locale = new Zend_Locale('en_US');                   ◁─────  Specifies the
$date = Zend_Locale_Format::getDate('3/2/2007',               U.S. locale
    array('locale' => $locale));          Prints "3"
                                          for March
print $date['month'];    ◁───────
```

As usual, we create a locale object for the correct language and region and use it with the getDate() function. We've used the en_US locale for the U.S., so getDate() correctly determines that the month is March. If we changed the locale to en_GB, the month would be February.

Similarly, we can use checkDateFormat() to ensure that the date string received is valid for the locale, and once we have the date information separated into its components, we can manipulate it in any way we like.

Now that we know the basics of using Zend_Locale to help our international visitors feel at home, let's have a look at Zend_Translate's ability to help us present our site in different languages.

15.2.2 *Translating with Zend_Translate*

As we've already seen, website translation requires, at a minimum, ensuring that every string that is displayed has a translated version. The most common way to do this is with gettext(), which is powerful but fairly complicated. Zend_Translate supports the gettext() format but also supports other popular formats such as arrays, CSV, TBX, Qt, XLIFF, and XmlTm. Zend_Translate is also thread-safe, which can be very helpful if you're running a multithreaded web server, such as IIS.

Zend_Translate supports multiple input formats using an adapter system. This approach is very common in Zend Framework and allows for further adapters to be added as required. We'll look at the array adapter first, because that's a very simple format and very quick to learn. Its most common use is with Zend_Cache, to cache the translations from one of the other input formats.

Using Zend_Translate is simple enough. In listing 15.4, we output text using pretty ordinary PHP and repeat the exercise in listing 15.5 using Zend_Translate's array adapter. In this case, we make life easier by "translating" to uppercase, but we could equally have translated to German (if any of us knew enough German to avoid embarrassing ourselves).

Listing 15.4   Standard PHP output

```
print "Welcome\n";
print "=======\n";                                    Outputs UK
print "Today's date is " . date("d/m/Y") . "\n";   ◄──── format date
```

Listing 15.4 is a very simple piece of code that displays three lines of text, maybe for a command-line script. To provide a translation, we need to create an array of translation data for the target language. The array consists of identifying keys mapped against the actual text to be displayed. The keys can be anything, but it makes things easier if it's essentially the same as the source language.

Listing 15.5   Translated version of listing 15.4

```
$data = array();                                       Creates a        Creates an
$data['hello'] = 'WELCOME';                            translation      instance of
$data['today %1$s'] = 'TODAY\'S DATE IS %1$s';         array            Zend_
                                                                        Translate
$translate = new Zend_Translate('array', $data, 'en');  ◄──────

print $translate->_("hello")."\n";              ◄──────
print "=======\n";                                      ❶ Prints the "hello"
printf($translate->_('today %1$s')."\n",                   translation text
    date('d/m/Y'));                          ❷ Uses printf()
                                                placeholders
```

In this example, we use the _() function to do the translation ❶. This is a very common function name in many programming languages and frameworks for translation. It's a very frequently used function, and it's less distracting in the source code if it's short. As you can see, the _() function also supports the use of printf() placeholders so you can embed dynamic text into the correct place within a string ❷. The current date is a good example, because in English we say, "Today's date is {date}," whereas in another language the idiom may be, "{date} is today's date." By using printf() placeholders, we're able to move the dynamic data to the correct place for the language construct used.

The array adapter is mainly useful for very small projects, where the PHP developers update the translation strings. For a large project, the gettext() format or CSV format is much more useful. For gettext(), the translation text is stored in .po files, which are best managed using a specialized editor, such as the open source poEdit application. These applications provide a list of the source language strings, and next to each one the translator can type the target-language equivalent string. This makes creating translation files relatively easy and completely independent of the website source code.

The process of using gettext() source files with Zend_Translate is as simple as picking a different adapter, as shown in listing 15.6.

Listing 15.6   Zend_Translate using the gettext() adapter

```
$filename = 'translations/uppercase.po';        Uses the
$translate = new Zend_Translate('gettext',       gettext
           $filename, 'en');                      adapter

print $translate->_("hello")."\n";
print "=======\n";
printf($translate->_('today %1$s')."\n", date('d/m/Y'));
```

As you can see, the use of the translation object is exactly the same, regardless of the translation source adapter used.

Now let's look at integrating what we've learned into a real application. We'll use our *Places* application and adapt it to support two languages.

15.3   Adding a second language to the **Places** *application*

Our initial goal for making *Places* multilingual is to present the user interface in the language of the viewer. We'll use the same view templates for all languages and ensure that all phrases are translated appropriately. Each language will have its own translation file stored, in our case using the array adapter to keep things simple. If the user requests a language for which we don't have a translation, we'll use English. The result can be seen in figure 15.1, which shows the German version of *Places*. (Note that most of the translation text was done using Google Translate—a professional translator would do a much better job of it!)

These are the key steps we'll be taking to make *Places* multilingual:

- Change the default router to support a language element.
- Create a front controller plug-in to create a Zend_Translate object and load the correct language file. It will also create a Zend_Locale object.
- Update the controllers and views to translate text.

We'll start by looking at how to make the front controller's router multi-language aware so that the user can select a language.

15.3.1   *Selecting the language*

The first decision to make is how to determine the user's language choice. The easiest solution is to ask the web browser by using Zend_Locale's getLanguage() function, and then to store this into the session. There are a few problems with this approach. First, sessions rely on cookies, so the user would have to have cookies enabled in order to view the site in another language. Second, creating a session for every user involves overhead that we may not want to bear. Third, search engines like Google would see only the English version of the site.

To solve these problems, the code for the language of choice should be held within the URL, and there are two places we can put it: the domain or the path. To use the domain, we'd need to buy the relevant domains, such as placestotakethekids.de,

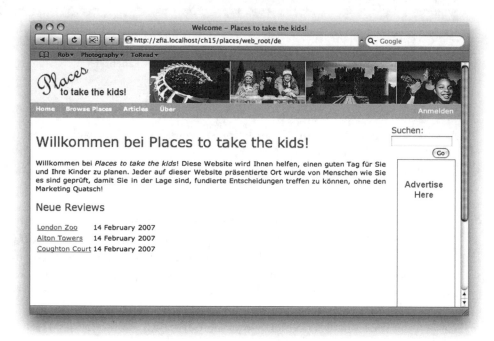

Figure 15.1   The text on the German version of *Places* is translated, but the same view templates are used to ensure that adding additional languages doesn't require too much work.

placestotakethekids.fr, and so on. These country-specific domains offer a very simple solution and, for a commercial operation, can show your customers that you're serious about doing business in their country. Problems that may arise are that the domain name may not be available for the country of choice (for example, apple.co.uk isn't owned by Apple Inc.) and for some country-specific domains you need to have proof of business incorporation within that country in order to purchase the domain name. One alternative is to include the language code as part of the path, such as www.placestotakethekids.com/fr for French and www.placestotakethekids.com/de for the German language. We'll use this approach.

Because we wish to use full locales for each language code, we need to map from the language code used in the URL to the full locale code. For example, /en will be mapped to en_GB, /fr to fr_FR, and so on for all supported languages. We'll use our configuration INI file to store this mapping, as shown in listing 15.7.

Listing 15.7   Setting locale information in config.ini

```
languages.en = en_GB
languages.fr = fr_FR
languages.de = de_DE
```

The list of valid language codes and their associated locales are now available in the `$config` object that was loaded in the `Bootstrap` class and stored in the `Zend_Registry`. We can retrieve the list of supported language codes like this:

```
$config = Zend_Registry::get('config');
$languages = array_keys($config->languages->toArray());
```

To use the language codes within the address, we need to alter the routing system to account for the additional parameter. The standard router interprets paths of the form

```
/{module}/{controller}/{action}/{other_parameters}
```

where {module} is optional. A typical path for *Places* is

```
/place/index/id/4
```

This calls the `index` action of the `place` controller with the `id` parameter set to 4. For our multilingual site, we need to introduce the language as the first parameter, so that the path now looks like this:

```
/{language}/{controller}/{action}/{other parameters}
```

We'll use the standard two-character codes for the language, so that a typical path for the German language version of *Places* is

```
/de/place/index/id/4
```

To change this, we need to implement a new routing rule and replace the default route with it. The front controller will then be able to do its magic and ensure that the correct controller and action are called. This is done in the `Bootstrap` class's `runApp()` method, as shown in listing 15.8.

Listing 15.8 Implementing a new routing rule for language support

```
$config = Zend_Registry::get('config');                      Loads list of allowed
$languages = array_keys($config->languages->toArray());      language codes from
$zl = new Zend_Locale();                                      config
$lang = in_array($zl->getLanguage(), $languages)             Uses browser's language code
        ? $zl->getLanguage() : 'en';                         if it's in allowed list

// add language to default route
$route = new Zend_Controller_Router_Route(
    ':lang/:controller/:action/*',
    array('controller'=>'index',                    ❶ Creates
        'action' => 'index',                            new route
        'module'=>'default',
        'lang'=>$lang));

$router = $frontController->getRouter();             Updates
$router->addRoute('default', $route);               router with
$frontController->setRouter($router);               new route
```

We use `Zend_Controller_Router_Route` to define the route using the colon (:) character to define the variable parts with language first, then the controller, the action, and the asterisk, which means "all other parameters" ❶.

We also define the defaults for each part of the route, for when it's missing. Because we're replacing the default route with our new route, we keep the same defaults so that the index action of the index controller is called for an empty address. We set the default language to the browser's default language, as determined by `Zend_Locale`'s `getLanguage()` method. However, setting this as a default means that if the user chooses a specific language, the choice will take precedence. This allows people using a Spanish browser to view the site in English, for instance.

Now that we have routing working, we need to load the translation files. We need to do this after the routing has happened, but before we get to the action methods. The `dispatchLoopStartup()` method hook of a front controller plug-in is the ideal vehicle to perform this work.

15.3.2 *The LanguageSetup front controller plug-in*

A front controller plug-in has a number of different hooks into the various stages of the dispatch process. In this case, we're interested in the `dispatchLoopStartup()` hook, because we want to load the language files after routing has happened but we only need it to be called once per request. Our plug-in, `LanguageSetup`, will be stored in the Places library and follows Zend Framework naming guidelines in order to take advantage of `Zend_Loader`. The full class name is `Places_Controller_Plugin_LanguageSetup`, and it's stored in library/Places/Controller/Action/Helper/LanguageSetup.php. These are the main functions it performs:

- Loads language file containing array of translations
- Instantiates `Zend_Translate` object for the selected language
- Assigns language string and `Zend_Translate` object to the controller and view

All this is done in the `dispatchLoopStartup()` method. In order to do its work, it will need to know the directory where the language files are stored and also the list of languages available. This information is in the `Bootstrap` class, so we pass it to the plug-in via its constructor.

The plug-in's constructor takes two parameters: the directory where the translation files can be found and the list of languages from the config file. We could get the plug-in to figure out these values, but we prefer to leave the specific knowledge of the directory system to the `Bootstrap` class so that if we change anything, all changes will be in one place. Similarly, the plug-in could retrieve the list of languages from the `Zend_Config` object directly, but this would introduce a coupling to this component that isn't needed.

Let's start building the `LanguageSetup` plug-in now. The first part is the constructor, shown in listing 15.9.

Listing 15.9   `LanguageSetup` front controller plug-in

```
class Places_Controller_Plugin_LanguageSetup
    extends Zend_Controller_Plugin_Abstract
{

  protected $_languages;
  protected $_directory;

  public function __construct($directory, $languages)
  {
    $this->_dir = $directory;            Stores to member
    $this->_languages = $languages;      variables
  }

  public function dispatchLoopStartup(
      Zend_Controller_Request_Abstract $request)
  {
                                Does actual
  }                             work here
}
```

We need to register the new plug-in with the front controller in the `runApp()` method of the `Bootstrap` class. This is done in the same way as registering the `ActionSetup` plug-in back in chapter 3, and it looks like this:

```
$frontController->registerPlugin(
    new Places_Controller_Plugin_LanguageSetup(
        ROOT_DIR . '/application/configuration/translations',
        $config->languages->toArray()));
```

We take advantage of the `ROOT_DIR` to absolutely specify the translations directory.

Now that we've registered the plug-in and have stored the required data in local member variables, we can write the `dispatchLoopStartup()` method that sets up the locale and translation objects. This is shown in listing 15.10.

Listing 15.10   The `LanguageSetup`'s `dispatchLoopStartup()` method

```
public function dispatchLoopStartup(
            Zend_Controller_Request_Abstract $request)
{
  $lang = $this->getRequest()->getParam('lang');       ❶ Retrieves
  if (!in_array($lang,                                     chosen language
            array_keys($this->_languages))) {           ❷ Ensures language
    $lang = 'en';                                          chosen is allowed
  }

  $localeString = $this->_languages[$lang];            Sets up
  $locale = new Zend_Locale($localeString);            locale object

  $file = $this->_dir . '/'. $localeString . '.php';
  if (file_exists($file)) {
    $translationStrings = include $file;               ❸ Loads
  } else {                                                translation
    $translationStrings = include $this->_dir            file
      . '/en_GB.php';
  }
```

```
    if (empty($translationStrings)) {
       throw new Exception('Missing $translationStrings
             ➥  in language file');
    }

    $translate = new Zend_Translate('array',              ❹  Creates Zend_
          $translationStrings, $localeString);               Translate object

    Zend_Registry::set('lang', $lang);
    Zend_Registry::set('localeString', $localeString);   ❺  Assigns to
    Zend_Registry::set('locale', $locale);                  registry
    Zend_Registry::set('Zend_Translate', $translate);
}
```

The code in `dispatchLoopStartup()` consists of as much error checking as actual code, which isn't uncommon. First, we collect the language that the user has chosen. This is in the `Request` object, so it is accessible via `getParam()` ❶.

Before we load a language file, we first check that the selected language is available ❷, because the user could, in theory, type any text within the language element of the address path. Because we only have a limited number of language files in the translations directory, we check that the user's choice is available. If not, we pick English instead. Similarly, if the language is valid, we double-check that the file actually exists ❸, in order to avoid errors later, and we load the file using a simple `include` statement. An assumption is made that the language file returns an array which we assign to `$translationStrings`. The array contains the actual translations, so we throw an exception if this array doesn't exist.

Having completed our error checking, we instantiate a new `Zend_Translate` object ❹. Finally, we register everything with `Zend_Registry` so that the information can be used later ❺. Registering the `Zend_Translate` object with the registry also means that `Zend_Form` and `Zend_Validate` will use it for translating form labels, form buttons, and validation error messages.

As we discovered when we looked at `Zend_Translate`, the system supports multiple adapters to allow for a variety of input sources for the translation strings. For *Places*, we've chosen arrays, because they're the simplest to get going, but if the site grows significantly, moving to `gettext()` would be easy to do and would require changes to just this `init()` method.

The next stage is to use the `translate` object to translate our website.

15.3.3 *Translating the view*

For our website to be multilingual, we need every piece of English text on every page to be changed so it runs through the `_()` method of `Zend_Translate`. Zend Framework provides the `translate` view helper to make this easy. This view helper needs access to a `Zend_Translate` object, and the easiest way to give it one is to register one with `Zend_Registry` using the key "Zend_Translate", as we did in listing 15.10.

In the view scripts we can change the original `<h2>Recent reviews</h2>` on the home page to `<?php echo $this->translate('Recent reviews'); ?>`. Let's look at it in use on the home page. Listing 15.11 shows the top part of the index.phtml view template for the home page before localization.

Listing 15.11 The top part of the non-localized index.phtml

```
<h1><?php echo $this->escape($this->title);?></h1>

<p>Welcome to <em>Places to take the kids</em>! This site will
help you to plan a good day out for you and your children. Every
place featured on this site has been reviewed by people like you,
so you'll be able to make informed decisions with no marketing
waffle!</p>

<h2>Recent reviews</h2>
```

As you can see, with the exception of the title, all the text in the view template is hard-coded directly, so we have to change this, as shown in listing 15.12.

Listing 15.12 The localized version of index.phtml

```
<h1><?php echo $this->escape($this->translate($this->title));?></h1>
<p><?php echo $this->translate('welcome-body'); ?></p>        Uses a simple
                                                              key for the
<h2><?php echo $this->translate('Recent reviews'); ?></h2>  1  long text
```

With the localized template, every string is passed through the translate() view helper. For the very long body of text, we use a simple key (1) in order to make the template easier to understand and the language file simpler.

The relevant parts of the language files for English and German are shown in listings 15.13 and 15.14. The full files are provided in the accompanying source code.

Listing 15.13 The English translation file, en_GB.php

```
<?php
$translationStrings = array(
    'Welcome to Places to take the kids!' => 'Welcome to Places to take the
kids!',
    'welcome-body' => 'Welcome to <i>Places to take the kids</i>! This site
will help you to plan a good day out for you and your children. Every place
featured on this site has been reviewed by people like you, so you\'ll be
able to make informed decisions with no marketing waffle!',
    'Recent reviews' => 'Recent reviews',
);
```

And the equivalent file in German is shown in listing 15.14

Listing 15.14 The German translation file, de_DE.php

```
<?php
$translationStrings = array(
    'Welcome to Places to take the kids!' => 'Willkommen bei Places to take
the kids!',
    'welcome-body' => 'Willkommen bei <i>Places to take the kids</i>! Diese
Website wird Ihnen helfen, einen guten Tag für Sie und Ihre Kinder zu
```

```
planen. Jeder auf dieser Website präsentierte Ort wurde von Menschen wie
Sie es sind geprüft, damit Sie in der Lage sind, fundierte Entscheidungen
treffen zu können, ohne den Marketing Quatsch!',
);
```

We had a little help with the translation of welcome-body. Thomas Wiedner looked at what Google Translate had come up with and provided the correct translation, because Google's wasn't very good! But it's quite clear when looking at listings 15.11 and 15.12 how easy array-based translations are to create.

The final area we need to look at is creating links from one page to another. Fortunately, Zend Framework provides a URL builder for us in the shape of the url() view helper. Listing 15.15 shows how we can use it.

Listing 15.15   Creating URLs using the url() view helper

```
<a href="<?php echo $this->url(array(          ❶ Sets language
    'lang'=>$this->localeString,                   parameter
    'module'=>'default'
    'controller'=>'review',       Sets other
    'action'=>'add',              parameters
    'placeId'=>$this->place->id   for routing
    ), null, true);?>">
  Add review</a>
```

As can be seen in listing 15.15, creating a URL is simplified by using the url() view helper. It can be further simplified by not passing true as the last parameter, which is called $reset. When $reset is false (the default) the helper will "remember" the state of any parameters you don't override. Because the lang parameter would never be overridden, it only has to be specified if the $reset parameter is set to true.

We've now provided comprehensive support for all aspects of translation using Zend_Translate, and adding languages can be done very easily by adding the language to config.ini and writing a translation file.

It's traditional to provide a mechanism for allowing users to choose the language that they wish to view the site in. One common mechanism is the flag, because it works in all languages, although it can annoy UK citizens when they see the U.S. flag indicating English. An alternative is to use text in each language, but that can be quite hard to integrate into a site's design.

To complete our conversion of *Places* into a multilingual website and make our visitors feel at home, we need to ensure that we translate the dates displayed throughout the site using Zend_Locale.

15.3.4 *Displaying the correct date with Zend_Locale*

If you look closely at Figure 15.1, you'll notice that the dates are in the wrong format and are displaying the English month name rather than the German one. This is due to our view helper, displayDate(), which isn't correctly localized. We'll now look at how to localize dates. As a reminder, the original code for displaying dates is shown in listing 15.16.

Listing 15.16   Naïve localization of dates

```
class Zend_View_Helper_displayDate
{
    function displayDate($timestamp, $format='%d %B %Y')
    {
        return strftime($format,                Returns the
            strtotime($timestamp));             formatted date
    }
}
```

We're using `strftime()` in listing 15.16, which, according to the PHP manual, is locale aware. Unfortunately, although we know which locale we want, `strftime()` uses the locale of the server unless you tell it otherwise. There are two solutions: use `setlocale()` or Zend_Date.

At first glance, using `setlocale()` is very tempting. We just need to add the following line to our LanguageSetup front controller plug-in:

```
setlocale(LC_TIME, $lang);
```

However, this doesn't work as expected. The first problem with `setlocale()` is that it isn't thread-safe. This means that if you're using a threaded web server, you need to call `setlocale()` before every use of a locale-aware PHP function. The second issue is that on Windows, the string that is passed to the `setlocale()` function isn't the same as the string we're using in our config.ini file. That is, we're using "de" for German, but the Windows version of `setlocale()` expects "deu". Zend_Date, as a member of Zend Framework, works more predictably for us.

Zend_Date is a class that comprehensively handles date and time manipulation and display. It's also locale-aware, and if you pass it a Zend_Locale object, it will use it to translate all date- and time-related strings. Our immediate requirement is simply to retrieve dates in the correct format for the user, so we modify our `displayDate()` view helper, which is stored in views/helpers/DisplayDate.php, as shown in listing 15.17.

Listing 15.17   Localization of dates using `Zend_Date`

```
class Zend_View_Helper_displayDate
{
    function displayDate($timestamp, $format = Zend_Date::DATE_LONG)
    {                                                            ❶ Retrieves
                                                                    locale
        $locale = Zend_Registry::get('locale');   ◄─────────
        $date = new Zend_Date($timestamp, null,        ❷ Creates Zend_Date
            $locale);                                     object

        return $date->get($format);   ◄──────────────
    }                                              ❸ Gets date as a
}                                                     formatted string
```

The LanguageSetup front controller plug-in stored the `locale` object into the registry, so we can simply retrieve it for use with Zend_Date ❶. Displaying a locale-aware date is simply a matter of creating the Zend_Date object from the `$timestamp` to be displayed ❷, then calling `get()` ❸. The `get()` method takes a `format` parameter that can be a

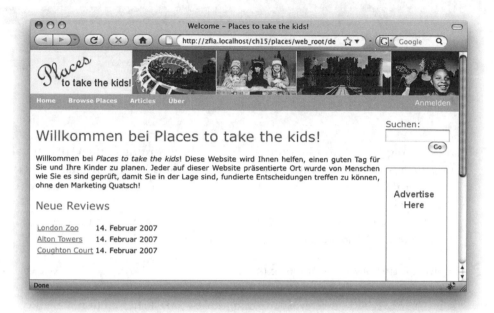

Figure 15.2   Using the locale-aware Zend_Date, we can display the date in the correct language

string or a Zend_Date constant. These constants are locale-aware so that DATE_LONG will display the month name in the correct language. Similarly, Zend_Date::DATE_SHORT knows that the format of the short date is dd/mm/yy in the UK and mm/dd/yy in the U.S. In general, we recommend staying away from short dates, because they can confuse users who aren't used to locale-aware websites.

The German version of *Places*, including localized dates can be seen in figure 15.2.

As you can see in figure 15.2, the date string created by Zend_Date::DATE_LONG for our German users is as they'd expect. As a result, our German guests realize that they're first-class citizens on this site, and not an afterthought.

15.4   *Summary*

Zend_Locale and Zend_Translate make creating multilingual, locale-aware websites much easier. Of course, creating a website in multiple languages isn't *easy*, because care needs to be taken to ensure that the text fits in the spaces provided, and you need to make sure you have translations that work!

Zend_Locale is the heart of localization in Zend Framework. It allows for normalizing numbers and dates written in different formats so that they can be stored consistently and used within the application.

Zend_Translate translates text into a different language using the _() method. It supports multiple input formats, including the widespread gettext() format, so that you can choose the most appropriate format for your project. Small projects will use array and CSV formats, whereas larger projects are more likely to use gettext, TBX, Qt,

XLIFF, and XmlTm. Through the flexibility of Zend_Translate's adapter system, migrating from a simpler system to a more robust one doesn't affect the main code base at all.

That covers the use of the internationalization and localization of applications, so we'll move on to a different sort of translation: output formats. Although all websites can be printed, it's sometimes easier and better to provide a PDF version of a page. Zend_Pdf enables the creation and editing of PDF documents with a minimum of fuss, so we'll look at it in the next chapter.

Creating PDFs

This chapter covers

- Creating, loading, and saving PDF documents with `Zend_PDF`
- Drawing text and shapes on the page
- Adding color and styles
- Rotating and clipping objects
- Building an example PDF report generator

Surprising as it may seem to those of us who spend an unhealthy amount of time in the digital world, there are still people who use and need documents in paper format. Having said that, although clever use of HTML and CSS can produce well-formatted web pages, there are still limits to how pixel-perfect web pages can be, especially when it comes to printing them.

Adobe Systems created the PDF (Portable Document Format) to bridge the gap between printed and digital documents, and it has since become the standard for web-based printable documents, as well as an integral part of a modern graphics workflow. The precision of the PDF format is particularly important for documents such as specifically formatted copies of web page content, emailed invoices, site statistics, and other reports.

In this chapter, we'll be using Zend Framework's `Zend_Pdf` component to generate an example report, and we'll work through some of its features. But before doing so, we should properly introduce the component, starting with the basics.

16.1 Zend_Pdf basics

Using only PHP, `Zend_Pdf` allows you to create, load, and save PDF v1.4 documents and provides commands for drawing shapes, text, and images.

The number of classes that make up this component suggests that creating it involved a large amount of work, but you may still find it currently lacking some functionality you might expect. For example, you'll be forced to do some things, like text wrapping and pagination, manually or with workarounds. Also, documentation is still a little sparse. On the positive side, there are already motions to add such requested features, so some effort at this stage won't be wasted in the future.

On that note, let's look at how to create or load PDF documents.

16.1.1 Creating or loading documents

`Zend_Pdf` has various ways of creating and loading PDF documents. The basic way to create a PDF document is to instantiate a new `Zend_Pdf` object, like so:

```
$pdf = new Zend_Pdf();
```

There are two ways to load an existing PDF document, both of which use a static method. The first loads from a file:

```
$file = '/path/to/example.pdf';
$pdf = Zend_Pdf::load($file);
```

The second loads from a string containing the contents of a PDF document:

```
$pdf = Zend_Pdf::parse($pdfString);
```

Whether you have created or loaded a PDF document, you work with it in the same way. Each document is made up of pages on which you draw your text, image, or shape elements.

16.1.2 Creating pages in your PDF document

Once you have created your `Zend_Pdf` object, you can work with the pages of your document as if you were working with a regular PHP array. The `pages` array is `$pdf->pages`, and all of the normal PHP array functions will work.

To create a new page, you can create a `Zend_Pdf_Page` object and set its page size as follows:

```
$page = new Zend_Pdf_Page(Zend_Pdf_Page::SIZE_A4);
```

The `Zend_Pdf_Page::SIZE_A4` argument used here uses a constant to define what size and orientation we want the page to be. Table 16.1 shows the available predefined constants, together with their measurements.

Table 16.1 Predefined `Zend_Pdf_Page` **page-size constants with width and height measurements**

Constant	Size in inches	Size in millimeters	Size in points (1/72 of an inch)
SIZE_A4	8.27 x 11.69	210 x 297	595 x 842
SIZE_A4_LANDSCAPE	11.69 x 8.27	297 x 210	842 x 595
SIZE_LETTER	8.5 x 11	215.9 x 279.4	612 x 792
SIZE_LETTER_LANDSCAPE	11 x 8.5	279.4 x 215.9	792 x 612

You are not limited to the predefined sizes. Each page can have its own size and orientation, so you can use any value for width and height, ordering your arguments like so:

```
$page = new Zend_Pdf_Page($width, $height);
```

You may prefer to work in inches or millimeters, but the values entered here will be treated as points, so you'll need to convert them.

NOTE   All measurements in `Zend_Pdf` are in points. If you prefer to use inches or millimeters, you should convert them to points using `$inches * 72` or `$millimeters / 25.4 * 72`.

If we had chosen to use the `Zend_Pdf::newPage()` static method to create our page, that page would be already attached to the document. In contrast, `Zend_Pdf_Page` objects instantiated directly are independent and need to be added to the document like this:

```
$pdf->pages[] = $page;
```

While we're now able to set up our document and add pages to it, those pages will be blank. Before we get into filling them with content, we should add some information about the document itself in the document's meta-information.

16.1.3 Adding document meta-information

One of the advantages that digital documents have over paper is the ease with which they can be managed based on file content and document information. This document meta-information can be added to your document by setting values in the `properties` array of the `Zend_Pdf` object. The title of the document, for example, is set like so:

```
$pdf->properties['Title'] = 'Zend_Pdf makes great PDFs';
```

Of course, there are more properties than just the title property. Table 16.2 shows the keys available in PDF v1.4 that `Zend_Pdf` can use.

Table 16.2   The PDF v1.4 document meta-information keys available for use by `Zend_Pdf`

Name	Type	Description
Title	String	The document title.
Author	String	The name of the person who created the document.
Subject	String	The document subject.
Keywords	String	Keywords associated with the document.
Creator	String	The application that created the original document prior to conversion, if the document was converted from another format to PDF.
Producer	String	The application that performed the conversion, if the document was converted from another format to PDF.
CreationDate	String	The date and time the document was created; populated using `Zend_Pdf::pdfDate()` to correctly format the date.
ModDate	String	The date and time the document was last modified; populated using `Zend_Pdf::pdfDate()` to correctly format the date.
Trapped	Boolean	Indicates whether trapping has been done (`true`) or still needs to be done (`false`); trapping masks printing-registration problems by making overlaps between neighboring colors, but it is only relevant for certain printing processes.

Opening the generated document in a PDF reader and looking at the document properties is a quick way to check that the meta-information has been set correctly.

NOTE   Because `Zend_Pdf` can read PDF document meta-information via the `properties` array, it could itself be used in a data management situation where, for example, cataloguing of PDF documents was required.

We now know how to create a document of blank pages containing meta-information. While this may not seem very useful, it's enough to save or output.

16.1.4 *Saving the PDF document*

Once you have finished working with your PDF document, you can use the `Zend_Pdf::save()` method to save it to a file, like so:

```
$file = '/path/to/shiny/new/example.pdf';
$pdf->save($file);
```

Or, you can have the `Zend_Pdf::render()` method return the PDF document as a string, like this:

```
$pdfString = $pdf->render();
```

The resulting string could then, for example, be saved to a file or database, added to a zip archive, attached to an email, or output to the browser with the correct MIME header.

We've now covered enough to make the first component of this chapter's example report, so let's start actually building it.

16.2   *Building a PDF report generator*

We're going to imagine that *Places to take the kids!* has launched and been running for a long enough time for us to have gathered some statistics about its use. After numerous meetings in which we based the progress and future direction of the site on various rough pieces of information, we've decided that Zend_Pdf could help us produce something a bit more organized.

What we want is a single page with an introduction and a simple annual graph of the performance of any piece of functionality on the site. We'll use this during meetings to guide decision-making, so we'll also want some space for meeting notes on each page.

16.2.1   *Our report document model*

Our report-generating code, shown in listing 16.1, is going to start with a model class for the document itself. We'll call the class Report_Document and store it in the application/models/Report/Document.php file, following the Zend Framework naming convention mapping the class name to the directory structure. Creating this class allows us to set up some default features, such as the document meta-information, and it presents a clean interface we can use to build our reports later.

> **Listing 16.1   The report document model class forms the basis for our report generator**

```
class Report_Document
{
    protected $_pdf;

    public function __construct()
    {
        $this->_pdf = new Zend_Pdf();           ⟵  Creates new
        $this->_pdf->properties['Title'] =          Zend_Pdf object
                'Yearly Statistics Report';
        $this->_pdf->properties['Author'] =     Sets document
                'Places to take the kids';          meta-information
    }

    public function addPage(Report_Page $page)
    {                                                       Adds our page object
        $this->_pdf->pages[] = $page->render();   ⟵        to document
    }

    public function getDocument()
    {
        return $this->_pdf;
    }
}
```

We could have extended Zend_Pdf to build this class, but, partly for the sake of providing a clearer example, we've favored composition over inheritance and made $_pdf (an instance of Zend_Pdf) a property. The basic function of Report_Document is to set up a PDF document with some meta-information, then only allow pages to be instances of the Report_Page class, which we'll start on next.

16.2.2 *Our report page model*

Over the course of the rest of this chapter, we're going to build up our report page by adding content while also covering the different ways that content can be added using Zend_Pdf.

Before we do that, we'll use the initial setup of our Report_Page class, shown in listing 16.2, to cover a few pointers about working with Zend_Pdf. Again, due to the underscore in the class name, this class lives in the application/models/Report directory.

Listing 16.2   The initial setup code for our Report_Page model class

```
class Report_Page
{
    protected $_page;
    protected $_yPosition;
    protected $_leftMargin;
    protected $_pageWidth;
    protected $_pageHeight;
    protected $_normalFont;
    protected $_boldFont;
    protected $_year;
    protected $_headTitle;
    protected $_introText;
    protected $_graphData;

    public function __construct()
    {
        $this->_page = new Zend_Pdf_Page(
                Zend_Pdf_Page::SIZE_A4);
        $this->_yPosition = 60;
        $this->_leftMargin = 50;
        $this->_pageHeight = $this->_page->getHeight();
        $this->_pageWidth = $this->_page->getWidth();
        $this->_normalFont =
                Zend_Pdf_Font::fontWithName(
                Zend_Pdf_Font::FONT_HELVETICA);
        $this->_boldFont =
                Zend_Pdf_Font::fontWithName(
                Zend_Pdf_Font::FONT_HELVETICA_BOLD);
    }
}
```

1 Instantiates Zend_Pdf_Page as a property

2 Sets starting vertical position

3 Sets left margin

4 Gets page height and width

5 Chooses default fonts

For much the same reasons as for our report document model, we've decided not to extend Zend_Pdf_Page for this class, and to instead use it as a property **1**.

One of the first things that we need to come to grips with is that, like the PDF standard, all drawing in Zend_Pdf works from the bottom left of the page. This takes a little readjustment for those of us used to desktop applications that work from the top left down. To get around that, we've decided to work with what can be pictured as a sliding *y*-axis marker that is initially set at 60 points up from the page bottom ❷. Similarly, we've set a left margin at the *x*-axis position 50 points in from the left side ❸. The use of these two settings will become clearer when we start drawing items on the page.

Having set some points of reference with the *y* position marker and left-margin setting, we need to know how big the page is, which we've determined using the `Zend_Pdf_Page::getHeight()` and `Zend_Pdf_Page::getWidth()` methods ❹. Because we're working with an A4 page, these will return the point values 595 and 842 respectively. If we chose to change our page size to something like `Size_Letter`, these settings would allow our layout to adapt as needed.

The final settings in our constructor are some default font choices ❺, which brings us to the first `Zend_Pdf` drawing features we'll be covering: adding text.

16.3   *Drawing text on the page*

Text is drawn as a single nonwrapping line along a baseline that starts from an *x* and *y* position on the page. Before adding text, it's a requirement that a font has been set, which can be one of the 14 standard PDF fonts or a custom one.

16.3.1   *Choosing fonts*

In our `Report_Page` class in listing 16.2, we specified using the Helvetica and Helvetica bold fonts by name by using `Zend_Pdf_Font::fontWithName()` and the relevant `Zend_Pdf_Font` constant. If we wanted to stick with the standard fonts, we could have chosen any of the following options:

- `Zend_Pdf_Font::FONT_COURIER`
- `Zend_Pdf_Font::FONT_COURIER_BOLD`
- `Zend_Pdf_Font::FONT_COURIER_OBLIQUE`
- `Zend_Pdf_Font::FONT_COURIER_BOLD_OBLIQUE`
- `Zend_Pdf_Font::FONT_HELVETICA`
- `Zend_Pdf_Font::FONT_HELVETICA_BOLD`
- `Zend_Pdf_Font::FONT_HELVETICA_OBLIQUE`
- `Zend_Pdf_Font::FONT_HELVETICA_BOLD_OBLIQUE`
- `Zend_Pdf_Font::FONT_SYMBOL`
- `Zend_Pdf_Font::FONT_TIMES_ROMAN`
- `Zend_Pdf_Font::FONT_TIMES_BOLD`
- `Zend_Pdf_Font::FONT_TIMES_ITALIC`
- `Zend_Pdf_Font::FONT_TIMES_BOLD_ITALIC`
- `Zend_Pdf_Font::FONT_ZAPFDINGBATS`

Alternatively, we could load and use a TrueType or OpenType font from a file with a statement like the following:

```
$font = Zend_Pdf_Font::fontWithPath('arial.ttf');
```

Note that custom fonts are embedded in the PDF document by default. If you really need to keep file sizes down and are sure that your end user has the fonts on his system, you could use the Zend_Pdf_Font::EMBED_DONT_EMBED constant as the optional second argument to fontWithPath().

Once you have your font object ready, you're ready to apply it to the page.

16.3.2 *Setting the font and adding text*

The first thing our report page is going to need is a header, and in listing 16.3 we've created a setHeader() method that will produce a simple title with a horizontal line underneath it.

Listing 16.3   The setHeader() method of our Report_Page class

```
public function setHeader()
{
    $this->_page->saveGS();                          ❶ Saves graphics state
    $this->_page->setFont($this->_boldFont, 20);     ❷ Sets font
    $this->_page->drawText($this->_headTitle,        ❸ Draws title text
                    $this->_leftMargin,
                    $this->_pageHeight - 50);
    $this->_page->drawLine($this->_leftMargin,       ❹ Draws horizontal line
                    $this->_pageHeight - 60,
                    $this->_pageWidth - $this->_leftMargin,
                    $this->_pageHeight - 60);
    $this->_page->restoreGS();                        ❺ Restores graphics state
}
```

After setting the font for our title (bold font at 20 point size) using Zend_Pdf_Page::setFont() ❷, we can draw it on the page. The first argument to Zend_Pdf_Page::drawText() is the text you want to place on the page, followed by the *x* and *y* locations, for which we've used the left margin and a position 50 points below the full page height ❸. A further 10 points below that title text we then add a horizontal line from left margin to right margin ❹.

You'll notice that before we worked on the text, we made a call to Zend_Pdf_Page::saveGS() ❶, and we finished up with a call to Zend_Pdf_Page:: restoreGS() ❺. The reason for doing this was to keep any changes to the document settings we made earlier isolated to this method, so we could revert back to those document settings once finished.

NOTE   Working in a way that reminds us of PHP's output buffering, Zend_Pdf_Page can make isolated changes to styles by first saving the current graphics state using saveGS() and then using restoreGS() to return to it after any isolated changes have been made.

While we're talking about adding text, you may remember that one of the requirements for our example report was to have introductory text about the information on each page. Since it's most likely that this introduction will be more than a single line, we're going to have to implement a bit of a workaround to wrap the text.

16.3.3 Adding wrapped text

Text is drawn as a single nonwrapping line, which means that if we try to add a large amount of text, it will run off the side of the page. To get around this, we'll create a wrapText() method, as shown in listing 16.4.

Listing 16.4 Our `wrapText()` method, which will allow us to draw wrapped text

```
protected function wrapText($text)          Wraps provided text ❶
{                                           to a specific width
    $wrappedText = wordwrap($text, 110, "\n", false);   ◁         ❷ Splits wrapped
    $token = strtok($wrappedText, "\n");   ◁                         text
    $this->_yPosition = $this->_pageHeight - 80;   ◁
                                                    Sets y position
                         ❹ Loops over each        ❸ to start from
                           tokenized string
    while ($token !== false) {   ◁
        $this->_page->drawText($token,      ❺ Draws tokenized
                    $this->_leftMargin,        string
                    $this->_yPosition);
        $token = strtok("\n");   ◁                  Tokenizes
        $this->_yPosition -= 15;   ◁            ❻ string
    }                         Shifts y position
}                         ❼ down 15 points
```

Our wrapText() method first uses PHP's wordwrap function to set the supplied text to a width that will fit in our report page, and wraps it using the linefeed delimiter ❶. That delimiter is then used to split the text into smaller strings ❷, which are then looped over ❹. Each string segment is then drawn onto the page at the left margin point, and the current *y* position ❺, which we initially set as 80 points down from the top of the page ❸. The remaining string is split again (remembering that when using strtok() only the first call needs a string argument) ❻, and the *y* position is moved down 15 points, ready for the next line of text to be drawn ❼.

Drawing our introductory text is now as simple as passing it to the wrapText() method from within our Report_Page class, like so:

```
$this->wrapText($this->_introText);
```

Of course, this method isn't the only way of wrapping the text, but it works for the needs of our Report_Page class, and we expect that Zend_Pdf will gain its own solution in future enhancements. In figure 16.1, you can see the results of our labors to date.

Underneath our title, we drew a horizontal line ❹, which we'll cover a bit later in this chapter. But before we do so, there are a few more things to set, starting with colors.

16.4 Working with color

Together with the grayscale, RGB, and CMYK color spaces, Zend_Pdf also supports the use of HTML colors, which is a convenient addition for web developers. We can use

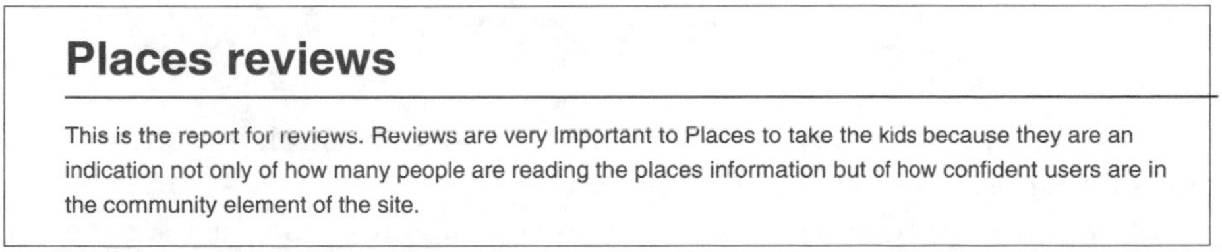

Places reviews

This is the report for reviews. Reviews are very Important to Places to take the kids because they are an indication not only of how many people are reading the places information but of how confident users are in the community element of the site.

Figure 16.1   The generated header and introductory text for our PDF report

colors in our PDF document by creating a `Zend_Pdf_Color` object chosen from any of these four color spaces.

16.4.1 Choosing colors

Since the color setting methods in `Zend_Pdf_Page` all expect a `Zend_Pdf_Color` object as their argument, the first thing we need to do is choose and create one.

A grayscale object is created with the single argument being a value between 0 (black) and 1 (white):

```
$grayLevel = 0.5;
$color = new Zend_Pdf_Color_GrayScale ($grayLevel);
```

An RGB object accepts three arguments—red, green, and blue—based on an intensity scale from 0 (minimum) to 1 (maximum):

```
$red = 0;
$green = 0.5;
$blue = 1;
$color = new Zend_Pdf_Color_Rgb ($red, $green, $blue);
```

A CMYK object accepts four arguments—cyan, magenta, yellow, and black—also based on an intensity scale from 0 (minimum) to 1 (maximum):

```
$cyan = 0;
$magenta = 0.5;
$yellow = 1;
$black = 0;
$color = new Zend_Pdf_Color_Cmyk ($cyan, $magenta, $yellow, $black);
```

An HTML color object accepts the usual hex values or HTML color names:

```
$color = new Zend_Pdf_Color_Html ('#333333');
$color = new Zend_Pdf_Color_Html('silver');
```

Having created a `Zend_Pdf_Color` object, we can move on to setting objects to use them.

16.4.2 Setting colors

As you might expect, there are the usual two ways to set colors for drawn objects: by fill and by line or stroke.

The fill color is set by passing a color object as an argument:

```
$page->setFillColor($color);
```

The line color is set the same way:

```
$page->setLineColor($color);
```

Line settings apply not only to drawn lines but also to the strokes (outlines) of shapes. Fill colors apply to text as well as to shapes.

So far, we've covered setting fonts and colors, and in the next section on styles, we'll look at ways of organizing those settings.

16.5 *Using Styles*

By using Zend_Pdf_Style, settings such as fill color, line color, line width, and font preferences are combined into style sets that can be applied to the page as a group. This saves us lines of code and makes it easier to make widespread style changes.

In listing 16.5, you can see that we've created a setStyle() method in our Report_Page class that builds a style object for our report pages. If our report generator were to get more complicated, this method could easily be refactored into its own class if needed.

Listing 16.5   Creating a style set for our `Report_Page` class

```
public function setStyle()
{                                               Creates style
    $style = new Zend_Pdf_Style();      ◁────   object
    $style->setFont(Zend_Pdf_Font::fontWithName(
        Zend_Pdf_Font::FONT_HELVETICA), 10);    Sets default
    $style->setFillColor(                       style settings
        new Zend_Pdf_Color_Html('#333333'));
    $style->setLineColor(
        new Zend_Pdf_Color_Html('#990033'));
    $style->setLineWidth(1);                     Adds style to
    $this->_page->setStyle($style);     ◁────    page object
}
```

Aside from the line-width setting, the style settings should now be quite familiar, except that they have been applied to the style object, which is then passed as an argument to Zend_Pdf_Page::setStyle(). Once set, these style settings will become the defaults for our document, unless overridden. Styles only apply to elements drawn after you set the style; they won't apply to elements that have already been drawn.

Our report page now has lots of settings and only a minimal amount of content, so it's about time we added some. This will include using shapes to draw those graphs we needed.

16.6 *Drawing shapes*

Using Zend_Pdf, we're able to draw lines, rectangles, polygons, circles, and ellipses. Before doing so, though, we may want to define settings such as color (discussed in section 16.4), or the line width, which we set in listing 16.5:

```
$style->setLineWidth(1);
```

The line width, here, is specified in points, like all measurements in Zend_Pdf.

While we're discussing line widths we should also explain how to draw that horizontal line underneath our page title. Let's look at that now.

16.6.1 Drawing lines

In the setHeader() method in listing 16.3, we drew a line under our page title using the following command:

```
$this->_page->drawLine($this->_leftMargin,
                $this->_pageHeight - 60,
                $this->_pageWidth - $this->_leftMargin,
                $this->_pageHeight - 60);
```

In this function, we specify two points with their *x* and *y* positions, and a line is drawn between them. We have therefore used the fixed and relative values in our report class to set the first point at 50,782 and the second at 545,782, so it's a simple horizontal line.

We didn't specify otherwise, so it is a solid line, but it could be made into a dashed line.

16.6.2 Setting up dashed lines

Another requirement of our report page was to have a section for meeting notes. Putting aside any personal preferences for lined or blank notepaper, we're going to add a series of faint dashed lines to our notes section.

In listing 16.6, you can see how that setting features in our getNotesSection() method and also how we use the graphics state to make temporary changes to lines.

Listing 16.6   Drawing dashed lines in a notes section

```
protected function getNotesSection()
{
    $this->_yPosition -= 20;
    $this->_page->drawText('Meeting Notes',
            $this->_leftMargin,
            $this->_yPosition);                    Draws section
    $this->_yPosition -= 10;                        header
    $this->_page->drawLine($this->_leftMargin,
                $this->_yPosition,
                $this->_pageWidth -
                    $this->_leftMargin,
                $this->_yPosition);
    $noteLineHeight = 30;          <──────────────  Sets line height
    $this->_yPosition -= $noteLineHeight;           for note lines

    $this->_page->saveGS();        <──────────────  Saves current
    $this->_page->setLineColor(                     graphics state
            new Zend_Pdf_Color_Html('#999999'));   Sets line
    $this->_page->setLineWidth(0.5);                style
    $this->_page->setLineDashingPattern(array(2, 2));  Sets line
    while($this->_yPosition > 70) {                     dash
        $this->_page->drawLine($this->_leftMargin,  Draws lines  pattern
                $this->_yPosition,                  in a loop
```

```
                    $this->_pageWidth -
                        $this->_leftMargin,
                    $this->_yPosition);
        $this->_yPosition -= $noteLineHeight;
    }
    $this->_page->restoreGS();        ◁
}
```

Restores graphics state

The first argument to `Zend_Pdf_Page::setLineDashingPattern()` is an array of lengths of dashes and spaces in sequence, with the first number being a dash and the second a space. This dash-space sequence can be repeated as many times as needed. The setting we used in listing 16.6 is a simple 2-point dash followed by a 2-point space, which can be seen in figure 16.2.

Figure 16.2   The meeting notes section, showing the use of lines and dashed lines

Having used dashed lines to draw our meeting notes section, we've actually jumped too far ahead and need to go back and draw our graph. For that, we're going to need to look at drawing rectangular shapes.

16.6.3 *Drawing rectangles and polygons*

Rectangular shapes are drawn with many of the same arguments as drawing lines. The first two arguments refer to the *x* and *y* positions of the bottom-left corner of the rectangle, and the next two arguments specify the *x* and *y* positions of the top-right corner:

```
$page->drawRectangle($x1, $y1, $x2, $y2, $fillType);
```

To draw a polygon, you can use the following command:

```
$page->drawPolygon(
    array($x1, $x2 …, $xn),
    array($y1, $y2 ..., $yn),
    $fillType, $fillMethod
);
```

The first argument is an array of all the *x* values in order, while the second is an array of the corresponding *y* values.

The third argument defines the type of fill and stroke to be used, which can be one of three options:

- `Zend_Pdf_Page::SHAPE_DRAW_FILL_AND_STROKE`—This will draw both the fill color and the stroke according to the page's current settings.
- `Zend_Pdf_Page::SHAPE_DRAW_FILL`—This will draw only the fill, leaving out the stroke.
- `Zend_Pdf_Page::SHAPE_DRAW_STROKE`—This will draw just the stroke, resulting in an outline of the shape.

The fourth argument is complex enough that describing what it does could take up a page in itself. It is also one you're unlikely to need unless, for example, you want one shape to knock out another below it, in which case we'll point you to the PDF specification at http://www.adobe.com/devnet/pdf/pdf_reference.html where you can research the following two options:

- `Zend_Pdf_Page::FILL_METHOD_EVEN_ODD`
- `Zend_Pdf_Page::FILL_METHOD_NON_ZERO_WINDING`

For our reports, we're going to use the `drawRectangle()` method to draw a bar graph, where each rectangle represents a month of data. Listing 16.7 shows the `getGraphSection()` method that will produce the graph.

Listing 16.7   The `getGraphSection()` method of our `Report_Page` class

```
protected function getGraphSection()           ① Saves graphics
{                                                 state
    $this->_page->saveGS();          ◄──────┘
    $this->_page->setFont($this->_boldFont, 16);
    $this->_yPosition -= 20;
    $this->_page->drawText('Monthly statistics for '
                    . $this->_year,
                    $this->_leftMargin,             ② Draws
                    $this->_yPosition);                graph
    $this->_yPosition -= 10;                           heading
    $this->_page->drawLine($this->_leftMargin,
                    $this->_yPosition,
                    $this->_pageWidth
                        - $this->_leftMargin,
                    $this->_yPosition);
    $this->_yPosition -= 40;

    $graphY = $this->_yPosition                    ③ Sets initial x- and
            - max($this->_graphData);                 y-axes for graph
    $graphX = $this->_leftMargin;
    $columnWidth = 40;          ◄──────┐
                                        ④ Sets column width
    $date = new Zend_Date();              of graphic
                                                     ⑤ Loops over
    foreach ($this->_graphData as $key => $value ) {  ◄──────   graph data
        $graphFill = $key % 2 == 1 ?                ⑥ Sets
                ➥ '#FA9300' : '#990033';               alternating
        $this->_page->setFillColor(                    column
                new Zend_Pdf_Color_Html(               color
                    $graphFill));
```

```
$this->_page->drawText($value,
            $graphX + ($columnWidth/3),
            $graphY + $value);
$this->_page->drawRectangle($graphX, $graphY,
            $graphX + $columnWidth,
            $graphY + $value,
            Zend_Pdf_Page::SHAPE_DRAW_FILL
            );
$yPosition = $graphY - 20;
$date->set($key + 1, Zend_Date::MONTH_SHORT);
$this->_page->drawText($date->get(
            Zend_Date::MONTH_NAME_SHORT),
            $graphX + ($columnWidth/8),
            $yPosition);
$graphX += $columnWidth;
}

$this->_yPosition = $yPosition - 20;
$this->_page->restoreGS();
}
```

7 Draws column value

8 Draws rectangle for column

9 Sets *y* position 20 points below graph

10 Sets and draws short month text

11 Moves *x* position to draw next column

12 Makes space under graph

13 Restores graphics state

Our getGraphSection() method starts by saving the current graphics state **1**, and adds a header for the graph **2**. The initial *x* and *y* positions are then set, the *y* position based on the current *y* position marker and the maximum value of our graph data **3**, followed by the column width **4**.

Looping over our data **5**, we use the $key value to alternate the color setting for the columns **6**. Each column's value is drawn at its top **7**, and then a rectangle is drawn for the column itself, which we've set to not have a stroke **8**. After setting the *y* position marker to 20 points below the column **9**, we use Zend_Date to get and draw the shortened text for the month **10**.

With one column complete, we shuffle the *x* position along by the column width, ready for the next column to be drawn **11**. Once all months have been drawn, we add some space below the graph section by setting the *y* position marker 20 points down **12**, and we restore the graphics state **13**. When called, this method produces the final output shown in figure 16.3.

Astute readers will notice the shortcomings in the preceding method, one being that its height is based on the largest data value, which means large values will generate an overly tall graph. We've done that to keep this example simple, but for actual use we'd obviously want to add calculations to keep that height proportional to the page height.

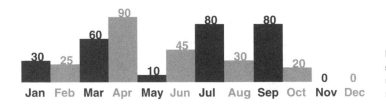

Figure 16.3   Demonstrating drawing rectangles with our report graph

Because we're plotting the month-by-month performance of our site, a bar graph is a suitable choice. Had we been dealing with the kind of data that would suit a pie chart better, we'd have had to draw circles or ellipses.

16.6.4 *Drawing circles and ellipses*

Before you get too excited, we're not actually going to draw a pie chart in this section, but we'll give you a start on drawing circles and ellipses so that you're at least part way there.

The commands for drawing circles and ellipses are fairly similar, with the variation being due to the difference in the way they're drawn. A circle is drawn out the length of the radius from a center marked with the *x* and *y* values, as in the following command:

```
$page->drawCircle($x, $y, $radius, $startAngle, $endAngle, $fillType);
```

An ellipse is drawn within a rectangular bounding box specified with two sets of *x* and *y* coordinates like `drawRectangle()`:

```
$page->drawEllipse($x1, $y1, $x2, $y2, $startAngle, $endAngle, $fillType);
```

Had we been drawing pie charts, the `$startAngle` and `$endAngle` arguments would have been useful for drawing slices of a circle, as shown in figure 16.4.

Circles are drawn in a counter-clockwise direction, so the example on the left of figure 16.4 starts at 90 degrees and moves around to 0 or 360 degrees and could be drawn with the following code:

```
$this->_page->drawCircle(300, 300, 50, deg2rad(90), deg2rad(360));
```

The example on the right of figure 16.4 has a start angle of 0 degrees and an end angle of 90 degrees, which could be done like so:

```
$this->_page->drawCircle(300, 300, 50, 0, deg2rad(90));
```

The final argument for both methods is used to define the fill type in the same way we did when drawing rectangles.

You'll probably have noticed that we used the PHP function `deg2rad()` when specifying the angles in the preceding code. This is because angles are specified in radians rather than degrees. Whether or not you see this as intuitive, at least it's consistent because it's also the value used when rotating objects.

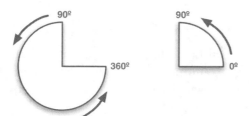

Figure 16.4 Slices of a circle are drawn in a counter-clockwise direction

16.7   *Rotating objects*

You rotate an object by rotating the page, drawing the element, then rotating the page back to its original position (or to the next angle required). This may initially seem an odd way to do it, but a quick look at the command to do so makes the logic clearer:

```
$page->rotate($x, $y, $angle);
```

By rotating the page on an angle (in radians) around an *x* and *y* position, we can rotate any object, be it text, rectangle, circle, or any other item, without the need for each item to have its own methods of rotation.

In figure 16.5, we demonstrate how page rotation works by first rotating the page 10 degrees from its normal position, then drawing text at the top of the page. More objects could be drawn at this point, and they would also adopt the rotation settings. The page is then rotated back to its original position, with the text remaining at the angle of 10 degrees to the page.

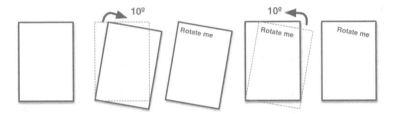

Figure 16.5   Demonstrating how rotation works by setting some text at a 10 degree angle

To make it easier to return the page to the original angle, you can save the graphics state, perform the rotation or rotations, draw the element, and then restore the graphics state:

```
$page->saveGS();
$page->rotate($x, $y, $angle);
// Draw your element here
$page->restoreGS();
```

The rotation will only apply to the elements you draw after rotating. Everything drawn before rotation will remain as is.

So far we've covered adding various types of objects to the page, but we've left out one fairly major one: images.

16.8   *Adding images to the page*

Adding images to your PDF document starts by loading your image file, which must be in TIFF, PNG, or JPEG format, passing its full path to the Zend_Pdf_Image::image-WithPath() method, then adding it to the page like so:

```
$file = '/path/to/image.jpg';
$image = Zend_Pdf_Image::imageWithPath($file);
```

```
$page->drawImage($image, $x1, $y1, $x2, $y2);
```

The *x* and *y* values here are the same as you'd use for drawing a rectangle. Your image will be stretched to fit the specified size if it isn't the same as, or proportional to, the original image size.

If you need to load alternative image formats, or you want better image resizing, you might consider using the GD library to save a modified version of the image file to be loaded into your PDF.

In cases where we want to show only a part of an image or object in our document, we can use clipping masks.

16.9 Drawing objects within clipping masks

Any of the drawn shapes described in this chapter can be used as clipping masks to exclude parts of an image, such as an unwanted background, in a picture.

The methods for creating the clipping masks are almost identical to the methods for drawing the shapes, except that there are no fill types:

```
$page->clipCircle(...);
$page->clipEllipse(...);
$page->clipPolygon(...);
$page->clipRectangle(...);
```

All elements drawn after a clipping mask has been defined will be affected by the mask. If you want to continue to draw elements that aren't affected by the clipping mask, you can do so by saving the graphics state, defining a clipping mask, drawing your elements, and restoring the graphics state.

We've now covered the main functions of `Zend_Pdf`, which means we just need to use our report generator models.

16.10 Generating PDF reports

Throughout this chapter, we've been going through the various parts of our report document and page model, but we haven't yet demonstrated how to use it. The actual `Report_Page` class is quite a bit bigger than we've been able to show in this chapter, but we've covered the key methods. You can view the full class in the source code accompanying this book.

One final method that we do need to cover before moving on to the controller is the `Report_Page::render()` method that is shown in listing 16.8.

Listing 16.8   The `render()` method of our `Report_Page` class

```
public function render()
{
    $this->setStyle();
    $this->setHeader();
    $this->wrapText($this->_introText);
    $this->getGraphSection();
    $this->getNotesSection();
    $this->setFooter();
```

```
        return $this->_page;
    }
```

This method simply calls together the various pieces of our report page, and it is grouped this way so that, at a later date, we could move it to an interface or an abstract class as our reporting needs grow. You should recognize all the methods called within it, except for the setFooter() method, which, as you can probably guess, produces a page footer.

Having shown that last method, we can turn to listing 16.9, which shows how our models are used to construct the PDF document within the indexAction() method of our ReportController controller class.

Listing 16.9   Using the report models in our `ReportController` controller action

```
public function indexAction()
{                                              ❶ Creates document
    $report = new Report_Document;    ◁────────   object
                                                        ❷ Creates page
    $page1 = new Report_Page;         ◁────────────────    object
    $page1->setYear(2008);
    $page1->setHeadTitle('Places reviews');      ❸ Sets some
    $page1->setIntroText('This is the report for      text content
    reviews. Reviews are very important to Places to
    take the kids because they are an indication not
    only of how many people are reading the places
    information but of how confident users are in the
    community element of the site.');    ❹ Sets some
    $page1->setGraphData(              ◁────   graph data
        array(30,25,60,90,10,45,80,30,80,20,0,0)
    );                                           ❺ Adds page to
    $report->addPage($page1);         ◁────────────   document

    header(                           ◁────────
        'Content-Type: application/pdf; charset=UTF-8'   Sets correct
    );                                           ❻ HTTP headers
    echo $report->getDocument()->render();                   ◁────

    $this->_helper->viewRenderer->setNoRender();   ❽ Disables view and
    $this->_helper->layout->disableLayout();          layout rendering
}
                                              Outputs rendered
                                                  document ❼
```

After creating a document object ❶ and a page object ❷, we add some text content to that page object ❸. Following that, we add graph data ❹, which in actual use would be real data gathered from another source, such as a database; but for this example is just some fictitious data. With that page object now complete, we can add it to the document ❺.

At this stage, we could repeat the process of adding as many pages to our document as needed. We'll skip doing so and generate the document, starting by setting the correct HTTP headers to be sent to the browser,❻ then outputting the document,

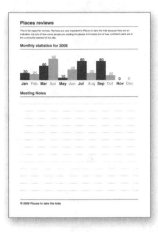

Figure 16.6   The final PDF report page generated by our PDF report generator

rendered by the `render()` method from listing 16.9 **7**. Finally, since we're outputting a PDF document, we disable view and layout rendering for the action **8**. The final rendered document can be seen in figure 16.6.

With our PDF report generator built, we can now look forward to many an exciting progress meeting, armed with accurate and up-to-date information about our website!

16.11 *Summary*

In this chapter, we covered how to use `Zend_Pdf` to load or create a PDF document, add meta-information, add pages, and then save it. You learned how to set page styles, such as colors and fonts, which apply as the default to any drawn objects. You also learned how to draw shapes and text, style and rotate them, add images, and apply clipping masks to them.

Along the way, you'll have noticed some of the quirks we alluded to at the start of the chapter regarding working with the current version of `Zend_PDF`. Hopefully, you can see that they aren't too difficult to work around, and they should be ironed out as the component is developed further.

On the subject of ongoing work, ever since we began writing this book, Zend Framework development has been moving along at a pace that was sometimes hard to keep up with. Our parting recommendation, now that we've come to the end of our coverage of Zend Framework, is to go to the community section of the Zend Framework website (http://framework.zend.com/community/overview) and join the mailing lists, subscribe to the development newsfeeds, get on the #zftalk IRC channel, and anything else that helps you keep in touch with those developments.

Thanks for reading, and remember that if you find us at any of those Zend Framework hangouts, feel free to say hello and tell us what you thought of this book, whether good or bad.

appendix A:
A whistle-stop tour
of PHP syntax

This appendix covers

- Fundamental PHP syntax
- Variables and types
- How loops and conditionals work in PHP
- The basics of PHP functions

Zend Framework is a powerful framework and it's piquing the interest of a wide range of users, from PHP developers who want to take their sites and skills to the next level to developers from other languages and environments looking to build sites in PHP. The content of this book isn't for beginners, and the code assumes a reasonable level of PHP knowledge. This appendix and the next are intended to provide a whistle-stop tour of the core PHP concepts you'll need to know. Obviously, these appendices aren't a substitute for a complete book on the subject.

This appendix covers the key points of the PHP language that you'll need to know to make sense of this book. It's intended for people who understand programming but aren't well versed in the nuances of PHP. If you don't know the fundamentals of programming, we suggest that you consider *PHP and MySQL Web Development* by Welling and Thompson—it's an excellent introduction to PHP development and programming for the Web. Another good book that goes beyond the basics is *PHP in Action* by Reiersøl, Baker, and Shiflett.

We'll start our tour with a look at the fundamentals of PHP then move on to consider the most common PHP operations using arrays and string manipulation. Finally, we'll look at how PHP interacts with a web server. Appendix B will pick up from there and discuss object orientation in PHP, along with the more advanced concepts of the Standard PHP Library and software design patterns.

A.1   *PHP fundamentals*

PHP is very much a pragmatic language designed to enable you to create web pages easily and quickly. It inherits much of its syntax from C and Perl, with a smattering of other inspirations, such as Java for its object-oriented additions.

Listing A.1 shows a basic program with most of the fundamental constructs.

Listing A.1   A simple PHP script, listing1.php

```php
<?php
function say($name)          ❶ Declares function
{                              called say()
    if ($name == 'Nick') {   ❷ Checks value
        echo "G'Day $name\n";    of $name
    } else {
        echo "Hello $name\n"; ❸ Prints out string
    }                            containing variable
}
                             ❹ Calls say()
say('Rob');                     function
say('Nick');

?>
```

To run this code, we simply type `php listing1.php` on the command line. Alternatively, if the file is stored within the web root directory of a web server, we can navigate to it in a web browser. This code is very simple and produces the following output:

```
Hello Rob
G'Day Nick
```

As you can see in listing A.1, each line in PHP ends with a semicolon, and all structures are bounded by braces. Also, because it's a web language designed to be interspersed with HTML, you must start a PHP code block with the `<?php` statement and end it with `?>`. If there is no other code in the file, you can omit the final closing `?>`.

A function in PHP uses the `function` keyword followed by the function name and then parentheses enclosing any function arguments ❶. The content of the function is enclosed in braces and is executed as shown ❹. All conditional statements have the same basic structure as the `if()` statement ❷. There are two key types of strings in PHP: single-quoted strings and double-quoted strings. When using single quotes, the text is output exactly as typed, but with double quotes, any variables within the string are changed to the value of the variable ❸ (also called variable interpolation).

PHP programs are usually separated into many files. The `include` and `require` keywords are used to load and execute a file from within another one. For example, to load the b.php file, the following code would be used:

```
include 'b.php';
```

As the number of files in a project grows, it can be quite hard to keep track of all the times a given file is included. To prevent loading the same file twice, the keywords `include_once` and `require_once` can be used. These work exactly like `include` and `require`, except that they don't load the file a second time if it has already been loaded.

Let's look in more detail at some of the basic constructs within PHP, starting with variables and types.

A.2   *Variables and types*

Variables in PHP start with a $ symbol and are loosely typed, as opposed to C or Java variables, which are strongly typed. This means that you can store any type of data into a variable without worry. Also, the language will automatically convert between types as required by the context of use. For example, if you have a string in one variable and a number in another, PHP will convert the string to a number in order to add them together.

A full explanation of PHP's type-juggling rules can be found at http://www.php.net/language.types.type-juggling. Table A.1 lists the most important types found in PHP.

Table A.1   PHP data types

Data type	Description
`boolean`	A scalar type that can be either `true` or `false` (case insensitive).
`int`	Any number without a decimal point, such as −2 or `0x34` (hexadecimal).
`float`	Any arbitrary precision number including a decimal point, such as `3.142` or `6.626e−34`.
`string`	Any series of characters, each one byte long, such as "`hello world`".
`array`	A map of values to keys. The key can be either numeric, starting at 0, or an arbitrary string, such as `$a=array('a', 'b', 'c');` or `$a[0]='a';`

Table A.1 PHP data types *(continued)*

Data type	Description

object	A grouping of variables and functions, such as
	``
	class user
	{
	    protected $_name;
	    function getName() {
	        return $this->_name;
	    }
	}
	``

resource	A reference to an external resource, such as a file pointer or a database handle. For example, a resource is created when opening a file using `$fp=fopen('filename');`
null	A variable with no value. The keyword `null` is case insensitive.

In PHP, you don't need to declare a variable before first use, so the act of assigning a value to a variable using = will create the variable if it doesn't exist. If it does exist, the value of that variable is overwritten.

It's also possible in PHP to create a variable variable. This is a variable whose name is set dynamically using another variable. Here's an example:

```
$a = 'name';
$$a = 'Rob';
```

This means that there is now a variable called name whose value is Rob. Hence, we can display this using

```
echo $name;
```

This will produce the output Rob.

The string type in PHP is fully featured and contains a number of *gotchas*, so let's look at those next.

A.2.1 *Strings*

Strings in PHP can be declared in four different ways:

- Single quoted
- Double quoted
- Heredoc syntax
- Nowdoc syntax (PHP5.3 or higher)

We'll look at each one in turn.

SINGLE-QUOTED STRINGS

The simplest string is the string literal, which is defined using the single quote character, like this:

```
$name = 'Rob';
```

There are two special characters within a string literal: the single quote and the backslash. To use either within a string, escape it with a backslash, like this:

```php
$name = 'Rob\'s to do list';
```

If you want to store a backslash in the string literal, you can escape it with a backslash, which is known as a double backslash.

DOUBLE-QUOTED STRINGS

Double-quoted strings allow for special escape sequences to be used for special characters. This includes \n for line feed and \t for tab. For example, to display a multi-line string, you'd write this:

```php
echo "This is line one\nThis is line two\n"';
```

You can also create a string over multiple lines in the file and PHP will create it as multiline too.

The full list of escape characters can be found in the PHP online manual at http://www.php.net/manual/en/language.types.string.php. Again, a double backslash is used if you want a literal backslash in the string.

More importantly, as we noted when looking at listing A.1, variables within double-quoted strings are expanded to their values. There are two types of syntax for variable parsing within strings: simple and complex (which adds braces to the simple syntax).

Simple variable parsing is used more often. When a dollar sign is found in the string, PHP takes the next sequence of characters up to a punctuation mark as the variable name to be expanded. Listing A.2 shows examples of simple variable expansion within double quoted strings.

Listing A.2   Simple variable expansion within strings

```php
<?php
echo "My name is $name.";
echo "My name is $names[rob].";          Prints the value of
echo "My name is $user->name.";          array element
                                                  Prints the value of
?>                                                object's property
```

Note that the use of an array within a string is a special case, and usually you need to delimit a string that is within an array's square brackets with quotation marks.

The complex syntax merely adds braces around the variable name, as shown in listing A.3.

Listing A.3   Complex variable expansion within strings

```php
<?php                         Prints the value of
echo "My name is {$name}.";   a multidimensional
                                    array
echo "My name is {$users['names']['rob']}.";    Prints the result of
echo "My name is {$user->getName()}.";          a member method
                                                 of an object
?>
```

As you can see, when using the complex variable expansion syntax, you can use multi-dimensional arrays, and even object methods will work.

HEREDOC STRINGS

Heredoc strings allow for both single and double quotes within a string block without escaping. This format uses the `<<<` operator followed by an identifier to start the string. The string is terminated when the identifier is next encountered at the start of its own line. Here's an example:

```
$name = 'Rob';

echo <<<EOT
There's "$name".

EOT;
```

That produces this output:

```
There's "Rob".
```

As you can see, any variables within a heredoc string are expanded using the same rules as for double-quoted strings.

NOWDOC STRINGS

Nowdoc strings are simply heredoc strings without any parsing. They work exactly like single-quoted strings but use the heredoc syntax. They're created in the same way as heredoc strings except that the identifier is enclosed in single quotes. Here's an example:

```
$name = 'Rob';
echo <<<'EOT'
There's "$name".
EOT;
```

That code produces this output:

```
There's "$name".
```

This means that nowdoc strings are ideal for large bodies of text, such as PHP code, without worrying about escaping.

That's all the ways a string can be created, so let's look at the array syntax next.

A.2.2 Arrays

Arrays are used for lots of different data structures within PHP, because there are lots of functions available that manipulate arrays. Arrays can be treated as arrays, lists, hash tables, dictionaries, collections, stacks, and queues.

In comparison to strings, arrays are relatively simple, because they can only be specified in two ways. The first is by using the `array()` keyword, like this:

```
$users = array('Rob', 'Nick', 'Steven');
```

The second is directly by assignment, like this:

```
$users[] = 'Rob';
$users[] = 'Nick';
$users[] = 'Steven';
```

Both examples result in an array with three elements that have indexes 0, 1, and 2.

Arrays can also be associative, using strings for the key, like this:

```
$['author'] = 'Rob';
$['reader'] = 'Fred';
```

Finally, arrays can be multidimensional:

```
$users = array(

    array('name'=>'Rob', 'country'=>'UK'),
    array('name'=>'Nick', 'country'=>'Australia'),
    array('name'=>'Steven', 'country'=>'Australia')
);
print_r($users);
```

The preceding example will generate this output:

```
Array
(
    [0] => Array
        (
            [name] => Rob
            [country] => UK
        )

    [1] => Array
        (
            [name] => Nick
            [country] => Australia
        )

    [2] => Array
        (
            [name] => Steven
            [country] => Australia
        )

)
```

Note that the key for an array can be either an integer or a string. If the key isn't specified, 1 is added to the maximum integer already in use within the array. If there isn't an integer in the array, 0 is used.

We've now looked at all the data types in PHP, so we'll move on to look at looping and conditional structures.

A.3   Conditionals and loops

As a PHP script is simply a series of statements, the loops and control structures are the part of the script that does the work to achieve a specific goal. A loop allows for executing the same code multiple times, usually with changing variables so that similar, but different, results occur. Conditionals allow for branching the code so that only certain parts of the code execute if a condition is met. We'll start with conditionals.

A.3.1   *Conditionals*

There are two main conditional constructs: `if` and `switch`. The syntax of the `if` statement is shown in listing A.4.

Listing A.4   The `if()` syntax

```php
<?php

if ($a > b) {
    echo '$a is bigger than $b';
} elseif ($b > $a) {
    echo '$b is bigger than $a';
} else {
    echo '$a and $b are equal';
}
?>
```

Testing for alternative condition

Listing A.4 shows that an `if` construct contains a conditional statement between parentheses, and the code to be executed if the conditional evaluates to `true` is between braces. The `elseif` statement, which works exactly the same as using `else if`, provides for multiple conditionals to be tested for. Finally, an `else` statement allows for a block of code to be executed if all the other conditionals fail.

The `switch` statement is essentially a series of `if-else` statements, where you compare the same variable with a series of alternative values, as shown in listing A.5.

Listing A.5   The `switch()` syntax

```php
<?php

switch ($error) {
    case '403':
        echo 'Forbidden';
        break;
    case '404':
        echo 'Not found';
        break;
    default:
        echo 'any other error';
        break;
}

?>
```

Finishes execution of this case

Executes if no other case matches

Note that the `switch` statement will continue executing from the first matching case statement until the end unless you `break` out. The `default` keyword is matched if all the preceding cases fail, and it must come last if you use it.

Both `if` and `switch` alter the flow of operation based on conditions. We'll now look at looping, which allows you to perform the same task multiple times.

A.3.2 *Looping*

There are four main looping constructs: while, do-while, for, and foreach. They all allow for a statement or block to be executed a number of times. We'll start with the while loop.

USING WHILE() AND DO-WHILE()

The while loop is the simplest loop. Here's an example:

```
$i = 0;
while ($i < 10) {
    $i++;
    echo "$i\n";
}
```

This code tells PHP to execute the block repeatedly until $i is 10 or greater. Note that execution doesn't stop until the end of the block. Also, if the conditional evaluates to false immediately, the block doesn't execute at all.

If you need the block to execute at least once, use do-while, like this:

```
$i = 0;
do {
    echo "$i\n";
    $i++;
} while ($i < 10);
```

In the case of do-while, the conditional is checked at the end of each iteration rather than at the start.

You can finish the execution of a loop early by using the break statement; the continue statement is used to restart the loop before it gets to the end of this iteration. These are shown in listing A.6.

Listing A.6 Using break and continue within loops

```
<?php

$i = 0;
while ($i < 10) {

    $i++;
    if ($i == 1) {
        echo "first\n";          ❶ Returns execution to
        continue;                    the start of the loop
    }
    if ($i == 5) {               ❷ Finishes
        break;                       the loop
    }
    echo "$i\n";
}

?>
```

The code in listing A.6 executes the loop five times and produces the following output:

```
first
2
3
4
```

The `continue` statement ❶ sends execution back to the `while()` statement without the echo of `$i`. The `break` statement ❷ stops the `while` loop completely when `$i` is 5.

The `while` and `do-while` loops are generally used when you don't know how many iterations are required. When you know how many times you want the loop to execute, the `for` loop is used.

USING FOR()

The `for` loop constructs are the most complex in PHP, and they work like `for` loops in C. Listing A.7 shows a `for` loop in action.

Listing A.7   The `for()` syntax

```php
<?php

for ($i = 0; $i < 10; $i++) {          Loops 10
    echo "$i\n";                       times
}

?>
```

A `for` loop contains three expressions within the parentheses. The first expression (`$i =0` in listing A.7) is run once before the loop starts. The second expression (`$i < 10` in listing A.7) is evaluated at the start of each loop, and if it's `true`, the block of statements within the brackets is run. If it's `false`, the loop ends. After the block of statements has executed, the third expression (`$i++` in listing A.7) is executed. All expressions can contain multiple statements separated by commas.

The final looping construct, `foreach`, is a simplified version of the `for` loop for iterating over arrays.

USING FOREACH()

The `foreach` loop only works with arrays and objects. It iterates over each element in the array and executes a block of statements for each one in turn. This is shown in listing A.8.

Listing A.8   The `foreach()` syntax

```php
<?php

$users = array('Rob', 'Nick', 'Steven');       Assigns current element
foreach ($users as $key=>$user) {               to $value in each iteration
    echo "$key: $user\n";
}

?>
```

Each time through the `foreach` loop, the value of the current element is assigned to `$value` and the key to `$key`. The code in listing A.8 would produce the following output:

```
0: Rob
1: Nick
2: Steven
```

The key is optional, but the value part is not. Note that the value variable (`$user` in this case) is a copy of the value from the `$users` array. If you want to modify the original array, you need to reference it using a & symbol, like this:

```
foreach ($users as &$user) {
    echo "$key: $user\n";
}
```

We've now covered the major looping constructs in PHP. To wrap up this section, we're going to look at an alternative syntax that allows us to forego the braces around the nested blocks of code.

A.3.3 *Alternative syntax for the nested block*

There is an alternative syntax for both loop and conditional control structures that is widely used in Zend Framework view scripts. This form replaces the opening brace with a colon and the closing brace with a new keyword—endif, endwhile, endfor, endforeach, or endswitch, as appropriate. This is shown in listing A.9.

Listing A.9 Alternative syntax for control structures

```
<?php

<?php if ($a > b) : ?>          ◁────┐  Uses a colon instead
$a is bigger than $b                    of an opening {
<?php elseif ($b > $a) : ?>
$b is bigger than $a
<?php else : ?>
$a and $b are equal             ┌── Finishes statement
<?php endif; ?>         ◁───────┘   with closing keyword
```

The alternative version is most commonly used when PHP is mixed directly with HTML. In this scenario, each PHP statement is surrounded by PHP's opening and closing statements so that plain HTML can be used between each conditional test. The example in listing A.9 has only one line of text, but in a real application there would usually be many lines. The alternative syntax is used because it's relatively difficult to match up braces when opening and closing the PHP blocks so often.

We've now looked at the key features of PHP's looping and conditional control structures, so it's time to move on and look at organizing our executable code using functions.

A.4   *Functions*

A function is a block of code that is separated from everything else. This allows us to reuse a block of code multiple times without having to copy and paste the same code. The code within a function is also isolated from other PHP code and so is easier to test, and we can be sure that it isn't dependent on any other code. Listing A.10 shows an example function.

Listing A.10   An example of a function to display a name

```php
<?php

function hello($name)          ◄──────┐  Declares
{                                         function
    echo 'Greetings ';         ❶ Prints result of a
    echo ucfirst($name);       ◄──────┘    function call

    return true;    ◄──────┐
}                  ❷ Returns value to
                      calling code
?>
```

A function is declared using the `function` keyword followed by the name of the function and parentheses. If the function takes any parameters, these are listed between the parentheses. The function in listing A.10 takes one parameter (`$name`) and displays it after it has converted the first character to uppercase using another function called `ucfirst()` ❶.

NOTE   All functions are in the global scope, and you can't have two functions of the same name. There are many thousands of PHP functions within all the extensions that are available to PHP. As a result, you should consider naming your functions with a prefix, such as your initials, to avoid clashes.

The function in listing A.10 is executed like this:

```php
$result = hello('rob');
```

It produces this output:

```
Greetings Rob
```

Obviously, most functions are considerably more complex than this.

Any variables created within the scope of a function aren't available outside the function definition. The easiest way to have a function provide information is to use the `return` keyword ❷. In the case of the `hello()` function in listing A.10, the returned value is `true`, which is assigned to the `$result` variable.

A.5 *Summary*

This concludes our look at the fundamental syntax of PHP. There is obviously much more to the language than we've covered here, and the online documentation should be consulted for the fine details on syntax and usage. PHP also comes with many extensions that provide additional built-in functions to the language. The range of functions give PHP its power as a web language. The most common extensions cover databases, XML parsing, file system interfaces, encryption, character encoding, image processing, email, and more.

As this is a whistle-stop tour, there is more we haven't covered than we have! We've covered the key areas of variables, loops, conditionals, and functions at a high level, which should be enough (along with appendix B) to understand the code in this book. The PHP manual's Language Reference has further details on the nuances of what has been covered (http://www.php.net/manual/en/langref.php). The rest of the PHP manual has full coverage of all the thousands of functions provided by extensions. Each function has its own page in the manual, which provides details on usage, return types, and examples.

PHP5 vastly improved the object-oriented features of the language. As Zend Framework is an object-oriented framework, all of the functionality it provides is in the form of objects. Appendix B looks at the key features of the PHP object-oriented system that you need to know in order to understand Zend Framework.

appendix B:
Object-Oriented PHP

This appendix covers

- The PHP object model
- An introduction to the iterators, arrays, and counting interfaces provided by the Standard PHP Library
- The basics of software design patterns, including the Singleton and Registry patterns

This appendix will refresh your knowledge of those bits of PHP that you haven't had a chance to deal with until now. Zend Framework is written in PHP5 and is fully object oriented, and you'll need to have a reasonable amount of knowledge about OOP in PHP to make sense of it. This chapter is no substitute for a full book, such as *PHP in Action* by Reiersøl, Baker, and Shiflett, but it should help you enough to get going with Zend Framework.

We'll look at what makes a class, including the visibility specifiers of `public`, `protected`, and `private`. And because the full power of object orientation is realized when classes are extended, we'll also investigate the use of abstract classes and interfaces to help document the API for a component.

PHP5 introduced the SPL, a library that allows you to make your classes easier to use. Zend Framework uses SPL internally, so we'll look at some of the powerful things that are possible with it.

We'll also look at software design patterns. A design pattern is an approach to a given problem used by many people. I use the word "approach" deliberately, as the actual code used to solve the problem is usually different, but all solutions share the same design. Design patterns give us a vocabulary we can use to share solutions and to also understand each other. They also have the benefit of having been tested in real applications, so you can be sure that the design pattern is a good solution to the class of problems that it helps to solve.

Let's dive right in and look at object orientation.

B.1 Object orientation in PHP

OOP is a way to group related functions and variables together. The fundamental goal is to produce more maintainable code—that is, code that doesn't accidentally break when you're working on something else.

In this section, we'll look at the basics of classes and objects, and how they can be related using inheritance. We'll then look at how interfaces and abstract classes can help to control how classes are used. Finally, we'll look at PHP5's so-called "magic" methods.

B.1.1 Classes, objects, and inheritance

In order to understand OOP, you need to understand classes and objects. While we're here, we'll also look at interfaces, which are closely related to classes.

A *class* is the code that groups methods and variables together. That's all. It's not scary! Listing B.1 shows the most simple class.

Listing B.1 The most basic implementation of a class

```
class ZFiA_Person    ◁─────────      Defines the
{                               ❶    class's name

}
```

As you can see, the class keyword is used to declare the class, and it's followed by the class's name, ZFiA_Person in this case ❶. The name of the class has to be unique across all your files, so it's a good idea to prefix every class name with a unique identifier. In our case, we'll use the prefix "ZFiA". While this is a bit more work when writing the code, the benefits down the line, when you need to integrate your code with someone else's, far outweigh any initial pain and using a prefix is recommended by the php.net manual.

An *object* is a runtime instantiation of a class. This means that it has a name and it's created using the new keyword:

```
$rob = new ZFiA_Person();
```

The variable $rob is an object, and it follows that you can have many objects of the same type. For instance, I can create a $nick object using the same syntax:

```
$nick = new ZFiA_Person();
```

I now have two objects that are of the same class. That is, there's only one class but two instance objects of it. You can create any number of objects from a particular class.

Let's look at how we can set up the object using a constructor so that it's ready to use immediately after creation.

CONSTRUCTING AND DESTRUCTING

Usually an object needs to set up its internal state; that is, it must set the initial values of its member variables. To do this, a special method, called a *constructor*, is used, which has the name __construct(). This method is called automatically when a new object is instantiated. It's very common for a class to have a constructor, and usually one or more function parameters are used to set the object's internal state. This is shown in listing B.2.

At the opposite end of the object's lifetime, another method is called, __destruct(), just as the object is about to be deleted. This method is called the destructor, and it's rarely used in PHP scripts intended for the web because of the "set-up and tear-down every request" nature of PHP. In PHP, all objects are destroyed automatically at the end of the request and recreated at the start of the next request.

Listing B.2   Adding a constructor to our class from listing B.1

```php
<?php                                                    Declares
                                                      constructor
class ZFiA_Person                                          method
{
    private $_firstName;        ❶ Declares member variables that
    private $_lastName;            are only visible to this class

    public function __construct($firstName, $lastName)  ◁
    {
        $this->_firstName = $firstName;    ❷ Assigns function parameters
        $this->_lastName = $lastName;         to member variables
    }
}
```

Listing B.2 introduces the private and public keywords that control the visibility of methods and variables within a class. These are discussed in more depth in the next section. As you can see in listing B.2, we've created two member variables ❶, which are set to their initial values using the constructor ❷.

PUBLIC, PROTECTED, AND PRIVATE VISIBILITY

As we've noted, a class can have methods and variables. This grouping is useful in its own right, to help organize code, but it really comes into its own when we add *information hiding* to the mix.

NOTE *Information hiding* is the ability to mark class methods and variables as invisible outside the class boundary. This leads to more maintainable code, because each class "publishes" an API for other classes to use, but is able to implement that API however it would like to.

There are three keywords involved: `public`, `protected`, and `private`. They follow the same usage as in other object-oriented languages, such as C++, Java, or C#:

- `public`—Available from any scope
- `protected`—Only available from within the class or any of its children
- `private`—Only available within the defining class itself

Let's look at this in use, and flesh out the `ZFiA_Person` class in listing B.3.

Listing B.3   A simple class

```php
<?php

class ZFiA_Person
{
    protected $_firstName;        Declares member variables visible
    protected $_lastName;         to the class and its children

    public function __construct($firstName, $lastName)
    {
        $this->_firstName = $firstName;    Assigns to member
        $this->_lastName = $lastName;      variables
    }

    public function fullName()
    {
        return $this->_firstName . ' '      Defines method used
            . $this->_lastName;             by consumers of class
    }
}
```

As you can see, we've marked the `$_firstName` and `$_lastName` member variables as `protected`. Because they're inaccessible to users of this class, we've provided a method, `fullName()`, to allow access to the data. We're now free to change how we store the first name and last name information, without affecting any code that uses this class.

We also may want to avoid having to repeat this code for a class that is conceptually similar. This is handled by the concept of class extension.

B.1.2   *Extending classes*

Extending classes is extremely powerful and can save you a lot of time by facilitating code reuse. When one class extends another, it will inherit the properties and methods of the class it extends, provided they're not `private`. The class being extended is called the *parent*, and the class that is extending the parent is called the *child*.

When you extend another class, you're creating an "is a" relationship. That is, your child class "is a" parent class with additional functionality. For example, we could create a `ZFiA_Author` class that extends `ZFiA_Person`, which means that an Author *is a* Person. This is shown in listing B.4.

Listing B.4   Extending `ZFiA_Person` to create `ZFiA_Author`

```
class ZFiA_Author extends ZFiA_Person          ◁─────────────        Uses extends to
{                                      ❶ Declares a variable only     inherit functionality
    protected $_title;          ◁──┘     available in ZFiA_Author

    public function setTitle($title)          ❷  Defines
    {                                             member
        $this->_title = $title;                   method
    }

}
```

The `ZFiA_Author` class inherits all the properties and methods of the `ZFiA_Person` class. It can also have its own properties ❶ and methods ❷. You can override the methods by creating new methods with the same name in the child class, or you can use the methods of the parent class simply by calling them. You don't need to redefine them. Also, the `final` keyword can be prepended to the declaration of a function next to the visibility keyword to prevent any child classes from overriding the method.

Another thing we may wish to do is create a class that implements common functionality for a series of child classes, but this class should not be instantiated itself. Abstract classes are designed to solve this problem.

B.1.3   *Abstract classes and interfaces*

Two new features of PHP5 are interfaces and abstract classes. These are special constructs that are used with classes to allow a library designer to specify how consumers of the library should use the provided code.

ABSTRACT CLASSES

Some classes are designed purely to be extended by other classes; these are known as *abstract classes* and act as a skeleton implementation of a concept that is then fleshed out by child classes. Abstract classes contain their own member variables and methods along with declarations of methods that must be defined by the concrete child classes.

For instance, we could make `ZFiA_Person` an abstract class, where we determine that all people will have a first name and surname, but leave the definition of how to present their formal name to be determined by the child classes, as shown in listing B.5.

Listing B.5   An abstract class contains undefined functions

```
abstract class ZFiA_Person              ◁──────────────   Declares an
{                                                          abstract class
    protected $_firstName;
    protected $_lastName;
                                                    Defines a standard
    public __construct($firstName, $lastName)   ◁──┘  member function
    {
        $this->_firstName = $firstName;
        $this->_lastName = $lastName;
    }
                                               Declares an abstract
    abstract public function fullName();   ◁──┘  function signature

}
```

Because ZFiA_Person is now declared as an abstract class, it can no longer be instantiated directly using new; it must be extended by the child class instantiated. The fullName() method is defined as abstract, so all child classes (that aren't themselves declared as abstract) must provide an implementation of this method. We can provide an implementation of ZFiA_Author as shown in listing B.6.

Listing B.6   Creating a concrete class from an abstract one

```
class ZFiA_Author extends ZFiA_Person
{
    public function fullName()
    {
        $name = $this->_firstName . ' '      Defines concrete
                    . $this->lastName;       implementation of
        $name .= ', Author';                 fullName()
        return $name;
    }
}
```

As you can see, the ZFiA_Author class provides a specific implementation of fullName() that isn't appropriate to any other child class of ZFiA_Person, because it appends the word "author" to the end of the person's name.

One limitation of the PHP object model is that a class may only inherit from one parent class. There are lots of good reasons for this, but it does mean that another mechanism is required to enable a class to conform to more than one "template." This is achieved using interfaces.

INTERFACES

Interfaces define a template for classes that implement the interface. The interface is an API or contract that the class must satisfy. In practical terms, this means that an interface is a list of methods that must be defined by implementing classes. Interfaces allow a class to be used by a method that depends upon the class implementing certain functionality.

If we were to make ZFiA_Person an interface, it would be declared as shown in listing B.7.

Listing B.7   An interface, specifying methods that must be defined in the class

```
interface ZFiA_Person
{                                                        Declares method to
    public function fullName();                          be implemented
}

class ZFiA_Author implements ZFiA_Person
{
    protected $_firstName;
    protected $_lastName;

    public function __construct($firstName, $lastName)
    {
        $this->_firstName = $firstName;
        $this->_lastName = $lastName;
    }

    public function fullName()
    {                                                    Defines
        return $this->_firstName . ' '                   implementation of
                . $this->_lastName;                      interface's method
    }
}
```

If the fullName method isn't defined in ZFiA_Author, it will result in a fatal error. Because PHP isn't a statically typed language, interfaces are a convenience mechanism for the programmer to help prevent logical errors, as they may be specified in type hints.

Type hinting tells the PHP interpreter information about the parameters passed to a function or method. Consider the function in listing B.8.

Listing B.8   Providing information about function parameters with type hinting

```
function displayPerson(ZFiA_Person $person)              Defines a type hint in
{                                                      ❶ function declaration
    echo $person->fullName();
}
```

To create a type hint, all we need to do is include the type of the function parameter, ZFiA_Person in this case ❶. If we try to pass any other kind of object to this function, we'll get this error message:

```
Catchable fatal error: Argument 1 passed to displayPerson() must be an
instance of ZFiA_Person, string given, called in type_hinting.php on line
18 and defined in type_hinting.php on line 11
```

As should be obvious, interfaces aren't required for PHP coding because PHP isn't a statically typed language and will do the right thing in the majority of cases. The main benefit of interfaces is for the programmer, because it helps make code self-documenting.

Another feature of PHP5 that is used by Zend Framework to make programmers' lives easier is *overloading*, via so-called "magic" methods. These are special methods that PHP calls automatically, when required, allowing the programmer to provide a cleaner interface to the class.

B.1.4 Magic methods

Magic methods are special methods used by PHP in certain circumstances. Any method whose name begins with "__" (double underscore) is reserved by the PHP language, so all magic methods are prefixed with __. The most common method is the constructor, __construct, which we looked at in section B.1.1. Table B.1 shows all the magic methods you can use in your class.

Table B.1 PHP5's magic methods are automatically called by PHP when required

Method name	Prototype	When called
__construct()	void __construct()	When the object is instantiated.
__destruct()	void __destruct()	When the object is cleaned up and removed from memory.
__call()	mixed __call(string $name, array $arguments)	When the member function doesn't exist; used to implement method handling that depends on the function name.
__get()	mixed __get (string $name)	When the member variable doesn't exist when retrieving.
__set()	void __set (string $name, mixed $value)	When the member variable doesn't exist when setting.
__isset()	bool __isset (string $name)	When the member variable doesn't exist when testing if it is set.
__unset()	void __unset (string $name)	When the member variable doesn't exist when unsetting.
__sleep()	void __sleep()	When the object is about to be serialized; used to commit any pending data that the object may be holding.
__wakeup()	void __wakeup()	When the object has been unserialized; used to reconnect to external resources (such as a database).
__toString()	void __toString()	When the object is converted to a string; used to output something sensible on echo().

Table B.1   PHP5's magic methods are automatically called by PHP when required *(continued)*

Method name	Prototype	When called
`__set_state()`	`static void __set_state(array $properties)`	When `var_export()` has been called on the object; used to enable recreation of an object using `eval()`.
`__clone()`	`void __clone()`	When the object is being copied; usually used to ensure that the copy of the object handles references.
`__autoload()`	`void __autoload($class_name)`	When the class can't be found when instantiating; used to load the class using `include()` by mapping the class's name to a file on disk.

Let's look at one use of `__set()` and `__get()` within `Zend_Config`. `Zend_Config` stores all of its variables within a protected member variable called `$data`, and uses the magic `__set()` and `__get()` methods to provide public access to the information, as shown in listing B.9.

Listing B.9   Zend_Config's use of `__get()` and `__set()`

```php
class Zend_Config implements Countable, Iterator        ◁————  Declares interface
{                                                              to implement
                                                  Declares member
    protected $_data;        ◁————                variable

    public function get($name, $default = null)    ◁————
    {                                                      ❶ Defines method to
        $result = $default;                                  retrieve data value
        if (array_key_exists($name, $this->_data)) {
            $result = $this->_data[$name];
        }
        return $result;
    }                                       ❷ Defines magic method
                                               that uses get()
    public function __get($name)    ◁————
    {
        return $this->get($name);
    }                                    ❸ Special conditions on
                                            setting a variable
    public function __set($name, $value)    ◁————
    {
        if ($this->_allowModifications) {
            if (is_array($value)) {
                $this->_data[$name] = new Zend_Config($value, true);
            } else {
                $this->_data[$name] = $value;
            }
            $this->_count = count($this->_data);
        } else {
            throw new Zend_Config_Exception('Zend_Config is read only');
        }
```

```
        }
    }
```

As you can see in listing B.9, Zend_Config has a public method, get(), that is used to retrieve a variable, and it provides for a default if the variable isn't set ❶. The magic method __get() uses the get() method that's already written ❷, and so allows for accessing a variable as if it were a native member variable. For example, calling this,

```
$adminEmail = $config->adminEmail
```

is identical to calling this,

```
$adminEmail = $config->get('adminEmail');
```

except that the first way is cleaner and easier to remember!

Similarly, __set() is used for setting a variable ❸. This method implements private business logic to only allow a variable to be set if the object has its __allowModifications variable set. If the object has been created as read-only, an exception is thrown instead.

This concludes our whistle-stop tour through the highlights of objects in PHP. For more in-depth information, I recommend reading chapters 2 through 6 of *PHP in Action* by Reiersøl, Baker, and Shiflett.

Another area of PHP5 that is used by Zend Framework is the Standard PHP Library, known as the SPL.

B.2   *The SPL*

The SPL is a library of useful interfaces designed to make data access easier. It provides the following categories of interfaces:

- Iterators—Allows you to loop over elements in collections, files, directories, or XML
- Array access—Makes objects act like arrays
- Counting—Allows objects to work with count()
- Observer—Implements the Observer software design pattern

As this is a tour of the SPL, we shall only look at iteration, array access, and counting because we looked at the Observer design pattern in chapter 9. We'll start with iterators, because these are the most common use of the SPL.

B.2.1   *Using iterators*

Iterators are objects that loop (or traverse) a structure such as an array, a database result set, or a directory listing. You need an iterator for each type of structure that you wish to iterate over, and the most common (arrays, directories) are built into PHP and the SPL directly.

A common situation is reading a directory, and this is done using the SPL's `DirectoryIterator` object, as shown in listing B.10.

Listing B.10　Iterating over a directory listing using `DirectoryIterator`

```
$dirList = new DirectoryIterator('/');                          ◁─┐  Creates
foreach ($dirList as $item) {   ◁─┐                               │  iterator
    echo $item . "\n";            │  Uses iterator in
}                                 │  foreach() to loop
```

As you can see, using an iterator is as easy as using a `foreach()` loop, and that's the whole point! Iterators make accessing collections of data very easy, and they come into their own when used with custom classes. This can be seen within Zend Framework in the `Zend_Db_Table_Rowset_Abstract` class, where iterators allow you to traverse all the results returned from a query.

Let's look at some highlights of the implementation. First, we use `Zend_Db_Table_Rowset` as shown in listing B.11.

Listing B.11　Using iteration with `Zend_Db_Table_Rowset`

```
class Users extends Zend_Db_Table {}          ◁─┐  Defines gateway
                                                 │  class to Users
$users = new Users();                Gets        │  database table
$userRowset = $users->fetchAll();  ◁─┘ rowset

foreach ($userRowset as $user) {   ◁─┐
    echo $user->name . "\n";          │  Iterates over
}                                     │  rowset class
```

As we'd expect, using a rowset is as easy as using an array. This is possible because `Zend_Db_Table_Rowset_Abstract` implements the `Iterator` SPL interface, as shown in listing B.12.

Listing B.12　Iterator implementation within `Zend_Db_Table_Rowset_Abstract`

```
abstract class Zend_Db_Table_Rowset_Abstract
                  implements Iterator, Countable
{                                                      ❶  Defines Iterator's
    public function current()    ◁─┐                      current() method
    {
        if ($this->valid() === false) {   Returns null at the end to break
            return null;   ◁─┘            out of a foreach() or while()
        }

        return $this->_rows[$this->_pointer];
    }                                            ❷  Defines Iterator's
    public function key()    ◁─┐                    key() method
    {
        return $this->_pointer;
    }                                 ❸  Defines Iterator's
    public function next()    ◁─┘        next() method
```

```
    {
        ++$this->_pointer;
    }
    public function rewind()      <─
    {
        $this->_pointer = 0;
    }
    public function valid()       <─
    {
        return $this->_pointer < $this->_count;
    }
}
```

④ **Defines Iterator's rewind() method**

⑤ **Defines Iterator's valid() method**

Zend_Db_Table_Rowset_Abstract holds its data in an array called $_rows and holds the count of how many items are in the array in $_count. We need to keep track of where we are in the array as the foreach() is progressing, and the $_pointer member variable is used for this. To implement Iterator, a class needs to provide five methods: current() ①, key() ②, next() ③, rewind() ④, and valid() ⑤. These methods, as you can see in listing B.12, simply manipulate the $_pointer variable as required and return the correct data in current().

One limitation of Iterator is that it is limited to forward traversal of the data and doesn't allow for random access. That is, you can't do this with an instance of Zend_Db_Table_Rowset_Abstract:

```
$aUser = $userRowset[4];
```

This is by design, because the underlying technology behind the class is a database that might not allow random access to a dataset. Other types of objects may require this, though, and for those cases the ArrayAccess interface is used.

B.2.2 *Using ArrayAccess and Countable*

The ArrayAccess interface allows a class to behave like an array. This means that a user of the class can randomly access any element within the collection using the [] notation, like this:

```
$element = $objectArray[4];
```

As with Iterator, this is achieved using a set of methods that must be implemented by the class. In this case, the methods are offsetExists(), offsetGet(), offsetSet(), and offsetUnset(). The names are self-explanatory and, as shown in listing B.13, allow for several array operations to be carried out.

Listing B.13   Array operations with an `ArrayAccess`-capable class

```
if(isset($rob['firstName']) {                          ◄────────────┐ Calls
    echo $rob['firstName'];     ◄────┐                 │            │ offsetExists()
    $rob['firstName'] = 'R.';   ◄──┐ │ Calls offsetGet()
}                                  │ └─ Calls offsetSet()
unset($rob['firstName']);   ◄──────┐
                                   │ Calls
                                   │ offsetUnset()
```

The only other array-based functionality that is useful to implement in the context of an object is the count() function. This is done via the Countable interface, which contains just one method, count(). As you'd expect, this function needs to return the number of items in the collection, and then we have all the tools to make a class behave like an array.

The SPL has many other iterators and other interfaces available for more complicated requirements, which are all documented in the excellent php.net manual.

B.3   PHP4

By now, everyone should be using PHP5 because it's over four years old and PHP4 is no longer supported. If your first steps into PHP5 are with Zend Framework, you should read the excellent migration guide available on the PHP web site at http://www.php.net/manual/en/migration5.php.

With the adoption of PHP5, the PHP world has seen the adoption of software design patterns, which describe how to solve common problems in a language-agnostic manner. Patterns are used throughout Zend Framework's core code, so we'll introduce some of the more common ones.

B.4   Software design patterns

Everyone who produces software soon discovers that they encounter problems similar to ones they've encountered before and that require the same approach to solve. This happens across all software development, and there tend to be best practice solutions for certain classes of problems. In order to make it easier to discuss these approaches to solving problems, the term *design pattern* has been coined, and catalogues of design patterns are available to help you solve software design problems.

The key thing about design patterns is that they're not about the code; they're all about guidelines on how to solve the problem. In this section, we'll look at the Singleton and Registry design patterns. These are both used within Zend Framework's core code.

B.4.1   The Singleton pattern

The Singleton design pattern is a very simple pattern intended to ensure that only one instance of an object can exist. This is used by Zend Framework's Zend_Controller_Front front controller to ensure that there is only one front controller in existence for the duration of the request.

Listing B.14 shows the relevant code for implementing the Singleton pattern in `Zend_Controller_Front`.

Listing B.14 The Singleton pattern as implemented by `Zend_Controller_Front`

```
class Zend_Controller_Front
{
    protected static $_instance = null;          ①  Declares static variable holds
                                                      the one instance of this object
    protected function __construct()             ②  Defines protected
    {                                                constructor

        $this->_plugins = new Zend_Controller_Plugin_Broker();

    }                                            ③  Defines method
    public static function getInstance()             to allow creation
    {
        if (null === self::$_instance) {         ④  Creates one
            self::$_instance = new self();           instance if not
        }                                            already created

        return self::$_instance;                 ⑤  Returns instance
    }                                                to user
}
```

There are three pieces in the Singleton jigsaw, as implemented by `Zend_Controller_Front`, and most other implementations are similar. A static variable is used to store the instance of the front controller ①. This is protected to prevent anyone outside of this class from accessing it directly. To prevent use of the new keyword, the constructor is `protected` ②, so the only way to create an instance of this class from outside its children is to call the static method `getInstance()` ③. `getInstance()` is static because we don't have an instance of the class when we call it; it returns an instance to us. Within `getInstance()`, we only instantiate the class once ④; otherwise we just return the previously created instance ⑤. Note that `Zend_Controller_Front` allows its child classes to implement their own constructor. It is also common to make the constructor `private`, and this can be seen in `Zend_Search_Lucene_Document_Html` and other classes within the Zend Framework.

The net result is that the code to access the front controller is as follows:

```
$frontController = Zend_Controller_Front::getInstance();
```

This code will work wherever it's required, and it will create a front controller for us if we don't have one; otherwise, it returns a reference to the one that has already been created.

Whilst the Singleton is easy to implement, there is a rather large caveat with it: it's a global variable by the back door. As the Singleton has a static method that returns a reference to the object, it can be called *anywhere*, and if used unwisely, could introduce coupling between disparate sections of a program. Singletons are also difficult to test, because you have to provide special methods to reset the object's state.

NOTE   *Coupling* is the term used when two sections of code are linked in some way. More coupling makes it harder to track down bugs because there are more places where the code could have been changed from.

As a result, care should be taken when designing a class to be a Singleton and also when choosing to use the `getInstance()` method elsewhere in the code. Usually, it's better to pass an object around so that it's easier to control access to it than to access the Singleton directly. An example of where we can do this is within the action controller class: `Zend_Controller_Action` provides a `getRequest()` method, which returns the `Request` object, and this method should be used in preference to `Zend_Controller_Front::getInstance()->getRequest()`.

Having said that, it isn't uncommon to need to access commonly used information from multiple places, such as configuration data. We can use the Registry pattern to ensure that managing such data works well.

B.4.2   *The Registry pattern*

The Registry pattern allows us to take any object and treat it as a Singleton, and it allows us to centrally manage these objects. The biggest improvement over the Singleton is that it is possible to have two instances of an object if required.

A typical scenario is a database connection object. Usually, you connect to one database for the duration of the request, so it's tempting to make the object a Singleton. However, you may need to connect to a second database every so often (for export or import, for example) and for those times you need two instances of the database connection object. A Singleton won't allow this, but using a Registry will give you the benefits of the easily accessible object without the drawbacks.

This problem is so common that Zend Framework provides the `Zend_Registry` class, which implements the Registry pattern. For simple access, there are two main functions that form the basic API of `Zend_Registry`, and their usage is shown in listings B.15 and B.16.

Listing B.15   Storing an object to the `Zend_Registry`

```
// bootstrap class
$config = $this->loadConfig();
Zend_Registry::set('config', $config);    ⟵——— Stores the object into
                                               the registry objects
```

To store an object into the registry, the `set()` method is used. Predictably, the `get()` method is used to retrieve an object at another place in the code.

Listing B.16   Retrieving an object from the `Zend_Registry`

```
// bookstrap class
$config = Zend_Registry::get('config');    ⟵——— Retrieves object via
                                               key name: 'config'
```

The only complication to be aware of with `Zend_Registry` is that you must ensure that you provide a unique key when you store the object into the registry; otherwise you'll overwrite the previously stored object of the same name. Other than that, it's easier to use a Registry than modifying a class to make it a Singleton.

The key components of the implementation are shown in listing B.17. Let's examine it.

Listing B.17 The Registry pattern as implemented by `Zend_Registry`

```
class Zend_Registry extends ArrayObject
{
    public static function getInstance()           ❶ Uses a Singleton
    {                                                 object internally
        if (self::$_registry === null) {
            self::init();
        }

        return self::$_registry;
    }

    public static function set($index, $value)
    {
        $instance = self::getInstance();            ❷ Sets element via
        $instance->offsetSet($index, $value);         ArrayObject interface
    }

    public static function get($index)
    {
        $instance = self::getInstance();

        if (!$instance->offsetExists($index)) {
            require_once 'Zend/Exception.php';       Checks that
            throw new Zend_Exception("No entry is    key exists
                ⮕ registered for key '$index'");
        }                                            ❸ Retrieves data
        return $instance->offsetGet($index);            and returns it
    }
}
```

Internally, `Zend_Registry` uses a Singleton-like method, `getInstance()`, to retrieve an instance of itself ❶. This is used in both `get()` and `set()`, and it ensures that both methods are using the same registry when setting and retrieving items. `Zend_Registry` extends `ArrayObject`, which means that you can treat an instance of it as if it were an array and so iterate over it or directly set and get elements as if they were array keys. `ArrayObject` is provided by the SPL and implements the methods required by the `ArrayAccess` interface, including `offsetGet()`, `offsetSet()`, and `offsetExists()`. This saves having to write these methods yourself, though they can be overridden if custom functionality is required. The static methods `set()` and `get()` need to perform the same actions, so `set()` calls `offsetSet()` to set an item into the registry ❷, and `offsetGet()` is used to retrieve an item from the registry within `get()` ❸.

Note that by using `offsetGet()` and `offsetSet()`, the code is oblivious of the underlying storage mechanism used to hold the items. This future-proofing allows for the storage mechanism to be changed if required, and this code won't need to be updated.

We've looked at two of the common design patterns used in web applications and, as noted earlier, there are many others. Zend Framework implements more too, and so is a good code base for studying them. These are some of the other patterns in use:

- MVC in the `Zend_Controller` family of functions
- Table Data Gateway in `Zend_Db_Table`
- Row Data Gateway in `Zend_Db_Table_Row`
- Strategy in `Zend_Layout_Controller_Action_Helper_Layout`
- Observer in `Zend_XmlRpc_Server_Fault`

There are a lot of patterns out there, and we recommend you read *Patterns of Enterprise Application Architecture* by Martin Fowler and *php|architect's Guide to PHP Design Patterns* by Jason Sweat for further information on many of the common Web-oriented patterns. Also, *PHP in Action*, by Reiersøl, Baker, and Shiflett, has a very accessible introduction to the finer points of using design patterns with PHP.

B.5   *Summary*

Zend Framework is a modern PHP5 framework and, as such, takes advantage of all the new goodies that PHP5 provides. Understanding of the key features of PHP5's object model is vital for writing applications with Zend framework. Every part of the Framework is written in Object Oriented PHP with careful use of the SPL interfaces such as ArrayAccess, its sibling ArrayObject, Countable, and Iterator. The SPL can be used to provide interfaces to classes that make them behave more like native PHP arrays. Software design patterns are an important part of modern web development and we've covered what they are and looked at how Zend Framework uses the Singleton and Registry patterns.

This chapter has provided an overview and for more information. We strongly recommend looking at other books that cover these topics in depth. Having said that, armed with the knowledge gleaned here, you're well placed to dive head first into Zend Framework and the main chapters of this book.

appendix C:
Tips and tricks

The appendix covers

- Using modules with Zend Framework's MVC components
- Understanding the effects of the case sensitivity of controller classes and action functions
- Zend Framework URL routing components
- Understanding your application using `Zend_Debug`, `Zend_Log`, and `Zend_Db_Profiler`

This is the where we think about the more advanced uses of some key Zend Framework components. Within the MVC components, we'll look at how modules can be used to further separate your code and also investigate how the dispatcher handles actions and controllers with uppercase letters. We'll also look at how the static and regex routing classes can provide more flexible and efficient URLs.

As a web application grows, logging the processes taking place becomes important. `Zend_Log` provides the features required to let your application tell you what's going on. We'll also look at the benefits of `Zend_Debug` for when you need a quick and dirty check while debugging your code.

Finally, we'll look at `Zend_Db_Profiler`, which will show you exactly which SQL statements are run and how long each one takes. This is very useful when trying to make your page load as quickly as possible.

Let's dive in and look at modules in the MVC system.

C.1   MVC tips and tricks

Within this section, we'll look at features of the MVC system that we've not addressed within the rest of the book either because they're more advanced or less likely to be used in most projects.

C.1.1   Modules

If you peruse the online documentation about `Zend_Controller`, you'll notice that Zend Framework's MVC system supports modules. Modules are designed to provide a further level of separation for your application and are usually used to separate different sections of your application to promote reuse of separate MVC mini-applications.

A simple CMS application may use two modules, blog and pages, each with its own directories for controllers, models, and views. Figure C.1 shows how the directories in this CMS application would look.

Each module has its own controllers directory containing the controller classes. The classes use the naming convention `{Module name}_{Controller name}Controller`, and they're stored in the file application/{Module name}/controllers/{Controller name}.php. For example, the index controller for the pages modules is stored in application/pages/controllers/IndexController.php and is called `Pages_IndexController`.

There is also the standard set of MVC directories in the application folder itself. These are the default modules and behave exactly the same as for a non-modularized

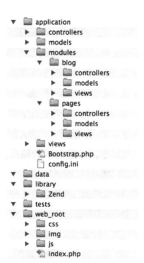

Figure C.1   A directory structure for a modular Zend Framework application may have its own set of MVC subdirectories.

application. That is, the controllers in the default module aren't prefixed with the module name, so the index controller in the default module is simply named `Index-Controller` and is stored in application/controllers/IndexController.php.

By default, once the additional modules are registered with the front controller, the standard router will use the URL scheme of {base url}/{module name}/{controller name}/{action name}. For example, http://example.com/pages/index/view will execute the view action within the default controller of the pages module (the `view-Action()` method within the `Pages_IndexController` class).

Let's look at how to register modules with the front controller, using the *Places* bootstrap code. Listing 3.1 in chapter 3 introduced the `Bootstrap` class and set up the controllers' directory, as shown in listing C.1.

Listing C.1   Front controller setup for *Places* in chapter 3

```
public function runApp()
{
    // setup front controller
    $frontController = Zend_Controller_Front::getInstance();
    $frontController->throwExceptions(false);
    $frontController->setControllerDirectory(
        ➡ ROOT_DIR . '/application/controllers');

    // ...
```

❶ Sets the controllers directory

The important line is the call to `setControllerDirectory()` ❶, where we tell the front controller where to find our controller classes. To include the additional ones in the modules, we can call the front controller's `addControllerDirectory()` for each module in turn like this:

```
$frontController->addControllerDirectory(
        ➡ ROOT_DIR . '/application/modules/blog, 'blog');
$frontController->addControllerDirectory(
        ➡ ROOT_DIR . '/application/modules/pages, 'pages');
```

If you have many modules, this gets very longwinded. An alternative is to make use of `addModuleDirectory()`, which iterates over a directory and adds each subdirectory's controllers directory for you. This is shown in listing C.2.

Listing C.2   Adding modules to the front controller setup for *Places* from chapter 3

```
public function runApp()
{
    // set up front controller
    $frontController = Zend_Controller_Front::getInstance();
    $frontController->throwExceptions(false);
    $frontController->setControllerDirectory(
        ➡ ROOT_DIR . '/application/controllers');
    $frontController->addModuleDirectory(
        ➡ ROOT_DIR . '/application/modules');

    // ...
```

❶ Adds all modules

As you can see, to add support for all the controllers directories within the child folders of the modules directory, we need only a single line of code added to our bootstrap ❶. Using addModuleDirectory() also solves a potential maintenance problem,
because we never have to think about this code again. If we used addController-
Directory(), we'd have to update this code every time a new module was added to
the application.

   In use, a modular application works the same way as a normal application. The
url() view helper works with modules the same way. To create a URL to the index
action of the index controller in another module, the code in the view script looks
like this:

```
$this->url(array('module'=>'another', controller=>'index',
          'action'=>'index'));
```

One issue that does come up is loading the module's models. One way to do this is to
dynamically alter the PHP include_path so the correct module's models directory is
on the path. This is best handled using a front controller plug-in, as shown in
listing C.3. To avoid naming clashes, we use a class prefix to provide a namespace for
the plug-in. The convention we will follow maps the class's name to its location on
disk. In this case, the class name is Places_Controller_Plugin_ModelDirSetup, so
the class is stored in the file library/Places/Controller/ModelDirSetup.php.

Listing C.3   Using `ModelDirSetup` to set the include path to the module's models

```
class Places_Controller_Plugin_ModelDirSetup extends
    ➥ Zend_Controller_Plugin_Abstract
{
    protected $_baseIncludePath;

    public function __construct()                                ❶ Stores
    {                                                               current
        $this->_baseIncludePath = get_include_path();  ◁───────     include path
    }

    public function preDispatch(Zend_Controller_Request_Abstract
            ➥ $request)
    {
        $moduleName = $request->getModuleName();

        $fc = Zend_Controller_Front::getInstance();
        $controllerDir = $fc->getControllerDirectory(
            $moduleName);                                       ❷ Sets models
        $moduleDir = dirname($controllerDir);                     directory
        $modelsDir = $moduleDir.'/models';

        set_include_path($moduleDir . PATH_SEPARATOR .          ❸ Sets include
            ➥ $this->_baseIncludePath);  ◁──────────────────      path
    }

}
```

As with the other two plug-ins, `ActionSetup` and `ViewSetup`, the `ModelDirSetup` plug-in is loaded in the `Bootstrap` class's `runApp()` function using this code:

```
$frontController->registerPlugin(new
    Places_Controller_Plugin_ModelDirSetup());
```

The class stores the current PHP `include_path` in the constructor ❶, so that we can use it later. We do the actual work in the `preDispatch()` method. This allows us to set up the models directory for each action, which is important because it's possible that each action in the dispatch loop will belong to a different module. We set the modules directory by calling `dirname()` on the controllers directory, which is obtained using the `getControllerDirectory()` method of the front controller and adding `'/models'` to it ❷. We then prepend the models directory onto the previously stored `include_path` ❸. This ensures that we don't have multiple models directories on the include path when each action in the dispatch loop is executed.

With care, modules can be used to divide a complex application with many controllers into more manageable segments. If you need to access the models of another module, though, there is nothing to help you directly within Zend Framework, and often it's easiest to use the full path in a `require()` statement.

Let's look next at how the MVC system deals with capital letters in controller and action names.

C.1.2 Case sensitivity

Zend Framework's router and dispatcher are sensitive to the case of action and controller names. This is for a very good reason: PHP's function and method names aren't case sensitive, but filenames generally are. This means that there are rules when using capital letters or other word separators as controller names to ensure that the correct class files can be found. For action names, it's important that the correct view script can be found. The following subsections outline the rules for controller and action URLs.

WORD SEPARATION WITHIN CONTROLLER URLS

The first letter of a controller class name must be uppercase—this is enforced by the dispatcher. The dispatcher also converts certain word-separator characters into directory separators when determining the filename for the class. Table C.1 shows the effect of different controller URLs on the filename and class name of the controller for a controller we wish to call "tech support".

Table C.1 Mapping of controller URLs to controller class name and filename

Action URL	Controller class name	Controller filename
/techsupport/	`TechsupportController`	TechsupportController.php
/techSupport/	`TechsupportController`	TechsupportController.php
/tech-support/	`TechSupportController`	TechSupportController.php
/tech.support/	`TechSupportController`	TechSupportController.php

Table C.1   Mapping of controller URLs to controller class name and filename *(continued)*

Action URL	Controller class name	Controller filename
/tech_support/	`Tech_SupportController`	Tech/SupportController.php

As you can see in table C.1, capital letters in controller names are always lowercased, and only period (.) and hyphen (-) word separators will result in a MixedCased class name and filename. In all cases, there is a direct mapping of class name to filename. This follows the standard Zend Framework conventions, so if an underscore is used in the controller's URL, it acts as a directory separator on disk.

Action names have similar but slightly different rules, because both the dispatcher and the ViewRenderer are involved in resolving an action URL through to an action method and then on to the associated view script file.

WORD SEPARATION WITHIN ACTION URLS

The dispatcher enforces case sensitivity in action method names. This means that it will expect your action method name to be lowercase unless you separate the words in the URL with a recognized word separator. By default, only the period (.) and the hyphen (-) are recognized word separators.

This means that if you name your action using camelCase naming (such as view-Details), the action called will be the all lowercase `viewdetailsAction()`. The View-Renderer will map both recognized word separators and also a capital letter change to a hyphen within the view script filename. This means that an action URL of viewDe-tails will be mapped to a view script filename of view-details.phtml.

Table C.2 shows the effect of different URL word separators on the action and view script called.

Table C.2   Mapping of action URLs to action functions and view script filenames

Action URL	Action function	View script filename
/viewdetails	`viewdetailsAction()`	viewdetails.phtml
/viewDetails	`viewdetailsAction()`	view-details.phtml
/view_details	`viewdetailsAction()`	view-details.phtml
/view-details	`viewDetailsAction()`	view-details.phtml
/view.details	`viewDetailsAction()`	view-details.phtml

As you can see from table C.3, a certain amount of care needs to be taken when using word separators in URLs. We recommend that you always use a hyphen in your URL if you want to have word separation. This will result in easy-to-read URLs, camelCase action function names, and a hyphen separator in your view script filenames, which is consistent with the action name in the URL.

The rules for word separation in controller and action names follow a predictable system. In general, using the hyphen is easiest and also results in URL separations that Google and other search engines like, so we recommend you use them if you want to separate out multiword controller and action names.

Let's look at how to use the router to our advantage for both speed and flexibility in converting URLs to action functions.

C.1.3 Routing

Routing is the process of converting a URL to an action to be run. The standard router is the rewrite router in the `Zend_Controller_Router_Rewrite` class, and by default it attaches the default route that a Zend Framework MVC application uses.

The default route translates URLs of the form module/controller/action/ variable1/value1/. For example, a URL of ncws/index/view/id/6 will be mapped to the "view" action in the "index" controller of the "news" module with the additional parameter id set to 6. The id parameter is accessible in the controller using `$this->_getParam('id')`.

Additional routes can be created and attached to the router, and these will also be used to map URLs to actions. Additional routes are usually set up to provide more easily comprehensible or shorter URLs. As an example, we could create a route that would allow the news/6 URL to map in exactly the same way as news/index/view/id/ 6. To do this, we'd need to create a route object and add it to the router in the bootstrap class before the front controller's `dispatch()` method is called. Listing C.4 shows how this is done.

Listing C.4 Creating a route for news/{id number} in the bootstrap class

```
$defaults = array(
    'module'=>'news',                        ① Sets action
    'controller'=>'index',                      for the route
    'action'=>'view');
$newsRoute = new Zend_Controller_Router_Route(    ② Sets up
    'news/:id', $defaults);                          new route

$router = $frontController->getRouter();     ③ Adds
$router->addRoute('news', $newsRoute);          route
```

To set up a new route, we first have to create a `Zend_Controller_Router_Route` instance and set the route template (news/:id in this case ②). The route template uses the colon character (:) as a prefix to indicate a variable placeholder name. Variable placeholders are then available within the request object and again are accessible from within the controller using the `_getParam()` member method. In this case, the id is set as a variable. If the route template doesn't contain enough information to resolve a route to an action (that is, to provide the module, controller, and action names to be used), they must be specified in the `$defaults` array ①. Once the route is defined, it's added to the router using the router's `addRoute()` method ③.

Obviously, as many routes as are required can be added. The route object allows for validating the variable placeholders in the route to ensure that they're of the required type, and it also allows for defaults, if the placeholder is missing. Listing C.5 shows the creation of a route that lists archived news entries for each year with URLs of the form news/archive/2008.

Listing C.5　Creating a route with defaults and requirements

```
$defaults = array(
    'module'=>'news',
    'controller'=>'index',
    'action'=>'view',              ❶ Sets value
    'year'=>2008);         ◄──         for :year      ❷ Requires digits
$requirements = array('year'=>'\d{4}');  ◄──               only for :year

$archiveRoute = new Zend_Controller_Router_Route('news/archive/:year',
    $defaults, $requirements);
```

Again, we set up the defaults for the module, controller, and action, but this time we also add a default for the :year placeholder. This means that if a value isn't specified, it will be set to 2008 ❶. The requirement for this route is that the :year placeholder must consist only of four digits. This is set using a regular expression in the $requirements array ❷. If the :year placeholder doesn't match the requirements, the route fails to match and the next route is tried. This means that a URL of news/archive/list wouldn't match this route and would instead be matched to the list action of the archive controller in the news module.

Some routes don't need the full flexibility of the standard route class. For instance, a route of /login, which maps to the login action of the auth controller, doesn't need any variable placeholders. In these situations, Zend_Controller_Router_Route_Static is faster, because it doesn't match variable placeholders. Its usage is similar to Zend_Controller_Router_Route, as shown in listing C.6, where we create a static route from the login/ URL to the login action of the auth controller in the default module.

Listing C.6　Creating a static route to /login

```
$defaults = array(
    'module'=>'default',                          Creates
    'controller'=>'auth',    ❶ Sets route      static route
    'action'=>'login');   ◄──    defaults

$loginRoute = new Zend_Controller_Router_Route_Static('login',
    $defaults);                                      ◄──
```

The creation of a static route is identical to a standard route except that you can't use variable placeholders and so must define the module, controller, and action within the defaults array ❶.

Alternatively, you may wish to have a URL that can't be routed using the standard route because it's too complex. In this situation, Zend_Controller_Router_Route_Regex can be used. This route is the most powerful and flexible, but also the most complex. It also has the added benefit of being slightly faster. Listing C.7 shows the new archive route expressed using the regex route.

Listing C.7 News archive route using `Zend_Controller_Router_Route_Regex`

```
$defaults = array(                          Uses a regular expression to
    'module'=>'news',                              define the route
    'controller'=>'index',
    'action'=>'view');
$archiveRoute = new Zend_Controller_Router_Route_Regex(
        ➡ 'news/archive/(\d{4})', $defaults);
```

Because the regex route doesn't use placeholder variables, the resultant data is available within the request object using numeric keys starting at 1 for the first regular expression in the route. In the case of the route in listing C.7, the year value is extracted within the controller like this:

```
$year = $this->_getParam('1');
```

This can complicate matters if the route is ever changed, because the numeric indexes may also change. Changes to routes are relatively rare, and judicious use of constants to hold the indexes would mitigate the cost of changes.

We've now covered some of the more advanced uses of the MVC system, so let's move on and look at how to diagnose problems in your application.

C.2   *Diagnostics with Zend_Log and Zend_Debug*

Zend Framework provides the `Zend_Log` and `Zend_Debug` components to make it easier to find problems in your application's logic. `Zend_Debug` is used more for transient checking of data and `Zend_Log` for longer-term logging of information about the application.

C.2.1   *Zend_Debug*

`Zend_Debug` is a simple class with one method, `dump()`, which either prints or returns information about a variable that is passed into it. It's used like this:

```
Zend_Debug::dump($var, 'title');
```

The first parameter is the variable you wish to display, and the second is a label or title for the data. Internally, the `dump()` method uses `var_dump()` and wraps the output in `<pre>` tags if it detects that the output stream is web-based. It will also escape the data if PHP isn't being used in CLI mode.

`Zend_Debug` is best used for quick and dirty testing. If you want to put some more long-term diagnostics into your application, `Zend_Log` is a better fit.

C.2.2   *Zend_Log*

Zend_Log is designed to log data to multiple backends, such as files or database tables. Using Zend_Log to store log info to a file is very simple, as shown in listing C.8.

> **Listing C.8   Logging data with Zend_Log**
>
> ```
> $writer = new Zend_Log_Writer_Stream(        ❶ Creates stream
>             '/tmp/zf_log.txt');                  to log to
>                                                              ❷ Creates
> $logger = new Zend_Log($writer);                               logger
>
> $logger->log('message to be stored', Zend_Log::INFO);
>                                              Logs an
>                                            ❸ info message
> ```

The Zend_Log object needs a writer object to store the data. In this case, we create a stream writer to a file called /tmp/zf_log.txt ❶ and attach it to the Zend_Log object ❷.

To store a message, the log() member function is used ❸. When you store a message using log() you need to specify the priority of the message. The available priorities are listed in table C.3.

Table C.3   Priorities for Zend_Log log() messages

Name	Value	Usage
Zend_Log::EMERGE	0	Emergency: system is unusable
Zend_Log::ALERT	1	Alert: action must be taken immediately
Zend_Log::CRIT	2	Critical: critical conditions
Zend_Log::ERR	3	Error: error conditions
Zend_Log::WARN	4	Warning: warning conditions
Zend_Log::NOTICE	5	Notice: normal but significant conditions
Zend_Log::INFO	6	Informational: informational messages
Zend_Log::DEBUG	7	Debug: debug messages

The priorities are from the BSD syslog protocol and are listed in order of importance, with EMERGE messages being the most important. For each priority, there is a shortcut method named after the priority name that acts as an alias to log() with the correct priority set. This means that these two commands log exactly the same thing:

```
$logger->log('Critical problem', Zend_Log::CRIT);
$logger->crit('Critical problem');
```

These convenience methods mainly serve as shortcuts so that you type less code.

In a typical application, you'd create the $logger object at the start of the application, within the bootstrap, and store it to the registry for use in the rest of the application, like this:

```
$writer = new Zend_Log_Writer_Stream(ROOT_DIR.'/tmp/log.txt');
$logger = new Zend_Log($writer);
Zend_Registry::set('logger', $logger);
```

When you create the Zend_Log object, you can choose which writer to use. There are four writers available, as shown in table C.4.

Table C.4 `Zend_Log_Writer` objects

Name	When to use
`Zend_Log_Writer_Stream`	Stores logs to files or other streams. The 'php://output' stream can be used to display logs to the output buffer.
`Zend_Log_Writer_Db`	Stores logs to database records. You need to map the level and message to two fields within a table.
`Zend_Log_Writer_Firebug`	Sends log messages to the console in the Firebug extension to Firefox.
`Zend_Log_Writer_Null`	Discards all the log messages. This can be useful for turning off logging during testing or for disabling logging.

To control the level of logging that is performed, a Zend_Log_Filter_Priority object is used. This sets the minimum priority of the message to be logged, and any messages of lower priority aren't logged. The filter is attached to the log object using addFilter() as and when required. Usually, this is added at creation time, and the priority chosen is usually higher for a live site than for a test site. To limit logging to messages of CRIT or above, this code is used:

```
$filter = new Zend_Log_Filter_Priority(Zend_Log::CRIT);
$logger->addFilter($filter);
```

This means all information messages are discarded and only the very important ones are logged. For the live site, this will ensure that the performance of the application isn't impeded by the time taken for logging.

We'll now turn our attention to the profiler component within Zend_Db and see how we can display the SQL statements that are run.

C.3 *Zend_Db_Profiler*

Zend_Db_Profiler attaches to a Zend_Db adapter and enables us to see the SQL of queries that are run and how long each one took. We can use this information to target our optimization efforts, either by caching the results of long-running queries or by optimizing the query itself, maybe by tweaking table indexes.

If you're configuring the database adapter using a config object, the easiest way to turn on the profiler is to set it within your INI or XML file. We use this mechanism for *Places*, and listing C.9 shows the *Places* config.ini with profiling enabled.

Listing C.9   Enabling database profiling within config.ini

```
[general]
db.adapter = PDO_MYSQL
db.params.host = localhost
db.params.username = zfia
db.params.password = zfia
db.params.dbname = places
db.params.profiler = true          ◁——┘   Enables
                                           profiler
```

All the data within the `params` section are passed to the `Zend_Db` database adapter, which then creates a `Zend_Db_Profiler` object and enables it.

To retrieve the profile information, the profiler's `getLastQueryProfile()` method can be used. Listing C.10 shows how to log the query data from the `fetchLatest()` method of the `Places` model in application/models/Places.php within the *Places* application.

Listing C.10   Logging SQL query data within the `fetchLatest()` model function

```
public function fetchLatest($count = 10)
{
    $result = $this->fetchAll(null,                  ❶ Runs        ❷ Retrieves
                'date_created DESC', $count);           query          profiler
                                                                       instance
    $profiler = $this->_db->getProfiler();   ◁————————┘

    $p = $profiler->getLastQueryProfile();                    ◁————

    $msg = 'Query: "' . $p->getQuery() . '"';
    $msg .= ', Params: ' . implode(',',                ❹ Formats
                $p->getQueryParams());                    profile
    $msg .= ', Time: ' . $p->getElapsedSecs() * 1000      data
                . 'ms';
                                                                  Collects
    $logger = Zend_Registry::get('logger');    ❺ Stores to        last
    $logger->debug($msg);                         logger          query's
                                                                  profile ❸
    return $result;
}
```

First, we run the `fetchAll()` query ❶ and store the results to be returned at the end of the method. We retrieve the profile data for this query by getting an instance of the profiler ❷ and then calling `getLastQueryProfile()` ❸. The query profile has some useful methods that we use to create a string to be logged ❹. As we discussed in section C.2.2, we can retrieve the instance of the `Zend_Log` object, `logger` in this case, from the `Zend_Registry`, and log the message to the debug priority ❺.
The resultant log entry looks like this:

```
2008-02-02T17:00:00+00:00 DEBUG (7): Query: "SELECT `places`.* FROM
`places` ORDER BY `date_created` DESC LIMIT 10", Params: , Time:
0.70691108703613ms
```

In this case, there weren't any bound parameters, so the Params section is empty. This is because the fetchAll() query simply orders the results by the date when they were created and limits them to the first time.

The profiler logs all events while it's switched on, so the data for all queries can be extracted right at the end of processing and logged if required. In this case, you don't need to alter any existing model methods and could just log the profile data after the call to dispatch() in the bootstrap. Listing C.11 shows an example of how to do this and assumes that the Zend_Log and Zend_Db objects have been stored to the registry.

Listing C.11   Logging all SQL profile data at the end of dispatching

```
$frontController->dispatch();                                    ◄─────┐  Runs
                                                                       ❶  application
$logger = Zend_Registry::get('logger');       ❷  Retrieves Db and
$db = Zend_Registry::get('db');                  Log from Registry

$profiler = $db->getProfiler();
$totalTime = $profiler->getTotalElapsedSecs() * 1000;       ❸  Collects overall
$queryCount = $profiler->getTotalNumQueries();                 numbers

foreach ($profiler->getQueryProfiles() as $i=>$query) {     ❹  Formats log
    $ms = $query->getElapsedSecs() * 1000;                     message for
                                                               each query
    $msg = $i . ' - Query: "' . $query->getQuery()

    $msg .= ', Params: ' . implode(',',
            $query->getQueryParams());
    $msg .= ', Time: ' . number_format($ms, 3) . ' ms';

    $messages[] = $msg;
}
$log = $queryCount . ' queries in ' .
            number_format($totalTime, 3)          ❺  Formats
        . ' milliseconds' . "\n";                    overall log
$log .= "Queries:\n";                                message
$log .= implode("\n", $messages);
                                                  ❻  Writes
$logger->debug($log);                    ◄─────────  to log
```

After dispatch() has completed ❶, we pick up the db and logger objects from the registry ❷, then pick up the profiler from the database object. The profiler object has some methods that provide overall metrics, and we use getTotalElapsedSecs() and getTotalNumQueries() to provide a sense of how many database calls were made and how long all the database querying took ❸.

The getQueryProfiles() method returns an array of Zend_Db_Profiler_Query objects, and we iterate over them, using the various member functions to create a single text string of information about each query within the $messages array ❹. We format a single string containing all the information we wish to log ❺ and store it to the log at debug priority ❻.

There's quite a lot going on there, so it would be wise to factor it into its own function. The log produced looks something like this:

```
2008-04-06T20:04:58+01:00 DEBUG (7): 3 queries in 3.029 milliseconds
Queries:
0 - Query: "connect", Params: , Time: 0.603 ms
1 - Query: "DESCRIBE `places`", Params: , Time: 1.895 ms
2 - Query: "SELECT `places`.* FROM `places` ORDER BY `date_created` DESC
LIMIT 10", Params: , Time: 0.531 ms
```

This information provides all we need to know about every query that took place in the generation of the page. In this case, we can see that the time taken to get the details of the places table using DESCRIBE was the largest, so we may choose to cache the database schema details using Zend_Db_Table_Abstract's setDefaultMetadata-Cache() method.

C.4   *Summary*

In this appendix, we've looked at less commonly used features within Zend Framework. The MVC system is very flexible, and the modules system, in particular, allows for further separation of your code base if you need it. Routing allows you to provide your users with URLs that are easy on the eye and also good for search engines. The three provided routes provide plenty of options, but if they don't meet your needs, the system is flexible enough to allow you to plug in your own router object or define your own routes to attach to the rewrite router.

   While we all believe that we write bug-free code, it's handy to have an easy way to inspect a variable or to log program flow to a file. Zend_Debug and Zend_Log provide opportunities to monitor what happens in your application when things go wrong and help you find problems. For database calls using Zend_Db, the built-in profiler can provide timing information along with the exact query that was executed. When integrated with Zend_Log, you have a powerful mechanism for finding database bottlenecks. This allows you to concentrate your optimization efforts on the queries where you'll gain the most.

index

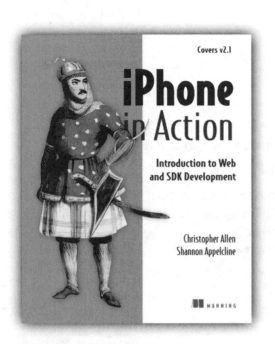

iPhone in Action

Introduction to Web and SDK Development

by Christophen Allen
and Shanon Appelcline

ISBN: 1-933988-86-X
350 pages
$39.99
December 2008

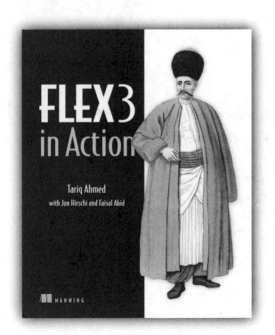

Flex 3 in Action

by Tariq Ahmed
with Jon Hirschi and Faisal Abid

ISBN: 1-933988-74-6
425 pages
$44.99
December 2008

For ordering information go to www.manning.com

MORE TITLES FROM MANNING

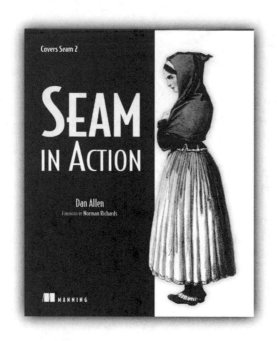

Seam in Action

by Dan Allen

> ISBN: 1-933988-40-1
> 624 pages
> $44.99
> September 2008

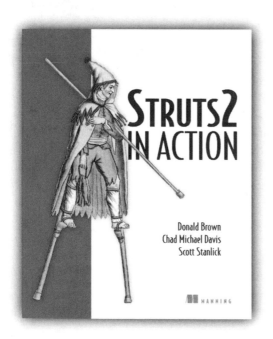

Struts 2 in Action

by Donald Brown, Chad Michael Davis,
  andScott Stanlick

> ISBN: 1-933988-07-X
> 424 pages
> $44.99
> May 2008

For ordering information go to www.manning.com

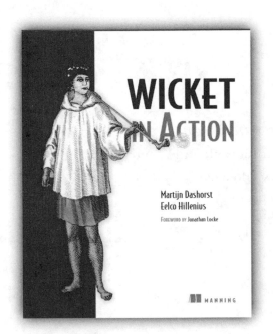

Wicket in Action

by Martijn Dashorst and Eeko Hillenius

ISBN: 1-932394-98-2
392 pages
$44.99
August 2008

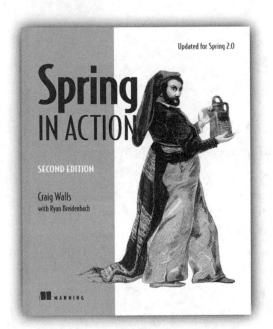

Spring in Action

Second Edition

by Craig Walls
   with Ryan Breidenbach

ISBN: 1-933988-13-4
768 pages
$49.99
August 2007

For ordering information go to www.manning.com

MORE TITLES FROM MANNING

jQuery in Action

by Bear Bibeault and Yehuda Katz

ISBN: 1-933988-35-5
376 pages
$39.99
February 2008

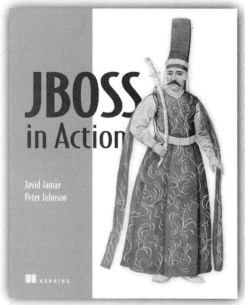

JBoss in Action

by Javid Jamae and Peter Johnson

ISBN: 1-933988-02-9
476 pages
$49.99
December 2008

For ordering information go to www.manning.com